Principles of Methodology

Principles of Methodology

Research Design in
Social Science

Perri 6 and Christine Bellamy

Los Angeles | London | New Delhi
Singapore | Washington DC

First published 2012

SAGE Publications Ltd
1 Oliver's Yard
55 City Road
London EC1Y 1SP

SAGE Publications Inc.
2455 Teller Road
Thousand Oaks, California 91320

SAGE Publications India Pvt Ltd
B 1/I 1 Mohan Cooperative Industrial Area
Mathura Road
New Delhi 110 044

SAGE Publications Asia-Pacific Pte Ltd
33 Pekin Street #02-01
Far East Square
Singapore 048763

Library of Congress Control Number: 2011920596

British Library Cataloguing in Publication data

A catalogue record for this book is available from the British Library

ISBN 978-0-85702-473-2
ISBN 978-0-85702-474-9

Typeset by C&M Digitals (P) Ltd, Chennai, India
Printed and bound by CPI Group (UK) Ltd, Croydon, CR0 4YY
Printed on paper from sustainable resources

Contents

Acknowledgements

We are very grateful to several cohorts of Nottingham Trent University graduate students for taking part in our uncontrolled experiment in teaching them by using materials on which we drew in writing this book, and for their comments and suggestions. The influence of our former colleague, Nick Tilley, on our thinking will be obvious, and we owe him a big debt. Rob Denny offered insightful comments on the material. We are very grateful to Patrick Brindle at Sage for encouraging us to write this book and to David Hodge and Ian Antcliff of Sage for their patience and their valuable guidance as we completed it, and for the reviewers' comments. All mistakes and infelicities are, of course, our own.

About the authors

Perri 6 is Professor of Social Policy in the Graduate School in the College of Business, Law and Social Science at Nottingham Trent University, where he teaches courses in methodology and advanced qualitative methods. He has worked at the universities of Birmingham, King's College London, Strathclyde and Bath. In recent years, he has published both qualitative and quantitative research on policies to change citizens' behaviour, tensions between joined-up government and client confidentiality (with Christine Bellamy and Charles Raab), policy implementation and policymakers' use of information in decision-making, as well as major theoretical work on institutions, emotions and networks and consumer choice in public services. Among his best-known books are *Paradoxes of modernisation* (ed with H Margetts and C Hood, 2010) *Institutional dynamics of culture: the new Durkheimians* (ed with G Mars, 2008), *Public emotion* (ed with S Radstone, C Squire and A Treacher, 2007), *Beyond delivery: policy implementation as sense-making and settlement* (with E Peck, 2006), *Managing networks of twenty-first century organisations* (with N Goodwin, E Peck and T Freeman, 2006), *E-governance: style of political judgment in the information age policy (2004)* and *Towards holistic governance* (with D Leat, K Seltzer and G Stoker). His book, *Explaining political judgement*, which develops a neo-Durkheimian causal theory of political decision-making, will be published by Cambridge University Press in 2011. Supported by the Leverhulme Trust, he is researching styles of political judgement and unintended consequences of policy decisions in British government between 1959 and 1974.

Christine Bellamy is Emeritus Professor of Public Administration in the Graduate School, Nottingham Trent University. She recently retired as Associate Dean (Research and Postgraduate Studies) in the College of Business, Law and Social Sciences at Nottingham Trent University, to spend more time on writing and research. She was responsible for the College's Graduate School for ten years, and played a key role in developing and delivering research training for students following masters, PhD and ProfD programmes throughout the College. She continues to participate in teaching methodology and methods to PhD students at both basic and advanced levels. Christine Bellamy is a member of the Academy of Social Sciences. She has served on the ESRC's Research Evaluation Committee and on the Steering Group for its International Benchmarking Exercise for Politics. She has also served on the Commissioning Panels for two ESRC-funded Programmes, and was a member of the Politics and International Relations Sub Panel for RAE2008. Christine's research interests lie in public administration and public policy, especially information policy. She recently completed a major ESRC-funded project (with Perri 6 and Charles Raab) on how public agencies deal with tensions between client confidentiality and data sharing, and is currently engaged in an administrative history of identity management and privacy in British government.

Introduction

We have written this book because, in our own teaching, we found that most text-books on methods or philosophy of social science say remarkably little about one of the most fundamental questions in research design: what will we be able to claim to know as a result of doing this research?

The book deals with the key issues in methodology – as opposed to methods – from basic through to advanced level. We have written it to address the needs of early career researchers, including graduate students taking masters' courses for which they are expected to carry out empirical research and doctoral researchers undertaking methods training in support of their PhDs. The early sections may also be useful for undergraduates preparing to undertake research-based dissertations. But we believe, too, that the important and original, and perhaps controversial, argument we develop will also engage experienced researchers, whether they work in universities or carry out or commission the growing volumes of social research now undertaken for businesses, government and social agencies.

What is 'methodology'?

This book is about methodology and research design. By 'methodology', we mean the understanding of how to proceed from the findings of empirical research to make inferences about the truth – or at least the adequacy – of theories. Its importance stems from the fundamental insight that findings about empirical facts are often most interesting when they enable us to make deeper judgements about what might be going on beneath those facts. The point of understanding 'methodology' is that it should enable us to design our research so that we can draw defensible conclusions about what might be *causing* the things we observe, including those causes stemming from ways in which people think about the world.

How to draw defensible conclusions is not the same problem as how to 'generalise' from our results. In its commonest form, generalisation is not a very deep problem. If we have looked at a set of cases – perhaps young people becoming homeless, or companies going bankrupt, or political parties recovering from electoral defeat – and we have good reason to think that those cases are typical of other cases in the same 'population', then most of us would risk generalising to cases that we have not actually observed.

A much deeper problem is that of drawing conclusions, even about the cases we *have* observed, from patterns of facts about such things to 'explanations' or 'interpretations'. 'Methodology' is the study of this problem. It differs from the study of 'research methods', which deals with techniques for collecting data and for analysing them. Good methods are, of course, essential to doing good research. A defensible methodology is no use at all, if the data are collected poorly or coded sloppily, or the wrong statistical tests or qualitative analyses are carried out. But the converse is also true. A sound understanding of methodology will help us avoid the risk of collecting and analysing the data competently, but finding ourselves unable to draw any sound conclusions because the research design is flawed.

The study of methods is commonly divided by the type of data they use. Broadly, different methods are used for collecting, coding and analysing quantitative and qualitative data. By contrast, many problems of research design and methodology are much the same, irrespective of whether the research uses numbers or strips of text. We still need to ensure that we can draw interesting conclusions from whatever we discover. For this reason, this book does not have separate chapters on qualitative and quantitative approaches to research.

Methodological disagreement: the impossibility of neutrality

Methodology is a subject about which social scientists disagree, probably more than they disagree about method. This means that there are few non-contentious issues with which to introduce social research methodology. We must therefore issue a health warning. No book on methodology can be entirely neutral between methodological arguments. As practising researchers we inevitably hold our own positions, which have influenced how we have conducted our own research. We have also found from teaching this subject over many years that students benefit from taking part in vigorous academic debates.

For these reasons, this book takes sides in some important, current disputes. We have endeavoured, nevertheless, to cover the main lines of methodological debate from a range of perspectives that accurately reveal the rationale for competing positions. We intend that, in this way, the book will equip you to develop your own views. A reader who does not share our approach, or who holds a rival one, can, we hope, use this book with confidence that we shall not smuggle in unacknowledged assumptions or disguise the space for rival positions. We have tried throughout to set out clearly the available contrary arguments, even as we indicate what we consider to be their weaknesses.

A multi-disciplinary approach to the study of methodology

We set out to write a book that will be useful across the social sciences, including sociology, political science, anthropology, development studies, business and management studies, criminology, public policy, social policy, and science and technology studies. Indeed, we draw examples from each of these disciplines and fields. We have both principled and practical reasons for believing that this cross-disciplinary approach is appropriate.

The principled reason is that all these disciplines share common foundations in methodology and research design. This is not surprising, because they have all developed from a common source. As late as the mid-nineteenth century, these disciplines were hardly distinguished from one another, save as empirical fields within the broad remit of social science. The practical reason is that it is increasingly common for students to learn about method and methodology in multi-disciplinary groups. Indeed, in many countries, including the UK, this practice is actively encouraged by the public bodies which fund research training.

We welcome multi-disciplinary approaches to research training, because we know from our own experience how much students and early career researchers benefit from seeing how colleagues in other disciplines work through methodological issues. Just as important, it can be easier to understand a complex issue from an example outside our own field, because it is easier to recognise the problem's logical structure, without being distracted by the empirical facts of the particular illustration. Contours and contrasts became clearer and easier to read, when we look at something from a distance. So, for example, political scientists should find considerable value in looking at methodological problems through the lens of examples taken, say, from anthropology, public policy or business studies.

The scope of the book

This is a book on methodology, so it will not cover much that is usually found in texts on research methods, either qualitative or quantitative. We say nothing here, for example, about how to carry out standard statistical tests or how to conduct interviews or analyse transcripts. Rather, this book addresses the problem of what inferences you might expect to be able to draw from findings produced by such methods. So it deals with the problem of how to design research that is methodologically defensible and provides confidence that good use can be made of its findings.

Nor is this book principally about the philosophy of the social sciences. We devote Chapters 2, 3 and 4 to philosophical issues that are of central importance to methodology, but this book does not provide a comprehensive guide to the thought of the key figures in the philosophy of the social sciences or to philosophical issues and problems.

We insist, too, that understanding research methods and the philosophy of the social sciences – important as they both are – is not enough to make a competent social researcher. Too many new researchers embark on their work with some background in method and philosophy, but too little in methodology. Worse still, they may not even realise that the methodology of research design deals with distinct issues from the study of method and philosophy.

The book is principally about what is often known as 'observational research'. We do not cover in any depth the methodological issues at stake in experimental work, although Chapter 4 does say some important things about experimental design in order to show what is distinctive about observational research.

The structure of the book

The book is divided into four parts covering, respectively:

- *Foundations* – what methodology is and does.
- *Designs* – the principal types of research design and the methodological challenges each type presents.
- *Achievements* – the kinds of products or arguments to which researchers can make inferences from the findings produced by analysis.
- *Combinations and trade-offs* – ways of bringing two or more research designs together to support each other, and how to think about the compromises that all types of research designs must make.

Part I raises two issues that recur throughout the book. We explain why the study of methodology is controversial in a manner and to a depth that, for example, the study of method is not. Second, all the good things prescribed by methodology do not go together well: we cannot have everything we would ideally like in the same research design. A research design may exhibit several different virtues, but we usually have to strike trade-offs between them. So a key part of any methodological defence of a piece of research is making the case that the trade-off struck between these virtues is a reasonable one.

The second part of the book deals with the concepts structuring the whole book. It describes the main types of research design by distinguishing between deductive and inductive design, within- and between-case analysis, and between variable-oriented, case-based and case-comparative research. The third part of the book is concerned with the main types of achievements, products or outcomes of social science research, or what research seeks to draw inferences *for*. These products are descriptions, explanations and interpretations.

In practice, however, some social science research combines these elements. In the final part, we examine the services that description, explanation and interpretation can provide for each other in a combined study. In the concluding chapter, we discuss some of the ways in which trade-offs can be struck between particular virtues appropriate to different research designs

Our experience of teaching this material to multi-disciplinary classes of masters and doctoral students suggests that the first nine chapters provide a basic or 'core' course, while the last nine chapters support an advanced-level course.

Methodology is a practical business, because understanding methodology allows us to deliver the goods promised by social science research. So, while this book deals with principles derived from the theory of methodology, it does so in the spirit of the old adage that 'there is nothing so useful as a good theory'. And so it is important that you should be able to see clearly how these principles may be applied to your own research. To this end, we provide two main kinds of pedagogical aids: examples and exercises. They appear in numbered boxes in each chapter.

Examples

The examples are taken from many disciplines, and are of two kinds. Some use influential pieces of published research as vehicles for showing how experienced researchers – including the authors of some classic studies in social science – have dealt with particular kinds of methodological challenges. We hope that you will want to read the original texts, because it is important for new researchers to become familiar with at least some of the principal items in the methodological canon. But we have attempted to provide a sufficiently clear explanation of each example for it to be useful to readers who do not have access to the original publications or the time to read them all. Others are fictional examples drafted to help you think about methodological problems that might well arise in your own research. We have taken both types of examples from a variety of social science disciplines, and have ensured that some of them deal with practical issues in business and policy research.

Running through the book are several fictional examples. Some are about investigating rough sleeping and household behaviour in recycling domestic waste. The purpose of creating linked examples is partly to show how different issues in methodology might play out in relation to the same research topic or even the same question. It also shows how different methodological strategies can illuminate different aspects of a problem and cumulate in providing an understanding of it. These series of examples speak to our overall purpose in this book, which is to help readers understand how different aspects of methodology contribute to good research design, sometimes, but not always, in the same study.

Exercises and further reading

We also include practical exercises in each chapter, to enable readers to test their understanding of key points. Some of these also run throughout the book. Most are appropriate for use in class discussion.

Suggestions for further reading at both basic and advanced level are offered at the end of each chapter. These are selective rather than comprehensive reading lists. We have indicated what we believe to be the most important and accessible articles or book chapters, whilst also encouraging readers to read some of the classic contributions to the methodology of social science. Because the list of references at the end of the book also includes all the recommended reading, it serves as a fairly comprehensive bibliography on methodology.

We are aware that even readers with a background in social sciences may not be familiar with some of the vocabulary used in this book. We have therefore provided a glossary of important technical terms.

PART I

Foundations

What methodology is and does

ONE

Inference and warrant in designing research

This chapter will:

- explain what is meant by methodology and how it differs from method;
- introduce the three main types of research question in social science, and how each is answered by drawing inferences from patterns found in data; and
- explain that methodology is always controversial, because all good things do not go together, and that trade-offs must be struck between the virtues of good research design.

How does methodology differ from the study of methods?

Since this book is about methodology, we should start with that term. But, first, we should point out that many standard textbooks use it loosely to refer to anything to do with research methods. So do not be surprised if you read books or articles that claim to be about methodology, but which deal with issues that are excluded from this book. Our definition, by contrast, is narrow and specific, and distinguishes clearly between method and methodology in social science.

In this book, we define *method* as the set of techniques recognised by most social scientists as being appropriate for the creation, collection, coding, organisation and analysis of data.

- *Data creation methods* are used to produce the raw material of research, namely well-structured data – or sets of information – that can be used to perform further investigations, of the kind described below. Data creation methods include ethnographic or participant observation, focus groups, individual interviews, questionnaire surveys and so on.

- *Data collection methods* are procedures for capturing what is important for answering the research question from the data that have been created. They may involve scanning text for particular themes, codes or content or undertaking counts or more advanced quantitative procedures. However, we can only count or code once we have decided how to identify what is important, as we show in Example 1.1.

EXAMPLE 1.1. STREET LIFE

It is claimed that the number of people sleeping rough on the streets in British cities fell fairly sharply in the four or five years after the British Labour government's initiative on rough sleeping in 1998. But it then levelled out, and at the time of writing appears to be increasing again.

However, as a consultation paper issued by the subsequent coalition government (Department of Communities and Local Government, 2010) shows, there is a major problem with this claim, in that no one believes that the data on rough sleeping are accurate, because counting the number of rough sleepers is far from straightforward.

The government is worried that its official definition of rough sleepers as 'people sleeping or bedded down in the open air' means that local councils do not count people who spend the night awake or sitting up in sleeping bags. But does it follow that councils should count all people on the street with sleeping bags? What, for example, about people who may use them as an aid to begging, but do not actually sleep rough? And should councils count people who sleep in tents, stairwells of blocks of flats or who take refuge on cold nights in shelters run by charities?

- *Data coding methods* are procedures for determining whether the information indicated by a particular datum or set of data meet the standards or thresholds required for them to be classified under a category, where that category is related to the research question or hypothesis.
- *Data organisation methods* are procedures for laying out whole sets or series of data, that have either been created, collected and coded by the researcher for the purposes of the project, or been taken from another source – for example, a national survey data set such as the British Crime Survey (BCS) or, as in Example 1.1, the British government's annual estimate of rough sleepers (available at http://www.communities. gov.uk/publications/corporate/statistics/roughsleepingcount2010). Data organisation involves setting out the data on a suitably common basis – for example, by tabulating them – so that they can be analysed.
- *Data analysis methods* are procedures for manipulating data so that the research question can be answered, usually by identifying important patterns. Statistical procedures are obvious examples. There are many qualitative analysis techniques too, such as open-ended content analysis, and a variety of theory-based comparative techniques for handling historical qualitative data of the kind we shall discuss in Chapter 17.

Interpretation

You will notice that nothing has yet been said about the 'interpretation' of data. The process of data collection almost always requires the researcher to 'interpret' the data, and that this is particularly so when – as in Example 1.1 – the things being studied do not fall neatly into convenient, unambiguous units. We shall consider some of these issues in more detail when we discuss the use and application of concepts in Chapter 9. Coding likewise involves interpretation, because the decision whether the data indicate that a case meets standards for a particular code is an interpretive act of scientific judgement.

'Interpretation' is also required in the process of determining whether the data analysis supports the general conclusions drawn from the research, to answer the research question. We call this support, its *warrant*. Warrant is a central issue in methodology, and therefore one that will be addressed throughout this book.

A third meaning of 'interpretation' in methodology is discussed briefly below and will be discussed again in detail in Chapters 15 and 16. This third meaning of interpretation is restricted to particular kinds of data and particular sorts of conclusions – namely, those which attribute beliefs, ideas, emotions or ways of classifying to people being studied.

But the point to emphasise here is that all methodological approaches rely to a large extent on 'data interpretation' and therefore 'interpretation' is not a separate stage or activity from the ones we list above. Although research proposals are often written with timetables describing 'data interpretation' as if it were the final stage of a project when conclusions are to be drawn about the theoretical or practical significance of the research, in fact interpretation is at the heart of the whole research process.

So what is 'methodology'?

The key lesson from this discussion is that *methodology* is not just – and is often *not very much at all* – a matter of method, in the sense of using appropriate techniques in the correct way. It is much more to do with how well we *argue* from the analyses of our data to draw and defend our conclusions. The *methodological* question posed by our rough sleepers example is just what would allow us to claim that an increase in rough sleeping has occurred; that is, to make inference to a *description*. If we went on to claim that a rise in rough sleeping is being caused by the economic downturn, then this would be an inference to an *explanation*. Or perhaps it would be illuminating to explore what rough sleepers themselves would count as rough sleeping and why. This would require an inference to an *interpretation* in the third sense discussed above.

Because methodology is about arguments that show warrant for inferences, it makes no sense to break down the study of methodology according to the different stages involved in the research process, in the way that we have just done above for methods. Rather, we shall distinguish in this book between different approaches to methodology, and discuss the strategies appropriate to these approaches. We shall begin this discussion later in this chapter, when we discuss the differences between research designed to lead, respectively, to *description*, *explanation* and *interpretation*. But we stress throughout the book that each of these approaches raises the same basic methodological question – how and how far can you argue from the particular data to the particular conclusions, or, to put it another way, what argument, if any, do these data actually support?

Being able to draw sound conclusions depends on designing all stages in the project on sound methodological principles. Conversely, it is entirely possible to follow pre-scribed methods carefully, but still produce methodologically suspect research, if the conclusions drawn from it are not soundly based. These problems are inescapably theoretical ones, because the study of methodology involves theories about how and how far the research design enables us to draw sound inferences to conclusions that provide answers to our research questions, or that determine how far our hypotheses are supported or undermined.

And that is what this book is all about.

Inference and warrant

The core concepts in methodology are those of inference and warrant, and we should explain here why they are so important.

We are used to opinion pollsters drawing conclusions about the voting preferences of over forty million electors by sampling the opinions of around a thousand people. They do this by using widely accepted principles of statistical inference. This example illustrates the problem that we often need to draw conclusions about a large population from what we can find out about a smaller sample. A second problem is that we cannot always observe the things we are interested in directly, but are forced to work with proxies or indicators. For example, psychologists make inferences about the working of human or animal brains from observing very fine movements of eyes. Industrial sociologists make inferences about organisational morale from the way workers behave or describe their feelings. And anthropologists interpret how human beings make sense of their worlds from their stories or other cultural artefacts. In none of these examples can synapses firing in brains, 'morale' or 'sense-making' be directly observed.

Furthermore, researchers could not confidently make inferences without theories – however implicit or provisional – about the relationships between the things in which they are interested and those things which they can directly observe. For example, using cultural artefacts to interpret sense-making depends on a theory of culture.

We can therefore define *inference* as (1) the process of making claims about one set of phenomena that cannot be directly observed (2) on the basis of what we know about a set of things that we have observed where (3) the choice of research instruments depends on a theory of how those instruments work.

We can define *warrant* as the degree of confidence that we have in an inference's capability to deliver truths about the things we cannot observe directly. Warrant involves particular standards, which we shall discuss in more detail in subsequent chapters. We shall see, too, that some of these standards are more straightforwardly related to methods than others.

Observation

In the course of the book, we shall have occasion to use this slippery but absolutely unavoidable word in several ways. There are four different ways in which this word is used in social science methodology:

1 The value taken by a unit of data that is collected for, defined by and organised in a scheme of measurement. For example, the value ascribed to a variable entered into a cell on a spreadsheet or table is an observation on that variable. 'Observation' is used in this sense in the question, 'what do the observations show?'
2 A unit of data, such as a case in a sample or data set, as in the question, 'how many observations do you have?'
3 The systematic collection of data about behaviour or action, where the researcher cannot exercise experimental control over the regime of stimulus and constraint under which the research participants act, as in the term, 'observational research', which is the alternative to experimental research.
4 The activity of a researcher undertaking visual and/or audio inspection of participants' behaviour, as in 'a period of fieldwork observations'.

When we discuss some philosophical questions in Chapters 2, 3 and 4, we shall use the word in sense 1 a good deal. Chapter 5 considers observational research, in sense 3. In Chapter 6, when we discuss variable-oriented research, 'observation' will be used in sense 2. Although we bear sense 4 in mind throughout, it will come to the fore particularly in Chapters 15 and 16. You are warned to pause whenever you see the word, to make sure that you know what is meant. It will always be clear from the context which meaning is intended, but you can check either this page or the entry in the glossary if you need a reminder.

Some controversial claims about methodology

With those definitions in mind, it is time for us to make some big claims. Some are going to be controversial. You will find, as you read this book, that almost anything that is said in the field of methodology will attract disagreement. This is another big difference from the study of methods, because most people who study methods agree on what counts as, for example, transcribing an interview, or calculating a chi-squared test.

Here is our first big claim. *Making warranted inferences is the whole point and the only point of doing social research*, irrespective of what type of data and what style of research we use. The contribution to knowledge of any research consists in the inferences that can be made from it. Inferences are the principal products; they provide support for findings; and they are what make findings into findings rather than speculations, on the one hand, or raw data, on the other.

There are two reasons for making this claim. The first is a semantic one and the second rests upon a normative claim about what our ambitions ought to be and why social scientists get out of bed in the morning.

The semantic reason is that careful attention to inference, and what warrants it, is what distinguishes *research* from other kinds of investigation. Good journalistic reportage does not generally try to make inferences, beyond telling us what the reporter found. Interesting speculative or theoretical writing does not have to be so concerned with warrant: pure theorists and social commentators leave that to empirical researchers. Detective work by police officers, however, *is* concerned with inference and warrant. But it differs from most social research – although it does resemble some kinds of historical work – in that it is concerned only with warranted inference about the particular case under examination, whereas a good deal of social science research is interested in drawing inferences beyond the particular case to a wider population.

The bigger, normative reason is that warranted inference is worth doing, because it represents a strategy for making a contribution to knowledge that none of these other investigative activities can achieve, given their entirely proper purposes and limitations. We need to understand how social processes generally work, and this cannot be done adequately by nailing 'whodunnit' in a particular criminal case, or by news-hounds ferreting out facts, or even by reading the insights of literary giants.

Critics of inferential ambition

We acknowledged that our first big claim would be controversial, and we should therefore tell you who would object to it, and why. Those who would resist this claim tend typically to argue one of the following positions:

- Social research can be justified if it 'gives voice' to people – such as rough sleepers – whose perspectives on homelessness would not otherwise be available. For this purpose, it is claimed, warranted inference to general theories is not necessary and, indeed, may actually be harmful. What, rather, is needed is researcherly observation and analysis that is faithful to the views of the individuals studied.

- Social research cannot, because of its inherently subjective nature, achieve warrant for general inferences, and should be considered just as lacking in fundamental – or 'foundational' – warrant as journalism, speculative writing, *belles lettres* and detective work. On this view, the accounts, say, of rough sleepers, national government ministers, local charity managers and local mayors of why rough sleeping is a problem, and how big and significant a problem it is, are bound to be different: we cannot achieve a perfectly accurate description, let alone a true explanation, of this state of affairs. This view is shared by several schools of social thought, ranging from scepticism through relativism to anti-foundationalism and postmodernism.

An answer to the critics

We are not persuaded by either of these claims, and, for the record, we shall offer a couple of remarks to indicate why we disagree with the first of these views. The second, we shall leave for Chapters 2–4.

'Giving voice' involves attributing thoughts, emotions, practices, aspirations, memories and so on to other human beings. Researchers often want to reveal the preferences, experiences or ways of understanding the lives of the people they study. But none of these things can be observed directly, nor can they be read off unproblematically from what people say in interviews or do when they are observed. There is no getting away from using information from outside the particular situation, because even the concepts we use are taken from a wider vocabulary. And when we try to work out just what people think, we draw on information about other people we believe to be similar to those we are studying.

The very concept of 'rough sleeping', for example, is one drawn from government policy documents, and we would find it difficult to escape from concepts such as the 'vulnerability' or 'social exclusion' of rough sleepers if we tried to describe the impact on their lives of, say, the closure of a winter shelter due to spending cuts. People in charge of public policy, and researchers who write and read scholarly articles or monographs, use language in a very different way from many of those studied by social science research. And so, 'giving voice' often involves risky acts of translation or making risky attributions.

The only way to do it well – and to do it in ways that make us accountable to other academics or to participants in our research – is to adopt procedures that force us to be conscious of the inferences we make and to reveal all our workings-out. That is to say, one characteristic of good research design is that it enables us to demonstrate how we got from interviews and other observations to our conclusions about research participants' lives. This process *is* warranted inference.

An alternative way of proceeding is available, of course. We could write down what we happen to think and perhaps publish it in journalistic outlets. But our research would then constitute a different kind of enquiry, undertaken for different purposes and with different kinds of accountabilities to the data, to research participants and to the wider academic community. Social research based on warranted inference makes a quite distinct – and distinctly valuable – contribution to understanding people from that made by journalism or any other type of enquiry. Specifically, the unique contribution of social science consists in the methodological care that we pay to the inferences we make.

Inference to what?

All this raises an important but obvious question: *to what* exactly do we make inferences? We have already seen that social scientists distinguish between three types of purposes for which inferences are made. These purposes are *description, explanation* and *interpretation*.

Descriptive inference

Descriptive inference is undertaken to answer certain questions about Xs (where X stands for any empirical topic for social research) when we cannot observe them at all, or cannot observe them all, or can observe only aspects of them, or cannot be sure that what we are observing of the Xs is quite what it seems. These questions are, 'what kinds of things are the Xs?', 'what kinds of statements can we make about them?' and 'how can we characterise them?' The product of descriptive inference is a set of claims about Xs. These claims may be about what is typical of Xs, what is generally true about Xs, or what is true about a subtype or across some spectrum of Xs.

One product of research on rough sleepers, for example, might be a description of how many rough sleepers there are in a particular town; what kind of people they are by age, gender and so on; how long, on average, they have been homeless; whether this period is becoming longer or shorter; and whether the number of long-term homeless people is rising or falling. This description would depend on inference, because – even if we could count directly everyone who sleeps rough in the town on a particular night – we would need to make assumptions about what proportion of rough sleepers we have observed. And we shall also have to make inferences from earlier data or from interviews with rough sleepers, about *changes* in patterns of rough sleeping and in the characteristics of the population of rough sleepers.

Some textbooks are very snooty about descriptive inference. This snootiness is – to coin a phrase – unwarranted. Description may be a modest ambition, but it is a necessary one. It is very difficult to go on to do anything more ambitious in social research if you have not got the descriptive inferences right. It is true that the most prestigious journals do not publish articles that offer *only* descriptive inferences. But the articles that they do publish rely, in a vital part of their overall argument, on the soundness of descriptive inferences, even if those parts of their workings are not shown.

Explanatory and counterfactual inference

Explanatory inferences are undertaken to answer the questions, 'why have the Xs done Z or become Y?', 'what brought this about?' and 'what *caused* the Xs to become Y or do Z?' In Chapters 10–13, we shall look in much more detail at what we understand by causation. We shall see that explaining how something came about raises methodological challenges of a higher order than describing it, although description can often be quite tricky too.

Suppose that we want to find out whether cuts in public spending have contributed, causally, to an increase in rough sleeping. Once the cuts have taken place, we can no longer look at rough sleeping in a particular town in the absence of those cuts. So we could never measure the impact of cuts on rough sleeping by comparing the situation we currently observe with one (in one and the same place) in which the cuts had never taken place. This difficulty is known as the fundamental problem of counterfactual causal inference. It is one reason why explanatory inference is tough. But it is often very important to try for explanations. Indeed, explaining why things happen is the main reason that anyone pays for social science research to be done, in the hope that explanation will help with the design of interventions in social problems.

There are weaker senses of the term 'explanation' which do not require *causes* to be revealed. For example, researchers write of *statistical* 'explanation'. This phrase refers to the process of showing that two variables are strongly associated with each other, but does not require us to draw any inferences about which direction any influence might run or to rule out the possibility that both variables are being influenced by a third variable. Other explanations are *logical* in character. That is, we may 'explain' a condition or event, by showing how it is derived logically from another. For example, we may explain the government's plans for extended sharing of personal information about individual citizens between government agencies on the grounds that this is a direct – that is, a logical – implication of an emphasis on multi-agency interventions in social problems such as homelessness.

Interpretive inference

Finally, there are *interpretive inferences*. Interpretive inference is addressed to a variety of questions, some of which we have already discussed.

We have seen that the most elementary interpretive inference is made when we determine whether something is to count, for a given research purpose, as falling within some category, and therefore decide that it is to be given a particular code or measure. We call this an interpretation of its *categorical significance*. Deciding, for example, who counts as a rough sleeper – a question which precedes the descriptive inference question of whether we can draw conclusions about the numbers of rough sleepers – is clearly a matter of interpreting the concept of a rough sleeper. And that, in turn, depends on our view of whether that concept captures the particular aspects of the underlying condition of utter homelessness in which we are interested.

Second, giving voice is only one way of accounting for how people think, feel, understand, frame issues and so on. Interpretive inference is not simply the development of descriptions of people's subjective experiences, but may also produce an *integrated* account – or interpretation – of the *subjective significance* for people's mental lives, in which the patterns observed make some larger sense. For example, in interpreting how managers of local council housing departments perceive the implications of the government's edict to count rough sleepers in new ways, we would probably need to go beyond a simple repetition of our descriptive data (e.g. 37% of respondents agreed with Proposal 1 put to them in our survey) by drawing inferences about the significance they attach to the government's proposals for the lives of their rough sleepers and for their capacity to help them. If the data allow, we could also, perhaps, make further inferences about what these managers believe to be the significance of these proposals more broadly for social justice or social inclusion and about the standards they appear implicitly to adopt in measuring justice and inclusion. Finally, there are inferences to integrated accounts in which the subject of the interpretation is not the mental life of a group – or groups – of people, but a set of events. Historical interpretation – which is very important in historical sociology, comparative political science, business history and even in institutional economics – is a case in point. Its aim is to detect overarching patterns of historical events – for example, those involved in the emergence of multinational business corporations in the period after the First World War or in the growth of a welfare state after 1945 – to provide the basis for an integrated account or interpretation of their *objective significance*.

Relationships between descriptive, explanatory and interpretive inferences

Much of the book will be devoted to considering separately the standards of warrant required for inferences in *explanatory* and in *interpretive* research. But we shall see that almost all explanatory and interpretive research rests upon descriptive and categorical interpretive inferences.

We shall see, too, that even those researchers who insist most fiercely on an exclusive focus on interpretation of *subjective* significance cannot, in practice, carry out that task without implying some kind of explanation of why people think as they do. It is very difficult to develop an account of, say, the ways in which people on low incomes think about or 'frame' the risks of health problems arising from their diets, without making some reference to categories that imply causation. For example, in trying to decide between interpretations that emphasise the limited dietary choices available to people on low incomes and those interpretations which emphasise their limited willingness seriously to consider eating health foods, researchers necessarily find themselves implying something about the causal role that beliefs might play in explaining unhealthy dietary behaviour.

This example illustrates the point that separating descriptive from causally explanatory categories is not straightforward, because we often describe by using categories that imply an explanation. For example, we might count the number of 'drug-dependent' people who are registered for treatment in the UK, but the very use of this category recognises addictive dependency as a significant *cause* of the use of illegal drugs and carries the implied claim that it should be treated rather than punished. We shall see in Chapters 15 and 16 that there are other and deeper reasons why it is difficult to do interpretive research without carrying any explanatory baggage.

The questions addressed by descriptive, explanatory and interpretive research are, nevertheless, analytically quite distinct. These three types of research ask, respectively, 'what's going on with the Xs?', 'why have the Xs done Y?', 'what do the Xs understand by the way they do Y?' and 'what is the wider significance of the fact that the Xs have done Y?'. It is therefore most helpful to consider separately the methodological challenges raised by each of these three approaches, and this is what we shall do in this book.

Trade-offs between virtues in warranting inference

In examining these challenges, we shall explore the virtues that should be exhibited by methodologically sound research, if it is to warrant the inferences that it seeks to support. Indeed, we have already noticed some of these virtues.

First, in discussing description, we have implied that a key virtue of a description is that it should be as *accurate* as possible within the limitations imposed by the ways in which the data have been created and collected. For example, the kind of accuracy we expect from a statistical description of broad trends is very different from the kind that can be achieved by a meticulous anthropologist who carefully checks each significant observation recorded in his or her field notes.

Second, we have assumed that our inferences should capture the significance of as many of the data in the set as is practicable. In other words, the account should summarise and integrate our findings, but with the minimum loss of the facts, nuances, differences and contrasts that are relevant to the question. The better our account does this, the better its *goodness of fit*.

Third, in contrasting social research with detective work and investigative journalism, we pointed out that social science researchers want to draw inferences beyond the particular case to some wider population of people, events or cases. That is, we are interested in achieving *generality* across some category.

Fourth, we mentioned that researchers often look for a few overarching patterns that are of the greatest significance in shaping thought styles or emotions or in explaining outcomes or events. Whilst it might be tempting to trace in great detail the interaction of a large number of complex factors that might *explain*, say, the rise in custodial sentences handed down by the criminal courts, it is both impractical and distracting to continue piling up lots of different factors over a large number of cases. It may be better to compare the influence of a few, important factors such as changes in national sentencing guidelines, judges' attitudes in interpreting them, and beliefs held by judges and juries about how community sentences work. That is, another virtue of both explanations and of interpretations is *parsimony*.

There are other virtues, which we shall consider in due course. However, we shall also see that it is often impossible in the same research design to maximise accuracy, goodness of fit, generality and parsimony, let alone other virtues (Przeworski and Teune, 1970). For example, the more accurate we try to be, the more detail we accumulate and the closer we stick to the granularity of particular cases, the more difficult it becomes to generalise across cases. It also becomes more difficult to identify the effects of a few really central factors, because they will not consistently perform their explanatory or their interpretive work at the level of close detail. Conversely, the more parsimonious we want to be, the more likely it is that we shall be forced to restrict the domain of cases over which we can generalise, because rather few things are common to every case, especially those falling in wide categories like 'homelessness' or 'judicial behaviour'. This problem means that we have to strike trade-offs between virtues in designing our research.

The need to strike trade-offs between virtues of good research design is one reason why there is no such thing as a piece of research that is completely beyond methodological impugning. It is possible to complain about something in every piece of social research, and social scientists, being a quarrelsome lot, are not slow to find it. But that does not mean that anything goes in striking trade-offs. There are always better and worse trade-offs to be found to address a particular research question, and there are some that lie so far behind the trade-off curve, or so far to one extreme of that curve, that they would clearly constitute poor research design.

What is 'research design'?

But what, actually, is 'research design'? By the *design* of a research project, social scientists usually mean (1) the specification of the way in which data will be created, collected, constructed, coded, analysed and interpreted (2) to enable the researcher to draw warranted descriptive, explanatory or interpretive inferences (3) where the warrant is calculated to strike a reasonable trade-off between competing virtues; and (4) where the standards of warrant may vary slightly, but are based on a core set of virtues for each type of inference.

A research design is usually set out in advance of undertaking a project, in a research plan or *proposal*. A more detailed statement of the methodological defence of a research proposal is often provided in a *protocol*, which lays out in detail the steps through which the inference will proceed and the degree to which the conclusion can be supported, given the nature of the data and the nature of the methods used to create, collect, code, construct and analyse them.

Standards of good research design

The simplest standards of soundness in methodology are those of *reliability* and *validity*.

Reliability

Reliability has to do with how we measure – or, if we are using qualitative data, code – the things in which we are interested. A reliable system of measurement or coding is *consistent* in that, each time it is used on the same data, it yields the same measure or code. If two researchers work together, and both follow the same procedure on the same data, they should produce the same measures or codes. Redoing the coding or measurement, to see how reliable the procedure is, is called the 'test/retest' method of assessing reliability.

A second way to assess reliability at the level of method is called the 'internal consistency' method. This does not rely on repeating the coding or measurement of the same data, but on gathering additional data using the same design. In a questionnaire survey, for example, we might insert several questions, each phrased slightly differently, to ask the same thing. If they elicit the same answers from the respondents as did the first, then they provide some evidence that the first question was reliable.

Validity

Validity is, loosely, the degree to which our statements approximate to truth. It is conventional to distinguish between construct and conclusion validity, and between internal and external validity.

Construct validity is the degree to which the measures or codes used to operationalise a concept really capture what we intend to capture. For example, suppose we want to know how much 'goodwill' people have toward their neighbours in their own street. Goodwill is not a straightforward concept. We might ask about people's attitudes to other people in general and to their neighbours in particular. Perhaps we should ask about hypothetical future neighbours who might differ in important ways – for example, in their ethnic origins – from the present ones. But we should surely want to know, too, about how people actually behave toward different neighbours. Perhaps we would want to know about how they think they would behave in certain hypothetical situations, such as a severe fall of snow in the neighbourhood. We might also want to know about how they expect their neighbours to behave toward them.

Having settled on a set of measures or codes, we could assess their construct validity in several ways. The simplest way might be to look at theories of goodwill, and compare our measures or codes with the features used in those theories. If we are collecting quantitative data, we might use statistical analysis to determine whether there are common factors that run through each of our chosen measures – such as whether goodwill is based, say, on 'social affinity' (sharing ideals and beliefs) or 'social reciprocity' (helping each other out), or whether in our observed cases, the values point in different directions: for example, goodwill may be strong where it depends on affinity but less so where it depends on reciprocity. If so, we might wonder whether, in fact, 'goodwill' is a single phenomenon after all, and instead stipulate different 'types' of goodwill. This process would increase the construct validity of our concept of goodwill, by giving it more operational precision.

Measurement validity is a subtype of construct validity. It captures the extent to which any given measure or code allows us to attribute values, say to different factors in, or dimensions of, 'goodwill' without importing systematic bias. Measurement validity is important whether we use cardinal (1, 2, 3…) or ordinal (1st, 2nd, 3rd…) numbers, on–off codes (yes/no) or qualitative values (such as 'strong/moderate/weak').

Conclusion validity concerns the warrant we have for making inferences from our conclusions. It relates to the degree of support which the patterns observed in the data provide for the conclusions drawn from them. If we conclude, for example, that goodwill based in social affinity tends to be stronger than that based in social reciprocity, the question is whether this conclusion is a reasonable statement of what the data show.

Internal validity applies within a study, regardless of whether we want to generalise to others. It concerns the warrant we have for inferring that an outcome can be explained by a particular causal factor. If we claim, for example, that our study shows that 'social reciprocity' becomes stronger the longer people are neighbours, regardless of factors such as race, then the test of the study's internal validity is the extent to which we can show from our data that this really is the case.

External validity concerns the warrant we have for inferring that our findings would hold in other situations or studies that were similar in relevant ways. Clearly, there is a gradient of similarity and dissimilarity. As samples or cases become less similar, external validity is bound to fall, along with our ability to generalise from the study. So, for example, the findings of a study of neighbourly goodwill in an American small town might be expected to hold in towns of a similar size and with a similar socio-demographic structure, but not in a city or in a small town with very different population. This means that a key issue in securing external validity is knowing what features of our cases or population are 'relevant' for this purpose, and what makes them 'similar' or dissimilar.

Trade-offs between validity and reliability

Just as there are trade-offs between different virtues in research design, so there can also be trade-offs between validity and reliability. At first blush, this might seem an odd claim. After all, as a measure or code declines in reliability, so it must also become less valid.

But there are some things we may want to measure or code in social science that are not amenable to straightforward measurement or coding. Suppose, for example, we want to understand the differences between people in respect of their capacity to make discriminating and thoughtful judgements in the fields of the arts such as music, theatre, literature and dance. Measuring taste, or aesthetic judgement, requires a cluster of different dimensions, because it is not just one thing. We should need to measure or code the breadth of the arts over which someone was capable of exercising judgement; whether they did so in consistent ways; and also the different ways in which they might be more and less articulate in their judgements; and so on.

Bringing all these measures or codes together into one composite indicator of taste could be done in a variety of different ways. We could, for example, increase the validity of our composite measure or code of taste by adding more subsidiary measures, such as scope, consistency and articulacy. That process would pick up more dimensions of this complex concept, but it would increase the difficulty of choosing a way of combining them, and our composite measure would be sensitive to whatever method we chose to weight and relate measures of particular dimensions of taste.

In other words, we would risk reliability for gains in validity. Beyond a certain point, too great a sacrifice of reliability will also ruin validity, and the range of *acceptable* trade-offs between the two values – for example, between reliable precision and valid relevance – especially in measuring complex or rich qualitative concepts such as taste is probably quite narrow. But there is usually more than one defensible trade-off to be struck dealing with this problem.

Sometimes, though, the trade-off problem can become vicious. Problems arise most acutely where the very process of doing the measurement or coding changes the thing being measured. For example, doing research about behaviours which are unlawful or which are regarded as immoral can cause the people being studied to behave more cautiously because they are being watched, or, alternatively, to show bravado by exaggerating their sinful behaviour. This is a problem that is well recognised, for example, among researchers who want to conduct ethnographic studies of institutional racism or bullying, where attempts directly to observe behaviour by means of non-participant observation end up by seriously undermining both validity and reliability.

This problem is also familiar to policy-makers. Goodhart's law was originally developed in the 1970s and 1980s, when new, more complex measures were developed by central banks of what counted as 'money'. The reason for measuring money in different ways was that central banks began to be charged with gaining control over the money supply, and needed to know how well they were doing. Unfortunately, the introduction of measurement and the use of policy measures to influence the money supply interacted in unexpected ways. Quite simply, when measures focused on one definition, people created money on some other definition instead: the central banks' work began to seem like squeezing a balloon in one part, only to expand the bulge at another.

The former Bank of England economist Charles Goodhart concluded that the very effort to measure money was making those measures less valid. He generalised his finding to any situation in which measurement was associated with policy action and so had behavioural consequences. Goodhart's original formulation of his law concerned the application of policy action – 'any observed statistical regularity will tend to collapse once pressure is placed upon it for control purposes'. Later formulations have extended it to make the point that even introducing or publishing a measure will have behavioural consequences that reduce its validity for capturing the phenomenon of interest. The problem of Goodhart's law matters most in research conducted over a period of time, when the people being studied have time to react to the research. So it particularly affects longitudinal research or where the activity being studied is one about which people have normative views.

We shall return to these concepts in Chapter 6 to explore how they are applied to research designs that use variables. In the more advanced chapters about explanation and interpretation, we shall look at various ways in which internal validity can be pursued in observational research, not least because many method textbooks give only experimental examples of internal validity. Construct validity is of central concern in Chapter 9 on concept formation and is at the heart of the methodological challenges for good interpretive work that we discuss in Chapters 15 and 16.

TWO

Methodology and social science knowledge

This chapter will:

- examine what it is that social science seeks to describe, interpret or explain, by distinguishing events, trends, states of affairs and conditions;
- discuss whether social science methodology for describing, explaining or interpreting is fundamentally different from that used in natural sciences;
- distinguish three levels of intellectual claim that social science examines, namely paradigms or frameworks, theories and models; and
- examine the relationships between them.

Why do practical social researchers need to know some philosophy?

In the next three chapters we enter the terrain within the philosophy of social science which is specifically concerned with the status of the knowledge we claim to be able to find by doing social research. We shall assume no prior knowledge of philosophy in general or of philosophy of science in particular. But to make sense of the rest of the book, it is important that you first acquire some understanding of the principal terms used in the philosophy of social science, along with some familiarity with the contours of philosophical debates that are relevant to methodology.

Everyday practice of research in the social sciences continues to have a close involvement with philosophical debate. Rival traditions of substantive theory often claim to rely on rival philosophical arguments, and advocates of particular methods – such as the statistical analysis of questionnaire-based attitudinal survey work or ethnographic participant observation – often justify their claims on the basis of philosophical arguments. Unsurprisingly, therefore, some of the mistakes and muddles we get ourselves into are as much philosophical as they are to do with the application of particular methods.

In this chapter, then, we shall first examine the kinds of phenomena about which we seek knowledge when we carry out social science research. We shall then consider the principal kinds of knowledge yielded by social science in the forms of *models*, *theories* and *paradigms* (or *frameworks*), before going on to explore in the next chapter what is meant when we claim that social science research can *empirically test*, *confirm* or *falsify* them on the basis of our data. Social scientists often aspire to decide between rival theoretical statements. We shall therefore examine what is involved in comparing, judging and, when necessary, replacing theories, and how far this process can be said to occur in a once-and-for-all manner in social science.

In Chapter 4, we shall revisit the same arguments, this time using the lenses provided by the main philosophical positions to which social scientists appeal when they seek to justify their methodologies, and when they criticise those of other social scientists. We shall see that each of these stances holds particular views about each of the questions examined in the next two chapters. This discussion will help us to draw out the methodological implications of these questions.

What do we try to describe, explain and interpret?

Consider the empirical claims in Example 2.1. Each has been taken from highly reputable research in the social sciences.

EXAMPLE 2.1. SOME KNOWLEDGE CLAIMS MADE AS A RESULT OF SOCIAL SCIENCE RESEARCH

- In April and early May 1962, as [Soviet premier] Khrushchev was finalising his decision to send missiles to Cuba, he was confronting an enormous problem with Berlin. (Allison and Zelikow, 1999: 106)
- Child poverty … has fallen by 600,000 to the nearest hundred thousand (or just under one-fifth) in the ten years since 1998–99 and needs to fall by a further 1.1 million in the remaining two years until 2010–11 to meet this element of the [government's] target. (Brewer *et al.*, 2001: 8–9)
- A loss of $x is more aversive [to people in general] than a gain of $x is attractive. (Kahneman and Tversky, 2000: 3)
- Azande speak of dreams as oracles, for they reveal hidden things (soroka). (Evans-Pritchard, 1976 [1937]: 174) [The Azande are a people living in an area today occupied by the states of Sudan, the Democratic Republic of Congo and the Central African Republic.]

The first statement in Example 2.1 describes an *event* – the Soviet leader's fateful decision that led to the Cuban Missile Crisis of 1962.

The second statement quantifies child poverty in the last ten years or so, and describes a once-and-for-all change that occurred over a defined period, or a *trend*.

Events, temporary states of affairs and trends have defined dates and places to bound them.

The third statement describes something that, if it is true, needs no bounding by time and place. The psychological generalisation of loss aversion is a *regularity*, a generalisation that rests on a very large number of observations, each of which shows the same consistent behaviour.

The fourth statement describes a *condition*, or a state of affairs which presumably has some boundaries in space or time but where those boundaries are not clearly defined. Moreover, a *condition* may or may not be tied to any regularity of *particular* behaviours or actions.

Social science research makes claims about each type of phenomena. To be sure, there are people who argue that events and *temporary* states of affairs might be proper matters for historians or political biographers, but not for social science research: so they could be properly consigned to the humanities. They would argue that social science should, like every other science, be interested in seeking *general* explanations, and should only be interested in particular cases – such as Khrushchev's decisions about Cuba and Berlin in 1962 – in so far as they are examples of more general phenomena, such as political decision-making.

This argument may be overstated. Individual cases may be of considerable interest for a number of reasons. They may offer an extreme example of something of great interest – such as political decision-making in an extreme crisis, such as the Cuban Missile Crisis – or because they are unique and thus provide us with important understanding of the limits to generalisation.

EXERCISE 2.1. IDENTIFYING EVENTS, TEMPORARY STATES OF AFFAIRS, TRENDS, REGULARITIES AND CONDITIONS

Think about a research project that you intend, or hope, to do.

Is the focus of this research an event, a temporary state of affairs, a trend, a regularity or a condition? And do you intend/hope to describe, explain or interpret it?

What do we get from social science research?

Each of the four statements in Example 2.1 sets out claims of fact. Moreover, each has been made on the basis of inference from data. The first statement is based on documents, such as state papers, memoirs, diaries and newspaper reportage. The second statement rests on published quantitative data about family income. The third statement rests heavily on results from laboratory experiments, rather than on data captured from people who are not subject to control by researchers. And the fourth statement rests on data captured by fieldwork conducted over several years in the 1920s and 1930s, during which the researcher lived among the Azande, taking detailed notes and asking questions.

The result, in each case, is a *descriptive inference*. The data on which they are based are taken from very different sources, but what they have in common is that statements of putative facts are made on the basis of more or less *structured* evidence.

Description is useful, but social scientists aspire to more than descriptive inference, in that we also want either to *explain* or to *interpret* our findings.

Social scientists present the products of explanation and interpretation as *theories*, *frameworks* and *models*. Theories, frameworks and models work by *reduction*. That is, they help us to see more clearly what lies behind the blooming, buzzing profusion and variety of empirical events, states of affairs, trends, regularities and conditions, by identifying a small number of general, abstract phenomena which characterise them or may, even, cause them. So they help us to see the shape of the theoretical wood in the empirical trees. Indeed, it is often held that the more convincingly we can show that a small number of more, rather than less, abstract phenomena account for a wide a range of empirical phenomena – that is, the more parsimonious our account – the better. Example 2.2 shows how a parsimonious theory helps us to understand and deal with crime.

EXAMPLE 2.2. HOW THEORIES ACHIEVE REDUCTION OF VARIETY IN EMPIRICAL DATA

In the field of crime prevention, a very simple but very influential theory – known as the theory of situational crime prevention (e.g. Clarke, 1980) – proposes that criminal acts which appear, empirically, to be very different can all be explained by the presence of an opportunity and an opportunistic individual. This is because it holds that crime is the outcome of how a *personal disposition to crime* interacts with *situational opportunities* (or temptation) through the mediation of a *criminal's decision-making* process.

The theory thus *reduces* the empirical diversity of crimes such as robberies, assaults, fiddling expenses and intellectual piracy to these three general, abstract factors. It proposes that crime can be prevented – or at least its volume reduced – by reducing opportunities for crime, and that this can be done by changing key aspects of the situations in which it is committed.

Such measures include redesigning cars to make them harder to steal and introducing visible CCTV cameras in car parks and elsewhere.

Social and natural sciences

Is there anything philosophically distinctive about the methodologies used for description, interpretation or explanation, or about the accounts offered for events, trends, states of affairs and conditions in social science, from those offered by natural and physical science?

This may seem to be a question of no great practical importance for most social scientists who expect to conduct most of their research work within the confines of social science. However, the trend is toward ever-deeper collaboration between social scientists and natural sciences, so this might well become a practical issue for many readers. In development studies, for example, it is now commonplace for anthropologists and sociologists to work alongside biotechnologists and agronomists to examine the ways that innovations in crops, weedkillers and pesticides are actually used in rural communities and how outcomes in such settings may be different from those observed in field trials in research centres. Vast sums are also spent on collaborations between social scientists and information technologists to understand the ways in which people's use of computing and telecommunications tools shapes, and is shaped by, new technologies, producing outcomes that could not have been predicted from either social science studies of behaviour in offices or computer science models of technological change.

In collaborations such as these, reconciling methodologies for drawing inferences from data becomes central to the success of research. So the claim that there is something fundamentally different in social and natural sciences is a practically important one. Four justifications for this claim are usually given special importance.

The first can be disposed of quickly. This is the claim that natural and technological science is fundamentally based on the experimental method, in which the researcher can control the independent variables, whereas social science is basically observational, and thus the researcher cannot achieve such control.

Quite simply, both parts of the proposition are false. Much of natural science is conducted through mathematical modelling before any experiments are considered, and sometimes several years – or even centuries – before the necessary technology is available to conduct them. In natural sciences such as astronomy, for example, direct experimentation is far beyond human powers: experiments can be done only with physical models in which the relationship between the phenomena the astronomers want to understand depends on theory. Geology works with time periods so vast that the possibility of experimentation is very limited. Oceanographers have many theories that work at the scale of whole oceans or whole global systems and that simply do not admit of direct experiment. In many specialist fields of zoology, such as the study of primates and cetaceans, observational studies probably comprise the majority of what is published for both ethical and practical reasons.

Conversely, there are experiments in the social sciences, and not just the laboratory experiments so beloved of psychologists. As we shall see in Chapter 5, a rich vein of work in political science is concerned with conducting field experiments to find out, for example, whether certain kinds of intervention have any effect on people's propensity to vote. Similarly, in social policy, many more randomised controlled trials are being funded today to examine the potential impact of particular approaches, for example to the treatment of addiction and to crime prevention.

The second claim is that causation in human systems is fundamentally different from that in any natural or animal system, requiring fundamentally different forms of modelling and therefore of research design. For many years, this was taken to be obviously true, but in fact it is far from clear that the premise is true or that, even if it is, the conclusion follows from it.

First, many animals clearly exhibit complex social organisation, perform rituals, engage in communication, collaborate, engage in competition and organised conflict, form kinship structures, exchange goods and services, use tools and so on. Human organisation may be more extensive, but it does not follow that the basic causal processes are fundamentally different. We used to believe that human systems are distinctive in being non-linear, complex in the sense of having sustaining self-organisation, and capable of irreversible causal processes and of exhibiting both positive and negative feedback dynamics. In fact, however, the social sciences have had to borrow every one of their models for these causal processes from natural sciences such as meteorology, oceanography and biology, and our use of such tools remains primitive by comparison with theirs.

A third claim is that natural science theories are more parsimonious than social science ones. It is true that the famous basic laws of physics, chemistry, microbiology and astronomy are indeed rather parsimonious. However, even in the natural sciences, the aspiration for reduction is sometimes qualified. For example, botany is committed to retaining quite a lot of blooming, buzzing profusion in its theories; so too are meteorology, geology, oceanography and many technological sciences such as agronomy.

Social science as the study of 'meanings'

The fourth claim is the only genuinely interesting one. This is the thesis that social scientists study '*meanings*'. This capacious term encompasses the full range of mental life including ideas, beliefs, desires, systems of classification, emotions, judgement and styles of thought. Some methodologists argue that studying meanings, in this sense, rather than just studying behaviour, makes a fundamental difference not only to the kinds of data with which we work, but also to our methods of analysis. It also makes, they claim, a fundamental difference to the methodologies we use for drawing inferences from data, and to what counts as an explanation.

The premise of this argument is true and no longer very controversial. Although in the 1950s and 1960s, behaviouralism in political science aimed to explain political behaviour and power without reference to meanings, it is not now judged to have been a success. Today, everyone is interested in meanings, from rational choice theorists who try to specify people's goals to describe their utility functions, through to ethnographers.

The second stage in the argument, likewise, is true. Data about meanings are different in kind from data about physical behaviour, whether they take the form of quantitative survey data about social attitudes or the less structured form of interview transcripts or observational field notes.

What remains deeply suspect, however, is the conclusion that methodologies used for data about meanings are, or ought to be, fundamentally different in character from those used for data about anything else. If we are engaged in causal explanation, we need to show how, for example, reasons or ideas operate to bring about action. And there can be true or false statements about what relationship a reason or an idea has to an action.

Think, for example, about Khrushchev's decision to deploy nuclear missiles in Cuba in 1962, which was mentioned in Example 2.1. We shall see later in this chapter that there are several theories about what was in his mind. But if one set of reasons was more important than the others, then that would change very fundamentally the way we explain the Cuban Missile Crisis. Beliefs and intentions have to be inferred, and form parts of coherent causal accounts exhibiting certain virtues before they can explain. Inference and building causal accounts are the core explanatory activities of all the sciences.

Later in the book, we shall discuss in more detail the argument that a science of meanings is methodologically distinct and that, furthermore, it must somehow eschew explanation altogether and deal with interpretation instead. In Chapters 15 and 16, we shall argue that one reason this argument fails is that it is very difficult indeed to produce an interpretation that does not imply some claims, however well disguised, about causal explanation. For the moment, we need only say that the argument is greatly overstated.

This conclusion is good news for those who engage in collaboration with natural scientists. But it does not follow from it that the social sciences should emulate the natural sciences. Indeed, this inference would make little sense. As indicated by some of the examples we listed above, there is no great consistency in the methodologies used by different natural sciences: those used by oceanography and fundamental physics are, for example, quite different and it would be impossible to emulate both at once.

The fundamental canon of methodology is all sciences must develop methods and methodologies that suit their theories, their puzzles and their data.

Paradigms, theories and models

Each social science discipline has its own theoretical traditions, but among those that cross several disciplines are rational choice, Marxism, Durkheimian and Weberian traditions, neo-realism and neo-liberalism, and various institutionalisms. We need not explain these traditions' ideas here, but we need to note the big methodological issue that it is quite easy to develop rival accounts from within the same tradition, as well as from different ones – to explain, say, an event or a regularity.

Paradigms

The intellectual core of a tradition consists in its *paradigms* or *frameworks* (the two terms are used interchangeably here). The canonical characterisation of a paradigm comes from the work of the historian and philosopher Thomas Kuhn, whose mono-graph, *The structure of scientific revolutions* (1970 [1962]), continues to be an important point of reference in both philosophical and methodological debates. For our present purposes, we can define a paradigm as a:

> shared commitment by an identifiable group of scientists about what is to be observed or examined and therefore what counts as relevant data for answering those research questions which are deemed important, how those data should be interpreted, and what structure we should expect in satisfying answers to those questions.

In particular, the paradigm specifies what is required by its peculiar tradition to be included in any satisfying explanation of an event, temporary state of affairs, trend, regularity or condition. Example 2.3 shows how a specific paradigm – neo-realism – works in the field of international relations.

EXAMPLE 2.3. THE PARADIGM OF NEO-REALISM IN INTERNATIONAL RELATIONS

This paradigm proposes that we should look for explanations of the foreign policy decisions of national governments by reference to the interests which those states have in securing a better relative position vis-à-vis other states. It further proposes that when, say, prime ministers claim to be acting for the good of the whole international community, we should not interpret this claim at face value, but look, rather, at the underlying national interests served by their rhetoric.

That is, the neo-realist paradigm tells us to weigh evidence about the expected benefits and costs to a state's position more heavily than claims to shared benefits, and proposes, further-more, that research questions about *interests* are much more important than research ques-tions about either *ideas* or *institutions*.

How paradigms change

It might be thought that – as the guardians of the cores of traditions – paradigms are unchanging and more or less impossible to challenge, and that people who wish to dispute anything they have to say about what constitutes good research will be forced to find homes in other traditions.

This assumption is too simple. The broad traditions in social sciences – such as rational choice, institutionalism or Durkheimian social theory – could not sur-vive unless they are sufficiently flexible to accommodate change. For example, Durkheimian social theorists used to explain arrangements such as family forms or industrial relations practices by referring to the function they performed for a 'soci-ety' as a whole. Today, Durkheimians would not do this. The idea that 'societies' – however they might be defined – have 'needs' has proven to be unhelpful, and can now be sustained only by being so heavily modified by other theoretical insights that it loses all claims to parsimony. Yet other kinds of functional explanations are still important in this tradition.

Again, conventional rational choice theory explains action by showing that people pursue their goals under constraints. Originally, this tradition assumed that people were basically neutral toward risk, but the advent of 'prospect theory' (Kahneman and Tversky, 2000) has challenged that assumption. This theory explains why people are averse to losses in some situations but willing to bear risks in others. However, prospect theory has preserved the basic idea of optimising subjective utility under constraint, and a debate is now going on about whether the change falls within the basic paradigm or breaks with it: for example, Levy (1997) finds the two approaches often empirically difficult to distinguish.

It appears from both these examples that 'peripheral propositions' – those which are less central to the identity of the tradition and less critical for its approach to explanation – can be surrendered if they prove unworkable, provided that 'core' or fundamental claims are maintained. Thus traditions persist, even though some aspects of their paradigms may change. Indeed, this view of how scientific traditions progress was set out in the work of an important philosopher of science, Imre Lakatos (1970).

Theories

Paradigms or frameworks do not, of themselves, describe, explain or interpret anything. But they tell us how descriptions, explanations and interpretations should be developed within the tradition in which we are working. We can then derive candidate explanations of particular regularities, trends or states of affairs or conditions from paradigms, so long, of course, as we have sufficient empirical data about these things. Candidate explanations of *particular* events, temporary state of affairs, trends, regularities or conditions are *theories*.

The theories with which we work for a particular piece of research may be extensions or refinements of ones that other people have previously developed, or they may be ones that we develop ourselves. But whenever we form a view about the *character*, *causes* or *significance* of events or conditions and so on, we are working, respectively, with a *descriptive*, *explanatory* or *interpretive theory* about them. Social researchers are, of course, usually aware of the theory from which they *deduce* the formal hypotheses that they propose to test in a piece of research. But, of course, the hunches or insights that lead us to stipulate research questions for more open-ended pieces of exploratory research are also based on ideas about states of affairs, conditions and so on. And so, the discussion in Chapter 13 about the use of deduction and induction in social science research will argue that there is necessarily an element of deduction from some kind of theory in the structure of all social science research.

Likewise, practical decisions made in government, business or social agencies depend on ideas, however implicit, about the character of particular social or business problems and the reasons why an intervention is likely to 'work' in the expected way. These ideas are, of course, theories, too. Indeed, some social scientists who work with such organisations (Pawson and Tilley, 1997) argue that one task of social science is to help decision-makers make explicit the theories on which practical decisions are based, partly so that these theories can be clearly stated and tested, but also to capture more systematically the tacit knowledge on which these decisions are based.

Suppose, for example, a local council decides to introduce CCTV cameras in the market square of their town. Their staff are, presumably, working with some ideas about why CCTV will reduce crime in that situation. These ideas – whether formulated in these terms or not – may be similar to, and can perhaps help further develop, those formally proposed by the theory of situational crime prevention we looked at in Example 2.2.

Rival theories within the same paradigm

Most paradigms allow us to generate several rival theories for the same phenomenon. So showing that one theory is false will not, by itself, falsify the paradigm. We discuss this point in Example 2.4.

EXAMPLE 2.4. THREE RIVAL THEORIES TO EXPLAIN ONE EVENT, ALL FROM ONE PARADIGM

Suppose we are interested in explaining why Soviet leader Nikita Khrushchev took the highly risky decision in 1962 to deploy nuclear missiles in Cuba, and to do so in secret.

The rational choice paradigm requires explanations based on individual desires, beliefs, capabilities and constraints. It assumes that a decision-maker has a set of intelligible goals derived from his or her strategic interests, and ranks them in a consistent and coherent manner. It assumes, too, that he or she arrives at this ranking using consistent inferences from the available information, and is not so constrained by circumstances that none of those goals can be pursued. Thus, a rational choice explanation asks for:

- a set of ranked preferences or goals, so that when the first preferences become unavailable, there are second preferences, and so on;
- a set of *beliefs* about how preferences can be pursued;
- a set of *capabilities* to act; and
- some *constraints on action*, such as limited information or resources, but not absolute constraints.

It is possible to develop several plausible theories that meet these requirements, indeed scholars of the Cuban Missile Crisis have done so.

(Continued)

One theory holds that Khrushchev was trying to protect Cuba from what he believed, on the basis of intelligence reports and inference from US policy, was a likely American invasion. Cuba had recently become a socialist republic following Fidel Castro's overthrow of the previous regime and the USA had sponsored an unsuccessful invasion by anti-Castro exiles in the previous year.

Another theory holds that Khrushchev was concerned only with trying to regain closer parity with the USA in terms of their mutual capability for threatening each other with nuclear war. This downplays Soviet concern for Cuba, other than as a theatre of superpower conflict.

A third theory holds that Khrushchev wanted to bind the fledgling Cuban socialist state into the Soviet system of alliances to stop it drifting under Chinese influence.

For each of these three theories, it is possible to supply plausible goals, reasons why Khrushchev might have believed that deploying Soviet missiles to Cuba would further them and reasons why he might have thought that the USSR had the capacity to do so.

Example 2.4 shows that three rival theories can be developed to account for Khrushchev's behaviour during the Cuban Missile Crisis, each consonant with the canons of rational choice. If, however, we could show that Khrushchev was not driven by any of the goals stipulated by these theories, we would not have shown that no satisfactory rational choice theory for his decisions could be developed – unless we were able to show, too, that there were *no* other goals that could provide a more convincing rational choice explanation.

Models

Each of the theories offered in Example 2.4 is schematic. By this we mean that, for each theory, we could specify slightly but *measurably* different accounts of the sets of:

- the constraints under which Khrushchev was working (financial, time, military and so on);
- the particular beliefs that the Soviet leader might have held; and
- the appetite among Soviet political and military leaders for different risks.

Each of the different ways of specifying the factors prescribed by the rational choice paradigm produces, in turn, a slightly different explanation of Khrushchev's decisions during the crisis, including their timing and the changing nature of his willingness to bargain with the Americans. So we could say that the different specifications of these factors prescribed by this paradigm would produce, for each of our three goal-based theories, a distinct *model* of Soviet decision-making in the Cuban Missile Crisis.

In social science, a model is a formal representation of exactly how a theory might be realised, showing how the explanatory factors are (1) to be measured, (2) predicted to be linked with each other and (3) how they relate to what is being described or explained. *Specification* is the development of precise statements of each of these three things.

In model-building, parsimony is usually weighted more heavily than goodness of fit or generalisability. This is because models are *reductionist* by intention: the main reason for building models is to isolate as clearly as possible the key factors and the relationships between them. This is why models are used in descriptive and particularly in explanatory inference, but to a lesser degree in interpretation which often tends to privilege other values, such as goodness of fit, over parsimony.

To revert to the example we used in Chapter 1, for example, a comprehensive model explaining a rise in the numbers of people sleeping rough in a town would need to include, say: changes in the characteristics of homeless people; routes out of homelessness; local labour markets; aspects of criminal justice policy and its implementation; demographic factors; and changes in national government policy or interventions by local councils. In practice, no one would attempt to construct a complete model of so complex a phenomenon. Instead, in striking trade-offs between various virtues of explanation, we would surely try to achieve more parsimony by excluding the less important variables, even at the expense of reduced goodness of fit or limiting the range of variance that could be explained.

A first test of a good model is that it is sufficiently 'specified'. In the case of an explanatory model, it must distinguish the important causal factors and specify their relationships with the outcome to be explained. And it must do this with sufficient clarity and detail to allow the model to be tested, provided the right data are available. Highly quantitative models often use algebraic specifications for testing statistical relationships between variables. But for other kinds of research, models can be specified adequately for testing using geometric representations (i.e. diagrams), or very rich, rigorous and careful qualitative statements.

The relationship between theories and models

Most theories are capable of being realised by several models, depending on how each factor is specified. Because theories can be realised by several models, it is usually easier to test a model than a whole theory. If one model fails, the same theory may yield another model that would be more consistent with the data.

It is sometimes possible to build a well-specified model, but lack a good theory to explain it. For example, we may be able to show a statistical association between a fall in gross domestic product (as a measure of economic activity in a country) and a rise in rough sleeping, but not know whether one causes the other. Our model will, nevertheless, still be of genuine interest if we believe that, sooner or later, we shall be able to develop a causal theory to explain the association. So when social scientists condemn someone else's work with that most damning of dismissals, that it is 'atheoretical', they may really be saying that a researcher has developed a model but has yet to specify a theory that provides a reason for being interested in it.

An important conclusion to be drawn from this discussion is that researchers should clarify both for themselves and for their readers just what inferential status they are claiming for their findings. For it is dangerously easy to claim more than the findings will warrant, for example by over-interpreting a finding as either supporting or undermining a theory, when, in fact, the research does no more than support or undermine a model. Similarly, it is dangerous to claim that a piece of research supports or undermines a paradigm when the findings do no more than support or disturb a theory.

EXERCISE 2.2. BUILDING THEORIES AND MODELS

Think about the rough sleepers example we have used in this chapter and the previous one, and try to formulate at least two, and preferably three, different *explanatory* theories that would account for a statistical association between an economic recession (defined as a fall in gross domestic product for two consecutive quarters) and the rise in the number of rough sleepers in a particular town in the same period.

Next, specify a model to test each theory. You can set it out in prose, if you prefer, or in diagrammatic form, or indeed algebraically.

Finally, identify the tradition(s) within which your theories are situated, and itemise the core features of its/their paradigms.

Basic reading

A good place to start for readers with little background in philosophical debates is Ford J, 1975, I beg your pardon, in J Ford, *Paradigms and fairy tales*, London: Routledge, 1–16.

Advanced reading

Kuhn TS, 1970 [1962], *The structure of scientific revolutions*, Chicago: University of Chicago Press.
A challenge to Kuhn which has attracted wide interest is Lakatos I, 1970, Falsification and the methodology of scientific research programmes, in I Lakatos and A Musgrave (eds), *Criticism and the growth of knowledge*, Cambridge: Cambridge University Press, 91–196.

THREE

Testing, confirming and falsifying

This chapter will:

- examine what is involved in confirming or disconfirming a model or a theory;
- discuss what counts as a test of a theory or model;
- examine how observations relate to theoretical claims made in theories and models;
- explore the risks presented by trying 'save a theory' by using auxiliary hypotheses;
- examine problems of comparing theories to see which works best; and
- consider the implications of this chapter for replacing theories and paradigms by better ones.

We have already introduced terms such as 'supporting', 'undermining', 'testing', 'confirming' and 'falsifying' to describe the relationships that data can have with models or theories. It is time to examine these terms in more detail.

Most theories of any interest have *something* going for them. Let us start with a simple example of a theory which is not deeply explanatory, but mainly descriptive. This is the widely discussed theory that since the 1960s, the way in which manufacturing production is organised has changed fundamentally. It holds that the system that held sway from the 1920s to the 1960s involved the mass production of highly standardised products for mass markets by vertically integrated firms that made their own tools and parts. This system was known as 'Fordism' because the Ford Motor Corporation was one of the earliest and most important companies to use it. According to this theory, Fordism has now broken down, and manufacturing has moved toward more flexible production systems capable of turning out a much greater variety of products aimed at small niches of consumers. These systems require shorter production runs, more variation in production tools and techniques, and thus more outsourcing of the supply chain for materials, parts and tools. Terms like 'post-Fordism' and 'flexible specialisation' are used to describe this new approach.

The theory does indeed have something going for it, and it is not hard to find examples that appear to confirm it. On the other hand, most theories also face at least *some* contrary evidence, as you will probably find if you do Exercise 3.1.

EXERCISE 3.1. IDENTIFYING CONFIRMING AND DISCONFIRMING INSTANCES

Write down some examples of trends in manufacturing and/or retailing that seem to be *consistent* with the theory of 'post-Fordism'.

Now write down some examples of trends in manufacturing and/or retailing that seem to be *inconsistent* with the theory of 'post-Fordism'.

If you are struggling to think of anything, it might to help to think about, say, ringtones for mobile phones or stores such as IKEA, and to consider what aspects of such phenomena are 'Fordist' or 'post-Fordist'.

Saving a theory from defeat by counter-examples

But if we rejected every theory that faced some contrary evidence, we would have to reject all or most theories in social science. This means that many – perhaps all – theories and models need to be refined in the course of their development, usually by supplying auxiliary hypotheses.

For example, many social scientists now offer explanations of welcome states of affairs such as low crime rates, good public health, impressive economic growth or peace between rival religions, by reference to 'social capital' (e.g. Putnam, 2000; Halpern, 2005). Social capital is defined and measured in somewhat different ways by different scholars, but a conventional characterisation emphasises the importance of benign social connections of acquaintanceship, friendship, mutual respect and trust. But only a moment's thought is needed to realise that successful criminals, too, must trust each other, and must have strong social bonds. So the simple version of the theory – that all positive social ties are beneficial in reducing crime – cannot be right.

But some auxiliary hypotheses can save the theory. For example, we can suggest (with Sampson *et al.*, 1997) that what is most important are the ties that connect law-abiding people (1) to criminals so that they know who is doing wrong and (2) to each other and to people in authority so that they will be willing to report crime. Thus, even if criminals are strongly bonded – provided other ties of the right kind exist – we might be able to explain reduced crime rates.

What have we done by adding these auxiliary hypotheses? First, we have added new content. Second, we have used that new content to qualify and modify the original theory, without abandoning the causal force it proposed. Third, we have made it much more specific. That is, we have moved closer to turning a general theory into a testable model. In doing so, we have saved the theory from falsification by some obvious contrary evidence.

Crucial tests of theories and models

Ideally, we want to design research that provides a *crucial test* of a theory, or at least of a model. To do this, we need a test that would show that there is no other *plausible* explanation than that offered by the theory or model. Thus, a *crucial disconfirmation* occurs when we can show that that no plausible auxiliary hypotheses can be developed that make the theory consistent with the data – the theory has to be wrong. *Crucial confirmation* occurs when we can show that no plausible auxiliary hypotheses can be developed that would make the theory *inconsistent* with the data – the theory has to be right. Crucial confirmation tests for anything interesting are rare in social sciences, and it is much debated whether crucial disconfirmation tests are available at all.

In practice, it is often possible to find alternative explanations for most findings produced by social science research, at least if we are prepared to make some changes in our models to accommodate them. This means that it is rare that we find a *crucial* test.

But this discussion raises an important question: what changes should we be prepared to make to our theory and what limits are there on making changes to save it?

Limits to saving theories and models

There is a view that it does not matter whether explanations in theories or in models *are plausible* or not, provided that they accurately fit the data – that is, if the predictions of the theory or model are borne out by the evidence, then that theory or model should be accepted. So any changes to a theory or model are also acceptable, as long as they fit the data. This view was famously argued by the economist Milton Friedman (1979 [1953]). One reason that he advocated this extreme position was that it enabled him to offer very parsimonious theories and models in economics, which posited little by way of unobservable mental life – beliefs, desires, motives, for example – among the people being studied, especially at the level of the firm. Provided the predictions of economic theory about how firms would behave in the face of changes in prices or whatever were borne out by their behaviour, it did not matter what was going on in the decision-making processes in the firms' board rooms to produce those outcomes.

Several criticisms have been made of Friedman's argument, not least that, to save our theories or models, we may have to pay too high a price in terms of their implausibility. Another is that it makes explanation just too easy to be interesting, because we can always come up with assumptions that will yield an exact fit with the data. In statistics, this inferentially risky procedure is called 'curve fitting'. There are situations in which two curves might show an equivalent goodness of fit with the distribution of the data points: so, on that ground alone, we could not choose between them. Requiring theories and models to be parsimonious may not allow us to choose between them.

So, when contrary evidence turns up for one or more of the things predicted by a theory or model, we have to make *scientific judgements* about what we are prepared to ditch. The problem is that, although various philosophers of science and methodologists have worried away at this issue for decades, there are no precise and generally accepted rules about the plausibility of auxiliary hypotheses and assumptions that could guide researchers.

But there are rules of thumb. Most people would say that if we find ourselves introducing more and more hypotheses to save a theory or a model, especially if they appear to be *ad hoc* in that they are not driven by the core ideas of the underlying theory or even the framework, and if they appear to do nothing but save the theory or model from one or two sets of recalcitrant pieces of evidence, then the theory or model is in deep trouble. The stock example in the textbooks is that of the attempt by Apollonius of Perga to save Ptolemy's theory of planetary movement. This attempt is described in Example 3.1.

EXAMPLE 3.1. AD HOC ADJUSTMENTS TO SAVE THE THEORY FROM THE DATA, BUT LOSING COHERENCE AND ADDING NO NEW EMPIRICAL CONTENT

Ptolemy's theory required the planets to move tidily in circles around the earth. Five of them persistently turned up in places in the sky that did not fit these circles. Undeterred by this inconvenient behaviour, Apollonius proposed to add some extra little circles (epicycles) to their paths, on top of the main circle (the deferent).

(Continued)

The resulting additional complexity produced some very odd-looking lines that did not seem to be driven by the basic idea of one big circle – but it did save the data.

One problem with these epicycles was that it was hard to derive any new predictions of observations from them. Put another way, they did not add any new 'empirical content' to the theory that could be tested against new observations: they just helped the theory better to fit the data that were already available.

Had there been a better theory available – one which did not require epicycles – then perhaps astronomers might have ditched Ptolemy's theory earlier than they did. Unfortunately, the only rival for a very long time was a theory – the heliocentric theory – that created more anomalies that also called for more epicycles to save the day. Trying ellipses worked better, because they required fewer *ad hoc* adjustments, but even they were not quite right. As a result, theory replacement took centuries.

The risk also arises in social science, of saving the data by means of *ad hoc* adjustments which can leave the theory appearing to degenerate. Marx, for example, famously propounded a theory of value which held that the value of a good or service was a function of the labour that went into making and distributing that good or administering that service, and that it had little to do with the capital investment involved. This required him to accept that prices and values could diverge very radically, but that was not a problem for Marx, who wanted to show that the capitalist system produced distorted prices. But as goods became steadily more capital intensive, and the amount of labour directly involved in making them fell, Marxists had to save the theory by arguing that the capital involved should be counted as a product of labour from other parts of the economy, perhaps even the distant past. This meant, however, that goods became progressively more valuable, even though they were getting cheaper. This stratagem detached the idea of a value from that of a price almost completely, so the theory was being saved from badly behaved evidence, but at the price of so extending the concept of labour that it had drifted far from its central theoretical imperative.

Observations and theory

This leads us to another important issue about how we should use observations to test, confirm or disconfirm models and theories.

In social science, we collect data in a variety of ways. We use social surveys based on questionnaires; we use semi-structured interviews; we ask participants to keep diaries for us; we use observation protocols to organise the collection of field notes; and, sometimes, we undertake either laboratory or field experiments. Each type of data rests on what we might call a *technology* of data collection. But this technology is, of course, itself a theory, one that makes claims, first, that the responses of people are capable of being captured by such instruments, and, second, that the data so produced will suffice to test a theory.

In order to analyse our data, we need to conduct some interpretation. Interpretation is done through the way we record and code data. This process too must rest on theory of some kind. Example 3.2 shows that this is because the *terms* in which data are recorded and coded depend, for their meaning and significance, on the theories in which they are based.

EXAMPLE 3.2. CODES TAKE MEANINGS FROM THEORY

Suppose we are coding responses from a transcript of an interview conducted in a doctor's surgery and that the purpose of the interview is to find out about the surgery's practice in handling patient records. We use a code that rates 'willingness to disclose details about a patient to the police on request if the police claim they have evidence of an urgent threat' – an example would be a threat to a child arising from the patient's mental health problems.

Next we develop other detailed codes to rate other aspects of the surgery's practice in relation to disclosure of information from patient records.

After examining the data entered in all the relevant codes, we infer that we can enter '*moderate* protection of patient confidentiality' in a higher-level code that summarises information in these codes.

You will notice that we have used the verb 'to disclose'. Its meaning in our coding scheme derives from the rules and conventions that we adopt to tell us what counts as a 'disclosure' of personal information for the purpose of *our* research. These rules and conventions are, in turn, derived from the substantive theory we wish to test.

Suppose, for example, the research is being conducted to test a theory about the organisational practices that shape how doctors make judgements about the circumstances that justify breaches of patient confidentiality. For such purposes, correspondence with a hospital specialist in the context of referring a patient for medical tests would not count as a relevant 'disclosure', but supplying details of a patient's illegal drug use to the police or social work agencies for the purpose of detecting crime or preventing child abuse would. We would also need conventions, justified by theory, enabling us to judge consistently what counted as 'weak', 'moderate' or 'strong' practices for regulating disclosures thus defined.

This example illustrates the point that, when we come to analyse coded data, we are analysing a set of data that are not in any sense 'raw'. If they were raw descriptions of sounds heard in the interview, they would be useless to us for the purposes of research.

The point illustrated in Example 3.2 has important consequences for using data to reject theories. For example, suppose that our analysis of our coded data suggests that our initial theory about the kinds of confidentiality protection to be expected from doctors appears to be wrong. One possibility is to write an article showing that another poor theory has bitten the dust. But before doing that, we should consider other possibilities.

Could the theory about confidentiality be right, but could there, instead, be something wrong with the theories that underpin the technology we used for data collection, instrument design and coding? It might be possible, for example, to defend our theory of organisational practice by arguing that our empirical test was not a fair one, because the other theories embedded in our 'technology' of interview schedules, coding frames, coding rules – including the meanings given to such terms as 'disclosure' – were faulty.

Some philosophers of science have suggested that there is potentially no limit to the number of theories that could be involved in a piece of research, because, in principle, each term or code we use will rest on still other theories and conventions that could also be challenged. The logic of this argument is that almost the whole of human theorising could be up for grabs in any one piece of research, if we are prepared to be sufficiently imaginative about saving some theories at the expense of others.

But in practice, of course, the situation is rarely so serious. Typically, we bound the set of theories we need to consider by refusing to sacrifice well-established ones about what terms mean or what a particular method does. Conversely, we also avoid defending theories that require *ad hoc* or degenerating adjustments unless there really is no practicable alternative. This brings us to a rule of thumb for deciding which theories to accept and reject when we find anomalous evidence. This can be called a *provisional rule of caution*, and it states that we should normally reject the fewest theories, and particularly those theories the loss of which would be most damaging for the body of social science knowledge. This is to recognise that all social science research necessarily stands on the shoulders of wider bodies of knowledge, including those relating to theories about method and methodology.

But this rule does not relieve researchers of the responsibility to specify models as clearly as possible and to focus empirical tests upon the principal, and especially the more controversial, theories upon which their judgements rely. In particular, methods and methodology sections in articles and theories require us to defend these specifications and designs on which our data collection, coding, analysis and interpretation rest. Exercise 3.4 illustrates this important point.

EXERCISE 3.4. DISTINGUISHING CORE FROM AUXILIARY THEORIES; MAKING SCIENTIFIC JUDGEMENTS ABOUT WHICH THEORIES TO AMEND, WHEN ANOMALOUS DATA ARISE

Go back to your work on rough sleeping for Exercise 2.2.

Take both your most plausible and your least plausible theory of the trend in rough sleeping. Now think about what you would do if some observations you made yield data which, apparently, conflict with these theories. If you were to save these theories, you would have to ditch other theories.

Write down some theories that you would, and some that you would not, be prepared to abandon for the sake of saving your explanation of the rise in rough sleeping, and explain your rationale.

Comparing rival theories

Some of the best, and certainly the most ambitious, social science is done when researchers take two bodies of theory, derive rival predictions from them and do some empirical work to decide which prediction is better supported by their data. In social science, it is probably done too rarely, because it is a hazardous process.

One reason that is so difficult has already been explored. Because paradigms do not yield only one possible theory about most matters of interest, and theories can be modelled in different ways by making changes to how dimensions are specified, achieving a genuinely crucial test to choose between theories is hard. Suppose, for example, that we want to choose between theories of acquisitive crime.

One theory – which is known as the 'market reduction' theory (e.g. Sutton *et al.*, 2001) and which is, in turn, a version of rational choice theory – predicts that overall levels of acquisitive crime, such as burglary, will fall when the demand for stolen goods falls, because criminals' motivation for committing acquisitive crime is reduced. We might develop another theory, derived from the 'prospect theory' approach of decision-making under conditions of risk. This theory would predict that if burglars see the price of stolen goods falling they may be tempted to risk more high-value burglaries to sustain the level of income from their trade.

If on the data from the UK, the market reduction theory outperforms this version of prospect theory, this fact would not enable us to infer that the latter theory is comprehensively defeated, even in the British case. For there may be yet other theories relating to the behaviour of burglars in response to risk that could outperform both theories. The most that we can claim for our work is that we have *shifted the onus of argument* onto those who still wish to defend the use of prospect theory in the study of acquisitive crime.

Is there a problem of incommensurability?

Another issue that has greatly preoccupied the philosophers of science is that the meanings of terms – like 'demand' and 'response to incentive' – may be defined *internally* so that they mean slightly different things in rational choice and the prospect theory. If that were true, then a test that compared the two theories would be misguided, because it would not be comparing like with like. Kuhn called this the problem of 'incommensurability' of meanings of theoretical terms.

**EXAMPLE 3.3. THE MEANING OF A TERM IN
TWO RIVAL THEORIES**

Consider two well-known theories of what drives the behaviour of top civil servants.

One theory developed in the early 1970s (Niskanen, 1971) says that what they really care about is increasing the size of their ministries, their budgets and their payrolls, because this process increases their importance and salaries as a result of giving them greater responsibilities.

(Continued)

The theory recognises that they will not be able to succeed in achieving those goals all the time, because they face constraints from politicians and ultimately from voters, who will not indefinitely elect parties which keep raising taxes. But subject to these constraints, the theory of 'bureau budget maximisation' predicts that this aim will shape the behaviour of civil servants. In its support, the advocates of the theory pointed to big spurts in the size of the civil service in several countries through the 1950s and 1960s.

A rival theory developed in the 1990s (Dunleavy, 1991) holds that their status and power – and the possibility of having a congenial working life – come from being able to influence policy. That requires having ready access to politicians, and having time and responsibility for leadership in developing policy. What they do not want, this theory says, is to spend huge amounts of time in managing large-scale service provision. Better instead to find ways to slough off that sort of dull, low-status work to specialist agencies.

Again, there may be constraints on the extent to which politicians will let civil servants shed these responsibilities, and there are limits, too, on the extent to which they will allow top civil servants to monopolise policy-making. But, nevertheless, top civil servants will engage in 'bureau shaping' by trying to shape their ministries into tight, influential, policy-focused machines with strategic rather than managerial functions, even if this means that they have smaller budgets.

In evidence, the advocates of the theory pointed to the support given in the 1980s and 1990s by top civil servants in the UK for the devolution of management responsibilities to specialist agencies and indeed for the privatisation of functions from government departments.

At first sight, these two theories appear comparable, but in fact they are difficult to compare directly. This is because some important terms that appear in both theories are defined rather differently in each of them. Furthermore, these differences become very important at the point where we try to find empirical evidence to compare their performance in explaining changes in the structure of government.

Let us take the concept of a bureau budget. The bureau budget maximisation theory does not restrict the size of the budget to the annual sums of expenditure spent directly by a government department. They may well include the budgets of agencies that have been 'hived off' to handle specialist functions on its behalf. There are, after all, many ways to measure the size of one's bureaucratic empire, if one needs to boast about it.

In contrast, the whole point of bureau-shaping theory is to draw a tight distinction between the 'core' budget directly spent by the department and the budgets of devolved or privatised agencies.

Furthermore, 'bureau budget maximisation' can be tested by financial data that admit of year-on-year comparison and between-department comparison. But 'bureau shaping' is also about nurturing certain kinds of capabilities that may change their meaning between periods and between departmental contexts and need to be qualitatively assessed.

The constraints on civil servants' behaviour are of different kinds in these theories, too. In 'bureau budget maximisation', the constraints come from political control on spending, whilst in 'bureau-shaping' theory the constraints come from changing opportunities for involvement in interesting policy work. But this latter theory does not predict what top civil servants will do once all the service provision that it is politically possible to slough off has been shed or outsourced. In contrast, we know what bureau budget maximisation theory predicts they will do in any given period, even if it is just 'more of the same'.

In each theory, then, the concept of 'optimisation under constraint' is central. In each theory, there is a goal to be optimised, and there are constraints imposed by political acceptability.

(Continued)

But the meaning of optimisation under constraint appears to be very different in the two theories. Should we infer that the meanings of the term are 'incommensurable', such that no direct test of their rival strengths can be carried out? Well, not necessarily.

To enable comparison, we shall need to move down from the level of theory to the level of the model. Here, we can itemise the differences of meaning in the term 'optimisation under constraint'. If one theory is underspecified in its meaning in one respect where the other is specified – as in the question of what the bureau-shapers do when they have sloughed off all the work they can – we shall need to supply new specifications, to force out a comparison.

The simplest thing one could supply is the null hypothesis, but even that might be unavailable: after all, what would count for a top civil servant as 'doing nothing very much' about the size, scope and functions of the organisation he or she runs? But even if we could conduct a comparison by this means, the advocates of the failed theory could claim that 'it's the model, not the theory, that has failed; another model might show it to be perfectly sound'.

But this leaves the advocates of these theories with a dilemma. Either they show us a way of comparing theories directly – without the need to specify particular models – or they accept that their theories are indeed incommensurable, so that they cannot criticise their opponents. Otherwise, they must let us specify some models, to see whether we can test them in ways that will at least shift the onus of argument one way or the other.

Change and replacement of theories and paradigms

Much philosophy of science is concerned with the ways in which paradigms are replaced by others. This is not just a philosophical problem: it is also a practical problem about how we should understand developments in a body of research to which we are seeking to contribute.

Some writers who are familiar mainly with natural science tend to write as if they believed that paradigms succeed each other, and, once succeeded, die and become part of the history of science. And indeed there are some fields in the natural and the physical sciences of which that statement is not wholly false. It is not a complete travesty of the history of physics: for example, Newtonian dynamics has been replaced by a body of theory developed originally by Einstein.

In the social sciences, though, linear succession of traditions happens more rarely, with the consequence that traditions are hardly ever entirely superseded. For example, an emphasis on social and political institutions was very important in political economy of the 1920s and 1930s, as well as in the classical sociology of Weber and, in a different manner, of Durkheim. The behavioural turn after 1945 in political economy and sociology eclipsed institutionalism, which had come under fierce criticism. Yet institutionalism did not die. Some leading journals continued to publish some institutionalist work. By the 1980s, institutionalism had been reworked and recast but continued to draw on some of the same sources of theory as those which drove the interwar tradition. Today, it is a mainstream tradition of explanatory research in more or less all social sciences.

The same pattern can be observed in the history of the rational choice tradition. Rational choice of a kind flourished in eighteenth-century France, and was revived in late nineteenth-century England with the work of Herbert Spencer. Although it was eclipsed in the interwar years, it was revived immediately after the Second World War by several groups of mathematicians, mainly in the USA. Today, it is perhaps the pre-eminent approach in American social science and hugely influential everywhere else, too.

These examples emphasise the provisional character of what social science, or indeed any science, can offer. Better paradigms may, perhaps, emerge, or better theories than existing ones. Or perhaps not. Perhaps in a century from now, our descendants will still be reshuffling the same pack as the one that we now have and that was available in its main contours by the 1920s. But there is a significant possibility that over the next decades, social science will reject some, perhaps much, of what we believe that we have achieved. This possibility does not imply that there is no reason for confidence in what we are now able to do. Still less does it imply that any particular judgement about which theories to reject or to accept is defensible.

Basic reading

Ladyman J, 2002, *Understanding philosophy of science*, London: Routledge.
Okasha S, 2002, *Philosophy of science: a very short introduction*, Oxford: Oxford University Press.
Both texts are accessible, but are not specific to social science.

Advanced reading

A more advanced text which is specific to social science is Kincaid H, 1996, *Philosophical foundations of the social sciences: analysing controversies in social research*, Cambridge: Cambridge University Press.
Popper K, 1959, *The logic of scientific discovery*, London: Routledge, is the canonical statement of Popper's early argument about falsification, but the book is not easy reading for social scientists.

FOUR

Perspectives on findings from social research

This chapter will:

- show that the arguments we encountered in Chapter 3 represent some of the main positions in the philosophy of the social sciences;
- examine what is meant by 'positivism', 'relativism' and 'realism';
- briefly explore the meanings of 'constructivism' and 'constructionism'; and
- explain the implications of each position for deciding between rival theories.

Why philosophical disputes matter for methodology

The argument in Chapter 3 occupies some very specific terrain in the philosophical battles which have been fought over the status of claims to knowledge that can be made for the products of social science research.

There are some, very practical, reasons why it is useful for the study of methodology to understand the basic contours of these philosophical battles. The first is that when social scientists defend the methodology they have followed in their own research, or when they criticise the work of other social scientists, they often use labels for various '-isms' as shorthand for key issues at stake in these battles. Furthermore, even famous social scientists sometimes use these labels inexactly or as all-purpose terms of abuse for styles of research they do not like. As a result, mistaken notions have arisen as to what is implied by particular methodological choices. A more precise understanding of these labels, and what is implied by them, can help us recognise the more obvious elephant traps in such debates.

The most important reason for understanding philosophical arguments is that they are important for understanding the kinds of warrant that we can claim for our conclusions, especially when we want to confirm or undermine a model or theory. This is because different philosophical positions give quite different statuses to our claims about inference – that is, to our claims to know about things that we cannot directly observe, such as people's preferences or their social networks or their political institutions.

There are a great many positions and perspectives in the philosophy of social science. Philosophers have a penchant for classifying them, and setting up debates between them. In this chapter we shall concentrate on three of the most important labels that are used as campaign badges in the philosophical wars among social scientists. We shall offer some definitions and also some warnings about what is, and what is not, implied for methodology, in taking these positions, Finally, we shall show how the arguments we are making in the first part of this book offer support for one of these positions.

The three positions on which we shall concentrate are 'positivism', 'relativism' and 'realism'. They have been chosen because these are the most common labels attached to the insults thrown at each other by social scientists. We shall also, in passing, issue brief warnings about 'constructionism', 'constructivism' and 'pragmatism'.

Positivism

Positivism is one kind of empiricism. Its basic idea is that all knowledge comes from experience – that is, from what we observe, in sense 3 identified in Chapter 1. Here, observation refers not only to visual observations but, in the broader sense, to what we can detect with all our senses or with the instruments we possess to extend and enhance them.

Empiricism argues, further, that when we develop abstract concepts and theories, we are doing no more than summarising our experience. This process, empiricists would argue, involves identifying patterns that recur in the data. These recurrent patterns are the real content of explanations. *Explanation* consists in no more, and no less.

Empiricism has a long history in human thought. Defined thus, it refers to a philosophical outlook that can be found in ancient Greek, Indian and Chinese thought. It was brought to a high degree of development in European thought in the seventeenth and eighteenth centuries, not least by Scottish Enlightenment thinkers such as David Hume.

However, in the recent philosophy of science, positivism has a more specific meaning than this. It holds that all claims to theoretical knowledge should be capable of being *reduced to* statements about empirical observations and the patterns found in them. It follows that explanation consists in the ability to project these patterns from observed to unobserved cases, to *predict* successfully what will be found by further observations. The quotations in Box 4.1 offer as simple a statement of the positivist position as can be found, without resorting to caricature. They are all taken from the work of a philosopher of science, Larry Laudan.

You have already met, in Chapter 3, one example of a positivist position. That was Friedman's argument that we can explain economic behaviour *as if* people optimised under constraint. So long as this explanation fits the data and serves as a basis for prediction, we need not worry about the plausibility of the assumptions on which it rests.

The following distinctive methodological principles therefore follow from the positivist position:

1 Abstract, unobservable things that we introduce into our explanations in social science – such as rules, institutions, interests, networks, power, organisation or organisations, beliefs or ideas – should be treated not as special kinds of entities or facts that are different from the observable behaviour of human beings, but simply as convenient shorthand for structured patterns of relationships between the measures or codes captured from our observations of that behaviour (that is, they show strong goodness of fit). If those patterns are useful, they will be capable of being projected onto new cases (that is, they exhibit strong generality), thus demonstrating the power of our explanation to predict future observations.

2 If we design the right research instruments, a theory, in principle, could be reduced to a set of empirically testable statements of generalisation about expected patterns between things we can observe.

3 The patterns that hold the key to theories are *regularities*. Events, states of affairs, trends and conditions are of interest for *scientific* social research when they can be shown to form regularities.

4 If two theories predict the same behaviour – or events or trends or conditions and so on – then they are equivalent theories, whatever the abstract terms they use suggest about possible differences. It is still possible, however, that one theory might be *better supported* by the empirical evidence. For example, one theory might perform better in the number or severity of anomalous or apparently disconfirming cases (Laudan, 1990: 64).

Positivism, verification and falsification

One form of positivism which was widely influential in the first half of the twentieth century adopted a view of research which emphasised *verification*; that is, a commitment to testing theories empirically by searching for *confirming instances*. Thus, if we wanted to test the market reduction theory of crime reduction we looked at in the previous chapter, we might apply it to an increasingly wide range of markets for illicit goods, such as illegal drugs or counterfeit products, as well as stolen goods.

The arguments of Karl Popper were widely considered to have been devastating to the idea of verification, and thus to this form of positivism. He pointed out that confirming instances can be found for most theories, but simply adding more and more confirming instances is not a fair test. Piling up evermore cases where market reduction leads to crime reduction does not test the theory adequately, because we shall still not know whether there are cases in which it does not work in the predicted way. Instead, Popper (1959) argued, we should concentrate on what a theory predicts will *not* be observed and then design research to see whether it *can* be observed, thus providing a *disconfirming* instance.

The key methodological point that emerges from this controversy is that to be useful, and to meet scientific standards of rigour, theories must be stipulated in ways that make them empirically testable and, according to Popper, falsifiable, too. The proposition that 'reducing the market for illicit goods leads to a fall in the numbers of crimes' is, in principle, both a testable and a falsifiable one, because a single case where this relationship does not hold would undermine the theory. The problem that we have already seen is that failing to find disconfirming instances does not prove that the theory is true, though increasing the number, and particularly the variety, of cases we test *might* enable us to find out how widely it holds.

The really interesting scientific judgements are made when a process of disconfirmation allows us to see more clearly what has to be done to preserve our theory. If, for example, it were found that the market reduction theory of crime prevention is generally supported in certain markets for illicit goods – such as stolen goods fenced through local shops or bars – but disconfirming instances were found in other markets – such as those for stolen works of art – then the theory would be increased in precision, and market reduction interventions by police forces could be accordingly refined.

Contrary to what is often said, Popper's approach to methodology – concentrating on finding disconfirming instances and then making judgements about which patterns appear most consistently to predict new observations – is perfectly consistent with the four core positivist positions on the nature of data and explanation that we have identified above. Indeed, Popper's fundamental break with positivism was based on arguments other than the one about falsification, but we need not discuss those arguments here.

Likewise, the point we made in Chapter 3 – that all data are necessarily stated in forms that imply some theory – is not a fundamental problem for positivism, correctly understood. Unlike its predecessor, empiricism, positivism does not require that experience is always captured in terms that are free of any theoretical implications. Rather, positivism requires only that we should design research that relies on theories of observation, measurement and coding that are – to some degree at least – more dependable than the theories we are testing (Laudan, 1990: 47–8).

Misapprehensions about positivism

There are, too, some other misapprehensions about positivism that frequently appear in discussions of social science methodology, especially by those who think their positions require them to be hostile to it.

Many social scientists, for example, accuse their peers of 'positivism' when they use statistical analysis of quantitative data sets to model social phenomena. However, nothing in the characterisation of positivism requires the use of any particular *kind* of data. Conversely, the use of a particular method or a technique does not imply a particular philosophical position.

Someone who undertook statistical analysis of quantitative data would be a positivist, only if they went on to claim that achieving a successful statistical prediction *is all there is to explanation*. A genuinely positivist view of explanation would be that of Milton Friedman who, as we saw in the previous chapter, claimed that no further consideration need be given to a model's assumptions, or to their plausibility, or to the problem of *how* the model is supposed to work. All we need to do, the positivist argues, is carefully examine the consistency of the assumptions in the model with existing knowledge, which, for a positivist, means the patterns that have already proved to be successful in making predictions. However, most social scientists who use quantitative methods to test statistical models would *not* make that kind of philosophical claim about the status of what they achieve with their statistical tests.

Another mistake – one often made by some social scientists – is to suppose that positivism implies *behaviourism*. Behaviourism refers to a *practical* approach to research that aims to eliminate accounts of mental life or normative prescriptions from substantive theories, to focus exclusively on what can be observed – namely, behaviour.

The conflation of positivism with behaviourism is important because many social researchers who are interested in the significance of what they often call 'meanings' – a term that covers people's ideas, desires, beliefs, systems of classification, preferences and so on – often claim that their approach to explanation is inconsistent with positivism. Strictly, this is not the case. Positivists have no objection to setting theories out in ways that include terms for unobservable entities – including mental states – provided that we concentrate only on what those theories predict about observable things rather than what they purport to claim about unobservable ones. For positivism has no room for knowledge claims based on untestable assumptions about the existence and character of abstract, unobservable entities. That is, positivists accept that, in practice, it would be cumbersome and practically useless to 'reduce' all theoretical statements only to the observations they imply. The issue is what status we can claim for a theory's assumptions, not what terms are allowed in the statement of the theory.

Positivism and explanation

We can see, then, that many arguments that are frequently used to attack the methodological claims of positivism turn out to be flaky. But this does not mean that we cannot make more powerful criticisms of positivism than the ones discussed so far. It does mean, however, that if we wish to reject positivism, we should do so for the right, and for quite precise, reasons.

One of the most controversial claims of positivism, in social science at least, is that, so long as we are confident of the accuracy of our data, we should privilege goodness of fit – albeit one achieved as the result of a good deal of data reduction – in any trade-off that we might have to make with other methodological virtues, such as the plausibility of our assumptions or causality or even generality. This is because the positivists' understanding of 'explanation' prizes predictive power – the achievement of a good fit between prediction and observations – over the search for 'explanation' in its everyday sense of understanding of how observations relate to deeper causes.

But to be told that a pattern can be successfully projected from observed data to new sets of data does not amount to a *satisfying* explanation. It does not tell us *how* or *why* the pattern works. Positivists claim that the questions 'how?' and 'why?' are illegitimate ones. But the only support they can offer for this claim is to assert that an explanation that does not consist in an empirically observable pattern must be a piece of metaphysics about things that are unobservable. In our view, this argument limits positivism to explanations that are bound to be more or less unsatisfying.

For example, if we found that market reduction theory worked in some, but not other, markets for illicit goods, we could re-examine the data from our cases to see whether it is possible to establish *why* that might be the case. We might, as a result, be able to develop a more refined *explanatory* theory about how different kinds of illicit markets operate and how each affects criminal behaviour.

Causality matters for making explanations intellectually satisfying and meaningful in ways that positivism cannot capture, because positivism values explanation only in so far as it yields predictions. Furthermore, plausible accounts of causality depend on making inferences about entities or facts that cannot be directly observed – such as the very notion of 'markets' for illicit goods or the idea of burglars responding to particular incentives – which should also be taken more seriously than positivism allows.

This leads directly to the second criticism, which is that the positivist's conception of scientific progress – including progress in social science – is *empirically* inadequate. A great deal of scientific progress has consisted not in predicting yet more empirical observations, but rather in conceptual development (Laudan, 1977), and especially in the development of theories about *how* causal processes work. Often the research that supports this work is done with existing data sets, in ways that claim to produce explanations that are richer, more satisfying and conceptually better organised, even when they do not predict new observations. And this progress in better specifying theories is sustained, in practice, not by the pursuit of maximising variance predicted by correlations but by the pursuit of explanations which take causality seriously, by proposing causal explanations which use facts which cannot be directly observed but only inferred. This means that any philosophical position that aspires to do better for methodology than positivism must recognise the important role of conceptual and theoretical development in the development of social scientific knowledge.

Relativism

Too often, this term is also used rather loosely. A more precise statement follows shortly, but, broadly defined, relativism claims that we cannot account for what we observe, independently of the ways in which we recognise, classify, code and analyse our observations. So the truth of statements must always be 'relative to' the paradigms and conceptual frameworks within which we collect and analyse data.

To turn again to our crime prevention example, relativists would claim that is there no possibility of achieving an account of the causes of acquisitive crime, which captures a truth of the matter in ways that are independent of the paradigms we apply to its study. They would emphasise that the market reduction approach is situated in the rational choice paradigm which assumes that crime is committed by offenders who are autonomous and rational human beings. They might also point out that, for example, work situated in an institutionalist paradigm – such as the work of Sampson we cited in Chapter 3 – would look to very different sets of constraints and opportunities to explain increases or reductions in crime, such as the changing strength and nature of social ties in the relevant communities.

Relativism claims, then, that *if* we categorise the problem in the way that rational choice demands, then we establish measures and gather and code observations in one way, but if we follow institutionalist categories, then we would measure and then gather and code data in a different way. And there is no way of determining which approach is superior that does not appeal to one or other of these paradigms, or perhaps to a third paradigm which has no greater authority. It follows that, for relativists, there can be no such thing as a science of criminology, possessing knowledge of facts that have determinate existence independent of the means of classifying, categorising and measuring them.

For the purposes of this book, we shall use a definition of relativism which is consistent with mainstream usage in the philosophy of social science, and say that *relativism is the doctrine that (1) there is no compelling reason to accept that scientific explanations are true or false on the basis of determinate facts; and (2) scientific methods of research and inference do not alone supply such a compelling reason.*

Some relativists in both philosophy and social science have recently reclaimed the old term 'pragmatism' (e.g. Rorty, 1990). This is confusing, because the historical founders of pragmatist thought were by no means all relativists, and even the few who came close to relativism had rather nuanced and qualified views. Moreover, there are important contemporary philosophers of science who call themselves pragmatists but who argue fiercely against relativism (e.g. Laudan, 1977).

Responses to the main arguments for relativism

The main arguments offered in favour of relativism have in fact already been rehearsed and rejected in Chapter 3, although at that stage, we did not present them as such, but rather as criticisms of an overly mechanical understanding of how data can be used to establish whether a theory is 'true'. We recap them here, and the rejoinders we offered to them:

'Theory is underdetermined by data.' This is the argument that data alone do not suffice to choose between theories. This is certainly true, and no one denies it. Positivists recognise that simple counts of confirming and disconfirming instances alone do not determine which of two theories we should accept, and that, even when we conclude that the data leave a model in trouble, we are making inferences. But, so what? It does not follow that, just because an inference requires scientific judgement and is risky, the statement inferred cannot be true or false save within one paradigm.

'Terms are incommensurable between theories.' It is sometimes true that the same term has different meanings in rival theories. But it does not follow that the two theories cannot be compared, because we have ways of moving down from theories to models that force us to specify meanings in ways that will permit comparison. This procedure requires us to draw more limited conclusions about theories, but it does enable us to shift the onus of argument in very important ways.

'Theories do not confront data alone, but in larger bodies of theory, and we have choices to make about which elements to amend in the face of anomalous data.' Again, this is quite true, but it does not support the relativist conclusion. The choices that we make about which changes are *reasonable* are not arbitrary ones, even if there can be no algorithm for making scientific judgements about them. On the contrary, we can make judgements on the basis of defensible rules of thumb which allow us to preserve the more robust parts of our bodies of knowledge, to eschew *ad hoc* modifications, and to maximise the empirical content of our theories.

'Data are not pure, but theory-laden.' This argument, too, rests on a true premise, and, indeed, we cannot state or describe our observations without using some theoretical terms. But, again, the relativist conclusion does not follow. The key problem is to design research on the basis of theories which are more dependable than the ones we are trying to test.

'Scientific theories are constantly being replaced, and the ones we have now will look quaint in a century's time.' Again, this is true but does not provide much succour for relativism, because it does not suffice to show that, over time, there is no improvement in our capacity to make scientific judgements about which theories to accept as being the best available at the time.

The main point to take from these arguments is that we do not have to adopt a relativist position as the best, or only available, response to the deficiencies of positivism. And although it is still common in social science writing to discuss these arguments as if they are mainstream ones – as they were in the 1970s in the work of writers such as Kuhn (1970), Lakatos (1970) or Feyerabend (1975) – philosophers of science moved on long ago, and today interest in relativism among philosophers has waned considerably.

A note about related terms: 'constructivism' and 'constructionism'

Before leaving relativism, we should make some points about 'constructivism' and 'constructionism', to which it is – mistakenly – often assumed to be closely related.

Constructivism and constructionism come in many forms which it is unnecessary to discuss in detail here. But what they have in common is that they both emphasise – what is undoubtedly true – that people understand the issues they face in ways that are influenced by biases, frames, theories, accounts, narratives and conceptual frameworks of various kinds, and that these construals of their situation and their experiences have important consequences for how they act and organise.

It used to be the case that 'constructivism' referred to an *empirical* argument in psychology – going back to the work of the Soviet theorist Vygotsky – about how *individuals* develop understandings, misunderstandings and ways of framing issues. But, confusingly for those who would have reserved the term 'constructivism' for theories of individual learning, it has come to be widely used to refer to constructionist accounts of social institutions and practices.

'Constructionism' was and is understood to be the study of the *social* interactions that led to *shared* understandings – or indeed conflicting ones – and to the development of practices based on those understandings. Thus institutions – such as money, constitutions, rights and occupational statuses – all function in the way they do because enough people accept them, and they cease to function – or at least function in the same ways – when enough people cease to accept them. So institutions are human inventions and do not last for ever, as is shown by the substitution of electronic money for paper and metal tokens, or by the abolition of inherited titles in the French and Russian Revolutions (cf. Searle, 1995, 2009; Berger and Luckmann, 1991 [1966]).

But constructionists recognise, too, that so long as they last, these institutions are social facts. They constrain our actions. They subject us to disciplines when we violate them. This view is quite different from relativism, which holds that all categories in social theory are merely conventions and that none can be regarded as grounded in determinate facts about the world. To add to the confusion, relativism is sometimes called 'strong social constructionism', but we hope that you can see that it takes a quite different position from constructionism on whether facts about social life exist independently of the way we claim to know about them.

It follows that researchers who are interested in the *causal processes* by which such construals or framings cause action and social organisation are not required to hold relativistic views about the status of their explanations, and would probably find it intellectually uncomfortable to do so. This is simply another way of putting the obvious fact that in the social science we study meanings, but, of course, some of us also want to explain why people develop the meanings they do and how these meanings, in turn, affect their actions and social organisation.

This is not to say that some constructionists are *also* – or at least write in ways that suggest that they could claim to be – relativists. But this is a distinct philosophical step over and above the constructionist emphasis on the importance of framing. We shall not here enter the debate about whether those constructivists are *consistently* relativistic, but in Chapters 15 and 16, you will find some reasons to doubt that they will turn out to be so.

Ideational constructivism

Some theories that fly under the constructionist flag put forward causal explanations that take a further step, one that goes beyond an emphasis on the human invention of shared social practices and the dependence of these practices on our common acceptance of them.

It is one thing, for example, for political scientists or theorists of international relations to claim that the conventions governing exchanges between diplomats, or the conduct of business in the civil service, persist only because governments, civil servants and diplomats accept them. It is quite another thing for theorists to claim – as students of the history of British public administration have done (e.g. O'Toole, 2006) – that the practices, ethics and organisation of the British civil service were shaped directly by a particular set of ethical ideas developed in the late nineteenth century about the role of the state and the moral responsibilities of its agents. It would be quite consistent with the first claim to say that ideas and beliefs *follow* rather than precede institutions, but it might be more accurate to describe the second claim – that practices are created by the prior existence of specific ideas and beliefs – as 'ideational constructionism' to distinguish more clearly what is specific to this form of constructionism.

Ideational constructionism need not be interpreted relativistically: many who use the approach do consider that there are determinate facts on the basis of which statements about people holding particular ideas, and the consequences of their doing so, are true or false.

Positivism and relativism

Arguments about methodology often proceed as if the 'positivist' and 'relativist' positions were diametrically opposed in every respect. This is a mistake. Both positivism and relativism are based on a principle of caution about making inferences from data about observable facts to make claims about the substantive existence of determinate but unobservable facts about causal processes. Both positions claim that we should place confidence only in observations, and both assert that we should hesitate to draw any inferences beyond those which are about things that can be observed directly.

Positivism and relativism differ fundamentally only on one question. That is, the issue of whether scientific judgements about which theories to accept can be the outcome of independent reasoning, or whether they are essentially matters of convention that are influenced by the prevailing paradigms of the day.

Relativism and the practice of social science research

Just as there are many social scientists who confuse positivism with other philosophical positions, so both critics and advocates of relativism also confuse it with particular practices in social science research.

First, doing interpretive social science does not imply relativism. Most interpretive research is done by social scientists who are far from being relativists. Anthropologists have practised interpretive inference for decades without being relativists. Many have long argued that their interpretations of the mental worlds of those they study rest upon determinate facts about the way those people think, believe, hope and classify their worlds.

Interpretation, as we shall see in Chapters 15 and 16, is one product of social science research – along with description and explanation – and sometimes it is a precursor to explanation. There are many kinds of research questions that require interpretive work. Relativism – like positivism – is simply an argument about the status of the claims made in interpretations, and not the most convincing one. Nor is the converse position true, either. Relativists in social science are not required to eschew explanation and to confine themselves to interpretive research designs.

Second, just as there is no necessary relationship between positivism and the use of quantitative data, so there is no necessary relationship between relativism and the use of qualitative data. Most qualitative researchers do not take a relativistic view of the status of their explanations and interpretations, and there are relativists who use statistics. Neither group is being inconsistent. There is also no particular relationship between constructivism and qualitative research. Some of the ways that people construe and frame their experience lend themselves to quantitative survey research; others do not. Finally, for the record, interpretive work does not have to be qualitative, either. Later in the book we shall look at a study by a famous sociologist which offers an interpretive inference from quantitative data.

Realism

The argument thus far has led us to suggest some good, as opposed to the many bad, reasons for rejecting positivism, and we have discovered some good reasons for rejecting relativism too. The 'last position standing' in this chapter is realism, and so you probably expect to find that the arguments presented here turn out to support it. Indeed, this is the case, but there remain some important nuances to take into account.

For the last thirty years or so, more attention in the philosophy of science has probably been given to varieties of what is called 'realism' than to positivism or relativism. Realism, at its simplest, involves the claim that there are facts which are not directly observable about social phenomena – such as interests, preferences, institutions, bonds, norms, opportunities and constraints – and that, to make claims about these facts, we must make inferences from things that we can observe. Furthermore, realists claim that these inferences are true or false, depending on how well they conform with those facts.

A realist account of market reduction, for example, might depend on making inferences about the nature, and perhaps the volume, of the trade in stolen goods, from, say, interviews with thieves and fences, or from data in the British Crime Survey about respondents' experiences of purchasing stolen goods. Indeed, this is what Sutton and his colleagues did in the example cited in Chapter 3.

So a realist account of social science argues that we develop our understanding of such unobservable things by careful, progressive construction and empirical examination of testable theories and models. The following, simple, definition of scientific realism comprises two parts. The first refers to claims about what is going on in the social world – its *ontology*, to use the technical term. The second part adds the 'science' in 'scientific realism', and makes claims about the status of knowledge, or its *epistemology*.

Realistic ontology

Ontology is that sub-discipline of philosophy which is concerned with the question of what exists, and what status we are ascribing, especially to unobservable, abstract things, when we speak of them as existing, being 'real', and causing states-of-affairs or functioning in some way:

> Realism in ontology is the doctrine that there are determinate facts about unobservable processes, on the basis of which well-specified social scientific models and, thus, social science theories, are either true or false.

This definition contrasts realism sharply with both positivism and relativism. Thus, in the market reduction example above, realism departs from both positions in claiming that it is possible to make knowledge claims about things like trade or incentives that cannot be directly observed. By contrast, relativism denies that we can make ontological claims at all: its epistemology effectively precludes any ontological claims. Positivism argues that, because we should confine ourselves to predicting variance, we do not need to make ontological claims about unobservable things.

Note, too, that the realist ontological claim does *not* say that the 'basis' for judging the truth of theories and models is their 'correspondence' with the underlying reality. Those people who say that realism implies a 'correspondence theory of truth' are, strictly, mistaken. All that realism demands is that claims about truth must be rooted in more than convention or in the practical utility of our theories; they must be true or false, depending on the facts, which are determinate. 'Correspondence' might turn out to be the wrong way to understand that dependence on determinate facts. Realists recognise that our knowledge, at any one time, can never be more than an approximation to truth, because so much of it escapes direct observation, and because our grasp of it depends on the inferences we can make from what are bound to be partial observations. So we have no full access to 'truth', although we hope steadily to make advances in our approximations to it.

Two key questions are prompted by this discussion. The first is whether we are making *warranted* inferences from the facts we have observed to the claims we make about entities we cannot observe; and the second is whether we are using the most appropriate *concepts* to capture what is important about these unobservable and often abstract entities. These are, of course, questions about knowledge, but we shall discuss practical aspects of selecting appropriate concepts in Chapter 9 and procedures for inference in Chapters 13, 14 and 16.

Realist epistemology

Epistemology is the sub-discipline of philosophy concerned with the truth status of knowledge that can be achieved either by observation or by inference. We describe the theory which is principally under examination or test in any single piece of research as the 'focal theory' for that study.

Realism in epistemology is the doctrine that:

1 Scientific judgements about which focal theories to accept, and what trade-offs between such virtues as parsimony, goodness of fit, generality, causality and so on to draw, can be made on the basis of good reasons, based largely on valid inference from findings produced by sound application of correct methods using well-formed categories and evidenced propositions.
2 These scientific judgements rest on accepting, for the particular study, a network of other theories, which can be tested in other studies for which each of them would become focal theory.

3 Scientific judgements make inferences from findings to claims about determinate facts, on the basis of which a focal theory is true or false.
4 Predictions of determinate facts do not exhaust the content of the theories or models: they may begin with logical deductions from axioms; they also contain conceptual definitions and measurement statements.
5 The good reasons which can be provided for scientific judgements are not confined to the manner in which they support or undermine theories – important as this consideration certainly is – but may also involve theoretical and conceptual development.

As we saw above, making satisfying inferences depends on being able to capture what is important about determinate facts, a process that depends on the organising work supplied by concepts and the theories from which concepts are derived. But this dependence does not commit realists to defending the *present* body of theories and concepts as if they 'correctly' and permanently reflect some kind of fixed truth. A key tenet of realism, rather, is its claim that all empirical knowledge is bound to be provisional, as are all the theories and conceptual frameworks with which we organise our understanding of what cannot be directly observed. It follows that developing knowledge depends not only on developing more complete and accurate empirical accounts, but also on developing and refining the concepts and theories in which we capture them. Indeed, for realists, the two endeavours are inseparable.

Realism – but about what?

This doctrine captures what is central to realist ambitions, but what exactly does the task of theoretical and conceptual development consist in? This question can be discussed at three levels.

The first level of argument has to do with *particular empirical claims*. When we are trying to determine whether, for example, reducing the market for stolen goods does reduce the level of acquisitive theft – or whether there is, really, an increase in the number of rough sleepers in a particular town – then the methodological issue is the extent to which the cumulation of empirical findings is converging on some theoretical consensus that appears to be well founded.

The second level of argument has to do with whether or not the theories we use to design our research instruments, measures and codes really do allow us to claim an appropriate status for our findings. We saw the importance of this issue in Chapter 1, and need not discuss it further here.

The third level of argument concerns the models, theories and paradigms we use to organise knowledge as it develops. A key issue here is whether we should advance claims of truth about statements found only in models, or also in theories, or indeed also in paradigms or frameworks.

Consider again the example about the motivations of top civil servants that we explored in Example 2.5. We saw that it was probably easier to compare the two theories discussed in this example, once we moved from the level of the theory to the level of the model where we could work empirically with the specific concept of 'optimisation under constraint'. And many social scientists would be happy to be realists in working with a well-specified concept of that kind, but would baulk at accepting either theory in its entirety, let alone buying into all the concepts involved.

Another reason offered for restricting realism to models begins from the fact that we can only claim plausibly to have falsified theories when we have exhausted all the possible models that we can derive from them. We saw in the previous chapter that falsifying *theories* is a residual and indirect business. Some people argue that, therefore, we should restrict the scope of realism, at least as an *epistemological* position, to the level of models.

Why it is difficult to restrict realism to the level of models

The problem with this proposition will become clear if we think further about the budget maximisation and bureau-shaping theories, and also about the earlier example in Chapter 2, which used rational choice theory to analyse Khrushchev's decisions during the Cuban Missile Crisis of 1962. Statements in these theories use many of the same terms as those used in the models that can be derived from them. Conversely, models do not consist exclusively in purely operational, observational terms: they are not always free from statements about abstract entities such as preferences or intentions. So, restricting the scope of claims for truth to models seems rather arbitrary.

More fundamentally, it is typically the theory rather than the model which supplies the *semantic content* for a satisfying explanation. For example, it would be difficult to understand how market reduction or situational crime reduction theories are supposed to work, without a theory of causation. Being realist only at the level of the model would, therefore, leave us unable to make claims about the very things which make explanations interesting and satisfying. And that would not be a realism worth the making of serious ontological and epistemological claims.

EXERCISE 4.1. PARADIGMS WITHOUT HOMES TO GO TO

Go back to the work you did in Exercises 2.2 and 3.4 on verifying and explaining the possible increase in rough sleeping.

Say whether you think your conclusions fell within the positivist, relativist or realist understanding of social science, and why.

How would researchers from the other two positions approach the same problem? What would be the main differences in the knowledge claims made for the results of their research?

Conclusion

We have argued through the last four chapters that, to be a complete social scientist, the researcher needs to be able to combine design choices made at three levels, namely:

- *method* – the selection of appropriate types of data and of appropriate strategies for collecting and analysing those data;
- *methodology* – the theories that explain why the methods used provide warrant for inferences from the data to be collected and analysed, to the kind of explanation or interpretation required by the research questions; and
- *philosophy of social science* – the account of the status of the explanations and interpretations, and the justifications presented for granting them that status.

Each level has its place in a research design, and each supports the other two. Unfortunately, many textbooks either run them together or entirely miss out either methodology or philosophy. For example, it is still far too common to read research proposals that deal with methods and with philosophy, and assume that methodology is covered simply by combining them. However, we hope that you can now see that making a philosophical argument – and still less stating a philosophical position – does not justify, let alone require, *any* particular choice of research design.

On the other hand, philosophical issues are of real practical importance for methodology. They provide us with ways to *understand* what it is that we are claiming, when we use particular research designs to claim warrant for particular inferences. So they force social scientists to be aware of, and to think through, the full range of judgements they make when they argue for the acceptance and rejection of theories, and when they make trade-offs between rival virtues of a good explanation or a good interpretation. And understanding some philosophy of social science equips us to answer critics who challenge us to show why they should take seriously the description, explanation, interpretation we produce by doing our research.

In this chapter, we have argued that, in our view, the most convincing response to such issues takes the form of 'provisional realism' and that this position requires us to be clear about the models and theories that are at stake in our research.

Basic reading

For a series of accessible, fictional dialogues between stock positions, see Laudan L, 1990, *Science and relativism: some key controversies in the philosophy of social science*, Chicago: University of Chicago Press.

For an accessible guide to realism in social sciences, see Pawson R and Tilley N, 1997, *Realistic evaluation*, London: Sage.

Advanced reading

Kincaid H, 1996, *Philosophical foundations of the social sciences: analysing controversies in social research*, Cambridge: Cambridge University Press.

Those interested in realism might look at Manicas PT, 2006, *A realist philosophy of social science*, Cambridge: Cambridge University Press, and Sayer A, 1999, *Realism in social science*, London: Sage. (Be aware that Manicas combines his commitment to realism with a substantive commitment to methodological individualism and rational choice, and that Sayer holds a particular philosophical position known as 'critical realism' which goes far beyond the present argument.)

A well-known statement of 'pragmatism', regarded by many as effectively relativistic, is offered by Rorty R, 1979, *Philosophy and the mirror of nature*, Princeton, NJ: Princeton University Press.

A famous relativist statement is by Feyerabend P, 1993 [1975], *Against method*, London: Verso, although he qualified his views in later writings.

PART II

Designs

The main types of research design

FIVE

Types of research design

This chapter will:

- discuss what social science can teach us about the process of generalising from observational, or non-experimental, research;
- introduce the principal strategies for designing observational research from which sound inferences can be drawn; and
- show how these strategies are related in a typology of social research designs.

Research designs may be experimental or observational, or they may combine elements of both designs. This book is about observational research. But to understand what is distinctive about observational research designs, it is important to contrast them with experimental ones. So we begin this chapter by explaining the most important differences between observational and experimental research designs. We shall then construct a typology of the main ways of drawing inferences from observational research. This typology will frame the material we develop in the rest of this book.

Experimental and observational research

The central principle of experimental research is that control is exercised over all the factors that might exert causal influence upon the outcomes in which we are interested. We would hold all those potential influences constant, save for one which is allowed to vary to a degree, or in ways, we control. Finally, we would compare outcomes. If there are differences in outcomes, then we would conclude that those differences must be due to the one factor that was allowed to vary.

Most people have some idea about experimental methods used in the natural sciences from their school days. Many of us recall doing simple laboratory experiments in chemistry, in which the one thing that is allowed to vary is the presence, absence or perhaps the amount of one compound. Assuming that we kept the apparatus at constant heat, and did not turn it to a different angle or allow the amounts of the other compounds to vary, then, when our substances turned blue, crystalline or whatever, we were able to conclude that the only possible cause was the introduction – or a change in the amount – of the compound we were testing.

In social science, too, there is a place for experimental research. Psychologists do laboratory experiments as a normal part of their research. Occasionally, other social scientists do experiments, too. In sociology, economics and political science, for example, researchers who are interested in how people make decisions conduct laboratory experiments with volunteers, by asking them to carry out tasks, play decision-making games, or undertake exchanges with other participants. In each run, the researchers vary some variables – the information provided, the age or experience of the participants, the participants' abilities to communicate with each other, the nature of the tasks or games or exchanges, and so on – to see whether any of these variables affects the nature of decisions or the process of decision-making.

However, this kind of work represents a small proportion of the research done in political science, sociology, anthropology, development studies, business and management studies or economics.

Field experiments

A common critique of laboratory experiments is that their highly controlled conditions are not sufficiently like the ones we see in everyday life to warrant inferences from the controlled to the social environment. So a compromise is sometimes sought between control and external validity, by attempting a field experiment. In development studies, for example, studies have randomly assigned villages with similar social, educational, transport and infrastructure conditions, to different 'treatments' or programmes of economic development (e.g. Humphreys and Weinstein, 2009).

A different experimental design principle has been used, for example by political scientists interested in increasing turnout in elections. The approach described in Example 5.1 is based on the randomised controlled trial that is widely used in medical research. If the sample sizes are large enough for each 'treatment', then randomisation should obviate differences that might bias the results – in this case, education or past history of non-voting. This is because in a sufficiently large sample, the differences should cancel each other out: this is known in statistics as the law of large numbers. Put another way, what randomisation does is to substitute a general control for all those factors which cannot be controlled separately, both in drawing the overall sample of participants in the study and then in allocating them to different treatments.

EXAMPLE 5.1. VOTE EARLY, VOTE OFTEN

Suppose we want to find out how to encourage people who would not otherwise have done so to vote in national elections. In practice, most of the work done to increase turnout is done by political parties in first identifying which electors are likely to support their candidate and then in encouraging them turn out to vote, so that the total vote for the party is maximised.

Parties use a range of methods to increase turnout among their own voters, including mailshots, 'vote today' leaflets delivered to houses, telephone calls from party activists, telephone calls from commercial 'phone banks', door-to-door 'knocking-up' and so on. None of these methods can be reliably aimed at individual voters, but, for practical reasons, only at the households in which they live.

We could, perhaps, enlist the co-operation of parties in randomly assigning households with registered voters to these different 'treatments'. In addition, we could also randomly assign households to a control group, to be given no treatment at all.

We would then examine statistically the differences between the outcomes (i.e. turnout) between the groups that were treated and those that were not treated, on the assumption that the different 'treatments' are the most important factors explaining those differences.

Moreover, the differences between the outcomes for the control group and the outcomes for each of the other groups provide measures of the size of the effect for which those factors are assumed to be responsible.

For examples of similar studies, see the research published over many years by Donald P. Green (e.g. Green, 2004). A similar small-scale study was carried out during the 2005 British general election (John and Brannan, 2008).

Experimental research has great methodological strengths – if designed and executed well – because it can produce inferences with high capacity for generalisation. It is relatively straightforward to draw valid inferences from data obtained from laboratory experiments, where we can establish control over the phenomena we want to measure.

In some laboratory experiments, a high level of control can sometimes make unnecessary the large samples required for field experiments, where we already have strongly supportive evidence showing that variation in some variables is limited. For example, if we want to understand the effect of different levels of a particular kind of noise – say, very loud rock music – on people's moods, we could choose a modest sample of volunteers and screen them to exclude those with abnormal hearing or very disturbed emotional states. We would then place them in a sound-proofed laboratory from which all other noise was excluded, wire them up to machines capable of reading changes in the waves in their brains, and play them the same selection of rock music at carefully varied volumes or different types of music at the same volume. This procedure would allow us to control for all other obvious factors that might influence the outcome, so that we could be reasonably sure that we were picking up the effect of potentially important causal factors on the thing to be explained – namely, 'mood state'. These causal factors might be different levels or different types of 'volume', 'rhythm', 'lyrics', 'style of music' and so on. Although we would have measured their effects only on a small sample of individuals – small, that is, compared with the total population of people in the world – we would, nevertheless, feel justified in making inferences about the predicted effect of music displaying such factors on the mood states of all 'normal' human beings, so long as we could successfully meet various statistical significance tests. This relatively small sample is defensible here because we already have well-evidenced theories about the limited variation in hearing, mood and reception of music among the broad mass of healthy human beings.

We have seen however, that, in field experiments, randomisation can be a very powerful control tool when combined with samples that are sufficiently large to enable the researcher to disregard differences in the internal composition of treated and non-treated subgroups. So generalisation to the population from which the sample is drawn is warranted *if* the researcher has an adequate sample size for statistical inference, and *if* both random selection of the sample and random allocation to treatment and control are carried out carefully.

Why not all social science research can use experiments

But if experimental research has such strengths, why do observational research? And why are we devoting a whole book to discussing methodologies for it?

First, not all research questions are about causation. We might want to answer a question that calls for descriptive information, or we might want to answer a question that calls for interpretation. For such purposes, experiments would not be very helpful. For example, political opinion polls ask descriptive questions – such as 'which party would you vote for if there were to be an election tomorrow?' – but these are clearly not suitable questions for an experimental study.

Second, we might not yet understand enough about our research problem to know what factors to control for in designing an appropriate experiment. The experimental study described in Example 5.1 works because the methods used by political parties to increase their turnout are well understood and also limited in number. It would be more difficult, for example, to design a robust field experiment to examine whether, say, voters are more likely to vote if provision is made for online voting, because factors such as a voter's age, or whether or not a household has access to broadband, might well confound the results.

A third reason is that the phenomenon in which we are interested might not lend itself to experiment at all. If we are using historical cases, for example, the thing we want to research will no longer exist. Nevertheless, sociologists, political scientists, anthropologists, social policy researchers, and business and management researchers all study historical cases to answer descriptive, interpretive and explanatory questions: as we shall see from examples used later in this book, the past is not the domain only of historians.

Sometimes, we are interested in processes that we need to follow over long periods of time, but cannot hope to sustain experimental control over them for the duration.

For example, we could not design field experiments to measure the effect of different campaigning styles on voters' support for different parties over several months or years, for the simple reason that our participants have lives of their own, and many will move house, or become ill, or even die. So we would not be able to sustain or control our sample over the necessary period.

Or, perhaps, the phenomenon in which we are interested may exist in too few cases to admit of experiment. If we want to know about people who believe they have been abducted by aliens, we might be unable to assemble a large enough sample to allow for sufficient randomisation for experimental work.

Lastly, we might be interested in processes that are too big or important to control, even if it would be ethical for a researcher to try to do so. No research ethics committee is going to allow researchers to start wars or revolutions, or to drive companies to bankruptcy, even if it were practicable to conduct research in such ways. Research ethics committees may also have major objections to political scientists doing field experiments that might affect the outcome of a closely fought election, even though the researchers might argue that those studies are precisely the ones that ask the most interesting questions.

Social life is often too complicated for experimentation

A fourth – and perhaps the most important – reason for conducting observational research has already been mentioned, and it is an especially serious one if our research question is an explanatory one about causes. The carefully controlled environment of the experiment might not tell us much about the uncontrolled world of everyday life, especially where there are many potentially important factors. For example, getting people to vote online may not be a simple matter of changing the law to permit it, or even arranging for votes to be received from widely distributed gadgets such as mobile phones. There may also be complex issues to do with how far different groups in the population trust technology with their votes, or whether voters believe that they can protect the privacy of their vote against surveillance by family or friends.

Everyday life is, furthermore, often complicated by *interaction effects*. Think, for example, about the effects of such factors as gender, education or family contacts in determining career success in a particular industry such as financial services. Education and social networks may, for example, get young people their first jobs. Those jobs will give them skills, experiences, expectations and disappointments, but these factors may then set them on paths that could not be predicted simply from their education and networks. So, how well young people get on in their careers may not be a simple product of the sum – or the addition – of such factors, but may better be understood as result of complex interactions between them. We could control for these interaction effects in an experiment only if we *already* understood enough about them to sample for their expected presence or absence.

In other words, we may suspect that causation is the product either of many causes or of complex interactions between causes. To understand causation in such cases, we need to know not only *which* causes are at work, but also *how* they work. For such purposes, we may well be prepared to trade control for external validity and to use observational designs rather than experimental ones, even if it were practicable to follow such cases over long periods of time.

Being forced to make trade-offs in decisions between research design is a fact of life. We shall see over the course of the book that there are various trade-offs to be struck in designing research, and trading off control and external validity in the choice between experimental and observational research is only the first one we need to strike.

Observational research: types of control short of the experimental

In experimental research, data exist only because we carry out a procedure to create them. In so doing, we control the nature of this procedure, the resources used and the characteristics of our research participants.

Observational research *may*, at the opposite extreme, work entirely with *naturalistic data* – that is, data that would exist in the same form whether or not the researcher carried out any procedure to collect them and analyse them. Naturalistic data are of many kinds. Some – including administrative records of governments or firms, correspondence of dead or retired politicians or business leaders, newspapers, outputs of broadcasting companies and so on – are usually kept in archives dedicated to preserving these artefacts and making them available to researchers, such as the UK's National Archives at Kew, West London. Other records are kept privately by individuals and organisations.

Researchers often speak loosely of a situation in which a researcher literally observes – watches and takes detailed notes upon ('observation', in sense 4 as listed in Chapter 1) – what people do as the collection of 'naturalistic data'. An ethnographic study of the styles of management adopted by women managers in a blue-chip company might use this method of data collection, for example. Strictly speaking, it is incorrect to refer to data collected in this way as 'naturalistic', because these data are artefacts of the researcher's decisions about where he or she goes, what he or she looks at and to what he or she pays attention.

Of course, few data are entirely uncontrolled by human intervention – for example, every paper laid down in an archive reflects someone's decision about whether it is sufficiently important to keep. But, between the study of such relatively uncontrolled naturalistic data and the creation of fully controlled data in the laboratory lies a wide spectrum of research in which we exercise more or less control over our data and take a greater or smaller role in creating them. As we sacrifice experimental control by moving to observational research, we typically seek to substitute other forms of control, or at least to place greater reliance upon them.

In statistical work, we concentrate on the robustness of our *sample*. Statistical analysis is often regarded as the next strongest form of control after experimental control, and is often designed as far as possible to replicate it, through careful partitioning of the sample into subgroups characterised by variations in particular factors of interest, so that valid comparisons can be conducted among those subgroups. In studies of fewer cases, we still engage in comparison. If we study only a single case, we try to exercise control by designing a careful procedure, say for comparing sub-periods to study change over time, or contrasting different aspects of the same case within the same period. Being able to compare 'styles of management' for the ethnographic study mentioned above would depend on establishing an appropriate typology of management styles, perhaps using the approaches we discuss in Chapter 9.

We also exercise control through the analysis we perform on our data. In surveys and semi-structured interviews, we control the questions we administer and what counts as an answer worth recording or coding. In ethnographic studies in organisational settings, we control the topics about which we collect data, and determine what data we count as relevant to our questions. In using both kinds of methods, we control the selection of cases, whether those cases are individual respondents to surveys, or organisations, or events in the life of a single organisation, or whatever. For example, an ethnographic study of women's styles of management might well recruit individual women managers as 'cases', and our pre-stipulated 'types' of management styles would tell us what aspects of their behaviour we need to record, and why.

In observational research, then, we seek control over three elements in our research:

- the *categories* or types used to define the units of interest or attention, and to define the factors of interest about those units;
- the *means* by which data are created, collected, recorded and made capable of being analysed; and
- the *analytical procedures* used on those data, such as partitioning into periods, subgroups or sub-cases, identification of patterns, and comparison between cases and/or between patterns.

This list summarises most of what is presented in methods textbooks. But the *methodological* purpose served by method is control, even if the control used in observational research is necessarily short of that pursued in the ideal case of a laboratory experiment. But it gives us *some* leverage and traction over the warrant for the inferences we draw from observational research and thus allows us to study 'real-life' cases in our field of interest, rather than in highly artificial laboratory conditions.

The basic types of observational research designs

We shall work in this book with a typology of observational research designs, constructed from three ways of classifying research.

Classification by type of inference: descriptive, interpretive and explanatory research

The first classification captures the distinction between the fundamental types of inference in social science: that is, between descriptive, interpretive and explanatory research. To be precise, description, explanation and interpretation are different types of inference that can be made from empirical findings to conclusions about the significance of these findings for our research questions. We discussed the differences between these three types of inference in Chapter 1.

Under this first classification we are going to subsume a sub-classification. This captures the distinction between deductive and inductive research.

Deductive research

Deductive research begins with a *hypothesis*. That hypothesis may be derived deductively from a theory, or it may not. But it always consists in a precise statement of what we expect to find in our observations, given what we think we know, or suspect we know, in advance of doing our research. So the aim of deductive research is to test a statement that is formulated before we create or collect any data. The specification of the data to be collected, and the procedure to be followed in analysing them, is derived from that statement.

Ideally, for deductive work, we would design a piece of research that would enable us to tell definitively whether the statement is true, by ruling out any possibility other than the one which remains at the end of the test. That aspiration for a crucial test cannot often be achieved, but it represents a gold standard. Deductive research always proceeds by deducing what would be found to be the case if that statement or hypothesis were true, or what would not be observed if it were false. So we would design a procedure that would allow us to collect the necessary observations, and then we would determine whether the findings enable us to make the inference that the hypothesis is either true or false.

So – to revert to an example we used earlier in this chapter – we might hypothesise that family members already working in the industry are more important in achieving one's first post in financial services than gender or class of degree. This hypothesis might be tested by drawing a large-*N* sample of applicants for first-time posts, finding a way to measure 'family contacts' and then comparing its influence on the outcome with that of other factors.

Inductive research

Inductive research, on the other hand, starts with a question. Instead of seeking to find out whether a hypothesis is true or false, inductive research is used to develop such a statement from a position in which we have no real idea of what might turn out to be plausible, relevant or helpful about the subject of interest. Suppose, for example, that we suspect that 'family contacts' is actually a dimension of a set of wider social forces that we do not yet fully understand, but which we provisionally label 'social capital'. We could conduct some case studies of a smaller number of successful and unsuccessful applicants for entry into the financial services industry to find out whether our hunch is right and, if so, to find out more about how these forces work. We might, as a result, find out that what matters is the range and nature of a young person's social networks and those of their family; the nature and strength of the bonds connecting people in those networks; the person's understanding of the way the industry works; the kinds of social skills they possess; and their confidence in approaching high-status employers. Once we had developed a provisional understanding of how exactly such factors appear to determine career paths, we could stipulate a hypothesis to be tested in large-N research.

Deductive or inductive research?

Both inductive and deductive approaches carry risks. Inductive research risks error, because there are always several patterns, regression lines and hypotheses that could be developed to fit a set of data. It is usually hard conclusively to rule out any of them. Deductive research, on the other hand, can be rigid, because the scope of the enquiry is limited by the hypothesis. And if the research design does not enable us conclusively to rule out the truth or falsehood of our hypothesis, deductive approaches can be unsatisfying. However, deductive research does have the advantage of seeking to build on previous work: it is explicitly designed to be cumulative in relation to existing knowledge. By contrast, inductive research is not designed to be cumulative, which is why it is often used in fields where there is a dearth of previously published work.

Sometimes, research that appears to be deductive turns out on closer examination not to be deeply so. It is common in some kinds of statistical research to test models consisting in many variables, and to find goodness of fit. Yet, when the model is examined, it is often not clear that there is any particular theoretical reason for expecting those variables to be the important ones.

Furthermore, the most commonly used statistical technique is the conventional linear regression, in which the coefficients of the variables are treated *additively*: that is, their effects are regarded as cumulative. But unless we have good theoretical reasons for believing that the explanation relies on relationships that are linear and well represented by addition, then the facts that the statistical technique produces adequate goodness of fit, and that it passes tests for statistical significance, may not be sufficient to show that it really captures what is important about the case. As we saw above, for example, a study that fails to recognise the interaction between factors such as gender, educational qualifications and social capital in career progression may misunderstand the real nature of causation at work.

This kind of atheoretic modelling is often done when a researcher designs a project because he or she wants to use a particular method or a technique, not because he or she wants to test an interesting hypothesis derived from a specified causal theory about the relationships of variables. In other words, it is quite possible for studies that appear at first sight to be deductive – that is, driven by a hypothesis provided in advance – to turn out on closer examination to be quite inductive.

In principle, of course, it is possible to do descriptive, interpretive or explanatory research in either deductive or inductive ways. In practice, only explanatory research tends commonly to be done in both ways, though not often in the same project. Descriptive work is sometimes deductive, but much of it – including much standard survey work in such fields as market research or opinion polling – is essentially inductive.

By contrast, the greatest proportion of interpretive research currently done is inductive. Deductive interpretive work is, at least nowadays, rare. There is scope for a debate about whether more deductive interpretive work should be done in the social sciences but we shall postpone that question until Chapters 15 and 16.

EXERCISE 5.1. DEDUCTIVE OR INDUCTIVE?

Consider again the research you intend, or hope, to do yourself.
   Think about the degree to which it will be deductive and inductive, and explain how you would justify the particular combination of induction and deduction you describe.

Classification by type of analysis: between-case and within-case analysis

Our second classification captures the distinction between different types of observational research. This distinction has already been implicitly introduced, in a previous section of this chapter, where we discussed ways in which control is exercised in observational research. We saw there that, while this control may well be less tight than a laboratory experimentalist may seek to achieve, it is nonetheless important. We listed three things over which we need control. The third is of particular importance here – that is, the analytic procedures used in a piece of research. This is because, to create and collect data fit for different kinds of analytic procedures, we need different kinds of research design.

We also distinguished above between:

- *between-case analysis*, where we seek to isolate what we are interested in by comparing one case with others – or one unit with another – whether statistically or otherwise; and
- *within-case analysis*, where we seek to isolate what we are interested in by examining patterns and differences among elements within the same unit.

We had reason above to emphasise the *similarity* of these analytic procedures. Here we want to stress some important *differences*.

Within-case analysis is often concerned with questions of just *how* differences are generated, not simply with *what* those differences are. Think, for example, about doing within-case analysis on the course of an individual's career. We might develop a hypothesis about how gender affects long-term career trajectories in a particular industry. For this purpose, it would be insufficient to compare brute differences in the skills, experiences, social capital and so on possessed by a woman aged twenty five with those she possessed at the age of forty five. We would also want to know by what path she got from one state of affairs to the other. Tracing that path requires a different set of analytic procedures from undertaking a straight comparison of the two states of her affairs at these two ages.

Now think about a second study, to compare this woman's career trajectory with those of women of a different social class or academic background. For the comparative element of this study, we clearly need more than one case, but we also need to undertake within-case analysis of each case, to understand each woman's career trajectory. And, unless we have a very large team of researchers, we do not want too many cases to compare, or we shall never get the within-case analysis done, too. So there may be a trade-off to strike between the demands of within-case analysis and between-case analysis.

Variable-oriented research

If we use *between-case* analysis to determine the relationship of particular factors to various outcomes, then we shall treat factors and outcomes as *variables*. The outcomes will be treated as dependent variables (DVs) and the factors we believe are causing them as independent variables (IVs).

The type of design that creates, collects and categorises data for analysing relationships between variables is called variable-oriented research (VOR). VOR typically analyses the relationships between variables drawn from a large number of observations (large-*N* research), and aims to make inferences capable of being generalised to a much larger population than that used for the study.

This analysis is typically done statistically. For example, if – perhaps as a result of the within-case and between-case analysis described above – we developed a hypothesis that social capital was a bigger influence than class of degree or academic discipline on women's careers in the industry of interest, we might design a large-*N* study to compare the relationship of these three independent variables with the dependent variable, or career outcomes, which we might measure by pay and job grade. Thus, in VOR, the units of analysis are variables, and the aim is to make inferences from the population sampled for the study to the whole of the relevant population. In this case, we would hope to generalise about the factors influencing women's careers in the industry as a whole.

Case-based and case-oriented or comparative case research

If, by contrast, we are concerned only with within-case analysis, then our main unit of analysis is the *case* itself – the person, family, organisation, or whatever. Thus, in the within-case study described above, the woman's career path is the unit of analysis. Within the case, we are typically less concerned with isolating and measuring the effect of the most important individual factors than we are with developing a more holistic understanding of the case: how it relates to its particular context and perhaps how and why it changes over time.

Creating or collecting and coding data for this sort of analysis is done with a *case-based* research (CBR) design. This design involves a large number of observations *within* a single case study or a very small number of case studies ($N = 1$, or perhaps up to $N = 3$ or 4). It aims at in-depth understanding of theoretically important cases by developing an analytically structured pattern capable of linking observations into a plausible account of their connections with each other.

Finally, if we want to compare a modest number of cases on several dimensions or factors and also to do within-case analysis on each one, then we use *case-oriented research* (COR; the term is from Ragin, 1994). We can also call it comparative case research. This design aims to make comparisons *between* a relatively small number of cases (small-N research). It compares the behaviour of theoretically important variables *across* cases, but also uses within-case analysis to explore how these similarities and differences relate to the specific context and dynamics of each case. The second case study on women's career trajectories would be an example of COR.

Bringing it all together: a typology of research designs

The distinctions we have made in these classifications are not arbitrary ones, and are not simply a pile-up of ways of classifying designs. To show how they build on each other, we shall now bring together these ways of classifying observational research designs – by the type of inference and by type of analytical procedure – into a single typology.

Table 5.1 cross-tabulates our three types of inference with our three types of analytic procedure to yield nine cells. In each cell, we provide examples – but not an exhaustive list – of the kinds of social science that is practised in each cell. Some of these cells are largely empty, because, in practice, it is rare for social scientists to undertake research of these kinds. In particular, we believe comparative interpretive research to be rather rarely conducted and recently, most interpretive research has been case based.

For the remainder of this book, we shall focus on the distinctions between variable-oriented, case-based and comparative research, mainly among explanatory studies. When we consider interpretive research in Chapters 15 and 16, we shall mainly look at case-based and inductive work because that covers most of what is done in interpretive research.

But when we consider combinations of these research designs in Chapter 17, we shall examine a rare example of variable-oriented interpretive research. That chapter will discuss how we can produce hybrids between these types. Comparative research (COR) designs are, of course, combinations of within-case and between-case analysis; Chapter 17 will explain how we could be even more ambitious in combining research designs.

Table 5.1 Types of design for observational research

Type of sample and analytic procedure for generating findings	Type of inference from findings to significance (types of research question)		
	Descriptive *(either deductive or inductive; inductive is more common)*	*Interpretive* *(today, typically inductive)*	*Explanatory* *(either deductive or inductive)*
Between-case analysis on variables as units of analysis, large *N*, variable oriented	√ (e.g. descriptive statistics)	Very rare (but see Chapter 17 for an example)	√ (e.g. standard multivariate analysis)
Within-case analysis using whole case and context as unit of analysis, 1 or very small *N*, case based	√ (e.g. typical ethnographic study)	√ (e.g. typical interpretive study of ideas or beliefs, ideas, ways of classifying among a small group)	√ (e.g. historical case studies, process tracing)
Within-case and between-case analysis using whole case and context as unit of analysis, modest-sized *N*, comparative or case oriented	√ (e.g. multi-country review of trends)	Rare	√ (e.g. comparative historical research tradition, process tracing)

Qualitative and quantitative data

You may be surprised that we have given little weight to the distinction between qualitative and quantitative data – between describing and counting – especially since many textbooks divide their material between methods appropriate to these two types of data. And they sometimes refer to qualitative and quantitative 'research designs'.

Certainly, the difference between quantitative and qualitative data matters greatly for *method*. A researcher cannot easily undertake a chi-squared test of statistical significance if he or she is working with a bank of descriptions or strips of transcribed speech. Conversely, it is no use trying to do within-case causal process tracing on a spreadsheet summarising answers to a survey questionnaire. But are we claiming that this distinction does not matter for *methodology*? Not quite.

It is certainly true that much variable-oriented research uses quantitative data and much case-based research uses qualitative evidence. But this is by no means a universal rule, and it would be a great mistake to use 'variable-oriented' and 'quantitative' as synonyms. There are plenty of qualitative studies which explore factors in ways that treat them as variables, by weighing their relative importance. This is not uncommon, for example, in historical sociology or in business and management research where researchers use qualitative data to explain why some companies appear to do better than others.

Conversely, many case studies make extensive use of quantitative tables to explore patterns of change over time. Case-comparative researchers often employ multi-method designs to develop a more holistic understanding of the cases than is possible with a single method, and to this end the researchers may collect and analyse some quantitative data. For example, a study of the social dynamics of a professional football team might be usefully informed by some descriptive statistics relating to the changing commercial fortunes of the club: without this analysis, it would be impossible to understand fully how the business context might be affecting the behaviour of the team.

The important point here is that the research design should be chosen on the basis of the type of inference to be attempted to answer a particular research question. We must first decide whether it requires an inductive or a deductive approach, and whether we need to produce a description, explanation or interpretation. Having once settled what we are trying to do, we can then select appropriate analytic procedures. Only then should we worry about the kinds of data to use.

We shall see over the course of this book that it is possible to make sound inferences using either qualitative or quantitative data. It is important to understand, though, that the soundness of the inference is not determined by the type of data, but by the issues we have already begun to discuss, such as how well the research question is specified, the nature of the controls to be applied to various stages in the research process, and the trade-offs struck between these controls.

The type of data to be used may determine method, but not the type of inference: it is therefore not a key issue in methodology. We can design either inductive or deductive research using either kind of data. The really important determinant of the warrant we have for our conclusion rests on the type of inference, not the type of data. Indeed, *starting* with a decision about the type of data to use might lead an inexperienced researcher badly astray. There is a temptation to ask what data can be obtained about a topic and then what methods can be used to collect and analyse them, and only then to specify a research question that can be answered with those data and those methods, in the hope that the methodology will take care of itself. A central message of this book is that, if you follow that procedure, it will not.

Basic reading

For a simple introduction to deductive and inductive work, see Ragin CC, 1994, *Constructing social research*, Thousand Oaks, CA: Pine Forge Press, Sage, 14ff., or Blaikie N, 2007 [1993], *Approaches to social inquiry*, Cambridge: Polity Press, 56ff.

King G, Keohane R and Verba S, 1994, *Designing social inquiry: scientific inference in qualitative research*, Princeton, NJ: Princeton University Press, esp. 34ff, discuss differences between descriptive, explanatory and interpretive inference, although their view is different from ours, in arguing for always maximising sample size. They also emphasise the importance of inference.

For an experimentalist's critique of observational research, see Gerber A, Green DP and Kaplan EH, 2004, The illusion of learning from observational research, in I Shapiro *et al.*, (eds), *Problems and methods in the study of politics*, Cambridge: Cambridge University Press, 251–73.

Advanced reading

Tilly C, 2008, *Explaining social processes*, Boulder, CO: Paradigm, 108–17, offers a contrasting taxonomy of types of inference to ours.

For a critique of statistical studies which are driven by a method rather than a theory, see Taagepera R, 2007, Predictive versus postdictive models, *European political science*, 6, 2, 114–23, and Taagepera R, 2008, *Making social science more scientific: the need for predictive models*, Oxford: Oxford University Press.

For a general critique of method-driven social science see Shapiro I, Smith RM and Masoud TE (eds), 2004, *Problems and methods in the study of politics*, Cambridge: Cambridge University Press.

SIX
Variable-oriented research designs

This chapter will:

- discuss the benefits and limitations of 'variable-oriented research' (VOR) designs; and
- consider the problems of defining and specifying variables, measures and establishing causes in VOR designs.

In December 2010, the British coalition government published a consultation paper on reforming the criminal justice system (Ministry of Justice, 2010). The aim was to reduce reoffending by convicted criminals, but, in so doing, the government believed it would reduce the prison population, which had reached an all-time high. Predictably, the proposals attracted considerable opposition, not least on the grounds that the sharp rise in the use of imprisonment since 1997 had been accompanied by an equally sharp fall in the crime rate. These 'facts', it was claimed, show that 'prison works' in reducing crime.

So how would we test the claim that increasing use of prison is an important factor in the reduction in crime? Such a study would focus on the relationship between two 'variables' – in this case, variables selected to stand proxy for 'the use of prison' and for 'the reduction in crime' – and would thus be designed as 'variable-oriented research', or VOR.

VOR is typically used to test whether changes in the value of one variable are systematically related to changes in the value of another, so that theories about relationships between the factors and outcomes for which these variables stand proxy can be verified, refined or refuted. More specifically, VOR is typically used for testing relationships between the values of independent (or explanatory) variable(s) – or the things that do the explaining: here, increasing use of prison as a punishment – and those of dependent, or outcome, variable(s) – or the thing to be explained: here, falling rates of crime.

The characteristics of variables

But what, exactly, is a 'variable' and how are they specified and used in VOR? We can say that a variable:

1 is a discrete unit of analysis, defined and distinguished from other aspects of a situation, and analysed independently of them, to identify its distinct role;
2 is chosen as a valid proxy for an underlying phenomenon of interest, either a factor forming part of an explanation or the thing to be explained; and
3 takes one of a set of determinate values: on or off; strong, moderate or weak; between 0 and 1; 1st, 2nd, 3rd or whatever;
   where:
4 empirical features of the unit of analysis can be defined, specified and coded reliably to yield unambiguous measurements of those values; and
5 associations between values on the unit and those on other units can also be measured and can be represented as evidence for or against a claim that the associations tend to confirm or disconfirm a candidate explanation.

These five characteristics are also *standards* for VOR. Where all, or at least most of them can be met, VOR can be very powerful indeed. But if any of them fails for any proposed variable, then it cannot defensibly be used in VOR. Indeed, we shall see in the next two chapters that researchers sometimes use designs other than VOR because of difficulties in identifying sufficiently discrete units of analysis or where a focus on a factor's *independent* contribution would misrepresent its role.

Challenges in specifying and using variables

Meeting any and all of these standards is not always straightforward, as our 'prison works' example shows.

To test whether 'prison works', we first need to specify the variables of interest, in ways that distinguish them from other potentially relevant variables (standard 1). In this case, for example, it is not obvious what the most appropriate proxy for the independent variable would be (standard 2). Is the use of growing use of imprisonment best picked up by looking at the proportion of offenders given prison sentences, or by the number of people in gaol, or by the number of custodial sentences being passed? And what about changes in the availability of parole? Do these things operate separately, and, if so, which of them offers the most valid way to specify the independent variable?

Having specified our variables, we would need to find ways reliably to measure how they vary (standard 3). This is often difficult, because we may not be able directly to observe the required variation, and we may need to make inferences from data about things we can observe. The 'volume of crime', for example, is not directly observable, so inferences must be made from official crime statistics which in the UK – as in many other countries – are unreliable, mainly because of significant gaps in both the reporting of crimes by victims and the recording of reported crime by the police. The annual British Crime Survey (BCS) is more reliable, because it meets professional standards of social survey research and, as such, is subject to the controls we discussed in Chapter 5. As a result, it provides more reliable indicators of long-term trends. But the BCS, too, has gaps, because it surveys victims' experience of crime, which means that it underestimates murder and manslaughter and also so-called 'victimless crimes', such as fraud or drug-trafficking. So studies of changing crime rates are forced to seek measures of crime that are known to be incomplete but which are, nevertheless, the best available ways of representing general trends in crime levels (standards 3 and 4).

Finally, we need to specify the relationships between the independent and dependent variables (standard 5). It is one thing to demonstrate that two variables co-vary: that is a relatively straightforward matter of statistics. But the 'prison works' claim goes further, in inferring that change in the independent variable *explains* change in the dependent variable: causation is being claimed. We shall see in Chapters 10–13 that inferring causation on the basis of crude associations such as this one is highly risky. It can easily lead to spurious causal claims – as, indeed, the claim that 'prison works' might be.

The characteristics of VOR

VOR depends on specifying key variables in advance of conducting data collection and analysis: it therefore requires a strong element of deduction. The need to pre-specify variables and use them consistently means that VOR lends itself most easily to the use of either quantitative data or well-structured qualitative data. In focusing on a limited range of discrete variables, VOR tends to involve high levels of data reduction and privileges the design virtue of parsimony.

For these reasons – and especially when used with a large number of observations of a large population or universe of cases – VOR usually conforms more closely than do case-based (Chapter 7) and case-oriented research (Chapter 8) to the standards required for making statistically valid inferences from the data. Because statistical controls afford relatively high confidence in generalising from the results of VOR, it is often used to *test* theories about causal explanations and to see how widely such theories can be applied.

Among the characteristics of VOR designs, then, are that they:

- specify *a priori*, and as precisely as possible, relationships to be tested and therefore variables to be observed;
- establish as much control as possible over the impact of factors that might bias or confound the results;

- use techniques and standards borrowed from inferential statistics to determine what inferences can validly be drawn from particular data, taking into account the limitations of observational research; and
- therefore work with stable samples that cannot easily be changed once the research is under way.

Selecting variables

As we saw in the 'prison works' example, it is critically important to understand clearly why a certain variable is being selected for study, and particularly to resist the temptation to measure variation for no better reason that it *can* be measured.

Thus, air temperature can be measured by reference to well-established scales, for example the Celsius scale. It might be a relevant variable in a study concerned with the effect of different weather or climates on propensities to civil disorder. For example, we could use it as an independent variable to test the hypothesis that civil disorder (the dependent variable) increases in hot weather (the independent variable). However, for most social research, air temperature is not relevant and therefore need not be measured. Similarly, although it may be easy to collect demographic data about research participants – such as their age, gender, occupation, ethnic identity – collecting such data is not necessary to the research design unless such factors are variables of interest to the study.

Understanding distance between variables

Stinchcombe (2005) has pointed out that a key issue in VOR is the 'distance' between variables. By this he means that researchers should focus on understanding the 'difference between differences' – that is, the ways in which differences in the value of one variable are associated with differences in the value of another.

The most interesting findings are often associated with changes in values that are disproportionate – where a small change in the independent variable produces a big change in the dependent variable – or where the difference is qualitatively significant at a hypothesised threshold. For example, the difference in temperature between 20°C and 25°C is the difference between a mild and a warm summer's day in the UK. However, the difference between 25°C and 30°C would be a much more critical one for the study of civil disorder mentioned above, because it represents a difference between a warm summer's day and an exceptionally hot one. We might expect to find almost no changes in civil disorder associated with changes from mild to warm weather, but large changes in behaviour associated with changes from warm to hot weather. Indeed, it might be helpful to focus the investigation on days when we might find changes at this end of the temperature scale.

So, to design the most parsimonious research project – one that is likely to produce the most usable correlations for the least number of observations – a researcher would need to hypothesise a *qualitatively significant* threshold difference between warm and hot weather. Thus, designing quantitative studies requires qualitative judgements about the *significance* of – not just the *measurement* of – differences in value.

Proximate and distal variables

Another important judgement that might need to be made in selecting and defining variables is that between immediate causes – often referred to as 'proximate' causes – and underlying ones which are often referred to as 'distal' ones. Suppose, for example, we want to study the reasons for a rise in levels of *violent* crime. We might focus on the effect of changes in the law relating to the carrying of offensive weapons as *proximate* causes, but we might also be interested in underlying social or economic changes as *distal* causes. This is an important issue in understanding causation, and we shall discuss it at more length in Chapter 9.

A cross-design example

At this point, we introduce a problem that is currently of great interest in many countries: that is, how to encourage householders to recycle domestic waste. This problem is specified in Example 6.1.

EXAMPLE 6.1. USING A VOR DESIGN TO UNDERSTAND WHO RECYCLES HOUSEHOLD WASTE

This is what you might call a rubbish question. It is the question of what we do with rubbish. There is too much of it, and we keep making more. We are running out of landfill sites for dumping it. Burning the stuff is smelly and unpopular with people who live near incinerators. Burning rubbish releases greenhouse gases and contributes to global warming, whilst incinerators that break these products down into useful chemicals create the problem of how to store these chemicals until they are sold and taken away. So in every country, governments are putting increasing pressure on householders to sort their rubbish, so that some types of rubbish can be recycled.

Possible explanatory variables

But it turns out that a lot of us are, well, rubbish at separating waste for recycling. What is wrong with us? Idleness? Immorality? Inattention? Ignorance?

Yet some people are good at it. What is right with them? Too much time on their hands? Over-powerful conscience? Avid readers of *The Ecologist*? Do they simply do whatever governments tell them?

(Continued)

If we think about the problem as social scientists, we shall see that these stereotypes do not work very well. Not everyone with time on their hands recycles their rubbish. Nor do all the deeply moral people. Many people with weighty consciences put their time into combating hunger or trying to save the people of Darfur from slaughter rather than meticulously sorting the right from the wrong kind of plastic.

The converse is also true. Under-occupied, conscience-afflicted, compliant, ecology-minded people surely account for a small proportion of those who carefully fold newspapers into one box and place bottles in a differently coloured box.

So while factors such as time, morality, information and trust in government *may* well have *some* influence on behaviour, we do not know how much and we do not know whether other factors may also be at work. We need to find out.

Using variables in research

One way to answer the questions posed by Example 6.1 is to think of factors such as discretionary time, sense of moral duty, access to information about landfill and recycling, and trust in government as independent variables that take different values in different people. These values might be scored on scales from 0 to 10, or scored more simply as 'strong' or 'weak' (coded as 1 or 0).

A *dependent variable* might be the household's *propensity* to recycle (measured on a scale between 0% and 100%), or the household's actual *behaviour* in recycling (measured by a simple 'yes' or 'no', or perhaps measured by a scale running from 'always' to 'never').

Having specified our variables, we can then collect some data on each. If we can get information from a survey of residents in a given area, or – better still – a representative sample from several areas or of the whole population, then we could perform calculations on the resulting data set to tell how great a contribution each of our four variables might make to the aggregate propensity – across the whole sample – to sort household waste.

What is the 'level of analysis' for specifying variables?

It is also important to remember that the specification of variables depends on, and must therefore change with, the *level* of analysis, meaning the scale of aggregation. In Example 6.1, we assume that the best 'level of analysis' for studying the recycling of household waste is the *household*. But suppose we want to compare cities' recycling performance: the level would then be the urban area.

This change in level matters in specifying variables. A study of a city would require us to use, as our *dependent* variable, a *rate variable*, such as the percentage of households in each city that recycle household waste at least once a week. Similarly, instead of using as independent variables the individual household's time, information, conscience or trust, we would have to use *rate* variables, such as the percentage of householders in each city that can be shown to believe in recycling for environmental reasons, the percentage of households which are invited to join a recycling scheme, and so on.

Displaying patterns between variables

With such data, we can then examine the patterns – or relationships of association – between variables. Suppose X is the frequency with which the household recycles waste, scaled on frequency from 'never' to 'every week'. Suppose, further, that Y is the primary householder's *trust* in government advice about recycling, scaled from strong to weak. Now think of our households as arrayed as dots along lines showing X and Y. Then connect the dots representing the same households. We might end up with a diagram that looked like Figure 6.1.

For the sake of simplicity, we have entered data only for four households, but the figure displays graphically what is meant by measuring distances on variables. Here, the distance between the value taken by X (trust) and Y (recycling) is the product of the percentage of households which take a given pattern of values on both X and Y.

We would, of course, require data for a much larger number of households to produce statistically significant results.

Figure 6.1 shows a fairly strong, but less than perfect relationship between the values taken by the same units on X (trust) with those taken on Y (recycling). It shows that strong trusters typically recycle more than weak trusters. But some other variables must be important, too, because, for example, household D has a stronger, if still modest level of trust than C, but recycles less. This suggests that some other variables might be at work, too. One aim of this research is to identify what variables (e.g. Z, W, $U...$) might account for units like D, and to see what independent effect they might have on recycling (Y).

Figure 6.1   Distances on variables – significant positive correlations

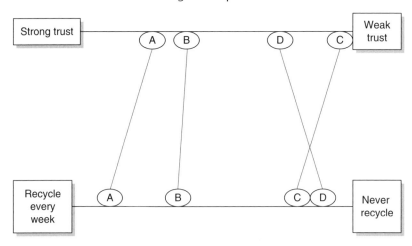

Clearly, the locations of C and D show that it is false to claim that weak trusters never recycle (C); equally, some strong trusters do not always recycle (B). So in this example, we might be able to say that X (trust), Z (time) and W (information) each help *explain some portion of the variance* on the dependent variable Y (recycling), but none explains it all. Alternatively, we can say that X has *some effect on Y*. That is, in a multivariate study, we want to isolate the separate contribution that each variable makes to explaining the outcome.

Now consider Figure 6.2. In this example, trust appears to have no very clear or stable relationship with recycling. Strong trusters sometimes recycle often (B) and sometimes do not (A); likewise weak trusters sometimes do (C) and sometimes do not (D). If there is no relationship between two variables, we can say that they *vary independently* of each other. So if we have a hypothesis proposing that trust (the IV) explains recycling (the DV), and it turns out that the IV and the DV vary independently of each other, then we can say that the hypothesis is not supported by the findings. In fact, the *null hypothesis* – that X has no effect on Y – does much better.

Now attempt Exercise 6.1.

Figure 6.2 Distances on variables – both positive and negative correlations

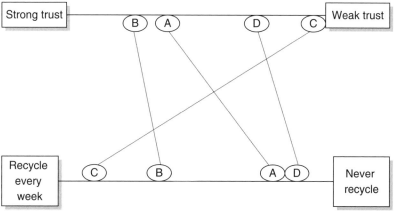

We now consider three key issues that influence the design of VOR: validity, reliability and determinacy. You may be familiar with these terms, but what do they mean in relation to VOR?

Validity, again

To recap the definition in Chapter 1, the term 'validity' refers the extent to which we can draw sound inferences from our data. Here, we focus more narrowly on *measurement validity*. This term refers to the extent to which measures actually measure what they claim to measure. For example, it would be highly problematic to use an expression of general support for action benefitting the environment as a measure of propensity to recycle. Thus, the aim of paying attention to measurement validity is to ensure that none of the measures and scores used in our research introduces *systematic biases* into our data.

It is often said that measurement validity involves three distinct aspects of research design:

- *content validity* – how well our measures accurately capture the construct being measured;
- *criterion validity* – whether the measures are in line with other measures of the same content that are generally accepted as valid in the wider research community; and
- *conceptual validity* – whether the measures are in line with the way we specify the relevant theoretical concepts.

Example 6.1 suggested four factors that might influence decisions about whether or how much to recycle household waste: namely, time, information, conscience and trust. But how would we specify these variables to pass these tests of validity? Let us look in more detail at how we might measure time, information and trust.

'Time' is shorthand for a bundle of resources, including the ease and convenience of the recycling scheme itself. Does the local authority provide the different-coloured bins or must households buy them? Are different kinds of waste collected frequently and on the same day of the week? If there are cash incentives, are they easy to understand?

'Information' includes knowing what will be collected and when; what rubbish householders have to take to the recycling centre; what incentives there are and how to claim them. It also involves knowing how to get help, and where to address queries. 'Trust' is also a vector of several things. To be sure, there is trusting government to tell the truth when it says that there is no sustainable and affordable alternative to the tiresome business of sorting household waste. But there is also trust in the local authority to do what it claims with different kinds of rubbish. If householders suspect that it is letting staff sell them at a private profit, or that rubbish is being shipped to landfill abroad, they will not feel motivated to spend time staring at bottoms of shampoo bottles to work out from which type of plastic they are made.

So, now we have broken down our initial set of three variables into several more valid ones: these are summarised in Example 6.2.

EXAMPLE 6.2. MORE VALID WAYS OF SPECIFYING TIME, INFORMATION AND TRUST

Under these headings, we can distinguish between the following specific and measurable factors:

1 discretionary time available in the household to sort rubbish;
2 ease of use of the scheme, including provision of bins for kerbside collection;
3 ease of access to a local recycling centre to dispose of uncollected waste;
4 intelligibility of any incentives;
5 information about how the scheme works;
6 information about how to solve problems that may arise;
7 trust that government advice is based on truth, or at least sincerity; and
8 trust that the local scheme is run honestly.

As a set, the measures in Example 6.2 have greater *measurement validity* than the ones we specified in 6.1, because they capture much better the underlying ideas that we are trying to test and thus give more specific content to our hypothesis. As a set, numbers 1–4 also have greater *content validity* than our initial, rather crude, idea of a single variable for measuring how and why time matters.

Measures 7 and 8 also have better *criterion validity* as measure of trust than our initial notion. In the literature on trust, it is now generally accepted that trust refers to an element in a relationship between two agents – say, a household and the local authority that runs the recycling scheme – in a context in which the first agent (the household) puts something of its own at hazard (its time and effort in recycling) in entrusting a specific task to a second agent. By contrast, the loose use of trust in our earlier examples would better describe the householder's general esteem for government advice rather than a relationship specifically of trust.

Internal and external validity

These different validity measures help us to examine how valid our measures and scores are for measuring variables in the present study: that is, their *internal validity*.

They also help us to examine how applicable they might be more widely within our field of interest: that is, their *external validity*. We might consider, for example, whether our IVs about information and trust can be applied to other environmentally-friendly behaviours, such as car-sharing or using public transport. Conversely, we might consider whether our IVs – for example, information and trust – might work differently for people who get most of the information they value from campaigning groups rather than from government.

EXERCISE 6.2. CONSCIENTIOUS, BUT IS IT VALID?

Consider whether the proposition that 'conscience' is an important factor in recycling behaviour offers adequate content, measurement and criterion validity.
  If you think it does, say why.
  If you think it does not, write down some changes you would make to it, or suggest a set of more specific and exact variables, to achieve greater content, measurement and criterion validity for this factor.

Reliability, again

To recap what we said in Chapter 1, 'reliability' refers to the consistency with which measures are used. It therefore refers to the problem that *random biases* may be introduced into our data because of the ways we gather and analyse these data.

Methodologists often claim that the most important test of reliability is replicability – that is, whether the same results would be obtained if the same study were repeated with the same methods, measures and samples. Replicability is easier to arrange with VOR than with other research designs, because measures are usually more precisely defined, measurement tends to rely less on the subjective judgement of the researcher, and the ways in which data are collected and analysed tend to be specified in more detail in the research protocol. So the two most important threats to reliability derive from the ways that

1 a single researcher uses and interprets the same measures at different times over the lifetime of a project (*intra-researcher reliability*); and
2 different researchers within the same project team use and interpret the same measures (*inter-researcher reliability*).

As in many other walks of life, reliability depends upon methodical attention to detail. Among the precautions we could take to maximise reliability are:

• clarifying definitions of observations to be collected, and agreeing unambiguous decision rules about how they should be identified, recorded, counted and displayed;
• drafting clear protocols stating these rules and procedures to be used in applying them;
• systematic piloting of data collection and analysis to identify possible problems in applying the protocol, before it is used extensively to collect observations;
• making regular inter- and intra-interviewer and coder checks to review how consistently the protocol is being applied; and
• regularly reviewing and revising protocols at key milestones in the project.

However, different combinations of precautions involve different trade-offs, including some trade-offs with validity. For example, consider the variable 'conscience'. Using in-depth, relatively unstructured, face-to-face interviews with householders who are strongly committed environmentalists, and who are also strongly committed to personal action to benefit the environment, may achieve a high degree of content validity for this variable. This is because such methods may directly capture a good understanding of how these people think, and why. However, these data may give rise to problems of reliability, if the very absence of structure causes the interviewer to lose track of the underlying concept – in this case 'conscience' – and the specific ways in which we have chosen to operationalise it. Moreover, a large set of transcripts with this kind of unstructured data may be quite problematic to code consistently because unstructured conversation may wander through many topics.

In contrast, some large-scale quantitative surveys can fail the test of content validity, by failing to pick up nuances in respondents' answers about their motivations for recycling. But a survey is relatively easy to apply and code consistently, so that analysis and findings may be more reliable.

Determinacy, sample size and parsimony

Determinacy is the measure of the extent to which the research design allows us to make the inferences we need to make. A crucial confirmation test on a hypothesis would have great determinacy: an inductive study on cases selected because they happened to be available would have much less determinacy.

Again, is what is proposed simply a fishing trip during which we throw a wide net overboard in the vague hope that it will catch something of interest? Or do we have good reasons for believing that the design of our project will yield data capable of producing inferences about matters that are theoretically interesting, and that will be accepted as valid and reliable?

In studies which meet statistical standards of inference, 'determinacy' is considered to depend on adherence to formal standards. One is that there should be a sufficient number of observations to back up the statistical inferences that the researcher wishes to draw.

Another important standard is *parsimony*. A research design that identifies a large number of possible, interlinked, factors to explain recycling behaviour, but attempts to test all of them at once in a small set of case studies, would fail this test. This is because it would not offer us a reasonable chance of systematically and reliably sorting out which of the multitude of rival factors carried the most promising explanatory weight. It would, therefore, not be possible to draw much in the way of useful inference from the results. The usual remedy is to increase the number of observations and reduce the number of variables. This procedure would produce a more parsimonious research design, because it makes fewer variables do more work.

Avoiding co-dependency and circularity

Another problem in VOR arises from selecting as IVs or DVs attributes that we already know, or might guess, to be connected with each other in ways that undermine the validity of the study.

For example, an important source of skew in results from VOR is the use of IVs which are neither logically or empirically genuinely independent of each other, so their effects are mutually reinforcing or mutually cancelling. For example, it might be a mistake to use both 'ideology' and 'commitment' as IVs, because 'commitment' might be an expression of 'ideology'. That is to say, they *are co-dependent*, not *independent* of each other. In statistical analysis, these two variables would be known as 'collinear' ones.

A closely related problem is 'circularity'. This refers to the risk that the results of a study are predetermined, because we set up the study in such a way that we are almost guaranteed to achieve positive confirmation or refutation of our hypothesis. One way to do this is to select, as IVs, factors that are, in practice, dependent on the DV. For example, we might be at risk of circularity if we selected 'providing separate bins in the house for paper, glass and plastic' as an IV, because it might be caused by the very phenomenon we are trying to explain, namely the householders' decision to separate waste of different types.

Sampling on the DV

There is always a temptation to conduct research among cases or populations that appear most strongly to exhibit the characteristics in which we are interested.

Suppose, for example, we want to find out which variables predict success in the implementation of local recycling schemes; it might be tempting – assuming there were enough of them – to draw a sample from areas where such schemes were considered to have worked, to find out what factors appear to be associated with success. Critics of this procedure argue, however, that sampling on successful *outcomes* encourages us to pre-judge what is important about them, and to overestimate the strength of factors appearing to cause them. If we select areas on the grounds that they are thought to exemplify 'success', then it is unsurprising if we end up inferring that the factors present in these areas appear to be associated with what we define as 'success'. The design encourages circularity. Worse, we cannot be sure that if we looked at failures, the same features would not turn up.

Sampling *both* successful and unsuccessful schemes might be better, but better still in VOR is to sample for diversity on, and so control, IVs. (We shall see, however, in Chapter 7 that in smaller-N studies, sampling across values on DVs is not always the worst trade-off.)

Necessary and sufficient conditions

In VOR we hope to make an inference to an explanation from finding that a measurable change in an IV is strongly associated with significant measurable change in a DV, without intervention by another variable. In VOR, in other words, to 'explain' is to do no more and no less than to say that a particular phenomenon must always be, or is usually, present for another phenomenon to occur.

An IV (or a set of them) may be 'sufficient' to explain the outcome variable. Or it may be 'necessary', in that, whilst it is always present, the independent factor does not, by itself, fully account for the phenomenon. We may claim that associations are 'deterministic': the specified outcome always follows a certain value on the independent value. Thus a single counter instance would be sufficient to falsify a generalisation. Or we may claim that the association is 'probabilistic' or 'stochastic': a specified outcome is *usually* associated with particular causes, but not invariably so. And so a single counter instance would be insufficient to falsify a generalisation.

The strengths of VOR

We postpone until Chapter 13 the question of when we can validly conclude such VOR explanations are causal. The important point to note here is that this understanding of explanation in VOR as a relationship of *influence* between variables – one which is at least *putatively causal* – underlies many common ways of reading VOR studies. It is helpful in social sciences because it facilitates the making of generalisations about social life, and can therefore be used to test the general application of theory. This is VOR's great strength, and it is the reason why some researchers believe that VOR designs set the gold standard for other kinds of social research. For them, other types of design may be useful, but will never amount to more than 'the best to be done in the circumstances'.

The limitations of VOR

VOR does, however, have some well-recognised limitations:

1 VOR designs focus on variables: this focus sometimes entails a high degree of abstraction from reality. It necessarily simplifies social phenomena and our understanding of them.
2 VOR tells us what causal factors appear to 'explain' certain outcomes, but it does not tell us much about causal mechanisms and *how* these mechanisms work.
3 VOR is often not much use in determining *how* multiple, causal factors *interact* with each other. It may be the case, for example, that outcomes are produced by the conjunction of causes in ways that are hidden by observations driven by our variables. For example, one causal factor might not 'work' as it is observed to do, if another factor were not present, too.

So how would these limitations impinge on recycling research? Consider Example 6.3.

EXAMPLE 6.3. VARIABLES AND CAUSALITY: PROBLEMS FOR RECYCLING RESEARCH

Unsurprisingly, extensive research has been carried out on the question of who does and who does not separate their household waste for recycling. Many factors have been found to be important, but no single factor appears to be pre-eminently responsible.

Studies tend to find that people from certain income brackets or particular educational backgrounds are more likely to recycle. A study of Scottish households found that rising income was significantly associated with greater propensities to recycle (Collins *et al.*, 2006). Women have been found more likely to recycle than men (Hunter *et al.*, 2004). But other studies found that socio-demographic variables, such as age, education, class and income, do not appear to be significantly associated with recycling household waste (e.g. Lober, 1996). However, studies that ask people what they care about, what they know or what they believe, tend to find that some attitudes or information matter more than others. A study in Exeter found that the variables that were significantly associated with household recycling were the presence or absence of a local collection scheme; whether or not people understood it and found it easy to use; and whether people thought recycling was the norm in the neighbourhood (Barr *et al.*, 2003). By contrast, a study in Hong Kong found that general attitudes were as important as the norm, along with a sense of being in control in using the scheme (Chan, 1998).

Slightly different variables appear to be important when we shift the level of analysis from households. For example, a study in the USA (Peretz *et al.*, 2005) found that *cities* with higher average incomes reported higher participation rates in their recycling schemes. Size seemed to matter, too: smaller cities could achieve comparable rates of participation with those found in the larger ones, but tended to rely more heavily on imposing mandatory duties or on financial incentives.

The findings set out in Example 6.3 leave us with two puzzles. The first is whether the socio-demographics are operating independently. For example, we know that higher education is highly correlated with higher income generally, and that both are associated with greater propensities to recycle. Is education or income more fundamental in explaining recycling? If income is the more fundamental factor, then the claim that the prevalence of higher education in a population leads to higher recycling rates might well be a spurious one. Or does one variable modify the effect of the other? What about rich entrepreneurs with little education but high incomes, and what about impoverished but highly educated people? Are there enough of them to test a hypothesis that education and income have distinct effects by discriminating between these two variables?

More fundamental, though, is the second puzzle. What is the relationship between socio-demographic variables and specific motivations to recycle? Being well educated, well-off or a woman is not an obviously plausible causal mechanism for recycling. On the other hand, it is neither surprising nor satisfying to be told that people who recycle want to do it, care about it and think they ought to do it. *Why* do they have these attitudes?

Variables as necessary and/or sufficient conditions

Because IVs cannot alone address such puzzles, we tend to write of them, in their causal role, as being *conditions*, not causes. This is because we cannot observe the causal process that leads from having, say, a certain level of education or possessing an environmental conscience to making the necessary household arrangements to separate different kinds of waste. Likewise, adequate time and convenience are conditions that make recycling possible, or at least easier. But they are not in themselves causal mechanisms.

Now consider 'conscience'. We might think that conscience alone is not enough to make many people recycle. But how much 'not enough' is 'not enough'? For example, is it the case that only people with some level of conscience will recycle their waste, however much time, information, trust they have and however great the incentives? That would make conscience a *necessary condition*. Or maybe it is time, information and trust that are necessary, but *either* conscience or financial incentives are needed, too. That sounds more plausible. But could a bit more conscience or a slightly greater level of incentive compensate – at least for some people (and then we would need to discover just which people are affected) – for time pressures, for having very limited information and or even for some dark suspicions about the way the scheme is being run? We invite you to think further about these issues in Exercise 6.4.

Conclusion

A VOR study will, then, not tell us *how* variables such as high income, educational achievement or the presence of a female household member contribute to willingness to recycle. Certainly, it will not tell us anything about how an individual household makes its decisions.

To answer such questions, we would need a design that focused in more detail on specific cases. Such a study would be designed to allow us to investigate how various social factors – and possibly psychological factors, too – interact with each other in particular historical, geographical or social contexts to create support or propensities for recycling. In other words, we would need a 'case-based' research design, focusing on complex conjunctures between multiple causes.

We conclude, therefore, that 'complete' social researchers need both VOR and case-based designs to understand all the dimensions of a complex problem. To this end, we shall turn in Chapter 7 to discuss the strengths and limitations of case-based approaches. We shall see, too, that there is considerable debate among methodologists about the strengths and weaknesses of the case-based approach, and how important they are. There is also considerable debate about how big and important the gulf really is between the kinds of inference involved in VOR and case-based designs.

Basic reading

For assistance in learning to handle the technical terms used in this chapter, and more discussion of VOR designs, see Brady HE and Collier D (eds), 2010 [2004], *Rethinking social inquiry: diverse tools, shared standards*, Lanham, MD: Rowman & Littlefield, Chapter Three.

Advanced reading

For a defence of variable-oriented social science against its critics, see Geddes B, 2003, *Paradigms and sand castles: theory building and research design in comparative politics*, Ann Arbor, MI: University of Michigan Press.

Lieberson S, 1985, *Making it count: the improvement of social research and theory*, Berkeley, CA: University of California Press, provides a thoughtful review of design issues in VOR.

SEVEN

Case-based research designs

> This chapter will:
>
> - describe case-based approaches to social research, and their differences from VOR;
> - examine their strengths and weaknesses; and
> - discuss key methodological issues to be taken into account in implementing case-based research designs, with particular reference to principles of case selection.

Chapter 6 ended by noting the tendency of VOR designs to abstraction, data reduction and simplification. These characteristics limit the kinds of research questions that they can address. VOR is central to social science, but cannot provide a complete design repertoire. It is therefore complemented by case-based approaches. Example 7.1 illustrates this point.

EXAMPLE 7.1. LIMITATIONS OF VOR IN UNDERSTANDING RECYCLING BEHAVIOUR – OR WHY WE ALSO NEED CASE-BASED APPROACHES

To understand recycling, we need to explain a range of behaviours, between full participation and outright refusal. Households might be prepared to recycle some things, but not others. They might not recycle for every collection. They might recycle for a kerbside collection but not those things that they must themselves take to the local recycling centre. So we might want to explain these activities separately.

Our explanatory factors turned out to be more complicated than we first thought, because – as we saw in Chapter 6 – our four variables turned out to be families or clusters of factors rather than single variables. We therefore need a way of understanding the influence of a multiplicity of factors and how they interact with each other.

Finally, we noted that a VOR design would not tell us much about how our four clusters of factors actually work in shaping household decision-making and behaviour. We therefore need a design that can investigate causal paths.

This example suggests that we could design better instruments for VOR if we first conduct in-depth research on a few cases, as a way of developing a better theory of decision-making and behaviour in recycling domestic waste. This might allow us to refine our explanatory hypotheses and state them more precisely.

We shall discuss the design of such a project throughout this chapter, as a way of exploring the advantages, limitations and methodological issues associated with 'case-based research' or CBR.

Case-based research

CBR refers to the classic 'case study' design, by which we mean the study in considerable depth, and as comprehensively as possible, of a single case ($N = 1$) or a few cases (small-N research).

The very modest numbers of cases used in CBR mean that it is often used to *develop* theory rather than to *test* it. The exception is where a theory proposes that something is a *necessary condition* for something else to occur. If the outcome arises, even in a single case where the condition is absent, then the theory fails. So CBR can be used to *falsify* theories which propose a necessary condition.

Whereas VOR focuses on discrete factors – for which variables are proxies – and looks for their independent contributions, CBR focuses on cases defined by interactions between factors that may not work independently, and looks for effects emerging, often in complex ways, from the whole set of interactions rather than from the principal or independent contribution of one, or a few, variables. CBR is used, therefore, to help us to understand the richness, complexity and nuances of social life, conceived holistically.

For this reason, CBR often works in much more detail than is possible with VOR designs. By contrast, VOR designs involve a great deal of 'data reduction' to focus on relationships between variables abstracted from a much larger population of cases.

What is a case?

If a 'variable' is a discrete unit of analysis which stands as a proxy for a factor of interest, then a case is a unit which is (Ragin and Becker, 1992; Stake, 1978):

1 defined and bounded by the researcher to answer a question about a particular phenomenon, either empirically and inductively, or theoretically and deductively;
2 sufficiently internally complex to enable within-case analysis of interacting forces and their combination; and
3 bounded in such a way that values of particular phenomena may change over the period of study or present a contrast between different elements.

Characteristics of CBR

CBR, then:

- typically focuses more on the dynamics of cases considered as *wholes* than on the relationships across cases among discrete variables;
- is more sensitive to temporal *chronology* and to the *context* of the case(s);
- enables us to study interactions between factors, or variables, in producing outcomes – it deals with *conjunctions* and *interactions* between, and *configurations* of, variables, and does not simply treat variables as having an 'additive' or cumulative effect;
- can be used to tease out *how* causal processes work (this is known as causal process tracing: see Chapter 14), and not just whether they are present;
- searches for emergent outcomes and properties;
- seeks to make use of a very full range of available data, of both qualitative and quantitative kinds: less data are 'eliminated' than in VOR, which abstracts data relating only to selected variables; and
- typically uses a *range of methods* to capture and analyse this variety of data.

Because they are less tightly structured, case-based designs are more flexible than VOR designs, and can more easily accommodate changes in the research frame. In very small-N, or N = 1 research designs, researchers can also develop much greater familiarity with their cases, and this familiarity may lead to insights that suggest new theoretical leads. In other words, it is much easier with CBR to identify and follow interesting leads, including those that might throw light on an important issue that may not have been identified before the research began.

Ragin (1994, 2004) therefore claims that CBR has a distinctive capacity to encourage iterative dialogue between theory and empirical evidence. Case-based researchers can, and should, he suggests, be prepared to recast theory in the light of changing empirical evidence. In turn, new ideas and evidence may cause them to develop new lines of theoretical enquiry, a process that is much more difficult with highly structured VOR projects. For example, it is possible to imagine that, as a result of greater familiarity with the effect of unemployment in middle-class households, a study that had been provisionally framed as a case study of the effects of environmental conscience and trust on recycling might be subsequently reframed as a study of the interplay of changing socio-economic status with changing attitudes to environmental issues and materialism.

These features of CBR afford important strengths, but as we shall show below, they also imply significant limitations.

Richness in use of data

A strength of CBR is its ability to capture the full significance of a complex data set. For example, CBR can achieve a nuanced, subtle, rich account of the complex sets of conditions that engender different kinds of householder responses to new, local recycling schemes. We might employ a mix of methods to capture the richest possible understanding of these conditions: how this might be done is discussed in Example 7.2.

EXAMPLE 7.2. COLLECTING DATA; USING A MIX OF METHODS IN THE CONTEXT OF CBR

We might ask households to keep diaries about their decision-making about rubbish. We might also interview household members; and we could even try some observation by spending time with our focal households at times when they are faced with putting out their waste.

Perhaps we could also talk to their relatives, friends, colleagues and acquaints about their understanding of how the people in these households make decisions. In particular, we would clearly need to collect rich data on the presence or absence, strength or weakness, of time, information, conscience and trust.

But, because our aim is to develop theory, we need, too, to collect data on *how* these factors are related.

We should also choose data collection methods that will enable us to collect data in a more open-ended fashion, to find out if any other factors are important.

Limitations of CBR

Among the limitations of CBR is that it cannot analyse large numbers of cases or large volumes of data. CBR is therefore prone to producing particularistic insights, the relevance of which to other contexts – let alone to general theory – may be unclear.

For example, a CBR project on the effects of introducing local recycling schemes might allow us to understand what causes some households in South London to make pragmatic decisions about their response to the scheme, with only scant discussion among household members. By contrast, a more politicised household in Sheffield might need an hour's debate over the Sunday lunch to agree on what exactly they are prepared to do. But this project would not allow us to apply these insights with confidence to British market towns with more established schemes, let alone to household decision-making about recycling in the *favelas* of Rio de Janeiro or the leafier suburbs of Munich.

Problems of generalising from CBR mean that researchers using single or small-N designs may be tempted to err in the other direction, by overstating the idiosyncratic or special nature of their cases(s), thus sacrificing the possibility of contributing to theory development.

Issues in case selection

Selecting cases is therefore a central issue in CBR designs. Example 7.3 considers how we might deal with it in our recycling project by selecting an appropriate *number* and *range* of cases, and also how we might select for appropriate *contextual factors*.

**EXAMPLE 7.3. THREE ISSUES IN SELECTING CASES FOR
A CBR PROJECT ON RECYCLING**

First, we want the right number of cases. Studying one case in considerable depth would be fascinating but it would offer too slender a base for developing theory. Three might still be too few. Twelve cases might be too many for our resources. Perhaps somewhere between four and eight might be practicable.

Although our sample will not be statistically *representative*, as would be required for VOR, we still want it to exhibit *adequate diversity* on at least some of the factors in which we are interested, for fear of prematurely shutting off promising lines of research. For this purpose, we might want diversity on *outcomes*, or the behaviours to be explained: this is the analogue of the dependent variables (DVs) in VOR. So we want households that have made different decisions about recycling and how much effort to put into it.

Most important, though, we need adequate diversity on some *factors or processes* that we expect to be *causally* important: these factors are the analogue of independent variables (IVs) in VOR. We shall probably be unable to assemble a set of cases exhibiting all of them. A reasonable compromise might be to ensure some diversity on factors we suspect are most important. For example, if we want to develop a hypothesis about the way in which conscience about environmental issues might influence decision-making about household waste, we might want to include households with people who are members of environmental or conservation associations, such as Friends of the Earth or the National Trust, and some who admit their ignorance of environmental issues.

CBR would enable us to explore both how conscience shapes decision-making about waste and how conscience might itself be shaped. So we could choose cases that would allow us to explore differences between households where all adult members are politicised or religious, households where no adults fall into these categories, and some which are mixed. Or we might choose cases that would enable us to explore the effects on behaviour of different local friendship patterns or of competing pressures on householders' time.

Third, we ideally want diversity on *contextual factors*, so that we can develop a theory about which are most important. However, this may be impossible to achieve within the available resources for intensive CBR, and we may have to restrict cases to a single context.

In researching recycling, 'context' might be a local authority area, or it might be a certain type of recycling scheme. Or maybe the 'context' in which we are interested may be peculiar to the period being studied: for example, we might be interested in the significance of the fact that an area has introduced a new recycling scheme, or in the impact of a major national or local publicity campaign.

Sampling on the dependent variable?

Example 7.3 illustrates another important issue in designing CBR projects. The combination of two constraints inherent in CBR – that is, the small number of cases it is possible to study and the need to achieve a sample with adequate diversity of *outcomes* – means that case selection in CBR is prone to the sin of 'sampling on the dependent variable (DV)' that we discussed in Chapter 6 in relation to VOR. Indeed, critics of case-based designs often focus on the tendency to seek out cases exhibiting the most extreme, the most pure, the most successful or unsuccessful, or the most advanced outcomes in which the researcher is interested.

In Chapter 8 we shall have something to say on the special conditions where small- to modestly-sized N *comparative case-oriented research* can legitimately sample across cases on the dependent variable. In CBR, too, there are some special situations where choosing a small number of cases, or even a single case, on the basis of *outcomes* may be appropriate. Indeed, Rogowski (2010 [2004]) points out that several landmark studies in social sciences have used this sampling strategy. This is because – even though this sampling strategy cannot be used to *test* a theory – sampling on outcomes can sometimes help CBR to realise its special contributions to building social science theory, by *developing* a theory, *specifying a causal mechanism* or *falsifying a necessary condition hypothesis*.

In particular, sampling on the DV may be justified in the context of very small-N research (Dion, 1998), if the purpose is to identify one sufficient cause, or to falsify a necessary condition hypothesis. This is because a CBR design allows us to show the absence of a supposedly necessary factor, or to establish specific conditions under which a sufficient factor works. Sampling on outcomes might also enable the researcher to establish what other conditions contribute to success. For example, it may be found that businesses employing people fluent in the language spoken in target countries are more successful in international marketing than those that do not, but that the marketing strategy is important, too. But the lack of comparison inherent in a small-N study would prevent us finding out whether these conditions are *necessary* for success.

Thus, a design that clearly distinguishes between necessary and sufficient conditions may escape the problem of circularity. Moreover, if we have *diversity* on the thing to be explained, and we have a sound prior reason – for example, an hypothesis, or perhaps a reasoned, pre-theoretical hunch – to believe that the things to be explained are good *proxies* for the factors that explain them, then there may be some justification for selecting on outcomes, especially in circumstances where we cannot select directly on explanatory factors.

The right strategy in our case?

We can illustrate these points by returning to Example 7.3. Selecting cases, at least in part, for diversity of outcomes may be the right thing to do in this case. We should remember that our explanatory purpose is different from that in VOR. We are not trying to *test* a theory, but to *develop* rich causal theory about how households make decisions, and perhaps how and why they stick to them, or not. For this purpose, we need to find out whether contrasting behaviours arise from different causal paths and, if so, to compare and contrast them, to establish the most important differences in those paths. Selecting cases to explain different outcomes – in this case, different recycling behaviours – is probably justified because we expect to find different outcomes associated with different explanatory factors, so 'outcomes' become a *proxy* for an expected underlying difference in explanatory factors, say 'conscience' or 'friendship patterns'.

Now think about how *you* would select cases for this study, by attempting Exercise 7.1.

EXERCISE 7.1. SORT YOUR EXPLANATIONS NEATLY INTO DIFFERENTLY COLOURED BOXES...

Write down an *exact statement* of one aspect of household decision-making about recycling – or not recycling, or not recycling much or not recycling often – that a well-designed case-based study could develop theory to explain.

Draw up a table of the factors on which you would want diversity in your selection of cases, for a study comprising eight households. Justify your choices.

Problems of small-*N* multi-variable research

CBR tends to draw its strongest criticisms from methodologists who hold to the gold standard of inferential statistics (e.g. Lieberson, 1992). Indeed, some of these critics believe that case-based designs are inherently problematic. First, they point to the problems of making generalisations on the basis of a small number of unrepresentative cases. Second, CBR is typically used to research situations that are inherently complex and multi-factorial, and that combine small-*N* observations with a much larger number of variables. Some critics conclude from this fact that CBR is therefore inherently prone to the problem of indeterminacy we discussed in Chapter 6. We show below that the situation is not so desperate as this would suggest, and that CBR can be used quite properly for certain kinds of research questions.

Debates about CBR

To what *extent* small-*N* studies are problematic, and how much their indeterminacy matters, are both much debated questions. King *et al.* (1994: Chapter One) argue, for example, that CBR should be judged by similar standards to VOR, and that under certain methodological conditions, CBR can be used to make inferences of a kind that parallel, but do not replicate, certain features of inferential statistics. Therefore, they argue, researchers ought, wherever possible, to improve design quality by increasing numbers of cases and reducing numbers of variables, and deny that theory development should follow a different inferential path from theory-testing.

Some advocates of CBR argue, however, that basing this debate on the standards of inferential statistics misses its point. They argue that CBR and VOR have different purposes, and that it is therefore inappropriate to judge the former by the standards of the latter.

Rogowski (2010 [2004]), for example, holds that, subject to further research, findings from CBR are provisionally generalisable to other cases through their theoretical insights into causal dynamics rather than through a process akin to statistical inference. He argues that we should use CBR to follow *theoretical* leads, to develop an in-depth, theoretically informed understanding of the relevant social dynamics of cases. For him, then, theory development can legitimately follow a different inferential logic.

Naturalistic generalisation and narrative exposition

Other advocates of CBR stress that understanding is made possible only by immersion in a very small number of cases.

Stake's influential (1978) article argued that human beings frequently perceive regularities in the social world and act with confidence on their perceptions. This confidence does not stem from conducting experiments or systematic observations to test whether general 'laws' are at work, but from experiential understanding of a range of similar situations and from developing intuitive skills in reading them. This process is referred to by Stake as 'naturalistic generalisation'. He claims that CBR can extend knowledge in a similar way.

Furthermore, an important way in which case study researchers can reveal and communicate their knowledge – particularly of complex cases – is through the development of narrative expositions of their empirical findings. 'Narrative' refers to the attempt to convey our understanding of the nature of events, relationships or processes, in ways that allow other people to 'make sense' of them. One way to do this is by using chronology as an organising framework: by asking and answering the simple question: what happened next? But it is also possible – and often more fruitful – to make connections between and within cases by organising our findings by 'themes'. For example, in writing up our case study of households' decision-making about recycling, we might organise our report to provide coherent accounts of the significance of common 'themes' such as 'neighbourliness', 'community', 'social networks', 'time-poverty' or 'environmentalism' in different cases.

However it is organised, what distinguishes the narrative form is its preoccupation with achieving inter-subjective connections between writer and reader. A kind of one-sided conversation ensues, in which, in the act of writing, the writer feels free to make assumptions about the tacit knowledge and intuitions that the reader will bring to the act of reading, to develop a richer sense of the meaning of the case and to convey more fully the experience of researching it.

Weber and the concept of *Verstehen*

In bringing forward this argument, Stake may appear to be aligning himself with the work of one of the founding fathers of social science, Max Weber (e.g. Weber, 1947). Weber argued that the relationship of social scientists with the social world is different from the relationship of physical scientists with the physical world, because social scientists share insights with the people they study. Social scientists can therefore draw on *Verstehen* – the German word for 'understanding' – a quality that comes from being able to bring subjective, tacit insights to develop an understanding of the social world.

In arguing this way, Weber was, in effect, announcing that the kind of positivist approach advocated by Friedman some fifty years later – and which we discussed in Chapter 3 – is wrong. To recap, Friedman argued that, if we can cajole any old data into yielding a model that faithfully reproduces the observed outcomes, then we can claim to have provided an 'explanation'. Weber would have regarded this claim as nonsense. If a model makes assumptions that bear no relation to the way that actors could plausibly understand matters, then the fact that it grinds out the right numbers is a party trick, not social science. Rather, Weber insisted that models and theories must be 'adequate at the level of meaning'.

In particular, Weber was interested in motives: the fundamental questions in social science are 'why do people act as they do?' and 'how do they understand their actions?' For example, it would be difficult to claim that the bankers who took large bonuses for making high-risk investments intended to put the whole financial system of Western capitalism into jeopardy, as seemed possible in the crisis of 2007. Indeed, these actions may well have caused this outcome, but, Weber would say, if we accept this claim as an *explanation* of the crisis, then we are in the wrong vocation in social science. An explanatory account that is adequate at the level of meaning should, rather, focus on what he called our habitual modes of thought and feeling, and should illuminate what is typical about those modes.

So the job of social science is to describe accurately the motivations, reasons, thought styles, understandings, emotions and heuristics which led bankers to act in the way they did. Such accounts must invoke common or typical features to be intelligible, and good accounts of anything very interesting will bring together accounts of such things for more than one group of people: in other words, the point is not simply to explain why a particular bank collapsed, but what our study shows us about the nature of financial services in the UK, or even more generally in the West.

Using deduction in CBR

The virtual debate we have just invented between Weber, Stake and Friedman is an important one. It is often assumed in the methods literature that CBR designs are most appropriately used in the context of *inductive* approaches to research, and, indeed, the thematic analysis and narratives advocated by Stake are often considered to be best done inductively, by letting them emerge from the data. However, the reference to Weber shows that the distinctive qualities of CBR can also be brought to bear in developing and refining explanatory theories. Furthermore – as we shall see further in Chapters 10–13 – explanatory theories can take account of people's ideas, motives and ways of seeing the world: indeed many scholars in the Weberian tradition insist that they should.

CBR may be used *deductively* to *develop* theory, by moving back and forth between theory and the empirical investigation of hypotheses deduced from it. As we saw above, an unexpected result in a particularly critical case – one, for example, that was predicted to display, in an especially pure form, the essential relationships identified by a theory – may undermine that theory, by showing decisively why it does not apply in that case. But that should not end the matter.

If, in one community, we were to find no positive connection at all between certain environmental attitudes and the making of principled decisions about recycling household waste, this might cause us seriously to rethink our hypothesis about linkages between particular forms of conscience and recycling behaviour. The question is: *why* is the result anomalous? Researching the anomalous case in more detail might lead to an insight that can be captured in a refined hypothesis to be explored in other cases.

For example, we might discover that some householders who seem to have strong environmental consciences do not, in practice, consistently recycle their domestic waste. Further investigation of these apparently anomalous households might lead us to develop a new hypothesis that 'conscience' leads to consistent recycling only in relatively time-rich households, and this might lead us to revisit other households in the study, or even select some new households, to look in more detail at the way in which behaviour is actually influenced by time constraints. In turn, this may lead us to formulate hypotheses about the ways in which the design of the recycling scheme makes more or fewer demands on the time of busy households.

The purpose, then, is to revise our hypothesis and perhaps develop fresh ones, until it becomes impossible to do more testing with the data that can be collected through a small-N CBR design. By that stage, we would hope to have a hypothesis that is sufficiently well developed and specified to justify testing it by means of a larger, more expensive and less flexible VOR design.

We can see, then, that a carefully structured and disciplined approach to the serial construction and assessment of deductive theories forms an important stage in theory-building.

Principles of case selection

Case-based researchers do not always have to claim that their cases are representative of wider populations of cases. But they do need to determine whether or not they can make warranted inferences from their cases to any wider population. The answer to this question depends in large part on what we think is interesting about the cases we select

One important reason for using a single case study design ($N = 1$) is to study a case that is of such intrinsic interest that its subject matter is sufficient justification for the time and effort spent on it. For example, Allison's famous study (Allison and Zelikow, 1999 [Allison, 1971]) of the US government's response to the Cuban Missile Crisis in 1962 needs no justification other than the importance of this event in the history of the Cold War – although as it happens, this study also represents a significant milestone in the development of the theory of public policy-making.

Most case study research designs deal with more prosaic matters, and need to be justified in other terms. One justification derives from their use as *illustration*. As many readers will know, case studies have long been used in medical education, business education and other professional development programmes, because well-chosen studies can be used to illustrate, or even to simulate, features commonly found in 'real-life' practice. Social scientists use case studies to provide similar insights.

Cases may also illustrate features that are widely found. They are therefore deemed worthy of in-depth study, because of their *typicality*. For example, a case researcher may develop a project to study the impact of 'institutional racism' on employment practices in the army or in a large corporation, on the assumption that these practices are not untypical of those occurring in large hierarchical organisations.

Third, the researcher may undertake a study of an *extreme* case – for example, a police force that is known to have a particularly difficult history of institutional racism – because it illustrates features of interest in a particularly pure and obvious way, and thus makes them easy to study. An extreme case may therefore be particularly revealing. Such a 'limit case' might, for example, help us to understand why the process under examination does not produce cases any *more* extreme than the outlier that was chosen for the study.

Similarly, case studies may be undertaken in organisations that are thought to be especially successful in a particular respect, as a way of understanding the factors that cause this success. For example, a case study of an organisation that has developed particularly advanced ways of using the Internet for communicating with its customers might fruitfully be studied to see what the future might look like for other organisations when they catch up. However, as we saw above, this case selection principle is particularly vulnerable to the accusation of sampling on the DV.

Clearly, however, using any of these justifications for a single case study or for a very small-N design places great pressure on us to show that the case or cases chosen for study do actually possess the characteristics claimed for them: that they are indeed 'intrinsically interesting', 'illustrative', 'typical' or 'extreme' cases. This may require reference to existing bodies of knowledge in social science, or may require additional research.

Theoretical sampling of cases

Alternatively, it may be possible to argue that the cases have been drawn according to a 'theoretical sample'. 'Theoretical sampling' is the process of making explicit the contribution that the cases can make to the development of theory, by showing why their particular features are of theoretical interest. This is a rather vague statement, and, in fact, 'theoretical sampling' is used in at least two contrasting senses.

One usage was developed for *inductive* qualitative research designs by Glaser, Strauss and Corbin (Glaser and Strauss, 1967; Strauss and Corbin, 1997). They use the term to refer to the practice of selecting cases specifically to examine features of particular interest for *questions* which require theories to answer them, by selecting a wide diversity of cases ('open sampling'), by selecting cases with sufficient diversity to examine particular kinds of variation ('variational sampling'), or by selecting cases with very limited diversity to undertake specific comparisons ('discriminate sampling'). The main purpose of case selection, for this school, is more often theory development than theory-testing.

Another usage of the term 'theoretical sampling' is rooted in *deductive* research designs. Suppose we have a theory that predicts that A will be associated with B, if C is also present, but will not be associated with B in C's absence. To examine this theory using both between-case and within-case analysis, we shall need cases where we expect A to be present and C absent, and also cases where both A and C are present. This set of cases would enable us to determine whether B turns up only in the latter group. However, claiming to use case studies for such purposes implies that the researcher *can* show that the case or cases *are* selected on the basis of factors of clear theoretical significance. This claim needs to be explicitly made in bringing forward a proposal for case study research, though the validity of such a claim can often only be definitively established *post hoc*, by inference from the research.

EXERCISE 7.2. THEORETICAL SAMPLING?

Return again to the discussion of case selection for our recycling project in Example 6.3.
   Consider whether the project you developed for Exercise 6.1 would count as an example of any of the principles of case selection discussed above.
   Explain your answer.

A note of caution about reliability and subjectivity

An important argument sometimes made for CBR is that it allows us to make much more faithful use of data than do VOR designs, which necessarily abstract and simplify 'reality'. However, the fact that CBR often uses less highly specified units of analysis and less complex analytic procedures than those typically used in VOR does not remove the need to be faithful to the empirical data. Indeed, the reverse is the case. The absence of highly specified variables of the kind associated with VOR designs often makes it less obvious how data collection and analysis can best be achieved, and this problem places considerable pressure on procedures for recording, coding, displaying and interpreting data. So protocols for recording and analysing case study data need to be constructed purposively, explicitly and transparently. The very richness and detail of data collected for CBR means, too, that recording, coding, analysis and interpretation are all labour-intensive, and the time needed to conduct a thorough and faithful analysis of relatively unstructured data is a significant cost in CBR, one that is often not fully appreciated in the project proposal stage.

Validity and reliability in CBR

This is another way of saying that, as with all approaches to social science research, case studies must meet certain standards of reliability and validity. However, by contrast with VOR designs, it is less clear what these standards are, and there is more room for contention as to whether they have been met. We conclude this chapter by discussing three proposals for increasing confidence in the validity and reliability in CBR.

Finding proxies for reliability and validity

Methodologists Denzin and Lincoln (1998) often use words like *dependability*, *confirmability* and *auditability* as proxies for replicability in case-based research. They imply that case studies should be undertaken in ways that allow us to demonstrate, by direct reference to our research instruments, coding frames and data sets, that the project was conducted with due attention to faithfulness to the data, that the research instruments were used consistently and that data were gathered and analysed in ways specified by the research design. For this reason, we should always be able to produce an audit trail, showing how we used the data to produce the findings reported at the conclusion of the project.

In practice, very few CBR projects are ever asked to produce this evidence, but it is a good test of the soundness of our procedures to draw up and implement a protocol on the basis that our procedures should be entirely transparent to other researchers. Thesis writers are certainly expected to explain in their theses, and/or in their oral defence, how much confidence they have in the reliability of their findings, and how this confidence was enhanced by the procedures they adopted in carrying out the project.

A second strategy, aimed mainly at increasing validity when dealing with people's ideas and motives, especially in interpretive research, is to find ways of checking back with participants to ensure that the project faithfully captured the subjective meaning to the people involved of the phenomena studied in the case study, and that the inferences drawn from the study make sense in the context of their experiences.

These two strategies do not find favour with all protagonists of case studies. For example, Hammersley (1992) regards the input of participants to the drafting of results as a threat to, rather than as a safeguard of, validity, because he fears that it might skew the results by causing the researcher to be captured by the interests of the people being studied rather than being faithful to the empirical evidence. Similarly, Morse *et al.* (2002) have argued that both of the above strategies are severely limited, in that they rely mainly on *post hoc* checks on reliability and validity: that is, they take place only after the research is finished.

Building verification procedures into the project

Morse *et al.* therefore argue for developing procedures that allow possible errors to be detected and corrected during the course of the research. They recommend establishing procedures that discourage researchers from mechanically collecting and analysing data according to pre-agreed procedures, and encourage them, instead, constantly to check their data and their findings against aims and purposes specified in the research protocol. They describe an approach to conducting CBR that forces the researcher to question and move constantly between the data, the theory and the research design, as the research proceeds.

Conclusion

This chapter has shown why the flexibility of CBR and its capacity for dealing with interactions of variables renders it well suited to the task of helping to develop theory, particularly theories about complex causal paths. But CBR is generally unsuited to testing theory, unless we are seeking to falsify a necessary condition hypothesis or unless the world only supplies a very small number of cases to which the theory, if it were true, could apply. In the next chapter, we shall see how the use of case studies to develop theory can be extended by the use of comparisons between cases and how they complement the kind of within-case analysis typical of CBR.

Basic reading

For an overview of the foundational issues about CBR and generalisation in CBR, see
Gomm R, *et al.*, 2000, Case study and generalisation, in R Gomm *et al.* (eds), *Case study method: key issues, key texts*, London: Sage, 98–116.

For a review of the issues at stake in using case studies for deductive theory-testing and inductive theory development, see Eisenhardt K, 1989 Building theories from case study research, *Academy of Management Review*, 14, 4, 532–50.

Chapter Five in Gerring J, 2007, *Case study research: principles and practices*, Cambridge: Cambridge University Press, is especially useful on principles of case selection.

Chapter 5 by Rogowski, and Chapter 6 by Collier *et al.*, in the first (2004) edition of Brady HE and Collier D (eds), 2004, *Rethinking social inquiry: diverse tools, shared standards*, Lanham, MD: Rowman & Littlefield, 75–102, address some standard critiques of small-*N* research. Chapter 8 (125–138) by Ragin is also helpful. The chapter by Rogowski is also in the second edition (2010: 89–98).

Advanced reading

Ragin CC and Becker HS, 1991, *What is a case? Exploring the foundations of social inquiry*, Cambridge: Cambridge University Press. See particularly Walton's review ('Making the theoretical case') of the issues involved in within-case analysis and in defining units of analysis.

For an overview of recent developments in case-based approaches, see Byrne D and Ragin CC (eds), 2009, *The Sage handbook of case-based methods*, London: Sage.

Dion D, 1998, Evidence and inference in the comparative case study, *Comparative Politics*, 30, 2, 127–45, addresses issues of inference.

Morse JM, Barrett M, Mayan M, Olson K and Spiers J, 2002, Verification strategies for establishing validity and reliability in qualitative research, *International Journal of Qualitative Methods*, 1, 2, 1–19, consider questions of validity.

Lieberson S, 1992, Small *N*'s and big conclusions: an examination of the reasoning in comparative studies based on a small number of cases, in CC Ragin and HS Becker (eds), *What is a case? Exploring the foundations of social inquiry*, Cambridge: Cambridge University Press, 105–18, offers a critique of reliance on small sample.

EIGHT

Comparative and case-oriented research designs

> This chapter will:
>
> - define and describe the nature and scope of comparative designs (sometimes called case-comparative or case-oriented research, or COR);
> - discuss the importance of comparison in social sciences and the reasons why it is difficult to select and compare cases in methodologically valid ways;
> - consider various strategies for undertaking comparison between cases; and
> - explore the importance of classification and typologies in selecting cases for comparison.

Comparative designs in small-*N* research

We saw in Chapter 7 that the simplest case-based designs are typically used to develop rich and detailed understandings, using within-case analysis, of the internal dynamics of one, or a very few, cases in context. In this chapter, we extend our understanding of the contribution of case-based approaches, by looking at comparative case study designs – and particularly 'case-oriented research' (COR) – in building and provisionally examining theories.

Ragin (1987, 1994) uses the term 'case-oriented research' to refer to the use of multiple case studies with modest-sized N – typically between four and twenty – to explore the causal effects of specific variables on particular outcomes, by comparing relationships between independent and dependent variables both within and between cases. Each case is studied in more depth, and especially with more regard to context, than is possible in traditional VOR designs, but the point of using this approach is not only to develop within-case analysis but also to compare the behaviour of particular variables, or analyse particular patterns, *between* cases.

Ragin (1994) assumes that COR will mainly, or exclusively, use qualitative methods, partly because they are more suitable for a limited number of cases. However, the logic of the comparative approach to inference – which imposes control by means of the principled selection of cases – is much the same as that which underpins many kinds of quantitative analysis, although the use of smaller samples means that we can attach lower confidence to inferences than would be the case for large-N VOR designs.

Ragin also favours qualitative methods for COR because they allow research instruments and analytical frameworks to be developed or amended in the course of the research. This is important, because as we began to see in Chapters 6 and 7, both CBR and COR designs should allow us to keep an open mind on the focus and scope of the project, and on the definition of themes and factors, as the research develops. This is illustrated in Example 8.1.

EXAMPLE 8.1. GO HYPOTHESISE! GO COMPARE!

Suppose we want to examine the relative efficacy of various new schemes to teach young schoolchildren to read. One obvious way to do this is to run a VOR study, comparing outcomes from different schemes, while controlling for factors such as the social class of children in the sampled schools. But this may not tell us *how* such schemes work – or fail.

Suppose, then, we conduct a COR study of a small number of schools, chosen on the basis that they have similar kinds of intakes but use different reading schemes. The initial hypothesis is that choice of reading scheme is the single most important factor explaining the different rates of success in teaching young children to read. But we might find in the first few cases that, in practice, the scheme used interacts with other factors such as the methods of the teacher, the experience of the teacher, class size and the language skills of the children to produce different outcomes. Thus, schemes work in different ways in different contexts.

We therefore refine our theory to reflect the complex multi-causality involved in success rates for reading, and then select other schools in which to examine a new hypothesis derived from this theory.

Iteration between empirical evidence and theory development

COR designs work, then, by promoting an iterative relationship between data collection, data analysis and provisional theoretical inferences. Coding data systematically to establish the behaviour of certain variables and displaying the results (using chronological timelines, tables, matrices and so on) reveals patterns both within and between cases. This process should stimulate us to ask questions about these patterns, and particularly about anomalies. We might ask, for example, 'why have we found these patterns and not others?', 'why are there these exceptions to the patterns?', 'are they significant, and if so why?', and 'why is this case behaving differently from other cases?'

These questions should lead us to formulate provisional answers to our research questions, or to refine our hypotheses, in ways that prompt further empirical research among a population of cases. In some circumstances, this process might lead us to increase the number of cases to see whether the same patterns hold in slightly different cases, or even to find a different set of cases more appropriate for studying the emergent patterns. New data are then coded and the process starts again. In this way, the shape of the project changes over its life course, and new theoretical insights emerge.

Although this process seems relatively straightforward, using between-case comparison raises important methodological issues. So we need to remind ourselves why social scientists aspire to compare.

Comparison in social sciences

Experimental controls in such disciplines as psychology systematically compare effects of common variables on different subjects, while controlling effects of other variables. Political scientists, macro-sociologists and historians have also aimed to develop statistical control methods for large, highly structured, quantitative, cross-country comparative studies, because they regard the development of capacity for such research as the *sine qua non* for aspiring to the same kind of authority as that enjoyed by many natural sciences. An example is Almond and Verba's well-known (1967) study of differences in civic culture among democratic political systems. But modest-N COR studies are also important. The work of Moore (1966) exemplifies the use of cross-country comparative methods in the history of fascist, socialist, liberal democratic and social democratic regimes, and Esping-Andersen's (1990) famous comparative study of welfare states was hugely influential.

Comparative social science is quite hard to do in non-experimental settings, for the good reasons that we discussed in some detail in Chapter 5. Particularly challenging methodological problems arise when we try to compare cases rigorously across significant geographical, historical or cultural gulfs, because it is very difficult to find reliable ways of establishing whether we are really looking at relevantly similar phenomena. We shall return to this important point again in Chapter 9, when we study 'concept formation' and the vexed issue of 'concept stretching'. The present chapter examines the ways in which methodologists think about comparison in the context of COR designs.

But whether controls are experimental, statistical or based on small-N case selection, the social science enterprise of discovering general patterns in the social world rests heavily on our capacity systematically to examine similarities and differences between social phenomena. Discovering that some things are identical or behave in similar ways allows social scientists to postulate general hypotheses. But observing differences allows us to delineate more precisely the situations or occasions when patterns apply and do not, so mapping *differences* adds greater precision to social science knowledge. Observing that a certain phenomenon does not behave as predicted by a general hypothesis prompts the social scientist to ask: *why*? Hence, discovering unpredicted differences or anomalies enables theories to be falsified, refined or changed. Identifying and weighing similarities and differences between cases selected on criteria of relevance is the task of comparative analysis.

So the fundamental presumptions of all comparative science are that:

- differences in outcomes among relevantly similar cases lead us to look for explanation by differences in causal forces (on which more in the next two chapters); and
- similarities in outcome in relevantly similar cases lead us to expect similarities in causal forces until shown otherwise.

Determining which cases are similar in relevant ways depends on what we want to know and on what we expect, on the basis of existing knowledge, to find.

Thus, *control* in COR consists in selecting only relevantly similar cases and in isolating differences and similarities that are most likely to carry explanatory weight. Indeed, the development of systematic, formal methods for so doing is at the heart of all science. The key question for control in COR is, therefore, how cases are selected for comparison.

How to select cases for comparison

What kinds of procedures should be developed to make valid comparisons capable of generating theoretically useful inferences? To address this question, social scientists often use one of two designs for comparing cases: the *method of agreement* and the *method of difference*. They were first proposed by the nineteenth-century philosopher John Stuart Mill (1967 [1843]), and are therefore often referred to as 'Millian' designs.

The method of agreement

This method involves selecting two or more cases displaying similar outcomes or dependent variables (DVs). A range of possible causes – independent variables (IVs) – are then explored, to see which, if any, is associated with these outcomes across the cases. The hope is that most IVs will be eliminated, leaving – ideally – a single IV standing. This IV is then regarded as the principal cause.

This procedure has the advantage of simplicity, and it can be used with very small-*N* case designs. However, it is easy to see why methodologists are sceptical about its value. In the first place, it explains only positive outcomes – why things happen, rather than why they do not happen.

Second, this method's effectiveness depends on being able to eliminate all but one or two causes: it cannot cope easily with cases where several factors are working simultaneously to bring about the effect (multi-causality); or where there are several paths to the same outcome (equifinality); or where several causes interact and affect each other (interaction).

Third, it requires us to 'sample on the DV': it is therefore prone to the problem encouraged by this procedure, namely a tendency to overestimate the explanatory power of whatever variable is present in the chosen case(s).

Despite these very real problems, we might find this design useful for some small-N case-based projects for theory development. In case-oriented and comparative research, it is usually operationalised as a 'most similar case' – or, in cross-national research, 'most similar country' – design. It involves choosing a few, carefully selected cases, on the basis that the IVs are similar in most respects, but differ in a way, or in a very few ways, that are important to the theory. It therefore allows us to focus on the relationship between a DV and a few IVs that we believe to be particularly significant. A small-N study allows us to study these relationships in some detail in their specific contexts, while systematically comparing their effects across the small population of cases.

The method of difference

This method, by contrast, involves choosing a number of cases – for example, countries or organisations – that display different characteristics or outcomes, where the DV varies in theoretically interesting ways. By analysing effects of several IVs, we hope to identify the one that varies systematically in line with the DV. The assumption is that most IVs will either be constant across selected cases or act in non-systematic ways, thus allowing the true 'cause' or 'causes' to be exposed.

This method is often preferred to the method of agreement, because it allows a wider variety and a larger number of cases to be used, thus increasing the number (N) of observations that are available for analysis. It can also cope to some extent with multi-causality, but it does not cope any better than the method of agreement with interaction, because it focuses on the independent effects of the IVs.

The method of difference is often operationalised in case study or comparative research as a 'most different case' design. It encourages us to choose cases displaying greater variety than the 'most similar case' design. Despite its name, we should not assume, however, that a 'most different' design values variation or diversity at any price. If the method of difference is to work effectively in isolating causal factors, there must be some homogeneity among the broad range of both IVs and DVs. If cases differ on all their attributes, between-case analysis cannot identify key difference(s). 'Difference' must therefore be bounded by relevant similarities. For example, it would not be fruitful to implement the project proposed in Exercise 8.1 below in a country where local government offers no kerbside collections of domestic waste.

The indirect method of difference

Ragin has pointed out that limitations in both the methods of agreement and of difference undermine a great deal of the point of undertaking COR rather than VOR. Indeed, the obvious limitations of these methods led Mill himself to advocate the use of 'the indirect method of difference'. This involves the double use of the method of agreement.

To explain this method, Ragin (1987: 39–42) uses the example of COR to examine the hypothesis that in certain historical circumstances, rapid commercialisation of an economy causes peasant revolts. The method involves first checking a number of cases to see whether rapid commercialisation is, indeed, correlated with peasant revolts, then checking the same cases to find out whether the absence of peasant revolts correlates with the absence of commercialisation. This allows the set of cases to be arranged in a two-by-two matrix with four possible combinations of variables, as set out in Table 8.1.

Unlike the method of agreement, this procedure can deal with negative cases; that is, ones displaying the absence of an outcome. More importantly, it allows the researcher to subdivide his or her set of cases. This in turn allows us to identify potentially fruitful questions about the reasons *why* different countries fall into these four different types. This example therefore allows us to see the particular value for comparative study of organising multiple cases into groups or classes and thus identifying interesting patterns between and among these cases. In Chapter 9, we shall examine in much more detail the varieties of ways in which this can be done by constructing 'typologies'. In the meantime, Table 8.1 provides a simple example of how typologies can be developed for this purpose.

Table 8.1 A two-by-two matrix showing four types of country

Cause? Rapid commercialisation	Outcome? Peasant revolt	
	Absent	*Present*
Present	Type A: commercialisation but not peasant revolt	Type C: both commercialisation and peasant revolt
Absent	Type B: neither commercialisation nor peasant revolt	Type D: peasant revolt but not commercialisation

Drawing samples for understanding causes

So far, we have discussed the standard textbook comparison between 'most similar' and 'most different' case designs, and noted that both designs have limitations in explaining outcomes across a range of cases. Table 8.2 summarises the definitions that have been given above of these two types of case design and the nature of these limitations. This table also shows that, depending on the number of cases used, COR designs allow us to achieve differing degrees of inferential leverage on a hypothesised causal relationship.

Type A designs use a few cases, carefully chosen to illustrate what we already know about a larger population of cases, on the basis of similarity on many attributes but a few potentially very important differences. We can learn something from research designed in this way: at least, we might be able to claim that our evidence 'tends to support' a hypothesis.

Clearly, if we had more cases – as in type C – we might hope to mount a full test of our hypothesis, which might warrant us in claiming to have 'confirmed' or 'disconfirmed' it. By contrast, in working with cases that differ on a wide range of attributes, it is only when we have, at least, a moderate N – as in type D – that we can exercise sufficient control – whether by statistical or other methods – to isolate the effect of any of these differences.

Table 8.2 Inferential leverage from most-similar and most-different case designs compared

	Many similarities but a few potentially key differences on independent variables	*Many differences on many independent variables*
Small number of cases	A: Most similar case design: adequate control to achieve some inferential leverage on hypothesised causal effects; may be possible to identify some information tending to support or not to support the hypothesis	B: Inadequate control to achieve sufficient inferential leverage for a test, even one only tending to support or not to support; may be possible to use the design to develop a hypothesis
Moderate to large number of cases	C: Strong control to achieve sufficient inferential leverage for a full test that would disconfirm or confirm the hypothesis	D: Most different case design: adequate control to achieve some inferential leverage on hypothesised causal effects; may be possible to identify some information tending to support or not to support the hypothesis

The use of these different designs is discussed in Example 8.2.

EXAMPLE 8.2. A RUBBISH LEAGUE TABLE

Let us return to the project set out in Examples 7.1 and 7.2. Instead of studying a number of households, we now want to compare and contrast the outcomes from recycling schemes in several local government areas, to identify success factors.

Suppose that our literature survey – including reports of several single case studies of introducing recycling schemes – suggests that two factors are associated with success, defined as a substantial increase in overall levels of recycling in the area. These factors are the design of the scheme: for example, regular kerbside collections of different types of waste on the same day of each week, and good-quality information about the scheme; and high levels of householder trust in the local authority.

A type A study (Table 8.2) might be undertaken by selecting a few local authorities which have introduced schemes of similar design with similar outcomes for overall levels of recycling. Differences between local authorities might be further controlled by selecting authorities with similarly sized areas and socio-economic structures, if the literature survey suggests these are contextual factors on which similarity matters. Representative surveys or interviews or focus groups with illustrative samples of households in the case study areas might then be conducted to ascertain whether there are similar levels of trust in the local authority in each case. We could similarly investigate the effects on outcomes of householders' level of information about recycling. If neither IV were found to be important, we could then vary the sample to include schemes with different design features.

The aim is to examine each IV in turn, in the hope of finding one, and preferable only one, that works. This would give us confidence that this IV is a critical variable in achieving success. Indeed, data from our qualitative methods might allow us to develop some insights into *how* the IV works, which might increase confidence in the hypothesis.

We could then proceed to test it with a larger sample, in conditions where we can achieve stronger control over our remaining causal relationships, by having discounted certain rival IVs (type C).

Note that, as we said above, this method can show us only that a certain IV, or perhaps two or three IVs, are key to success, but it does not enable us to show that *only* these IVs are important, because it does not exclude the effects of other possible variables that did not form part of the study. So at best we can say that the IV – say, having well-informed householders – is necessary but not sufficient to predict success. Nor does it allow us systematically to examine whether success is caused in some way by the interaction of variables rather than by their simple or additive action, although some insights might be achieved by means of in-depth qualitative work within each case. Indeed, it is the strength of COR that it allows for this kind of within-case, as well as between-case, analysis.

It would be much more difficult to design a small-*N* case-oriented study of the causal relationships involved when similar schemes lead to different outcomes (type B), because the number of variables is too great in proportion to the number of cases to display any clear patterns. So the study would be insufficiently parsimonious. However, it might be possible to gain some insights into possible causes of different outcomes by using the same methods as in the type A study above. This might allow us to develop a hypothesis which might be explored further in a larger set of cases (type D).

What then of the situation where we have a modest number of cases, which differ on many attributes (type B)? This is the condition about which methodologists worry most. Critics of small-N research fear that case-oriented and comparative work might collapse into a condition where there are more variables than cases.

Would this condition leave us unable to say anything useful at all? Not necessarily. But it does limit the confidence with which we can proclaim any findings we make on the basis of patterns we discern in our data. At most, we might be able to develop, or enrich, or better specify, a hypothesis. It would then have to await further testing, using a different kind of design. On the other hand, developing theory can sometimes be a useful contribution to knowledge, although one of a different kind from testing it.

Selecting on the dependent variable?

One widely held view is that, when we select cases, we should use information only about the IVs for fear of 'selecting on the DV'. We saw in Chapter 7 that there are some situations in which this is not the best advice. For example, if we want to falsify a necessary condition hypothesis, then we might do well to select cases where the outcomes might be the same, to find out whether the supposed necessary condition really was operating – and operating in the same way – in all the cases. This is what was done in the case selection used in Example 8.1. But there are other situations, too, where a hypothesis positively requires us to draw a sample by using information about known outcomes. To see why, think about the kinds of causal relations for which we might want to look, irrespective of the number of cases. Table 8.3 summarises the possibilities.

Table 8.3 Types of causation on which to draw samples

Values on the outcomes	Values on the possible causes	
	Same values on independent variables of interest (hypothesised causes)	*Different values on independent variables (hypothesised causes)*
Same values on the dependent variable (hypothesised outcome)	1 Linear causation: A causes B	2 Convergent causation (equifinality/multi-causality): C or D might both cause E
Different values on the dependent variable (hypothesised outcome)	3 Divergent or branching causation: F might cause either G or H	4 Diverse causation: no pattern of causation common to the cases studied; J might cause K while L might cause M

Type 4 is a situation we want to avoid. It might arise if, in the case we used in Example 8.2, we carelessly selected cases that displayed several different levels of success in increasing household recycling and that were also drawn from local authorities with several different kinds of area, a wide range of socio-economic conditions and differently designed recycling schemes. The only thing to do with type 4 is to develop some more finely grained hypotheses and better most similar or most different samples.

Types 1, 2 and 3 present interesting hypotheses. Type 1 is the simplest structure: it might postulate, for example, that the single key factor in recycling success is the design of the scheme, but we cannot assume in advance that all causal relations can be reduced to such simple issues. Type 3 is a *provisional* explanation. It suggests, for example, that schemes of similar designs sometimes lead to a sustained, long-term increase in the level of recycling, but that sometimes they lead only to a short-term increase. So we would still want to know what contextual factor might be at work: what makes the difference as to whether F – in this case, scheme design – brings about a successful outcome? If we find no contextual differences, then we might have to fall back on the claim that perhaps the scheme has some inherently stochastic feature that makes it sometimes work and sometimes not, but, especially in small- or modest-N studies, we should want both to exhaust all other possibilities first and to identify precisely what the feature of the scheme was that generated such probabilistic outcomes.

Even an initial finding of divergent causation teaches us something interesting. Type 2 brings forward the possibility of multiple causal factors or of *equifinality* – that is, the possibility that the same outcome can also be caused by different causal mechanisms. This type suggests that R (the socio-economic structure of the local authority) leads C (the design of the scheme) to bring about E (an overall increase in the level of recycling in the area). It also suggests, however, that D (introducing financial incentives for recycling household waste) would have achieved the same outcome: this postulates equifinality. But where R is not operating, C might bring about something else entirely. But again, finding the possibility of convergence is still worth learning.

What sort of sample would we use to find out whether convergent or divergent causation might be operating? In such cases, we would certainly need a sample drawn by using information about outcomes. Table 8.4 sets out what we might be able to hope for from samples drawn in this way, in the context of modest-sized N comparative research designs.

The situation in the bottom right hand quadrant (type IV) is hopeless. There is just too much going on in this sample to sort out anything useful, especially with small numbers of cases. In the top left hand cell (type I), we have a sample that, with small to moderate numbers, is probably too risky to rely on to stand up a claim to have found a linear causal relationship. But types II and III are precisely the kinds of samples we should draw, if we want to do some provisional work of a comparative kind empirically to *explore* hypotheses about convergent and divergent causation. With a small to moderate-sized N, we cannot hope to *test* such hypotheses, in a way that would confirm or disconfirm them. But we might be able to do something that would *tend to support* or tend not to support them. And that is a perfectly reasonable ambition for small- to moderate-sized N comparative case research.

Table 8.4 Drawing samples on outcomes and on candidates for causal roles

Small to moderate-sized number of cases as a sample exhibiting...	Same values on independent variables of interest (hypothesised causes)	Different values on independent variables (hypothesised causes)
Same values on the dependent variable (hypothesised outcome)	I: Sample may lack sufficient diversity to test for causal relationship	II: May be sufficient to examine a hypothesis about equifinality
Different values on the dependent variable (hypothesised outcome)	III: May be sufficient to examine a hypothesis about divergent or branching causation	IV: Sample may exhibit too much diversity to enable control

To explore further the issues about case selection we have discussed in this chapter, we suggest that you now attempt Exercise 8.1.

EXERCISE 8.1. DESIGNING APPROPRIATE SAMPLES

Suppose we want to design a comparative study using a modest number of cases to find out whether either or both of the following hypotheses are true:

- Left-wing local authorities are more likely than right-wing authorities to be early adopters of, and to invest money in, local recycling schemes with kerbside collections, because right-wing local authorities will prefer to keep costs down rather than increase taxes.
- Authorities with geographical catchment areas including some rural land on the edge of built-up areas will be more likely than wholly urban areas to adopt local recycling schemes early, because they can more easily find space to process recycled waste. They are also more likely to do so than wholly rural areas, which can more cheaply find space for landfill.

Which method would you use to draw a sample of cases of local authorities and why? Think carefully about the possibilities of equifinality, convergent and divergent causation.

Basic reading

For an overview of issues in working with multiple cases, see Stake R, 2005, *Multiple case study analysis*, New York: Guilford Press.
Ragin's chapter in Brady HE and Collier D, (eds) 2004, *Rethinking social inquiry: diverse tools, shared standards*, Lanham, MD: Rowman & Littlefield, 125–139,

provides a good introduction to his arguments. This chapter is not in the second edition, 2010.

For a book-length introduction to comparative case design, see Peters BG, 1998, *Comparative politics: theory and methods*. Basingstoke: Palgrave Macmillan, Chapter 2.

Dogan M and Pelassy D, 1990 [1984], *How to compare nations: strategies in comparative politics*, Chatham, NJ: Chatham House, is widely used, specifically on *cross-national* comparisons.

Social policy students interested in cross-national comparisons should read Cochrane A, Clarke J and Gewirtz S, 2001 [1991], *Comparing welfare states,* London: Sage and Buckingham: Open University Press.

Similarly, business studies students should read Eisenhardt K, 1989, Building theories from case study research, *Academy of Management Review*, 14, 4, 532–50. Eisenhardt's argument about case study research depends not only on the use of within-case analysis, but also on drawing systematic comparisons between cases.

Advanced reading

Ragin CC, 1987, *The comparative method: moving beyond quantitative and qualitative strategies*, Berkeley, CA: University of California Press, presents his ideas at an advanced level.

Ragin CC, 1994, *Constructing social research*, Thousand Oaks, CA: Pine Forge Press, Sage, offers a rationale of qualitative comparative analysis and its methodology.

Ragin later developed an important refinement in the approach, using fuzzy sets. See Ragin CC, 2000, *Fuzzy-set social science*, Chicago: Chicago University Press, and Rihoux B and Ragin C (eds), 2008, *Configurational comparative methods: qualitative comparative analysis (QCA) and related techniques*, Los Angeles: Sage.

For a review of advanced approaches in comparative analysis for social policy, historical sociology and political science, see Janoski, T and Hicks, AM, 1994, *The comparative political economy of the welfare state*. Cambridge: Cambridge University Press.

NINE

Concept formation

This chapter will:

- consider why concept formation matters in methodology;
- explore problems involved in defining the intension and extension of concepts, and explain why we may need to strike trade-offs between them;
- explain the structure of concepts, and why understanding their structure is important to good research design;
- discuss the use of typologies in social science and construct a typology of typologies; and
- consider how researchers can work effectively with typologies which are not jointly exhaustive or not mutually exclusive.

Framing research projects

For most purposes in everyday life, we implicitly assume that we share sufficient agreement with other people about what words mean to sustain mutual communication. So we do not spend much energy worrying about the terms in which we frame our understanding of the world.

In social science research, however, common sense approaches to key terms will not do, because, as we shall see below, constructing a relevant, clear and useful set of concepts to frame research is critically important to the successful conduct of each stage of a study, and thus for the confidence with which we can draw inferences from it. So, in this chapter, we shall discuss the critical role of 'concept formation' in the methodology of social science.

The use of concepts in social science research

A 'concept' for this purpose means a set of attributes – labelled with a word or phrase – that capture in abstract terms the common features of the class of empirical phenomena to which they refer.

To use one of the stock examples in the literature on concept formation (see e.g. Collier and Mahon, 1993), while 'democracy' takes many different forms in the real world, it has nevertheless been helpful for social theorists to use this concept to refer to the common and distinctive features of 'democratic' political systems. 'Democracy' is the term that captures these features in abstract form, and it allows us to refer to democratic political systems without continually having to list all the features we have in mind.

We shall call an initial, intuitive list of such features, the 'background notion'. We use it in research to capture our best, provisional sense of what our concept means, but, for background notions to serve well for research purposes, we need to tidy them up to ensure coherence, consistency, intelligibility, measurability and other virtues that we shall discuss in this chapter.

Using a concept often requires questions to be addressed about precisely which features should be captured by it. This is a particular problem for social science, because so many of our concepts are also used frequently in the mass media or in popular conversation, but in ways that are far too loose to be useful in social science research. Consider, for example, the expression 'lone parent'. Just how lone does a person have to be, and just how much parenting do they have to do, to count as a member of this class? What about a woman whose partner is absent, for work-related reasons, for months at a time? Is such a woman sufficiently 'lone' to count? And what about a woman who lives in an extended family in which parenting is shared with grandparents and siblings: when does she, or indeed any other person in the family, do enough parenting to count as a parent, let alone a lone one? And does a person become a 'former lone parent' when the child reaches eighteen?

It becomes obvious, as soon as we try to apply this expression to the design of an empirical research project, that one of our first and most important tasks is 'concept formation'. The aims of concept formation are to bring background notions to the fore, give them precision, define their scope and say how we propose to use them specifically for the purposes of our research. For example, a woman whose partner works away from home might count as a 'lone parent' for a project on parenting styles, but probably not for one concerned with the association of lone parenting with low family income.

EXAMPLE 9.1. THE VAGUENESS OF KILLING ONESELF TO KILL OTHER PEOPLE

Consider, too, the challenges of defining another term which is often used very loosely – 'terrorism'. For some research purposes, we could define this term in a way that includes all religion-incited violence against other people. But for others, it might better be reserved for violent acts aimed at terrorising a specific population to bring about political change, as was the case, for example, in Northern Ireland. Or perhaps we should treat acts involving suicide as a particular type of terrorism, distinct from other types?

(Continued)

If so, we might design a research project in which the secular suicide terrorism of those seeking national liberation, such as the Tamil Tigers, might appropriately be regarded as falling into the same category as that of al-Qaeda members, on the grounds that, in both cases, the agent brings about his or her own death in the act of killing others for ends regarded within their group as heroic. But perhaps, for other projects, the distinction between secular and religious motivation might be critical. So, to address a research question about the effect of religious motivations upon the strategy of terrorist groups, we should avoid treating these cases alike, but for a question about the impact of suicide terrorism on victim communities we might place less weight on *motivation* or *purpose*, and instead concentrate on forming a concept of terrorism defined by *means*. Choosing the right boundaries for our concept depends on the exact research question and purpose.

Securing external validity

There are four closely related methodological reasons for ensuring that concepts are sound and appropriately structured.

First, as we have already seen from examples discussed above, if we define and/or operationalise concepts wrongly, then our research questions will lack precision, and we shall not be able to choose the right cases or population to test them. That is to say, our research will lose external validity.

This point can be illustrated by considering the following research question: is it really true that democracies do not go to war with each other? This question derives from the so-called 'democratic peace' hypothesis, much debated in international relations research. We could define democracy as a simple concept, combining a number of *conjunctive conditions*. We could say that any country which meets the following conditions counts as a democracy: (1) the present government came to power as a result of a free and fair national election in which either (2) a majority of the votes counted were in favour of the government or else (3) a majority of seats in the legislature went to candidates sponsored by the governing party.

At first sight, these conditions sound reasonable, but they make Nazi Germany a democracy, because Hitler came to power in 1933 as a result of a national election that was widely regarded as free and fair. And indeed the Nazi regime went on to start wars with a great many countries. So is the proposition therefore false, that democracies do not go to war with each other? Well, not necessarily.

We would have to ask ourselves, first, whether there is something wrong with our concept of democracy if these are the only conditions that our concept requires. Suppose we add some extra requirements that would enable us to treat 'democracy' as a typological concept, because we could specify subtypes more precisely. For example, suppose we rule out states where the government has suspended elections, after coming to power. We could also require not only majoritarian rule, but also the presence of effective and legitimate constitutional constraints on the power of government, thus forming a new subtype, 'liberal democracy'. These changes would exclude the

Nazi state, but might raise new issues. What about a state that gives the government emergency powers that temporarily remove certain constitutional restrictions on governmental power?

We could also re-specify the proposition to claim that 'liberal democracies do not go to war with each other' but that might open the question of what is meant by 'war'. Do the so-called Cod Wars of the 1950s and 1970s between the UK and Iceland about fishing rights in the North Atlantic count as 'wars'? If you recall the debates in Chapters 2, 3 and 4 about when and how far it is acceptable to adjust theories to fit data, you will recognise a risk in the procedure described above: that we re-specify our concept of war in *ad hoc* ways to save the hypothesis of the democratic peace. Indeed, we could run the risk that whatever truth we save in the hypothesis is very largely an artefact of an increasingly rarefied definition. This definition might make the hypothesis true, but it might also make it uninteresting for the everyday concepts of democracy used by politicians, journalists and citizens.

Achieving measurement validity and reliability

The *second* reason is that if we specify and structure our concepts poorly, we cannot develop appropriate research instruments and apply them accurately and consistently. So the research will not achieve measurement validity and reliability.

For example, a widely read literature in the business and management studies field attempts to tell us both what an organisational culture is and what its consequences are. There is, however, very little agreement about how it can and should be operationalised for the purposes of collecting and analysing data. This is because researchers in the field disagree about what kind of concept 'culture' is. Is culture something that can be strong or weak? Or are there different degrees of 'strength'? Or are there different types of organisational culture? The answers to these questions matter, because they determine whether culture is coded or measured as a dichotomous variable (strong or weak), or as a phenomenon that can be measured along a continuous scale (more or less strong) or as a set of different types of culture.

Selecting populations and cases

The *third* reason the specification and structure of concepts matter is that, without getting them right, we cannot select appropriate populations and cases and thus make appropriate *comparisons* between them.

To illustrate this point, we shall take another example, this time from the sociology of professions. Some professions are given special legal status. Doctors, for example, have a legal monopoly: it is illegal in most countries for non-qualified people to provide medical care. In return for their licensed monopoly, professions are usually subject to special regulation. Practitioners are required to submit to discipline by professional institutes that can withdraw a doctor's right to practice. But this is not true of all professions. Some professions, such as social work, have enjoyed no system of this kind, although arguably things have changed in recent years in the UK. Many human resource managers would insist that they are professionals, yet in the UK they have no body equivalent to the General Medical Council.

So we might design some research to ask the question: why do some professions get licensed monopolies of this kind, and others do not? To answer that question, we need to compare those professions that were successful in achieving licensed monopolies and control over practitioners with *those that did not*. But which are they? Presumably, sole traders, entrepreneurs and janitors would fall into the category of occupations that could not hope for such status or would not have wanted it. But what about town planners? The British Town and Country Planning Association is a respected professional institute, but it has none of the disciplinary powers over planners that the General Medical Council has over doctors. Do town planners fall into a class *that could have* secured licensed monopolies, and could thus serve as a comparison with medical doctors? The answer will depend on how exactly we specify our concept of an eligible profession and on the hypotheses that we want to test about what might make the critical difference, as well as on our purposes for our research. Whether a given profession is one of the set of those that could have secured a licensed monopoly turns on other bodies of substantive theory about professions, not tested in the same study.

This issue is important in any research that uses the concept of an 'opportunity' or a 'constraint', either in the things that are to be explained or in those that constitute the explanation. If groups of people or organisations are confronted with an opportunity that some take and some do not, then it matters hugely *which* really did have that opportunity. If an organisation is constrained, for example by its rules, or by legislation or by its lack of resources, then we might decide that it falls outside the set of those who could have achieved professional status, thus defined. So in drawing a sample of organisations for a comparative study, we would need to decide how strong 'constraints' have to be before concluding that an organisation had insufficient opportunities to behave in ways in which we are interested, thus ruling them out of the study.

Drawing inferences

The *fourth* reason that precision about concepts is so important follows from the previous two. Quite simply, if we specify concepts wrongly, we will draw incorrect inferences in explanations and interpretations.

If we limit the concept of a profession to occupations whose members provide services to individual clients, then corporate accountants, town planners, project managers, management consultants and the like would all be excluded from the set of those who could have been licensed as monopolies. We would probably look for explanations in terms of the risks that clients might face from being exploited by rogue professionals. But if we have a broader definition of a profession, then we might look for explanations in terms of much more contingent facts about which occupations organised themselves most effectively, and which ones had most members elected to Parliament, in the period those professions secured their legal monopoly.

Intension

If we are to develop concepts on which we can safely design research, then we need to understand the relationship between two fundamental elements in the meaning of any concepts.

The first is what philosophers call the concept's *intension* or *sense*, or what it 'connotes'. This refers to the properties or attributes we consider to be captured by it. Thus, the process of confirming a concept's intension involves identifying – either through preliminary empirical research or through a literature review, or both – that the attributes we attach to it are coherent, consistent, meaningful and relevant to our research purpose.

We could, for example, stipulate that, for the purpose of our research, a lone parent must have a child under eighteen, for whom they have the principal legal responsibility, living with them full time, and have no present or past sexual partner who can be called upon to assist with the child's upbringing. That would be quite a narrow definition. For some research questions, it might be sensible to relax it. For example, we might have reason to include in our study people whose children live part-time with a previous partner.

So there is no answer to the question 'what is a lone parent?' which is correct for every research project. The right intension depends on what we want to know about these parents. If we want to know how lone parents cope with the primary responsibility of bringing up children alone, then we should not relax the definition to include ones whose children live most of the time with a previous partner. But we probably should include them, if we want to know how lone parents deal with their children's relations with the other parent and their partner.

Extension

The second element is what philosophers call the concept's *extension* or *reference*, or what it 'denotes'. This refers to the range of observations or cases to which the concept can properly be applied. For example, having decided what is connoted (intension) by the term 'lone parent', we could then determine whether a particular parent falls within the set (extension) from which we might draw our sample.

The extension of a concept may raise the important problem of deciding whether phenomena which look the same really are examples of the same concept or whether they are sometimes better connoted by a different concept. For example – to return to our running example – we might find that many households which recycle waste are driven by normative considerations. But it may not be helpful to subsume all these considerations under a single concept of 'conscience', because some households might be driven by environmental issues, whilst others may instead see recycling as a way of addressing larger issues to do with the distribution of economic wealth between developed and developing countries, and still others may be motivated by a simple aversion to profligacy and waste. So, paying attention to a concept's extension may reveal that it has more dimensions than we first thought, and this may lead us to revisit its intension.

The problem of equivalence

Concepts must be applied consistently for research to achieve reliability and validity. If we are not consistent in applying the attributes we select for 'lone parents', then our population – and sample – will be too heterogeneous for us to base any valid conclusions on it. The cases will not be equivalent to each other, and so we cannot validly compare them.

We mentioned briefly in Chapter 8 that, in the 1960s and 1970s, many social scientists aspired to conduct large-scale comparisons, sometimes between very different countries, societies or political regimes. One of the methodological problems posed by comparing very different countries or very different historical periods is deciding whether phenomena are, at bottom, the same or not, even though they are called by different names in different social or historical contexts. Thus, phenomena may sometimes be more similar than their label suggests. They may perform the same social function, or may act in the same way in shaping characteristics of systems, or in determining outcomes of social processes, and can therefore be studied as if they were versions of the same thing. Rites of passage from childhood into adulthood, for example, may take many different forms, ranging from religious ceremonies, such as the Jewish *bar mitzvah* ceremony, through non-religious ceremonies (such as high school graduation), to parties in which young men are inducted into drinking games. But there may well be common features that would allow valid comparison.

Conversely, phenomena may be labelled with the same name, but may turn out to be very different. For example, political 'parties' in eighteenth-century Britain were open only to a very tightly circumscribed, aristocratic elite who operated almost entirely within the confines of parliamentary politics. But by the end of the nineteenth century 'parties' had become mechanisms for mobilising large numbers of voters from a much wider range of social classes, and their focus was much more on grass-roots politics. For some questions, assuming that these 'parties' are 'equivalent' organisations could lead to invalid research. The only way to ensure equivalence is to develop well-formed sets of attributes, or intensions, and apply them consistently.

Concept stretching

Worried about social scientists' failure to do this properly, Giovanni Sartori, one of the biggest names in political science, wrote a famous article denouncing the practice of – what he called – 'concept stretching' (Sartori, 1970). This is the practice of making concepts travel too far from their original context and meaning (intension), such that they lose precision and cease to be useful.

An obvious example is the term 'fascist', which started life by describing a particular type of political movement of the 1920s and 1930s and is now used to connote any kind of extreme right-wing or authoritarian movement. Sometimes, it is even used to label any bold prescription about how people ought to behave, as in the weary tabloid cliché about health fascists in the world of dietary advice.

Sartori points out that we need concepts to serve two purposes, and that these purposes are often in tension. First, concepts are most useful when they have large powers of discrimination; that is, when they allow us to determine clearly for the purposes of a specific research project which attributes are or are not connoted by a concept, and whether a particular case is denoted by it or not. That calls for tight intension. But, second, we also want to use concepts to help us achieve greater generalisation, so we want them to have more powers of abstraction. In other words, we want concepts to apply to a wider range of phenomena with a greater range of attributes. That calls for wide extension.

Very few concepts have both tight intension and wide extension. It is dangerously tempting to loosen their meaning just to enable wide generalisation. The danger is that concepts lose equivalence and cases lose comparability. For example, think about the notion of 'democracy': it would be difficult to compare democratic politics in Europe, the middle east and Africa if we conceive of democracy in ways that are specific to Western liberal democracies.

Stretching versus travelling

Sartori goes on to point out that there is strong pressure for scholars to make concepts take on more power of generalisation, and that one way of doing this is bad while the other is good:

- *The bad way – stretching*: Stretching allows concepts to become vague, fuzzy or obscure to the point where their utility in framing empirical research is seriously undermined. For example, if we try to apply the concept 'democracy' to all regimes that claim to be democratic, it might cease to mean anything that is at all precise or meaningful. There is, for example, a well-known – albeit contested – rule of thumb among political scientists that says that any state that calls itself the 'The Democratic Republic of...' is probably not democratic. If the concept of democracy is 'stretched' to the point where it completely loses its original shape, it ceases to be a clear guide for designing research instruments, data are collected on the wrong cases and miscoded, and findings lack any claim to reliability and validity.

- *The good way – travelling*: A well-constructed concept, however, should be capable of supporting an appropriate level of generalisation to the sorts of cases that we want to capture for a particular piece of research.

Sartori teaches us that, to make a concept travel without also stretching it too far, we need to think carefully about the tension between 'abstraction' – or generalisation – on the one hand and particularity and context specificity, on the other. Resolving this tension involves a conscious trade-off between a concept's intension and extension. This is illustrated in Table 9.1.

Sartori's argument, in effect, is that the more precise a concept's intension, the less it is capable of being validly extended, and *vice versa*. For example, to gain more intension, we might use the term 'parliamentary democracy' to denote only regimes – such as that in the UK – where a party can form a government only if it has majority support in Parliament and must therefore resign if it loses this majority. Using this concept in this precise way would allow us to do a great deal of rich, context-specific research to develop narrow-gauge theory about contemporary British politics. It might also help frame comparisons between the UK, Australia and Canada which all have parliamentary regimes. But it would not frame research into more fundamental questions about the conditions necessary to sustain democratic politics in a wider range of regimes.

Table 9.1 Sartori's ladder of abstraction

	Aspect of meaning		
Level of abstraction	Connotation (intension)	Denotation (extension)	Comparative scope and purpose
High – high-level categories, universal conceptualisations	Minimal – low level of precision and specificity Low contextual reference	Maximal – wide scope and applicability	Cross-area/period comparisons among heterogeneous contexts, supporting global theory
Medium – general conceptualisations	Connotation balanced with denotation	Intermediate	Inter-case comparisons among relatively homogeneous contexts Middle-range theory
Low – configurative conceptualisations	Maximal – high level of precision and specificity	High contextual reference	Minimal – low scope Within-case analysis – narrow-gauge theory

Source: adapted freely from Sartori (1970: 1033–53, esp. 1044); used with permission of Cambridge University Press

It follows that, if Sartori is right, the trade-off between intension and extension will vary according to the nature of (1) the research design and (2) the kind of theory a researcher wants to test or build. Put simply, researchers who want to do context-specific, case-based research designed to develop narrow gauge theory will tend to prefer concepts with low levels of abstraction and high powers of intension. In contrast, researchers who want to test theory with high powers of generalisation might be prepared to trade off intension against extension, such that intension is reduced and extension increased.

EXERCISE 9.1. HERE'S ONE I PREPARED EARLIER

Think about your own research interests and identify two or three 'concepts' that are relevant to your field and which will probably frame any research you undertake in it.

Experiment by first forming these concepts so that they have (1) low abstraction, with maximal intension and minimal extension, and then try to form the same concepts with (2) high abstraction, with minimal intension and maximal extension.

If the planning of your own research project is sufficiently far advanced, think about whether it involves concepts with high or low abstraction, and explain why.

Types of concepts

Sartori thought that the ideal was for concepts to have tidy boundaries, so that each case should unambiguously fall either within or outside a concept. He focused on the trade-off between intension and extension, because that was central to his aspiration for clear boundaries. More recently, social scientists have come to acknowledge that researchers unavoidably use more types of concepts than Sartori recognised. In consequence, they now believe that there is more at stake than the relationship between intension and extension, and that we must recognise more trade-offs in forming concepts than this one. This section introduces the principal types of concept recognised by social scientists today, and shows how each one is structured.

Simple, conjunctive, disjunctive, scalar and typological concepts

The *simplest* concepts are ones where if a case meets a single condition, then it falls under the concept. If the liquid is chemically H_2O, then it is water. Slightly more complex are concepts which require the *conjunction*, or combination, of two or more conditions. A case must satisfy all of them. If the person has been (1) elected to Parliament (2) for a constituency (3) in a legal, free and fair election, they are an MP. For a payment to be a wage, it must be paid in money, not goods; it must be paid regularly, either weekly or monthly; and it must be for work undertaken in an employment relationship and not, for example, be a fee to a self-employed contractor.

Then there are concepts that cases can satisfy in several alternative ways: they allow for a *disjunction* of attributes. What is a mother? Well, clearly she is a woman and she has a child, who may be grown up. But beyond that? She could be the biological parent. Alternatively, she could adopt, or be a legal guardian, or foster, or *de facto* be the main female carer. Any of those conditions will qualify, at least for some research questions.

Then we come to concepts for which a case will qualify, if it falls anywhere on a wide *scale*. For example, what is a 'rent'? There is an old legal term called a 'peppercorn rent'. It means that the tenant pays no money to the landlord: the tenant is technically obliged to hand over a single peppercorn each year, but in practice few landlords bother to collect it. At the other end of the scale, rents for commercial property in downtown Manhattan and harbour-side Hong Kong are sums that most of us cannot imagine earning in our lifetimes. But the point is that payment for the right to use a piece of real estate is 'rent' if it falls anywhere on that scale. Money is a quantitative scale, but many scalar concepts use qualitative ones. What work do carers do, when they care? For some research questions, activities ranging from simple house-cleaning through to intensive emotional and practical support, including nursing or speech therapy, by way of bathing and toileting, might count.

Next, there are concepts which include cases only if those cases fall under sub-concepts or *types*. We shall say more about typologies shortly. But for the moment, think about the concept 'tax base'. Tax paid by a resident or a company is defined against one of several bases. Broadly, tax bases are income (income tax, corporate income tax, special taxes on dividends and so on), wealth (e.g. on the value of houses – as in the UK's 'council tax' or land taxes in other countries), or transactions (such as Value Added Tax in Europe, sales and purchase taxes in the USA, or stamp duty on the sale of houses). If something is 'income', 'wealth' or a 'transaction', it can be the base for a tax, but not otherwise in most tax systems.

'Family resemblance' concepts

Then there is a class of concepts that are rather hard to work with in social science, but for some kinds of research there is no avoiding their use. The most famous example of this class is the concept of a game (Wittgenstein, 1976 [1953]).

There is no clear way of limiting or bounding the phenomena to which the concept of a game refers. Some games are co-operative, others are competitive. Some involve using physical layouts such as tracks or boards, but others are purely verbal. More than that, the term 'game' is not confined to play, but, as a metaphor, is extended to many other types of activities. For example, we may refer to the 'rules of the game', to convey the idea that only people who understand the informal rules of business or political life can compete in it successfully. Whilst each 'game' has some features in common with some other games, the list of features that could count is indefinitely long.

Wittgenstein therefore used the example of the concept of a 'game' to introduce a class of concept, which he called 'family resemblance' concepts. Each member of a family has some similarity in some respect to at least one other member, but there is no set of criteria on which everyone is similar to everyone else. The name has stuck, for there are many situations where there is no bounded set of conditions that would capture all, but only, cases of the concept. But, as Wittgenstein pointed out, we cannot specify a single set of criteria that will be met by all games and only by games: we can recognise a new game as being one, if it is sufficiently similar to other games that we know.

Social scientists try to avoid using family resemblance concepts, for the obvious reason that using one to frame a new case is likely to be contestable. However, sometimes we have to use them, and may even want positively to do so. In interpretive research, for example, we often need to ask whether cases fall under *concepts used by the people we are studying*. If they use family resemblance concepts, then we must do so, too. For example, anthropologists are interested in what people count as a 'gift'. In different settings, gifts may be given either by compulsion or voluntarily; they may or may not give rise to obligations on the part of the receiver; and they may consist in physical objects or entirely abstract goods such as rights, entitlements or even statuses. Consider, for example, the tradition by which British monarchs bestow the title of Prince of Wales on their eldest son. Some gifts must be kept, others must be passed on. There are gifts that require public ceremonial to count as being made – think of a father 'giving away' his daughter in a traditional patriarchal European marriage – and others that must be given in secrecy, silence and anonymity, as required by some Islamic schools for charitable *waqf*.

So the set of conditions for being a gift has no finite boundary. But working out who counts what as a gift, and what rules govern different kinds of gifts, can tell us a great deal about how people are organised, whether we are studying the tradition among Women's Institutes in England of selling cakes and jam made and donated by members to raise funds, or complicated gift-giving systems found among aboriginal American people. Indeed, we cannot adequately understand the Women's Institute in England or the Tlingit people of north western Canada unless we understand their gift-giving. A gift is therefore a family resemblance concept that, in many settings, is central to social science research.

Radial concepts

Finally, there are some concepts that fall between family resemblance concepts, on the one hand, and simple, conjunctive, disjunctive, scalar and typological concepts, on the other. We mentioned earlier as an example of the dangers of concept stretching, the case of 'fascism'. How might we tidy up that particular conceptual mare's nest?

Some regimes which we might call 'fascist' have come to power by elections (Hitler's), some by military coups (Franco's in Spain) and some by legal appointment (Tojo's government in 1940s' Japan). Some centralise all power in one person (the Nazi regime), but some do not (Tojo's). Some engage in racial persecution (the Nazis), some do so under external pressure (Mussolini's in Italy by the 1940s) and some not greatly at all (Franco's regime). All fall, however, toward the upper end of the spectrum of authoritarianism, although that condition is surely not enough to make a regime fascist. For example, the USSR under Stalin was definitely not fascist but it was an extreme case of authoritarianism.

To make the concept usable, then, we might take one – or, at most, two very similar – *empirical cases* as *central* examples of the concept of fascism, chosen empirically on the 'we know a really strong case when we see one' principle. We could then map how distant each of the other cases is from the central one, on each of a number of attributes: authoritarianism, dictatorship, racial persecution, militarism, warmongering, violation of citizens' rights and so on. The result would be a gradation of cases on multiple scales from the central point. So, we might say that, the further away a regime is, on several scalar attributes or dimensions, from Mussolini's self-described fascist regime, the less fascist it is. We might then stipulate a cut-off point on each dimension, below which we would not call a regime 'fascist' at all. Concepts that can only be defined and measured in these ways are called 'radial concepts', because the gradations radiate from the central case(s).

Figure 9.1 shows in graphical form the elementary relationships for each of these types of concept. It shows the conditions that might be observed in a case; how to think about the relationships between them; and, thus, how to distinguish what type of concept structure is relevant for a given type of research question and background notion to be captured.

EXERCISE 9.2. CRISIS? WHAT CRISIS?

Consider the concept of a 'crisis'. Individuals go through crises in their lives, caused for example by bereavement, or by an episode of illness, or by losing a job. Business firms may face them. Newspapers often announce a crisis in the political or the economic system.

If you were researching either the causes or the consequences of a crisis in each of these settings, which kind of concept do you think that of a 'crisis' would best be understood to be? Would it be best to treat it as being of one kind when studying individuals and another when studying organisations or systems?

Give reasons, as fully as you can, for your answers.

Typologies

The previous discussion shows that the process of concept formation may sometimes require us to distinguish different types or subtypes of a concept, according to the different ways its attributes are combined. 'Typologies' enable us to do this systematically and rigorously.

First, a word of warning. Many social scientists disparage typologies: this is because researchers sometimes try to use them inappropriately to provide explanations. It may be tempting to claim, for example, that an organisation's interests, or a person's

Figure 9.1 Comparing the structures of different types of concepts

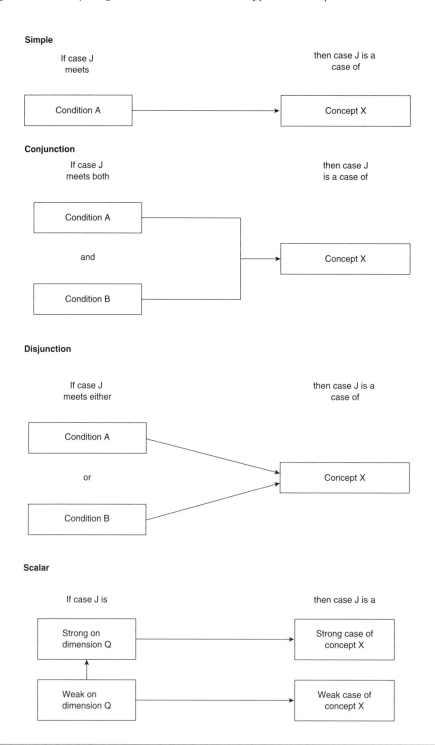

DESIGNS

Typological

If case J is any one of the following cases

then case J falls under

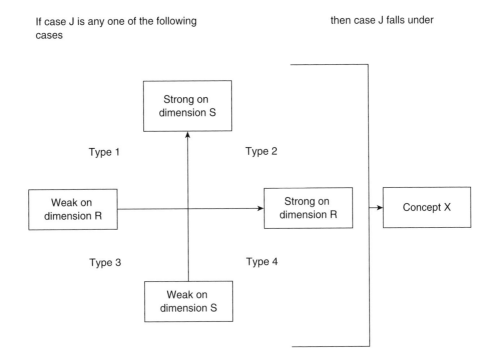

Family resemblance

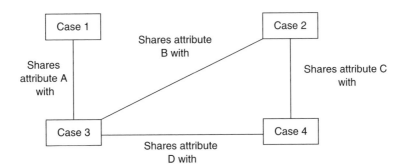

Radial

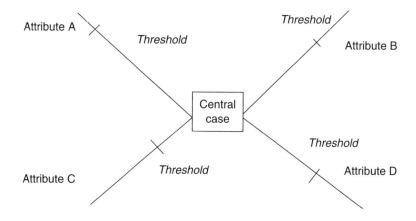

behaviour or attitudes, can be explained by the fact that they belong to a particular type of association or social group. Such typological explanations tend to be banal or simply unsatisfying. This is the problem, for example, with the statement that 'these people are engaged in proselytising for their faith because they are evangelical Christians': evangelicals vary in the effort they put into proselytising. Moreover, referring to a typology cannot explain *why*, for example, evangelical Christianity attracts certain kinds of people.

So, as we shall see further in Chapter 11, constructing a typology is no substitute for explanation. In this chapter, we shall show, though, that it can be a necessary precursor to *developing* explanations.

Constructing typologies

Let us look first at how typologies are constructed. The simplest way of classifying phenomena is to assume that things with the most attributes in common are the most similar to each other, and that this similarity is important in some way. If we started with a potentially unlimited number of attributes, then mapping attributes observed empirically in a population of cases would probably produce a scattergram distribution. Nevertheless, this kind of *empirical approach* to classification may also yield clusters of phenomena that seem to belong together and which can then be named. Early attempts to build classifications of diseases were undertaken in this way: for example, for centuries before medical researchers reformed the categories, 'leprosy' referred to any skin-wasting condition.

For the purposes of concept formation, we are more interested in a *conceptual approach* to classification. This approach proceeds by deriving attributes *a priori* from a predefined concept, and therefore limits attention to those which are logically possible. For example, researchers use the concept 'social capital' to capture the social significance of ties of friendship, acquaintance, collegiality or trust (Putnam, 2000; Halpern, 2005). They distinguish *from first principles* ties to people within a bounded group ('bonding'), from ties that span groups ('bridging') or that extend beyond bounded groups altogether ('reaching'). Next they distinguish ties between people of the same social status ('horizontal') from those between people of different social status ('vertical'). Cross-tabulating these two dimensions would yield a three-by-two matrix of types of social capital.

A typology of typologies

Like many other social constructs, typologies come in distinct types. The typology of typologies set out in Table 9.2 classifies typologies on two dimensions.

The first is whether they are *jointly exhaustive*. Jointly exhaustive typologies are formed, when, given the dimensions we are using, there cannot logically be any more types. Consider, for example, the distinction between types of political constitution famously put forward by the Greek philosopher Aristotle. He asks, 'who is sovereign in a state?' Logically, the possibilities are that a single person might hold sovereign power, in which the state is an autocracy; or a limited number of people might jointly

Table 9.2 A typology of typologies

Exclusive?	Exhaustive?	Jointly exhaustive		Not jointly exhaustive
	Conceptual or empirical?	Conceptual classification: finite number of attributes, all defined *a priori*, cases subsumed *a posteriori*		Empirical classification: indefinite number of attributes, similarity determined *a posteriori* by numbers of attributes shared
Mutually exclusive		Classical typology	Principled but incomplete	Not principled and incomplete
Not mutually exclusive	Fuzzy	Principled, complete, but scalar	Principled, incomplete, scalar	Not principled, incomplete, scalar
	Overlapping	Principled, complete, but overlapping	Principled, incomplete, overlapping	Not principled, incomplete, overlapping
	Hybrid	Principled, complete, but hybrid	Principled, incomplete, hybrid	Not principled, incomplete, hybrid

hold sovereign power, in which case it is an oligarchy; or most citizens might jointly hold sovereign power, in which case it is a democracy.

This simple typology follows from the fact that the categories 'one, some, all' exhaust the logical possibilities. But not all conceptual typologies are jointly exhaustive ones. Consider the concept, 'policy'. Governments of different countries divide the fields in which they need to develop policies very differently, and these fields change significantly through time. In Elizabethan England, for example, the government had policies on vagrancy, which cannot be mapped readily onto contemporary policy fields of homelessness or travellers or migrant labour. Similarly, 'land use' has been regarded in recent times as the preserve, variously, of environmental policy, business development policy, and town and country planning.

These simple examples show that there is no way, even in principle, to produce a jointly exhaustive classification of all possible fields of public policy. So, we tend only to use broad categories, such as the distinction between foreign and domestic policy. Indeed, in the case of a concept like policy, it may be more useful to rely on empirical lists of policy fields, for which no claims to be exhaustive are made.

The second dimension used in the typology of typologies in Table 9.2 is whether types are *mutually exclusive*: whether, that is, any case must fall into just one type. Legally, a firm is either solvent or bankrupt. A television is either on or off. Someone is either of pensionable age or not. To give an example with more cases, a member of the British House of Commons belongs only to one party: Labour, Conservative, Liberal Democrat, Scottish Nationalist, Plaid Cymru, Ulster Unionist, Green and so on.

Non-mutually exclusive types

Many concepts do not admit of types that are mutually exclusive. The case of foreign and domestic policy reminds us why this is so, because many matters of concern to governments fall under both foreign and domestic policy. Governments worry a good deal about cocaine, heroin, cannabis and other recreational drugs. On the one hand, this is matter for domestic legislation and policing priorities. On the other hand, it is of concern to diplomats who must negotiate with both countries from which drugs are exported, such as Colombia or Afghanistan, and powerful countries trying to establish a global strategy toward such drugs, including the USA. Likewise, there has recently been much political concern in the UK about the impact on medical training of the effect of the EU's Working Time Directive on the working hours of trainee doctors. And so on.

It does not follow from these examples that making a distinction between domestic and foreign policy is useless. Rather, it means that we cannot expect to use the distinction between domestic and foreign policy in the same way as that between a solvent or insolvent firm. Furthermore, when types are not mutually exclusive, they admit of several possible relationships.

Fuzzy types

The nearest condition to being mutually exclusive, without quite being so, is one where types can be ranged on a scale, but where the boundaries between adjacent types are *fuzzy*. Consider friendliness and hostility. These are concepts used both by sociologists interested in networks of ties between individuals and by political scientists interested in governments' relationships with other states or with interest groups such as trade unions and employers' federations. There are clearly *degrees* of friendliness and hostility in such relationships, and there is a mid-point – indifference – of being neither friendly nor hostile. Furthermore 'friendliness' covers a range of well-meaning stances from committed affection, through companionship, to more reserved, diffuse support. That is, the exclusivity is partial. We can probably distinguish broad and also extreme types of friendship, but the fuzziness of the boundaries between closely related types leaves us unable to be sure that they are sufficiently fine grained to provide total exclusivity.

Some famous classifications of types in social science have fuzzy edges of this kind. For example, many analysts have suggested that the distinction, which is commonly used in political science, between presidential and parliamentary democracies is one with very fuzzy edges. Consider the cases of British prime ministers, such as Tony Blair, whose large parliamentary majorities gave them a high degree of autonomy from Parliament, or of American presidents who, faced with adverse majorities in Congress, must negotiate their legislative programme with Congressional leaders.

Overlapping types

Next, there are typologies where types are *overlapping*. Let us assume, for example, that the same people adopt different stances on friendship and hostility in different fields of life. In politics and in business, this is very common. The US and UK governments, for example, tend to be very friendly to each other in matters of military security, but their relations over trade and environmental issues have often been very strained. In the same way, firms can co-operate with each other on some things and compete on others. There have even been times when big companies were simultaneously suing each other over one matter while pouring millions into joint investments.

These examples show how types of friendliness and hostility can overlap, and that any given case can exhibit the attributes of several broad, or even fuzzy, types, at the same time but in different fields. Again, some famous typologies in social sciences are overlapping ones. Marx offered a typology of 'modes of production', by which he meant the institutional arrangements that underpin the kinds of economy that prevail in different historical periods. He acknowledged that the periods of transition between ancient, feudal and capitalist forms were characterised by the overlapping presence of at least two types.

Hybrid types

Fuzzy-edged and overlapping typologies still try to make distinctions between types of cases. A greater divergence from mutual exclusivity is presented by situations where, even within the same field at the same time, a case is a *hybrid* one, containing attributes of more than one type.

Consider ways of organising social life. In the 1980s and 1990s, it was common to argue that there were three ways of organising any and all human relationships, whether they are between groups of friends or between firms. Scholars used to argue that the principal ways of organising were those of hierarchy – of which bureaucracy was the stock example – markets and networks, but in fact most relationships turned out to exhibit some elements of each. Some people then argued that this finding was devastating to the usefulness of this threefold classification, or trichotomy. Its advocates replied, perfectly reasonably, that 'it is the mix that matters', and defended the usefulness of this trichotomy by claiming that it was helpful to look at any given case and find out just how much hierarchy it showed, how greatly market-like its relations were, and just how strong the network elements were. That is to say, the trichotomy allowed researchers to compare cases exhibiting different forms of hybridity, thus allowing much finer comparative analysis than would be permitted by simply using three broad types.

Finally, we have cases with an indefinite number of types but where the researcher develops a typology of the ones considered to be the most important. We have already considered the concept of a policy field where, in principle, there is no limit to the number of possible types. But we could easily list the ones that are most important for studying British government in the 2000s or the former Soviet regime in the 1960s. But doing so takes us further away from conceptual and closer to empirical classification, that is to the distinction between empirical and conceptual classification with which we began.

Should we always aim to develop classical typologies?

Some social scientists hold the view that only *classical typologies* – those at the top left of Table 9.2 – are good, robust ones. This is too strong a claim, and it does not hold true in science generally.

Meteorologists work with classifications of weather that admit of scales and hybrids: think of the standard classifications of types of rain (drizzle, sleet, shower, squall, storm, etc.). Biologists aspire to a classical taxonomy of species, but because species constantly evolve, their taxonomy is always incomplete. Moreover, because the distinction between species and subspecies is not entirely capable of being applied consistently, some of the taxonomy is fuzzy edged. Indeed, there are hybrids too: think, for example, of mules. Similarly, we saw from the examples we used in the discussion above that big names and important fields in social sciences use typologies that are fuzzy or overlapping, or that employ hybrids to capture important states of affairs.

It should be clear, then, from our discussion that, just because types are conceptually distinct, it does not follow that any given case must fall unambiguously into one and only one type. Nor should we conclude that any typology which is not jointly exhaustive or mutually exclusive is necessarily deficient for all purposes. On the contrary, most typologies in practical use in social science lack either one attribute or both, and typologies are often usable even without both these attributes.

So it is not true to say that we should *always* try to develop and refine our typologies until they are jointly exhaustive and mutually exclusive, *if* the only way to do so is to focus on attributes that are of little explanatory interest. Rather than trying to produce classical typologies for the sake of it, researchers are better advised to develop typologies that are appropriate to the level of analysis required to answer their question.

For example, faced with a large number of potential cases, we could initially sort them into clusters by developing rules for dealing with their multiple attributes. In statistics, this procedure is known as cluster analysis. The aim is to identify patterns that may suggest a more principled, more strongly conceptualised basis of classification – one capable of providing a more powerful strategy for selecting cases and analysing data – and thus to move from the right toward the left in Table 9.2, that is, from an empirical to more highly conceptualised typology.

Our running example about recycling household waste illustrates how we might similarly move from the bottom toward the top of Table 9.2. We have used the concept of 'conscience' as a way of capturing one factor involved in motivating householders to recycle their waste, but, as we suggested above, further investigation would probably show that it is a hybrid type, in that 'conscience' has religious, social, economic and environmental dimensions. Case-based research among a few cases selected specifically for the purposes of exploring how householders understand and articulate these dimensions of conscientious recycling might allow us to develop a more refined concept of conscience in which more exclusive subtypes were identified, for example 'environmental conscientiousness', 'economic conscientiousness' and so on. Depending on just how exclusive these subtypes were found empirically to be, we could develop a new typology of overlapping, fuzzy or even mutually exclusive types. The new typology might then allow us to develop a hypothesis about the different behaviours associated with each type of conscientious recycling behaviour as the basis of comparative, case-oriented research (COR) or even large-N variable-oriented research (VOR).

EXERCISE 9.3. IS THIS CLUB A MEMBER OF ITSELF?

Consider the typology of typologies set out in Table 9.2, and decide which type of typology it is.

Clearly, the distinction between being mutually exclusive or not, jointly exhaustive or not, is itself one that is mutually exclusive and jointly exhaustive; so far, so classical. But what about the distinction between fuzzy, overlapping and hybrid types? Do you think this is principled, *a priori* and complete, and mutually exclusive?

Try to work out, too, whether you can enrich this table by thinking of other distinctions between types of typologies.

These examples illustrate how using attributes captured systematically by typologies to understand exactly how cases or populations are structured helps us draw good samples and to know what kinds of generalisations we can produce. Typologies thus help us to understand what kinds of theoretical inferences we are able to make from the data yielded from our research. This discussion has shown, too, how a willingness to develop and use non-classical typologies may help us generate more powerful ones.

Concept formation – a process

It should be clear, too, that the process of concept formation – including the construction and refinement of typologies – is just that: a *process*. The formation of useful concepts takes time, and may also involve preliminary fieldwork to explore the empirical terrain before a research project can be successfully framed by appropriate concepts.

For example, the authors recently carried out research for the UK's Economic and Social Research Council to compare the implementation of government policies about the sharing of personal information about clients among local social policy agencies, such as those concerned with child protection and crime prevention. A web-based review was used to conduct an empirical classification of a large number of potential cases to identify the main types of agency that could usefully be compared. We also conducted a major literature review of policy papers, and conducted twelve interviews with senior policy-makers in London, partly to validate these types but also to develop a more refined understanding of the concepts most likely to influence how local agency managers conceived these issues. All this preliminary empirical investigation was done *before* designing coding schemes and interview schedules for the main body of fieldwork.

This example illustrates how research always involves some element of iteration between the process of elucidating concepts to frame the research, developing instruments and samples to operationalise them, and reviewing concepts in the light of empirical investigation. Iteration is, of course, more difficult to achieve in VOR projects using structured methods of collecting and analysing data than in more open-ended, flexible, case-based designs. But confidence in the soundness of concepts used in VOR can be significantly enhanced if concepts are road-tested and refined by means of preliminary case-based empirical research. Furthermore, the utility of concepts can be further checked by piloting the measures and research instruments derived from them. Concepts can then be revisited in the light of operational experience before deploying them in the main stages of the project.

Striking trade-offs in concept formation

One of the most important aspects of the process of concept formation is the striking of trade-offs. Sartori stressed the importance of making thoughtful trade-offs between intension and extension, and we have seen that recognising the full range of concept types forces us to think about other trade-offs, too.

As we shall see in the next part of this book, a virtue of a good theory is that it should – all other things being equal – be parsimonious, by explaining many things with relatively modest intellectual machinery. So, if we can achieve it without too great a cost to other virtues, we should also like our concepts for explanatory factors to be parsimonious in the number of their attributes; in the limited complexity of the conjunctions and disjunctions of their attributes; and in the number of their types.

On the other hand, some problems are so complicated that parsimonious concepts probably do not help much. For example, anthropologists long ago gave up the search for parsimonious concepts for family relationships: most peoples around the world work, implicitly, with surprisingly complicated understandings of such apparently simple notions as being a 'cousin', and this issue can matter greatly for understanding marriage and incest rules and inheritance rights.

We also have good reasons – if we want to test theories that contribute to larger debates in social science – to want concepts to be derived from big theories, or even from frameworks. On the other hand, we would prefer to use concepts that are familiar to readers. Family resemblance and radial concepts are usually rather familiar ones, but they are not usually easy to derive from theories. Another problem with working with unfamiliar or rarefied concepts is that we might be tempted to invent special ones *ad hoc* to deal with particular problems.

Gerring (1999) has examined these trade-offs in detail. He argues that among the factors to be taken into account in forming concepts to frame research are their familiarity, coherence, parsimony, differentiation from other concepts, theoretical utility and field utility, and that these factors do not always make compatible demands. He recognises, therefore, that concept formation involves establishing the best available trade-off between many competing factors, taking into account the purposes of the research.

In a case-based project involving high levels of interaction with research participants who are unfamiliar with the language of social sciences, the 'field utility' of a concept – that is, the accuracy with which it captures meanings shared by participants or collaborators involved in the field of study – may be more important than its utility for developing or refining theory. Likewise, the theoretical open-mindedness which often characterises case-based research may be best served by concepts that are rich, inclusive but somewhat fuzzy, whereas the reliability of VOR may be best served by concepts that are precise, narrowly defined and unambiguous. A VOR study designed to test a theory might therefore score highly, to use Gerring's terms, on differentiation, parsimony and theoretical utility. The concept formation process is one, therefore, that often involves thinking through these various trade-offs, as we select and define concepts of the different types identified in this chapter.

This chapter has elucidated the methodology of concept formation in social science research, including the important business of building and using typologies. In so doing, we have explored the importance of sound concept formation for the practical business of research design, especially for stipulating research questions, sampling and comparing populations and cases, and designing research instruments.

Above all, careful concept formation allows us to understand the nature and the structure of inferences we can draw from our research. In drawing attention to the importance of concept formation, we have not, however, advocated a rigid, rule-based approach to forming and using concepts or an exclusive emphasis on building classical typologies. On the contrary, an open-minded approach to working with concepts can lead to the reframing of our research, and thus contribute to its development.

Basic reading

The obvious starting points on this topic are Sartori G, 1970, Concept misformation in comparative politics, *American Political Science Review*, 64, 4, 1033–53 and Gerring J, 1999, What makes a concept good? A criterial framework for understanding concept formation in the social sciences, *Polity*, 31, 3, 357–93.

The major text in this field, which sets out current thinking, and in so doing moves quickly from basic to advanced level, is Goertz G, 2006, *Social science concepts: a user's guide*, Princeton, NJ: Princeton University Press. This book discusses the systematic work of concept formation and the main types of concepts.

Advanced reading

On issues of measurement, an important place to start is Adcock R and Collier D, 2001, Measurement validity, *American Political Science Review*, 95, 3, 529–46.

Collier's work on concept formation is extensive: see particularly Collier D and Mahoney J, 1993, Conceptual 'stretching' revisited, *American Political Science Review*, 87, 4, 845–55.

For a discussion of the methodology of typologies, see Bailey KD, 1994, *Typologies and taxonomies: an introduction to classification techniques*, London: Sage, and the chapter by Collier *et al*, 2008, in Box-Steffensmeier J, Brady H. and Collier D (eds), *Oxford handbook of political methodology*, Oxford: Oxford University Press, 152–73.

For a review of thinking about concept formation since Sartori's 1970 article, both by Sartori himself and by others, see Collier D and Gerring J, 2008, *Concepts and method in social science: Giovanni Sartori and his legacy*, London: Routledge.

PART III

Achievements

What research makes inferences to

This part of the book comprises more advanced material. It is concerned with the nature of the explanations and interpretations that constitute the primary purpose of conducting social research, and, particularly, how we can provide warrant for them in the way we design our research.

The first four chapters of this part are concerned with explanation. We look first at what explanations are, why they matter and what makes them more or less satisfying. We then look at different kinds of explanation, before considering the particular challenges of ascribing causation. Finally we explore how we can warrant the inferences we make to explanations. The last two chapters in this part of the book cover the same range of issues, but in relation to interpretation.

TEN

Why ideas about explanation matter for methodology

This chapter will examine:

- the nature and importance of explanation;
- the things social science research explains;
- the fundamental problem of causal inference and the counterfactual claims implied whenever we assert causal relationships; and
- the features which make for more satisfying explanations.

Why explanation matters

In Chapter 1 we said that explanations are one of the three main types of product from social science, the others being description and interpretation. We also argued that making warranted inferences to explanations is, at once, the riskiest and the most important thing social scientists do.

What gets explained?

We need first to distinguish between the things that get explained and the things that do the explaining. Methodologists often use the Latin names:

- the *explanandum* (plural, *explananda*) is the phenomenon to be explained by research; and
- the *explanans* (plural, *explanantes*) is the phenomenon, or – more usually, with anything at all interesting – a set of phenomena that explain the *explanandum*.

We shall devote most of this part of the book to the things that do the explanatory heavy lifting – the *explanantes*. But we need to start by looking at what is being lifted – the *explanandum*. We noted in Chapter 2 that we usually conduct research to explain events, states of affairs and trends. The kinds of explanatory questions associated with each of these things are illustrated in Example 10.1.

EXAMPLE 10.1. EXPLAINING EVENTS, STATES OF AFFAIRS AND TRENDS

Mushroom cloud

1 Explaining an event or an action

Why did the North Korean government claim successfully to have tested a nuclear device in October 2006? Possible explanations are that the government did it:

- in the hope of increasing its negotiating power in talks on aid;
- to deter what it genuinely believed was an imminent attack; or perhaps
- in the hope of persuading other countries which have the same enemies to provide technical assistance.

Junk food nation

2 Explaining a state of affairs

Why is a higher proportion of British people clinically obese than that in any other European nation? Possible explanations might include:

- cultural factors – ingrained traditions of eating and exercise in the UK have prevented less well-off people from adjusting to the fact that working lives now consume fewer calories than those of their predecessors; and
- economic factors – British supermarkets and British advertising have greater power to persuade people to eat in less healthy but more profitable ways than their continental counterparts.

Pay no rent

3 Explaining a trend

Why do more British undergraduates live with their parents throughout their studies than was the case a few years ago? Possible explanations might include:

- financial factors – the advent of university tuition fees has reduced undergraduates' real incomes and the cost of independent housing has risen significantly in real terms; and
- cultural factors – young people have become much less interested in independence from their parents than they were a couple of decades ago, and even those who could afford to live independently choose not to, sometimes into their thirties.

Counterfactuals and the fundamental problem of causal explanation

Before considering the explanation of events, states of affairs and trends in detail, we must examine a fundamental problem, one that is relevant to all kinds of observational designs in social science research. This is the problem we raised in Chapter 5 about the claims that, in the absence of experimental controls, we can make about causation.

Suppose that we declare that the occupation of Iraq by US and British forces in 2003 was an important cause of the subsequent civil war. Are we claiming that, without the 2003 invasion, the civil war would not have occurred? If so, how could we warrant this claim?

The only history that we can observe is one in which the US-led coalition invaded Iraq; Saddam was removed from power; and the coalition's attempts to create an alternative government led to insurgency and inter-communal strife. But what if someone claims that, had Saddam continued in power in 2003, other forces might well have erupted within Iraq, perhaps in alliance with interests from the neighbouring states, and that such events might well have resulted in a civil war not dissimilar to the present one? This would be what is called a *counterfactual* claim.

We might doubt the claim in this case – or indeed in any similar case. We might try to argue about the relative strength of the various factors that would make this alternative scenario less or more likely. But as researchers, we cannot observe an Iraq that was not invaded in 2003. And, if we cannot absolutely say that in the absence of the cause, the effect would not have occurred, what are we saying?

Counterfactuals raise what is known as the fundamental problem of causal inference. The problem, put simply, is this: how, in the absence of a controlled experiment in which we observe outcomes on the same case but subject to different putatively causal factors, can we ever find out if a factor makes a causal difference?

Suppose, for example, that we want to know whether it would be possible to offer patients needing elective heart surgery an incentive that would encourage them to accept treatment at more distant hospitals, thereby creating more competition between heart surgery teams. Perhaps we could offer patients up to 66% of their travel costs and up to 40% of the costs of their relatives' hospital visits, on the calculation that, if even 30% were to take up this offer, the resulting savings from faster throughput of patients would pay for the scheme. (This is not actually true, but never mind!) Now, suppose that we run a pilot scheme in one area. We observe how many patients take up the offer, and extrapolate these findings to other areas with roughly similar populations, by income, health status, travel challenges and so on. Have we learned the size of the causal effect of the incentive, or even if there is one?

Perhaps. But the fundamental problem is that we cannot simultaneously observe more than one response from one and the same individual, so we cannot find out how many people would have taken up an offer of out-of-area treatment in the absence of financial incentives. If we were allowed to conduct a truly randomised controlled trial, then we could, perhaps, have more confidence in our results.

Coping with the fundamental problem of causal explanation

So how, in the absence of experiments such as randomised controlled trials, do social scientists cope with the fundamental problem of explaining causation? As we saw in Chapter 6, the next best thing is to rely on statistical inference, assuming that we have a sufficiently large-N sample to make this procedure reasonably reliable. Otherwise, we may have to use a small-N case-comparison design. Whatever strategy we use, we must employ some of the controls available in observational research to provide reasonable estimations of what is likely to have occurred; that is, to justify our inferences. So the key issue, here, is that the degree of confidence that we can place on our results is necessarily a function of the confidence that we have in our research design. That, in turn, depends on the confidence we have in the theories that inform it. In this case, such theories must involve claims which rest on theories not tested in this particular study about the characteristics of the populations of patients; the ways that we might control for those characteristics that are believed to matter for this study; and why we can confidently ignore other characteristics. There is no getting away from dependence on theories in methodology.

Nor can we escape dependence on substantive theory about the matter in question. If, for example, the widespread acceptance of the institution of queuing is an important factor in explaining the relative absence of conflict at bus stops, check-out tills and exits from theatres and sports stadiums, then we might want to know whether its causal force is a matter of degree or not. How many people would have to push and shove their way to the front before serious physical conflict breaks out?

Ethnomethodologists might research this question by trying out scenarios with varying numbers of postgraduate volunteers, assuming that they could get such an experiment approved by a university's research ethics committee. But if they did not already have good theories about the necessary and sufficient conditions of maintaining good order within crowds, it would be very difficult to infer with much confidence – even from such experimental studies – that a certain threshold number of pushers and shovers is required to precipitate various levels of disorder. This is because they could not estimate, in the absence of such theories, what would have happened if they had been able to change other characteristics of both the pushers and shovers and the pushed and shoved.

Any strategy for developing and warranting explanations is limited by this fundamental problem of causation. However, as we shall see in the next few chapters, there are ways of working with this problem. But, in so doing, we must always be clear in making claims about explanatory inferences that this problem limits our capacity for certainty.

Explanatory adequacy or satisfaction

We turn now to *explanantes*. Very often, people criticise social scientists for offering unsatisfying explanations. If true, it would be a serious methodological criticism of our research. A famous physicist once said that, as far as he could tell from listening to social scientists, they only have one law: 'some do, some don't'. Ouch.

Generally speaking, we can describe research as offering a high degree of explanatory satisfaction if it meets four criteria. First, it should pick out the most *critical* and important factors. In VOR, they might explain most of the variance; in CBR, they might drive the central analysis.

Second, an explanation is the more satisfying, the more *fundamental* are the factors it rests on. A fundamental factor is one that cannot be reduced to more basic factors. If 'educational attainment' disappears when we control for 'social class' in explaining attitudes to recycling, and we have independent evidence that class drives educational achievements, then we shall prefer an explanation that invokes class because it is the more basic force of the two.

Third, we usually find explanations to be more satisfying if they concentrate on *contingent* factors: the things that could have turned out differently than they did in the particular case(s). If our cases include households with different patterns of behaviour in recycling their household waste, then we shall look for explanations which point to factors which are *not constant* to all households. It is no help pointing to the introduction of kerbside collections to explain variation in behaviour, if all our households have access to that facility.

Finally, a satisfying explanation is one that also offers an explanation that is most relevant to the *purpose* for which the question is asked. Both sociologists and public policy researchers will be interested in explanations of household recycling behaviour which involve attitudes. But they will have different conceptions of a satisfying explanation. The policy researcher might want to know which aspects of attitudes are being influenced – and how directly or indirectly – by government campaigns, whilst a sociologist might be equally interested in the influences of family, friends and neighbours.

Distal and proximate explanations

Unfortunately, these four criteria are not enough to settle deep differences among social scientists about what explanations they will accept as satisfying. Often the debate comes down to the issue of whether the variables used – either individually or as a set – have the appropriate degree of *distance* from the thing being explained, to provide an interesting explanation. 'Distance' means something different here from the way we used it in Chapter 6 in the discussion of distances on variables. In the present discussion, distance refers to the issue of how *distinct in content* the explanatory variable is from the variable to be explained. This point is explained in Example 10.2.

EXAMPLE 10.2. WELL WORRIED

Consider the example of the things we do and do not worry about, and why we worry about some things more than others. In social psychology and some traditions of sociology, this is called 'risk perception'.

Psychometric psychologists working on public perceptions of risks sometimes use the notion of a 'dread factor' to explain why some things are widely believed to carry high risks. In most such studies, death from fallout in a nuclear war or from a terrorist attack scores a high 'dread factor', but death as a result of an accident in the home does not, even though it is much more likely to occur. 'Dread factor' is variously defined, but is generally taken to mean that a certain kind of emotion is attached to the very thought of a particular risk – whether it is nuclear radiation or an aeroplane crash – but not, typically, to other risks, such as radon emissions in our homes or asbestos in our office walls.

The problem with this explanation, argue some of their critics, is that it is banal. It amounts to pointing out that people rank some risks as severe ones – irrespective of their probability – because, well, they fear them greatly. That, the critics say, tells us very little. In short, 'dread factor' is too *proximate* to the fact of strong risk perception – which is what we want to explain – to be an interesting or a satisfying explanation.

Defenders of the psychometric approach, such as the hugely prolific Lennart Sjöberg (e.g. Sjöberg 2003), reply that proximate variable explanations are much better than ones that rely on reference to more *distal* factors, such as social organisation or overarching ideology, because proximate explanations can achieve much better *goodness of fit* with the data. For Sjöberg, what matters most is explaining as much of the variance as possible, and if that means we must use variables that are very close in meaning to what we want to explain, then that is just a fact of life in explaining anything.

The critics answer that it is true by definition that proximate variables will achieve stronger statistical associations. If our explanatory variables are so close to the ones to be explained, it is not surprising that we get strong correlations and high degrees of goodness of fit, but the price we pay is too great in that the explanation is just too boring. The advocates of theories of risk perception that privilege distal factors, such as ideology or location in social organisation, argue that social sciences are prepared to trade off some goodness of fit for gains in the level of causality that is captured, and in parsimony, explanatory power and relevance.

Sjöberg and other defenders of proximate explanation reply that such a trade-off is not warranted, because explanatory power in the statistical sense (i.e. percentage of variation 'explained') matters more than whether the explanation is satisfying.

There is, unfortunately, no general rule to tell us how distal a variable has to be before it provides a satisfying explanation. Worse than this, there is no agreement among social scientists about which characteristics matter most in defining the distal–proximate spectrum. However, the criteria set out in Table 10.1 can be found in the literature.

Trading off other virtues against explanatory satisfaction

Table 10.1 shows that it is difficult to use a single dimension to describe the spectrum running from distal to proximate variables. Furthermore, in the present

Table 10.1 Ways in which explanatory factors can be nearer to or further from what they are supposed to explain

Distal variables	Proximate variables
Effects more generalisable from the particular dependent variable to other types of case or context	Effects less generalisable
Contextual	Immediate
Background	Foreground
Collective matters, pertaining to significantly sized classes, sets or groups	Individual-level factors
Structures, institutions and conventions	Behaviour and/or condition of the focal person(s)
Macro-level	Micro-level
Upstream in a chain of causes	Downstream in a chain of causes
Indirectly causally linked to dependent variable	Directly causally linked to dependent variable
Long causal chain to dependent variable	Short causal chain to dependent variable
Distant in time and space from dependent variable	Close in time and space to dependent variable
Mediated: work through proximate on dependent variables	Unmediated: work directly on dependent variables
Not subject-matter specific to dependent variable	Subject-matter specific to dependent variable

state of the debate, there is no general theory of explanatory satisfaction that would specify thresholds, such that we could tell when a variable moves from being more proximate to more distal, and could thus be expected to provide a more satisfying, rather than a less satisfying, explanation. Nevertheless, these terms provide a vocabulary for the conduct of debate about appropriate trade-offs between the greater satisfaction that might be achieved by using variables that are more distal – on at least some of the measures in Table 10.1 – and other virtues in explanation.

But should we always prefer distal explanations? Are they always more satisfy-ing? Not necessarily. As ever, it depends on what we want to know – that is, on our research question and our purpose. If we want to know why a judge sentenced a convicted burglar to five years in prison, the fact that the judge followed the sen-tencing guidelines is a proximate explanation, but it can be a perfectly satisfying one in a simple case. On the other hand, suppose we want to know why the same judge gives very different sentences in apparently very similar cases, or why some judges appear to show much greater latitude and much less consistency in their interpretation of the sentencing guidelines, than others. In such cases, an explana-tion using a proximate variable – that is, some judges used their discretion more than others – is not a satisfying one. To answer this question, we want an explanation that uses more distal variables.

Using distal variables

The challenge in warranting explanations using distal factors is to specify clearly, and then evidence the mechanisms by which the distal factors are connected with the outcomes to be explained.

It is not uncommon in business studies to read claims that the reasons that businesses headquartered in China, South Korea or Japan engage in certain practices – such as adopting certain styles of decision-making, management–labour relations, or relationships with partners or regulators – is that they are driven by a 'Confucian' culture. Well, maybe. But the great sage died a long time ago, and over the centuries his teachings have been used to justify a great variety of things. Factors such as Buddhism, Taoism, Shinto, Japanese feudalism, nationalism, communism and military defeat will surely have shaped organisational 'cultures', too. Moreover, each of these countries is characterised by very different practices among large businesses and, in each of them, there is great internal variation between industries and firms of different sizes and ages. Unless we can specify just how the moral rules and conceptions of administrative authority developed by various schools claiming the sage as their inspiration have influenced the 'culture' of particular firms, and to what extent those schools have resisted the effects of rival imperatives and ideologies, the use of that particular distal variable does not make for a convincing explanation.

As we go on to examine the various types of explanation used in social science, you should be thinking about how satisfying each might be for the kinds of question that interest you. Exercise 10.1 should assist.

EXERCISE 10.1. PROXIMATE AND DISTAL CAUSES OF ROUGH SLEEPING

1 Go back to the exercises you did in Chapter 2 on the possible causes of an increase in rough sleeping.
2 Rank the explanations you suggested for this increase, in order of the proximity and distality of the principal variables used in each explanation.
3 Consider each explanation in turn. If you read a report that offered these explanations (and which provided enough evidence to convince you that each explanation was sound), how informative and how satisfying would you consider them to be? To what extent do you think that your answer should depend on why the report was commissioned?

Mistakes in explanation

If explanatory satisfaction is a critical virtue, there are also some vices to avoid in attempting to develop or test explanations. Research designs may be flawed in a number of ways:

- *Assuming explanations*: Choosing a VOR approach assumes that we need an explanation consisting in a set of variables, their values and coefficients – or at least, that these things are good proxies for the explanation. The problem is that – at least, in the same piece of research – we cannot test that assumption by comparing the results with a COR study which examines *how* those variables work and perhaps interact.
- Offering *unsatisfying* explanations: The explanations offered might be true but banal ('I joined the club because I wanted to'); true by definition ('this country runs free elections because it is a liberal democracy'); or true of such a restricted set of cases that the explanation becomes uninteresting ('households with a member who works in the waste disposal industry are particularly assiduous at recycling their household waste').
- Offering *insufficient* explanations, at least for the reasons that brought us to ask the question. For example, even if we were to find that big households do more recycling than smaller ones, we would probably think that household size was not by itself an adequate explanation of all recycling behaviour.
- Providing explanations *at the wrong level*. Some studies focus on producing an explanation at one *level* but not the level at which we might appropriately look for explanations. For example, a study of which *households* recycle their waste would not be able to explain why *individual* members are motivated to spend time and energy on doing it. Nor would an explanation of household behaviour necessarily tell us why different *areas* in a city have different rates of recycling waste.
- Providing *unwarranted* explanations: Some studies claim to make inferences from their data to particular forms of explanation that might not be *warranted*. For example, other explanations might be equally or more consistent with their data, might show better fit with the data, or might offer explanations that are more consistent with the findings from related bodies of research. This issue presents particularly tricky questions where the data do, indeed, allow alternative explanations. In such cases, we might plump for one of them on grounds supplied by empirical evidence in the wider literature or on the basis of a wider theoretical argument. In so doing, we would do well to adopt the principle of caution we noted in Chapter 2, which teaches us that, in cases of doubt, we should make inferences that do least damage to established bodies of knowledge.
- Offering *mistargeted* explanations: The facts or processes picked out by the explanation may be true and may even have something to do with what is explained, but not in the right way. For example, in studying the effects on household recycling of a new method of collecting household waste, it would be important to be sure that any changes in household behaviour were, in fact, due to the new collection method rather than to other factors operating at the same time, such as changes in public attitudes resulting from a national publicity campaign.

Some of these mistakes are illustrated by Exercise 10.2.

EXERCISE 10.2. HOW MUCH IN YEN FOR THIS BABY?

A group of economists and demographers once collaborated in a famous cross-national study of the relationship between exchange rates and birth rates. The study was provoked by a series of observations. First, they noted that in a data set spanning a couple of decades, the birth rate in Brazil rose when the exchange rate fell against the US dollar. Second, they noted that the birth rate in Malaysia fell over the same period whenever the exchange rate with the Indian rupee rose.

After several years of careful examination of the relationships between exchange rates and birth rates over five decades between twenty countries, they concluded that after all, there was no relationship.

Why are you not surprised by this result?

Trading off flaws

Of course, even explanations that we happen to like, and that might be true, satisfying, sufficient, correctly targeted and specified at the right level, may still not be warranted. Or they may even be warranted too, but only on the basis of evidence from other research. If so, this would raise the question of whether we learned much from our research or whether we could have offered the explanation without doing it.

Sometimes empirical research that offers to support an explanation that relies heavily on other research does add something worthwhile to the overall body of work and knowledge *if* it is designed to dovetail very carefully with the gaps in our knowledge. There is usually a trade-off here. If some research is very carefully designed to fill a hole in a wall that is being built by many hands, it is very difficult to use the same project to decide whether the wall is sound. So it is important to be clear what trade-offs are being made. Example 10.3 illustrates this point.

EXAMPLE 10.3. WHY DOES HOUSEHOLD SIZE TEND TO BE ASSOCIATED WITH A PROPENSITY TO RECYCLE HOUSEHOLD WASTE?

Suppose we noted from a VOR study that household size tends to be associated with propensities to recycle household waste. We would probably not find this a very satisfying explanation of the differences in household behaviour, but we might, nevertheless, decide to explore it further.

To do this, we might design a CBR study of six large households to explore how household size interacts with other factors found by our VOR study to be important, such as 'conscience' or 'information', 'trust' or certain design features in local authority schemes. As a result, we

(Continued)

---

might spot that household size reinforces the effects of such factors, rather than operating as an independent factor.

For example, the fact that several able-bodied people are available to sort and carry different bags of waste, and that household members feel accountable to each other for recycling consistently, offsets some of the factors – such as lack of time or fluctuating levels of conscience – that in most households tend to lead to inconsistent recycling.

This study would help us to solve an outstanding problem in our understanding of households' behaviour. But it would not have a sufficient large N, or a sufficiently representative set of cases, or study a sufficiently wide range of factors, either to confirm or challenge the main theory tested in our earlier VOR study.

The next three chapters will consider in detail what is involved in developing explanations in ways that offer reasonable hope of avoiding common mistakes, of achieving an acceptable degree of explanatory satisfaction, and of allowing us to draw valid inferences on the basis of a defensible warrant.

Basic reading

For an overview of the idea of causation, see Gerring J, 2001, *Social science methodology: a criterial approach*, Cambridge: Cambridge University Press, Chapter 7.

ELEVEN

Basic forms of explanation

This chapter will:

- distinguish the principal forms or structures of explanations used in social science;
- look briefly at non-causal forms of explanation, before turning to causal ones; and
- begin to examine the crucial question of just what does the causal explaining in theories and models.

Before we can discuss what kinds of explanatory inferences we are warranted in making from our research, we need to think about the different types of explanation used in social sciences. This is what this chapter is about.

Logical explanations

First, there are logical explanations. Mathematical proofs are perhaps the best-known type of logical explanation. But there are others. They are not often used in social science, but they can sometimes be important. Example 11.1 provides an example of how a geometrical fact – one that is, more or less, true by definition – can provide a satisfying explanation.

EXAMPLE 11.1. JUGGLING ACT

Two circus jugglers throw eight sticks high in the air so that they separate and tumble about as they fall. Alex brings his two children to see the circus stars practising. He takes some photos of the jugglers as they perform. One photo freezes the scene at a moment during the sticks' descent.

(Continued)

When Alex develops the photo some days later, he notices that almost all the sticks are nearer the horizontal axis than the vertical axis. He thinks about this for a while and realises that this outcome has nothing to do with the jugglers' actions.

There are a great many ways for a stick to be near the horizontal axis, but only a few ways for a stick to be near the vertical axis. Suppose 'near' means within 10° of either horizontal or vertical. Being within 10° of vertical implies that sticks are within a space shaped by a fairly narrow tube. But sticks can be pointing north–south, east–west, or anything in between, and still be within 10° of horizontal, so the available pancake-shaped space around the horizontal plane is a much larger one than the tube around the vertical axis. Figure 11.1 illustrates this fact.

Figure 11.1   More scope to be the horizontal than to be near the vertical

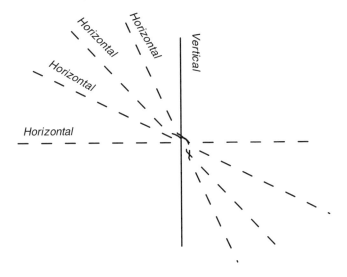

As Lipton (2004 [1991]: 31–2) says, the reason 'why more sticks are near the horizontal than near the vertical is that there are two horizontal dimensions but only one vertical one'. This explanation is 'not a causal one, since geometrical facts cannot be causes'.

Regression to the mean

Sometimes explanations can be surprisingly satisfying even when they rely only on quite general facts and do not invoke causation. 'Regression to the mean' is the most common explanatory factor of this type. Example 11.2 gives a famous case.

EXAMPLE 11.2. TOP GUN?

A research project found that trainee pilots in the Israeli Air Force tended to improve after their trainers had criticised them for unusually weak performances. If they were praised for unusually strong performances, they tended to do worse.

Should we conclude that criticism is more causally powerful than praise in improving performance?

As the researchers realised, this inference would be invalid, because the data are consistent with another explanation: namely, regression to the mean.

This refers to the fact that, on average, any really good performance is as likely, or even more likely, to be followed by a lousy one as by another good one. In short, it is possible that neither praise nor criticism has much long-run effect on performance among pilots (Kahneman *et al.*, 1982).

'Regression to the mean' is neither a mysterious nor an independent force. It simply refers to the well-known statistical phenomenon that, in any sufficiently large bivariate series with random variations and a normal distribution, extreme values will soon be followed by ones closer to the average. Indeed, the less the correlation between variables, the sharper the gradient of regression to the mean.

Regression to the mean can be an informative explanation, and has proven very useful in the past for debunking some fanciful claims.

Typological explanations: are there any?

In the terms we have used in this book, regression to the mean might be thought to be a sophisticated kind of *typological* explanation, because it claims that the events or processes we observe can be explained as cases of a certain statistical type. It so happens that the type is one that has features which – although they follow logically from the specification of the type – are often sufficiently surprising in any given case to make the explanation a satisfying one.

There are plenty of attempts to use typologies for explanation in the social sciences, but they offer varying degrees of explanatory satisfaction. Example 11.3 demonstrates their limits.

EXAMPLE 11.3. A SLICE OF THE CAKE? HOW TO PRODUCE UNSATISFYING EXPLANATIONS USING TYPOLOGIES

Why do people who are members of employee share ownership schemes (ESOPs) seem to be more committed to their organisations than people who are not?

Typological explanation – it results from the quasi-mutual character of the organisation.

(Continued)

We doubt that you are very impressed: this explanation is banal. It just says that people have a stake, so they feel that they have a stake. Read another way, it is missing the central thing that we really wanted to explain: that is, it does not tell us what kind of *difference* shareholding by employees can make to commitment, even, for example, in firms where managers do not treat their shareholding-employees particularly well, or in firms that are doing badly because of market conditions, and so on.

In short, the fact that a case falls within a type often tells us too little. Typological explanations often appear to be spurious or uninformative. They also have a tendency to instability because they often boil down to logical or causal explanations.

Typological explanations are sometimes shorthand for causal explanations. Try this one for size: 'There is no socialism in the United States because it could never gain a significant hold in a society which had never known feudalism, where social mobility was always high and where capital had great power from the beginning.' This statement means that socialism is not present in the USA because it is not the kind of place that would encourage socialism. But it does, at least, tell us something about which features of the type might stand proxy for a causal explanation, by pointing to the importance of history, social structure and type of economy.

Similarly, the hypothesis we discussed in Chapter 9, that 'liberal democracies do not go to war with each other', could mask an appeal to a causal process at work in liberal democracies. We might believe that the availability of the notion of a 'just war' to legitimate mobilisation allows them to go to war with more authoritarian countries and only with more authoritarian countries, but appealing to a typological explanation enables us to avoid having to specify this causal process in detail. Many explanations that at first blush appear to be typological ones are similarly unstable.

Now compare this explanation with Example 11.4, which is taken from anthropology.

EXAMPLE 11.4. ALL IN THE FAMILY

Why do men in a certain tribe go to live with their wives' families when they marry, while their property gets inherited from the male line but not through the women?

The rookie anthropologist answers that this particular tribal society is 'uxorilocal' (they live with the family of the wife) and 'patrilineal' (property passes down the male line). Furthermore, these characteristics have been noted as far back as records and local memories go. So these folks are doing what is expected of them around here.

The rookie anthropologist is offering an explanation which looks like a typological explanation: 'this is how this type of tribe behaves'. In fact, it is a causal explanation, one rooted in a theory about the way that the codes associated with kinship institutions affect the tribe's beliefs and social arrangements.

On the other hand, many social scientists would find the rookie anthropologist's explanation unsatisfying, because it says nothing about why people in this tribe *follow* the code. If the appeal to the institutional characteristics of the tribe were supplemented with an account of, for example, the sanctions applied to those who violate the rules, or of how alternative ideas are made unthinkable by the way children are brought up, it might form part of an explanation that satisfied them more.

Ideal types

Before leaving the issue of typological explanation, we need to say something about 'ideal types'. Readers may be familiar with Weber's (1946) argument that social explanation can use 'ideal types': for example, bureaucracy, patrimonialism and *qadi*-type justice. For each ideal type, he built up lists of characteristics, The characteristics of the ideal type of bureaucracy are set out in Example 11.5.

EXAMPLE 11.5. MAX WEBER'S IDEAL TYPE OF BUREAUCRACY

According to Weber, in the ideal typical case, a bureaucracy is characterised by:

1 fixed jurisdictions, explicit rules, regulations and laws;
2 specifically regulated authorisations for giving commands and duties for carrying them out;
3 positions awarded only to those who are qualified;
4 hierarchical grading of offices;
5 preservation of written documents, accounting for all decisions, processes, actions;
6 public funds, public decisions, succession to posts and so on, all kept entirely separate from individuals who happen to occupy those posts and their own interests;
7 posts awarded on the basis of training;
8 senior post-holders with distinct and high social status;
9 appointments made by senior authority on the basis of merit;
10 posts tenured for life;
11 officials rewarded by fixed salaries;
12 officials progressing upward through the ranks in a pattern that is recognised as career progression;
… and so on.

Why did he use 'ideal types'? Weber was careful to say that the characteristics of ideal types are not – and are not claimed or intended to be – found in pure form in any real-world social setting. But characterising what bureaucracy would look like in its *pure* – or 'ideal' – form could form part of three different causal explanations of the development of bureaucracy in *particular* cases:

---

1 *Ideal types are embedded in general thought.* If the people whose behaviour we want to explain turn out to possess concepts of things that are accurately described by the social scientists' reconstruction of ideal types, then we can use these types in accounts of the beliefs, hopes, fears and so on, on which these people act.
2 *Judging people's actions against certain ideal types is essential to explaining how far they have acted rationally.* Weber suggests that some ideal types describe processes that would be expected, to the extent that people are 'rational'. For example, he argues that the laws of neo-classical economics describe how ideal-typical buyers and sellers would behave, to the extent that they rationally respond to the incentives of an ideal-type market. So invoking ideal types can provide a satisfying explanation when we observe such behaviour.
3 *Some social processes have inherent logics that are captured by ideal types.* In his discussions of the development of bureaucracy, Weber suggests that – whether or not late nineteenth-century and early twentieth-century Prussian public administrators possessed a concept of an ideal-typical bureaucracy that resembled the one Weber described – the inherent logic of these organisations is such that they will tend to develop this set of characteristics, unless otherwise constrained.

Weber thought an ideal type explanation is really a claim that something is subject to a steady institutional tendency in the direction of a purer form of that type, subject to constraints by other forces. So 'ideal types', as he intended them to be used, rest on an underlying causal theory of institutional change. One way to reconstruct the implicit causal explanation in Example 11.4 would be to develop one or more hypotheses about how uxorilocal institutions are adopted, cultivated and reinforced, such that 'uxorilocal institutions' could become an anthropological ideal type.

Statistical explanation

Statisticians often talk about 'statistical explanation'. For example, they describe a coefficient estimated for one independent variable, while controlling for everything else in a multivariate regression, as 'explaining' the variance in another, dependent variable. Thus, statistical explanation is a measure of the association between the values on two or more variables. And very useful it can be, in helping us to find patterns that need more fundamental explanations.

But more importantly, a well-designed statistical test can also rule out other fundamental explanations, by enabling us to test and reject predictions that have been derived from them. This use of statistics can be very satisfying and whole bodies of social science can bite the dust in this way. In Chapter 13, we shall present a fully worked version of how this was done in a famous study.

But statistical association does not, *on its own*, produce fundamental or satisfying explanations. We can see this, if we think again about the 'prison works' example we used at the beginning of Chapter 6. It may be possible to show – once we have satisfactorily specified our variables – that there is a robust statistical association between the fall in crime and the rise in the use of prison in recent years in the UK. But this association says nothing about *how* it works. Does prison simply remove some offenders from opportunities to commit crime, for the duration of their sentence? Or does more use of prison, however measured, produce a direct and equivalent deterrent effect on people who are thinking of committing a crime? Or does it work less directly, by signalling to them something about a government's determination to crack down harder on crime, and, if so, is this what produces the deterrent effect? And what, more precisely, is it about 'prison' that produces this effect? Is it the greater chance that a custodial sentence will be passed, or that longer sentences become more likely, or is it the reduced availability of parole? To think about these issues further, try Exercise 11.1.

EXERCISE 11.1. BETTER LEVERAGE ON PRISONS AND CRIME

As we saw in Chapter 6, there is an apparent statistical association between the increased use of prison for punishing offenders and the fall in rates in crime in the UK.

Think of at least two, and preferably three, hypotheses to explain why the increased use of prison might lead to a reduction in levels of crime. How would you test them to see whether any of them have force? How could you be sure that it (or they) really have explanatory value?

Causal explanations

Finally, then, we come to causal explanations. Causation is concerned with identifying the prior events, states and processes that give rise to the outcome we want to explain.

Causal explanations differ from logical explanations in that they are *contingent*, rather than true by definition. So they could, in any particular case, be false. They differ from statistical explanations in that they tell us *why* the associations we observe between phenomena are significant – or not – and what brought them about. The reason that many social scientists are keen to pursue causal explanations is that combining contingency and fundamentality is significantly more satisfying than the alternatives.

A causal explanation consists in a schematic argument about how some forces act upon others, to produce an effect. In effect, a causal explanation has the status of a hypothesis that uses specific types of categories and relations.

Paradigms, theories, models and conceptual frameworks

You may recall that, in Chapter 2, we distinguished between paradigms, theories and models as three tiers of explanatory resources, and you may wish to remind yourself of that discussion before reading further into this chapter. You may also like to reread Chapter 9, where we examined the importance of concepts. The argument there serves to point up the importance of a fourth tier of explanatory resource – the conceptual framework – by which we mean a taxonomy and interlocking set of definitions defining key elements in the explanation.

In Chapters 2 and 3, we were concerned with the status of the first three tiers, and with how far we can expect research to falsify them. What matters for the present chapter are the differences between the four orders of explanatory resources in their content, completeness and structure, and in their roles in causal explanation.

The contribution to explanation made by a paradigm consists in setting explanatory standards and directing our attention to generic types of factors – interests, preferences, institutions, ideas, constraints, or whatever – and indicating their relative importance. It provides a strategy for making our explanations distinctive, and reasons for thinking them interesting, especially if they are likely to be controversial precisely because they downplay factors emphasised by other frameworks. General conceptual frameworks can fill out paradigms. More specific conceptual frameworks can, as we saw in Chapter 9, help us build theories and even models because we can use them to develop operational measures.

Theories do not offer candidate answers only to questions about which interests, ideas, institutions, or whatever, matter for explaining outcomes in a particular population of cases – which might be large or small, depending on the theory's scope. They also offer answers to the question about *how* those factors are expected to work.

From theories, models derive sets of predictions of precise weightings of these factors and the relations between them, in ways that are amenable to measurement or coding. This derivation is often done by adding assumptions to theories, so that models can be specified sufficiently precisely to enable the work of measurement or coding to be done.

Specifying paradigms, theories and models for explanatory work

In content, conceptual frameworks, paradigms and theories are generally specified qualitatively. Conceptual frameworks consist in interlocking sets of definitions and operational criteria for measurement. Even though a theory may be tested primarily with quantitative data, it is presented principally in a qualitative account of the factors, variables, mechanisms and contexts proposed for the particular phenomena of interest. See Chapter 12 for more on this point.

Models, by contrast, can be specified quantitatively. For example, a model might set out the expected ratios or relative weights among factors or variables, which would be expected on its particular implementation of the underlying theory. That implementation consists in rendering an exact statement of the relationships between factors, which flow from a particular set of assumptions about how precisely the underlying causal structures will yield observable patterns. Some models are specified qualitatively: this approach is preferred when the patterns predicted in the data by the model cannot be measured using cardinal or ordinal numbers.

The point of a model is that it should be sufficiently *complete* to enable a determinate result to be yielded by examining it against the data. This means that it must show either poor or good fit with the data, or that it should explain a high or a low proportion of the variance observed on the main factors. Explanatory completeness in a model means that the patterns it predicts are sufficiently clear and precise to be tested against data. It does not mean that the model must include *all* the plausibly relevant factors. Theories are nearly always incomplete, because there are in almost every case several sets of precise relationships that could be derived from them; the same is true of paradigms and of conceptual frameworks.

The rest of this chapter is concerned only with theories and models because, as we saw in Chapter 2, few research projects are concerned with verifying or falsifying paradigms. We now turn to the question of what actually does the explanatory heavy lifting in theories and models.

Factors and their proxy variables

In explanations that use conventional inferential statistics, we usually depend on *variables* to do the explaining. Variables get coefficients, and coefficients measure the explanatory power of the variables.

We saw in Chapter 6 that variables are proxies for what we have mostly – thus far in this book – called explanatory *factors*. A factor is nothing more than an empirical feature or phenomenon that may exert some causal influence upon an outcome (although *how* it exerts that influence is not always given by the specification of the factor: see Chapter 12). When we say that, in explaining the pattern of career peaks in the labour market of a particular industry, gender is still the main factor but that educational achievement is also a contributory factor, we are not speaking loosely. What is implied is a quite specific conception of a causal explanation.

We assume that the explanation of the pattern made by the peaks of occupational status and/or income across the labour market is the work of at least two – and perhaps many more – factors working in combination. We are assuming, too, that these factors can be isolated as variables that can take different, empirically measurable values, and that these values can be combined to measure their aggregate effect. The simplest way to combine variables is to add the contributions made by each of them. The contribution made by each variable is measured or estimated, independently of the others, so that the addition can proceed.

These are the basic assumptions lying behind the procedures involved in statistical regression. It follows that the variation that can be exhibited by a variable – strong or weak, high or low, effective or ineffective, present or absent, or whatever – must be capable of being reduced to numbers, which may be ordinal or cardinal, binary or multiple, indefinitely differentiable or only limitedly so, and so on.

In sum, the standard assumptions in statistical inferences are that:

- the causal force of the independent variables is *additive* – each one independently explains some part of the variance on the dependent variable;
- the total variance is the sum of differences made by all the variables in the model; and
- this sum accurately describes the underlying causal structure.

The use of factors and variables in qualitative research

Such assumptions are not only made by those who use numbers. The same basic approach can be followed qualitatively.

An historian trying to explain the end of the Roman Empire in Western Europe in the fourth and fifth centuries might well identify a series of factors, including: the growing strength and organisation of the peoples outside the empire; corruption within the empire; growing weaknesses in the administrative cohesion of the Roman civil administration; civil wars and the incentives for regional leaders to engage in internal competition within the empire; falling tax revenues as key parts of the tax base were eroded through loss to peoples outside the empire and by the splitting of the empire into eastern and western zones; and the growing dependence of the army on co-opting groups of tribal soldiers with greater loyalty to each other than to the army or the Roman state. And so on.

Our historian might try to attach weights to each of these factors, to identify their relative importance. Indeed, the historian might consider the contribution of his or her own argument to the wider literature to consist principally in the arguments he or she offers for one set of weightings rather than another. Sometimes this approach is called 'intuitive regression'. That description is in fact unfair, for the argument is based on the marshalling of evidence for relative weightings of factors, not on intuition. But the expression does capture something of importance, in pointing to the structural similarity between this kind of qualitative analysis of the relative contributions of different factors and that followed in statistical regression (Northcott, 2008).

The problem is that, as we have already noted, 'statistical explanation' – whether undertaken with numbers or not – is attenuated. We know what factors appear to do the work that produces the outcome, but not more than that.

Variables or configurations?

The assumption that variables bring causal influence to bear independently of each other, and that the independent influence of each variable is what needs to

---

be measured, can be, and has increasingly been challenged. The methodologist, Charles Ragin (e.g. Ragin, 1987) has argued at great length that there is something very odd indeed in the idea of a single variable holding up a specific portion of the explanatory burden, while relying on its fellows to hold up other portions. If one variable gets only a share of the explaining to do, then how sensible is it to talk about its doing any explaining at all? After all, a table cannot partly stand, using only one leg. Ragin would argue that the whole package – not only the separate variables but, just as important, the specific but complex *interconnections* between them – does the explanatory work.

Moreover, Ragin argues, an emphasis on the independent contribution of separate variables can easily mask the problem that the same outcome can arise from quite different causal paths: this is called 'equifinality' (see Chapter 8). For example, some businesses might fail for cash-flow problems. Others might fail for reasons to do with technological failures. Others might die from brain drains of talent, or from the failure to withstand the departure of a charismatic boss. Yet all these processes may involve similar financial factors such as problems in accessing credit or raising new equity; similar market factors such as failing or fickle demand for their goods and services; similar labour market problems, such as a shortage of critical skills or leadership; and similar competitive factors, such as those associated with adverse exchange rates. The fact that all these factors matter may be identified by analysing the *same* set of explanatory variables about finance, demand, labour and competition. But they may be related to each other in very different ways when companies die as a result of travelling different routes. Example 11.6 discusses a similar problem in another field.

EXAMPLE 11.6. WHY DO STATES BREAK DOWN?

There is a large literature in social science about states that collapse or suffer major revolutions. The examples that have most preoccupied social scientists are the *ancien régime* in France; the great European empires that came to various kinds of grief at the end of the First World War; and, more recently, the 1979 revolution in Iran, the 1991 collapse of the USSR and the descent of the Lebanon into civil war in the 1970s and 1980s.

There are lots of rival explanations in the literature. As you would expect, there is no one single pattern of causal explanation. The two diagrams in Figure 11.2 present two explanations, taken from the work of two comparative historical sociologists, Theda Skocpol (1979) and Jack Goldstone (1991), as summarised in graphical form by another, Randall Collins (Collins, 1999). Skocpol (1979) argues that international rivalry between states is the fundamental or most important distal cause, and it brings about state breakdown by forcing states to raise taxes, which exacerbates creating internal divisions. Goldstone (1991) argues, on the basis of a slightly different set of cases, that the fundamental distal variable is population growth and inflation. These are internal variables by contrast with Skocpol's emphasis on international causes.

Figure 11.2 Two rival explanations for state breakdown and revolution

Theda Skocpol's (1979) explanation

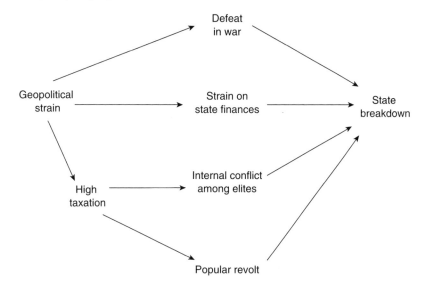

Jack Goldstone's (1991) explanation

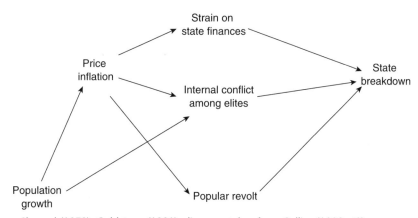

Sources: Skocpol (1979), Goldstone (1991); diagrams taken from Collins (1998: 48)

Using configurations

Each diagram in Example 11.6 offers a perfectly coherent explanation. Each is built up from variables. Quite likely, each captures something important, but probably about rather different cases. Perhaps we should think of state breakdown as being something that has at least these two, and probably several more, typical patterns of causes. But what, exactly, is doing the explaining in these cases? There are two rival answers. Each understands the causal relationships picked out by these arrows slightly differently.

One argument is that the variables on the left hand side of the diagrams are doing the heavy lifting. They are the ones that are most distal, and the ones that, at least for the purposes of these explanations, are not being treated as intermediate causes. On this reading, Skocpol is saying that geopolitics is a kind of aggregate variable that provides the ultimate cause, while Goldstone is making a similar claim for population pressure. For VOR, we should need enough cases of state breakdown and reliable ways of coding all these variables quantitatively – at least with dummy variables – to enable us to do, for example, a multivariate regression analysis. If this were possible, we would expect that the model showing the best combination of parsimony, variance explained and goodness of fit would effectively eliminate all those variables in the middle of each diagram in favour of the ones on the left.

But maybe we would be missing the central point that Skocpol and Goldstone are trying to make. After all, they are both arguing that it is the whole *set* of variables and their interactions that produce state breakdown. So perhaps state breakdown is something that can be explained by at least two distinct sets of variables and their interactions. Maybe eliminating all the variables in the middle is removing the very machinery by which causation gets done.

For Ragin the lifting machinery in such cases is what he calls the *configuration*, by which he means the set of values taken by variables as a set. Each of Skocpol's and Goldstone's diagrams describes a configuration. Ragin (1987) points out that configurations can also be described by a single row in a 'truth table' showing all the logically possible combinations of values on all the relevant independent variables, together with the relationships between those variables that may act together upon the dependent variable, or indeed upon a dependent configuration. However we choose to describe them, the advantage of using configurations to do the explaining is that they recognise the problem that the same outcome can be explained by different configurations and that there may be quite different explanatory routes to the same causal destination.

Defenders of standard statistical analysis offer several replies to Ragin. They suggest that if it is indeed the case that a variable A operates only with other variables B or C, and if it operates very differently when B takes the value 1 from the way it does when B takes the value 0, then one can simply derive a new set of conjoined variables, which would be $(A + B0)$ and $(A + B1)$, and conduct the analysis on each combination separately. Or they might suggest that if the issue has to do with whole configurations, one should use statistical approaches that estimate the goodness of fit of whole models rather than of individual variables. The best known of these techniques is structural equation modelling.

EXERCISE 11.2. FLOW YOUR OWN

Think again about the task we set in Exercise 11.1, and choose the two most promising hypotheses you developed to explain a possible causal relationship between the increased use of prison and falling crime rates. Draw *two* flow diagrams to represent the causal relationships between variables specified by your two candidate hypotheses.

Use the discussion above to decide whether both cases show a similar causal path. If so, what structure does it take? If not, what are the main differences in the structures of their paths?

What do your answers imply for your choice of research design?

By definition, of course, in historical or small-*N* comparative studies, the size of the sample does not permit the use of these statistical techniques. This chapter leaves us with an important question for comparative or case-oriented research (COR). This question is whether Ragin's move from factors to a configuration – as a set of factors working together – is sufficient to capture the nature of the causal work done by an ensemble of factors working together as a single structure.

In the next chapter, then, we shall consider how we can deepen causal explanation beyond the analysis of configurations of variables.

Basic reading

On methodological issues in causal explanation, see Gerring J, 2005, Causation: a unified framework for the social sciences, *Journal of Theoretical Politics*, 17, 2, 163–98.

Ragin C, 1987, *The comparative method: moving beyond qualitative and quantitative strategies*, Berkeley, CA: University of California Press, presents a critique of variable-based explanation and his argument for using configurations.

TWELVE

Mechanisms, contexts and trajectories

This chapter will:

- distinguish mechanisms from factors in causal explanation;
- show how mechanism explanations need to be modulated by context;
- examine the principal types of trajectory unleashed by mechanisms; and
- conclude with a review of the trade-offs involved in choosing these explanatory vehicles.

Factors or mechanisms?

Methodologists such as Pawson and Tilley (1997) would argue that in making the case for the position we discussed at the end of the previous chapter, Ragin has not gone nearly far enough in dispensing with variable-based thinking, even for within-case analysis. All that configurational explanation does, they would suggest, is to shift the explanatory burden from the solitary variable to a pile or aggregate of variables. Configurations are helpful, but they are still just sets of 'factors' and Ragin's techniques of configurational analysis are still based on associations. For example, in Example 11.6, the diagrams show arrows between the factors, but none of the arrows is labelled: we are given no verbs that might tell us *how* the causal relations among the set of factors work.

If we want to do genuinely causal explanation, Ragin's critics would argue, then factors do not capture what is doing the causal *work* (Hedström and Swedberg, 1998; Pawson and Tilley, 1997). Instead, explanation is something that can only be done by understanding *generative mechanisms*. A mechanism, for these writers, is the force that is responsible for *how* things happen: for example, *how* an independent variable works on a dependent one.

In explanatory research that does not use mechanisms, it is – or used to be – entirely acceptable to use terms like 'this causes that', 'this brings about that', or one thing 'yields' another. An example of this kind of limited causal analysis would be the kinds of flow charts from the work of Skocpol and Goldstone presented in the previous chapter. These flow charts are, from the perspective of those who argue for mechanisms, unredeemed IOUs. The whole point of causal process tracing is to describe the *semantic content* of the flows, not just to identify the principal factors. This means that providing clear labels for the arrows, with verbs that *describe* how mechanisms work is of central importance.

To use the helpful term offered by the philosopher of science Nancy Cartwright, we need 'thick causal concepts' (Cartwright, 2004). She writes that

> the pistons *compress* the air in the carburettor chamber, the sun *attracts* the planets, the loss of skill among long-term unemployed workers *discourages* firms from opening new jobs ... These are genuine facts, but more concrete than those reported in claims that use only the abstract vocabulary of 'cause' and 'prevent'. (Cartwright, 2004: 814)

For a mechanism, we must show how types of social organisation 'cultivate' particular ways of thinking, how being 'steeped' in a certain style of thought 'renders it painful even to think about' behaving in certain ways, or how a given event 'startled' a prime minister into reopening questions previously thought otiose or irrelevant.

Used in these ways, these verbs are – like 'compression' and 'attraction' in Cartwright's examples – not far from being metaphors. Using metaphors and flow charts to 'explain' things might sound too loose, too lacking in rigour and too literary to be appropriate for explanatory social science. Indeed, that can be a risk. Advocates of mechanisms argue, though, that the risk arises not in the metaphorical character of their content, but in the manner in which we evidence them and use them to label very precisely – or not – the arrows that give structure to our flow charts.

Understanding how interventions work through mechanisms

In business organisations or in public policy – to take some examples from practical fields – mechanisms are the forces that cause interventions in social or organisational problems to produce observable outcomes, though not always, of course, the intended or publicly stated ones.

In a classic criminological article, Pawson and Tilley (1994) suggest nine mechanisms by which closed-circuit television (CCTV) cameras in car parks can work to reduce crime. Only one of them is what they call the 'caught in the act mechanism': the detection of crime. More often, CCTV cameras 'work' in crime reduction by means of less obvious mechanisms. These mechanisms include the 'nosy parker mechanism' – which, by reducing the fear of crime and thus increasing the use of car parks, deters criminals by making them believe that it is more likely that some-one will spot them committing a crime – and the 'memory jogging mechanism', which reminds drivers of the possibility of crime and encourages them to take pre-cautions such as putting valuables out of sight.

In terms used in Chapter 4, these writers are realists. They are preoccupied with under-lying causation, with what is 'really' going on. Because they describe *how* causal factors work, mechanisms are, of course, not directly observable. Rather, their existence and nature must be inferred, for example from systematic observations of behaviour or from interviews that tell us how people involved in a situation believe things work. In other words, the attribution of mechanisms depends on the construction of a causal *theory*.

Many realist writers would argue that most social scientists concerned with rela-tionships between variables make implicit assumptions about mechanisms, just as most business managers and public policy-makers make implicit assumptions about why and how certain kinds of interventions in social or organisational life are likely to work or not. Thus, social scientists should bring to the surface these often half-formed and unarticulated theories about causal mechanisms, so that they can be formally stipulated, tested, and refuted, refined or replaced.

In working with mechanisms, it is important not to confuse them with simple intermediating variables that moderate the effect of independent upon dependent variables. Rather, mechanisms are better understood as underlying forces, not directly observable, which determine the observable relationships between variables. Thus, variables and factors alike are only of interest if they are valid and measurable proxies for underlying mechanisms.

Consider, for example, Example 12.1, which reports a dispute about mechanisms working on a much larger scale than CCTV cameras in car parks.

EXAMPLE 12.1. MECHANISMS FOR GETTING INTO THE EMPIRE

A slightly surprising success in high street and airport paperback bookshops in recent years is a book by the historian and archaeologist Peter Heather, called *Empires and barbarians: migra-tion, development and the birth of Europe* (2009; Basingstoke: Macmillan). Heather is interested in generative causal mechanisms that explain movements of people into the Roman Empire in the first millennium AD.

One school used to argue that this process resulted from the working of a process summar-ily called 'invasion'. This was assumed to mean the wholesale migration of ethnic groups with clear prior identities from one territory to another, leading to the slaughter and replacement of the people they found in their destination land. Invasions were thought to be triggered by 'displacement', as peoples even further to the east of Europe forced peoples nearer the Roman Empire to move west and to invade territories within that empire.

A more recent school argues that there are hardly any cases where this actually happened (save, perhaps for the Norman invasion of England in 1066). Instead, they argue, the breaking

(Continued)

---

and replacing of the states in the first millennium was largely the work of relatively small groups of warriors, who defeated armies of the incumbent state and then inserted their own members as the new governing leadership over the same population. Over time, they would influence the culture of the population they had conquered. This process is known as 'elite transfer'. If 'invasion' was driven by the negative 'push' of displacement, 'elite transfer' was driven by the 'pull' of searching for positive gains or opportunities.

Heather considers both accounts to be unconvincing. Instead, he argues for 'mass migration' over substantial distances of coalitions of people from several prior ethnic identities of varying degrees of fluidity. Migrant groups included some ten or twenty thousand warriors, but also women and children and long baggage trains with seedcorn, agricultural implements and livestock. The 'mass migration' process resulted, he argues, in more significant change than 'elite transfer', but also offered the opportunity for mutual cultural adaptation and learning between incumbent and incoming populations.

Contextual conditions for 'mass migration' included pressure from peoples further east, general population growth pressure and improved intelligence about greater trading opportunities within the empire than outside it. A critical mechanism for each migration process was generated by the external and internal balance of power. Externally, peoples outside the Roman Empire could secure sufficient concessions from that empire only if they arrived in sufficient numbers and with sufficient force to coerce the authorities. Yet this too was possible only if they prepared for campaigns over several years, during which time they would have to farm seized lands. Internally, new forms of kingship and organisation enabled the assembly of sufficiently large groups of people with adequate divisions of labour to enable mass migration on this basis.

Second, over time, successive mass migrations unleashed a ratchet mechanism, or self-reinforcing dynamic. Each successive mass migration deepened instability in the empire, making it more vulnerable to the next, and also gave subsequent peoples more information on how such endeavours might successfully be undertaken.

The structure of mechanisms

Whether or not Heather is right about what happened in the first millennium, what matters here is that his explanation has a similar structure to those offered by Pawson and Tilley. Broadly, a claim that a causal mechanism has been discovered depends on being able to link three elements in an explanation, to show *how* things happen:

- *Imperatives (or interventions)* – the phenomenon that triggers a response: in these cases, 'displacement' or trading opportunities, or the introduction of CCTV cameras.
- *Processes* – the means by which people respond to triggers: in these cases, coalition-building between peoples to effect relocation, or a ratchet effect of weakening in the empire and learning among those outside it, or putting valuables out of harm's way in parked cars.
- *Outcomes* – the results of the responses: in these cases, the making of new states or reductions in car park crime.

Mechanisms consist, then, in the causal connections between the three elements, and using a mechanism to explain an outcome depends on establishing a theory about how these connections integrate the three elements in the focal case or cases.

In Heather's mechanisms for mass migration, coalition-building among peoples to prepare for collective action in seeking new lands is an intelligible response both to the 'push' of threats from the east and the 'pull' of greater opportunities in the rich west. The collective organisation produced by new forms of kingship and inter-ethnic assembly enables the process of mass migration. In turn, this dictates a particular style of fighting and an overriding need to maintain cohesion. Successful occupation, for a period, of a new territory then creates a new ratio between incomers and incumbents, which, together with the degree of cohesion maintained among the incomers, determines the prevailing direction of cultural learning between the two populations. These, then, are the causal links between 'imperative', 'process' and 'outcome' to which Heather appeals in using the 'mass migration mechanism' to explain the pattern of state breaking and making in the first millennium AD.

Let us next return to our recycling example, by considering Example 12.2.

EXAMPLE 12.2. A RUBBISH POLICY?

Imagine that a local authority decides to encourage the sorting of household waste by a combination of sticks and carrots. Householders are provided free of charge with different-coloured bags for different kinds of waste – say, blue for paper and glass, green for organic waste and white for plastic waste – to make garbage easier to sort and store. But at the same time, the local authority tells householders that kerbside refuse collectors will no longer collect unsorted waste: waste must either be sorted for kerbside collection, or be taken to special waste disposal facilities which will charge a fee for receiving it.

In many parts of the town – though not all – the refusal of refuse collectors to take away unsorted waste appears to result in more 'fly-tipping' of garbage in canals, parks and other urban open spaces. An increase follows in inter-neighbour disputes and in disputes between householders and the local authority, apparently as a result of the nuisance arising from the accumulation on the streets of uncollected rubbish.

In this case, a researcher might infer that the local authority had an implicit causal theory which relied on a straightforward 'pressure to conform to rules' mechanism to link the new refuse collection arrangements (intervention) with a process, 'sorting garbage into different coloured bags', to produce the anticipated outcome, 'increase in waste recycling'. Instead, the researcher might conclude, the rule triggered a rather different 'rule evasion' mechanism, which led to unwelcome and unanticipated outcomes. However, as we shall see in the next section, there is room for discussion about what kinds of theories about what kinds of causal mechanisms might be needed to provide a full and satisfying explanation of the outcomes revealed by this example.

Distal and proximate mechanisms: explanatory satisfaction

The argument for using mechanisms in explanation is that we gain explanatory satisfaction, by learning how the causal process works. By contrast, analysing relationships between variables on the assumption that each variable makes an independent contribution gives us less genuinely satisfying explanatory information.

But is this always or necessarily true? Consider the argument in Example 12.3, which is taken from a minor classic of post-war social science.

EXAMPLE 12.3. HOW TO BOTCH UP WITHOUT REALLY TRYING

The American social policy researcher Sam D. Sieber spent much of the 1970s studying a variety of mechanisms by which policy interventions – especially those undertaken in welfare, policing, punishment and education – might not only fail, but even achieve the reverse outcome from that which was intended. Among his catalogue of mechanisms by which reverse outcomes were produced were the ways that interventions provoked counter-reactions, stigmatised clients and created new opportunities for people who were not originally in the target group to become clients.

He gave particular attention to mistakes in the diagnosis of the problem. For example, he documented a series of interventions in agricultural development that had relied on expert knowledge and ignored the lay knowledge of local people, with disastrous results (cf. Scott, 1998). He also looked at police reform programmes that were based on misunderstandings of the relationships between the work of police officers on the streets and their work in the courts (Sieber, 1981: 68ff.).

Sieber labelled the mechanism by which policy-makers develop initiatives on the basis of ignorance, arrogance or misunderstanding 'perverse diagnosis'. Understanding this mechanism, he argued, is a necessary part of explaining how and why initiatives sometimes produce the reverse of the intended outcomes.

The claim that 'perverse diagnosis' is a mechanism that – by explaining faults in policy design – can help to explain unwelcome outcomes of policy initiatives certainly is not wrong: empirically, there is a good deal of evidence that it matters. Sieber's concept of 'perverse diagnosis' is certainly an improvement on the kinds of simplistic explanation that rely on variables such as 'cognitive deficiency' to ascribe failures in public policy to the muddle-headedness of those who draw it up. It offers us a 'mechanism' that links cognitive deficiencies with the design of interventions and the particular kinds of perverse outcomes they produce. It could therefore provide the basis for constructing a – fairly short – flow diagram to show how we get from the *explanans* to the *explanandum*.

This explanation is still not, in our view, very satisfying, because it does not explain how particular policy-makers come to misinterpret, or be in ignorance of, facts, or develop unfeasible policy ambitions. Why do they suffer from particular biases and not others? Are their biases the result of psychological flaws in their personalities; of more systemic features of the institutions in which they work; the group dynamics among them; or some other factors entirely?

More generally, this kind of mechanism cannot help us answer these rather fundamental questions because – to use the terms we introduced in Chapter 10 – it offers only a proximate explanation. For a more satisfying explanation, we want a more distal mechanism that would take us further back along the causal chain and tell us more that is specific to the particular conditions that gave rise to the cognitive deficiencies that caused policy mis-design in the particular case(s) in question.

Consider, for example, one famous policy intervention that went disastrously wrong and produced the reverse outcome from that which the policy-makers intended. The USSR's model of domestic economic management was so disappointing by the 1980s that it was regarded as a failure even by many people in the Communist Party of the Soviet Union. The system was based on state-owned enterprises and collective farms, centrally set targets and control, administrative allocation of capital resources to meet planning goals, emphasis on production rather than consumption, and so on.

The proximate mechanisms for failure are well known. A key contextual factor was state economic dirigisme. The first factor contributing to the mechanism was the weakness of incentives. Lack of ownership rights meant that people had no claim on any surpluses they produced, so they faced weak incentives to create them, especially by way of efficiency improvement or investment. A second factor was price distortion. Over time, administrative allocation of resources and under-emphasis on consumption – as well as the direct use of subsidies – resulted in prices bearing little relationship either to true costs of production or to demand. The mechanism that resulted was, again, a ratchet, but in this case of disorganisation. The two factors combined to produce inefficiency, misallocation of resources and declining total factor productivity. These things reinforced the mechanism over time. For, as people adapted their expectations and behaviour to its effects, they siphoned resources and time into an informal or illegal economy, reduced effort in the formal economy and provided misinformation to the centre about resource usage and outputs.

Yet invoking these proximate mechanisms only raises the more fundamental question about the system's failure: why did Soviet leaders not recognise how these proximate mechanisms worked and change the system long before the deep failure of the 1980s? After all, they understood their problems very well. To explain the failure in ways that will satisfy us, we need explanations which also address this question. Such explanations call for more distal mechanisms.

At least for the period until Stalin's death in 1953, we might invoke political mechanisms of 'authoritarian imposition of ideology' which stifled reform. For the Brezhnev years after 1964, we might invoke 'fear of loss of power'. In those years, arguably, a leadership which had less commitment than previously to the communist ideology nonetheless avoided substantive economic reform, because they feared the political dynamic that it might unleash. Indeed, they were quite right to fear it. When economic reform was introduced in the 1980s, it immediately gave rise to a political dynamic which led to the Communist Party being swept from power by 1991. In this case, authoritarian imposition of ideology and fear of loss of power operate as distal mechanisms in explaining economic failure. But only when they supplement proximate ones – such as weakness of incentives and distortion of prices – is the explanation satisfying. So we need combinations of mechanisms, each working at a different level, in order to provide adequate explanations.

Similar mechanisms also work at less grand levels in organisations, in relation to less heroic policy problems. It would, for example, be tempting – and not inaccurate – to blame the – perhaps foreseeable – outcomes of the 'rubbish policy' we considered in Example 12.2 on the stupidity of the managers who imposed it. But it might produce more satisfying explanations to examine more distal mechanisms – such as those associated with the organisational dynamics of, and the thought-styles prevalent in, this local authority – to explain more precisely why these particular policy-makers adopted an implicit theory which overestimated the degree of householders' willingness consistently to comply with local authority rules.

Contexts and mechanisms

Suppose that one reason this local authority adopted the failed rubbish policy described in Example 12.2 was that it had been shown to work in a pilot exercise commissioned by national government, and that, as a result, local authorities throughout the country had been advised to adopt the same waste recycling scheme. The advice to replicate a pilot study in this rather mechanical way is not an uncommon outcome of research evaluations of successful policy interventions, but some methodologists insist that it is usually unwarranted and always risky (e.g. Pawson and Tilley, 1997). This is because the same imperatives or interventions may not, in all circumstances, trigger the same mechanisms.

Tilley and Laycock (2001) cite the example of an influential quasi-experiment in Minneapolis which randomly allocated perpetrators of domestic violence to different treatments, namely 'arrest', 'advice' and 'send away'. 'Arrest' was found to be associated with the lowest repeat offending rate, so several other cities tried the same experiment. But they achieved very different results: some found that arresting more perpetrators led to less repeat offending but some found that it led to more.

The explanation offered by Tilley and Laycock is that different mechanisms are triggered by the same imperatives or interventions in different 'contexts' – or situations where different background factors are at work to enable or disable, amplify or attenuate the mechanisms. In areas with low unemployment and high levels of marital stability, arrest triggers the mechanism 'shame', which discourages offending behaviour. In areas of high unemployment and high levels of marriage instability, arrest triggers 'anger', which leads to more domestic violence. The key message, they say, is 'Same problem. Same tactic. Different context. Different mechanism. Different outcome' (Tilley and Laycock, 2001: 19).

Another way of putting this point is that we should pay careful attention to the precise 'conditions' which constrain or enable particular mechanisms, before we attempt to make any general inferences about how mechanisms work (Kurki, 2008: 231). Thus, we saw that without contextual factors such as intelligence about economic opportunities within and military power of the Roman Empire, Heather's mechanisms for mass migration would not have worked in the way they did, or may not have been triggered at all. Likewise, in the absence of the scale and strength of Soviet state economic authoritarianism, weak incentives and price distortion alone might not have enabled the runaway ratchet mechanism to operate.

This discussion would lead us to expect, then, that the same mechanisms would not necessarily be triggered by adopting the same recycling scheme, even within the same local authority area, if the contexts in which the schemes were introduced differed in material ways. Suppose the perverse outcomes found in Example 12.2 occurred only in some parts of the city. Why? Well, putting out household waste for kerbside collection is highly visible to neighbours. So one possible hypothesis is that a mechanism 'strong social pressure to conform' might be triggered by the new policy in contexts where neighbours generally respect conforming behaviour or where there is a high prevalence of conscientiousness about environmental issues. Conversely, this same visibility might trigger 'fear of reprisal' or 'fear of being noticed' in areas characterised by high levels of anti-social behaviour, and might thus encourage rule avoidance associated with illicit tactics for disposing of household waste.

This hypothesis might be initially tested by finding ways of operationalising the factors which might be operating differently in different contexts. Assuming we have a sufficiently large sample of cases, we could then run a statistical test to determine whether there is a good fit between variables derived from these factors and the data about outcome distributions. Again, in both the domestic violence and waste recycling examples, the mechanisms cited depend on an underlying but unstated causal theory – this time about the effect of the social dynamics of neighbourhoods on facilitating or inhibiting policies aimed at behaviour change. If the findings of the large VOR study show strong goodness of fit with the hypothesis and statistically explain a high proportion of variance, it might be followed up by a case-oriented (COR) study designed to develop and refine that theory by comparing the detailed interaction of mechanisms, contexts and outcomes in a much smaller number of cases.

These examples illustrate why differences in *context* are thought to be the key modulators of mechanisms, and that considering mechanisms without contexts is likely to lead to explanations that are insufficiently specific and probably unwarranted.

EXERCISE 12.1. BREAKDOWN OF LAW AND ORDER, BUT IN CONTEXT, PLEASE

What combinations of particular contexts and mechanisms can you think of that might explain why some young people who are members of minority groups that frequently suffer discrimination might turn to violence and others might not?

How would you design a piece of research to distinguish which combinations of contexts and mechanisms were the important ones?

Loops and endogenous causation

Hitherto we have considered explanations where one group of forces (variables, configurations, factor, and now mechanisms and contexts) brings about an outcome. Unfortunately, much social life is not so linear. Causation often occurs in loops. That is, we often find causal processes where an outcome goes on to influence the very things that brought it about. For example, we have bad relations with our neighbours, because their children throw things into our garden. So we complain, resulting in even worse relations. In this example, our relations with the neighbours are no longer externally fixed independently of – or *exogenous* to – our complaints, but are influenced by the very thing they brought about. They are therefore *endogenous* factors. Causation occurs in a loop.

In this example, we can easily design research to test the explanation, because the process lasts over time: it is a case of what we have called above 'a ratchet'. So we can split the two processes by period. We can examine separately relations with the neighbours before the complaint and then again afterwards, to test how far each complaint deepens hostilities by comparing the outcome at different times. Splitting the forward and backward parts of the causal loop is indeed one of the standard ways in which social scientists deal with endogenous causation (King *et al.*, 1994: 195–6).

This procedure is more difficult to follow when all the interacting causes and effects occur simultaneously, and/or when the outcome does not change but the *status quo* is maintained, because there are no differences over time to compare. For example, many disciplines examine causal relations between the manner in which people think, what they want and what they do. Do we pray because we believe (ideas are more fundamental) or believe because we pray (practices and social relations are more fundamental)? This is not only an issue in studying religion: it arises in studying anything – from business to friendship – where stable and congruent practices and beliefs are observed together. We may not be able to find a period when people show only ideas or only social relations, and even if we could, the initiating force might not be the one that explains the long-run maintenance of beliefs and practices.

Social scientists have become increasingly interested in *emergent* effects, where interactions among several factors produce an outcome which characterises a system as a *whole*, and which then affects each of the particular forces. The best-known example is organisational culture. It is a feature of the whole organisation, produced by many beliefs, practices and interventions, but then, in turn, affects each of these beliefs and behaviours. Here, we have a loop that runs from facts about parts to facts about a whole unit of analysis – that is, it moves across at least two levels of analysis. Causation is both ongoing and simultaneous, and may result either in change or in maintenance.

At this point, some researchers give up on causal explanation altogether and fall back on description, or else resign themselves to being able to say little more than that practices and ideas interact and reinforce each other. But this is unsatisfying and we can do better.

We begin by changing the *explanandum*. In relation to religious beliefs and practices, for example, we should study separately the following questions:

- What initiated the interaction? What contexts and mechanisms triggered the interaction of praying and believing?
- What sustains the interaction over time? Are there are any *third* contextual factors or mechanisms which might contribute to the duration of both praying and believing?
- Is either of the two focal forces more fundamentally important in the long run? Is one direction of causation more contingent on local conditions and the other more universal and constant? Is one direction of causation more closely causally integrated into the wider social structure and organisation than the other?
- Do the two directions of causation use different mechanisms? For example, our complaining worsens relations with the neighbours by making them resentful of our tone, whereas the bad relations caused by our complaint leave their children with no compunction about throwing things into our garden; these are quite different causal mechanisms.
- Which direction of causation is stronger? Is either phenomenon subject more to influences by additional factors or mechanisms than the other, giving it a greater *degree* of independence?
- For emergent causation, are distinct sub-mechanisms working at the higher level, or the level of the system as a whole? Can we collect data on the causal processes separately at different levels of analysis?

Now consider how you might apply this approach in Exercise 12.2.

EXERCISE 12.2. ENDOGENOUS CAUSES IN CITY DOORWAYS

Rough sleepers often develop good peer relations with other rough sleepers. In some cases, these bonds can work to reinforce alcohol or drug abuse, which in turn can make it harder to secure or maintain accommodation. Support from others on the streets can even be so important that a few become unwilling to accept permanent housing at the cost of isolation from their sources of friendship.

Some researchers have suggested that in some cities among some networks of rough sleepers, peer solidarity, substance abuse, passing on information about promising opportunities for begging or casual (sometimes illegal) work, and a set of beliefs and values, all interact to sustain a distinct and integrated street culture.

How would you design research to distinguish the different causal relationships that might be at work, if this hypothesis were true?

Trajectories

Often researchers must find explanations which enable them to understand how particular mechanisms bring about change over significant periods of time. For

---

Table 12.1 General types of trajectory over time

	Organising or disorganising of effect	
Continuity or discontinuity of mechanism	Self-reinforcing	Self-undermining
Initial mechanism continues: 'ratchet'	1 Incremental cumulative development	2 Self-disorganisation
Initial mechanism triggers or gives way to another	3 Bandwaggoning	4 Indirect self-disorganisation

this purpose, we need to employ a *causal trajectory* as an analytic tool. A causal trajectory describes a sequence of mechanisms that leads, over time, in a particular direction of change. We have already seen examples in the ratchet effects identified by Heather in his work on mass migrations and in the economic decline of the USSR.

Trajectories might consist in continuations of originating mechanisms, which might be self-reinforcing or self-undermining. Alternatively, the initial mechanism might trigger others which become more important over time. Table 12.1 shows that there are therefore four general types of trajectory.

Feedback

These types all describe *feedback* processes. By feedback, we mean a causal effect looping back from the thing that, in the first instance, is to be explained to the factor that, in the first instance, does the explaining. This loop in turn creates a secondary effect and complicates the relationship between the two.

Feedback is found, very broadly, in two varieties. *Positive feedback* is the variety in which the causal effect works upon itself over and over again. *Negative feedback* is the opposite variety, where one causal force elicits a counter-reaction from another one. The two varieties of feedback might roughly balance each other, or one might overwhelm the other.

We consider positive feedback first. Figure 12.1 shows the most commonly invoked trajectories of positive feedback. On the horizontal dimension is time, running from the earlier left to the later right. On the vertical dimension is a notional measure of organisation. By this we mean the degree to which the phenomenon being studied can sustain its own viability or, alternatively, is vulnerable to instability, erosion, undermining and perhaps even to collapse.

Incrementalism is the simplest trajectory of all. Here, in each period, change follows the same path but with small increments that generally move in the same direction. Successful political constitutions – or indeed the conventions of behaviour we

Figure 12.1 Basic types of positive feedback trajectory

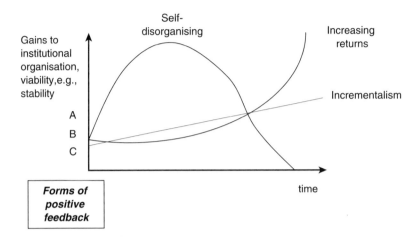

might find to be associated with certain kinds of sports or social clubs – might, in the ideal typical case, work in this way. They stabilise expectations about how people behave. These expectations would, in turn, lead people to expect that the constitution or club itself will remain broadly stable, with only modest or marginal developments.

Much bigger effects work, say, in social networks, where success depends on building a critical mass of committed customers or members. For example, in the case of a globally successful computer operating system, the creation of a sufficiently large base of users triggers a new mechanism that reinforces the effect of the initial one. More people write applications software for it, leading even more consumers to buy the system to a point where everyone who wants to share documents with other people has to use it too. Similar effects are found when devices such as mobile phones or email take off, or indeed when a particular sports league becomes so dominant that no one wants to participate in any other.

A third case is the most interesting. This is where a system undermines itself by being locked into its own main causal process. In the 1920s and 1930s, the Soviet economic system appears to have enabled the country to sustain capital-intensive development for very large projects, but over time its momentum slowed. The very centralism and reliance upon authority that may have worked initially to get large-scale projects of electrification and other infrastructure built also undermined a wide range of other capabilities for economic development. Some of the same kinds of self-disorganising rigidities might be found, for example, by studying a family firm or an academic department or a charitable agency, as the founding generation ages. These are cases of self-disorganising positive feedback.

Figure 12.1 shows the kind of trajectory that might be plotted for each case, using a simple line graph to represent each trajectory.

Now consider negative feedback. Here, we consider the contrary reaction of one causal force to another. One possibility is that there will be a continual sequence

Figure 12.2 Negative feedback of permanent conflict

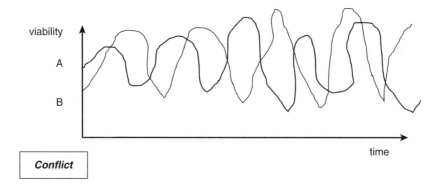

Conflict

of reaction and counter-reaction between constantly conflicting mechanisms. Figure 12.2 shows how this might look for two different but similarly shaped trajectories of change followed by organisations faced with unresolvable external pressures. This kind of line, for example, might represent the abrupt changes wrought in social work practices in conditions where one 'fear of blame' mechanism – say, for failing to intervene in high-profile child-abuse cases – is in constant tension with another, incompatible 'fear of blame' mechanism – say, the fear of blame for intervening unnecessarily in family life.

Thus, we may get oscillations or pendulum swings. When the fear of blame for too much intervention leads to scandals in which the authorities fail to identify children being abused, negative feedback will cut in, powering the opposite process until that leads to scandals produced by overzealous interventions in which children are taken into local authority care unnecessarily. And then the pendulum swings back.

Another trajectory, still, would be produced if one mechanism starts to dominate the other. If this happens, negative feedback stops and is overtaken by positive feedback of either an incremental or bandwaggoning variety. Figure 12.3 shows that case.

Figure 12.3 Negative feedback leading to hegemony

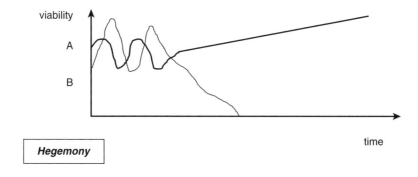

Hegemony

Third, it is possible that the two causal forces might simply exhaust each other (Figure 12.4). For example, it is conceivable that one outcome of the competing struggle between the two 'fear of blame' mechanisms would be that the social work profession might suffer increasing difficulties in retaining or recruiting child protection staff, such that it becomes impossible to retain the existing model of child protection based primarily on family-oriented social work.

Finally, and perhaps of greatest normative interest to many who do causal analysis for policy research, is the special case where the two (or more) forces balance each other more or less stably, and even support each other. The standard analogy here is the desktop angle-poise lamp. This lamp can be raised and lowered and its angle changed, but the careful balancing of its springs will provide for stability at all heights and angles. This is called, in the literature on systems theory, *homeostasis* or *collibration*. Once homeostasis is achieved in social settings, we should thereafter expect relative stability with, at most, incremental change (Figure 12.5).

Figure 12.4   Negative feedback leading to exhaustion

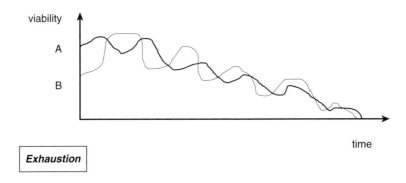

Figure 12.5   Negative feedback in homeostasis

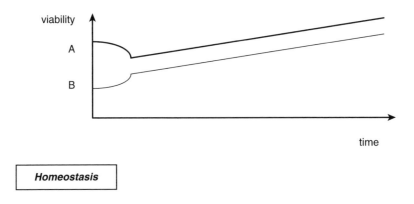

Reversible and irreversible causation: smooth and uneven causation

One could argue that the rise of American power in the world is not unlike the development of spoilt brats. This is not to suggest that the USA is like a spoilt brat. Rather, the similarity lies in how causal forces work.

Consider the causal forces that brought about American dominance. They would surely include the Cold War; the collapse of the old European empires in and after the First and Second World Wars; the fact that at a certain point in the 1940s, only the USA had developed and become capable of deploying nuclear weapons; and the weakening of the economy in the rest of the world in the wake of the Second World War. Today, none of these factors operates, yet their disappearance has not brought about a weakening of even the relative, let alone the absolute position, of the USA in either the political or the military spheres.

Likewise, when parents spoil a child, the causation involved may include inconsistent indulgence of whims and a tendency to appease the child's bad moods. By the time the child has grown and left home, he or she may still be a brat. Despite the ending of the causes that produced brattish behaviour, the young person remains a brat.

In short, the causes of American hegemony and of spoilt brats are examples of *irreversible* causation.

Contrast brats and superpowers with the explanation offered by the great sociologist Maurice Halbwachs, as to why we forget so much of our lives. In *The social frameworks of memory* (Halbwachs, 1952, trans. in Coser, 1992), Halbwachs shows that we tend to forget those things that are related to times when we were involved with people, social networks or institutions with which we no longer have contact. Conversely, when we renew lost friendships, we find that we recall events from our previous lives together that we had entirely forgotten during the years of separation. Memory of particular things is sustained only by the continuing availability of the relevant social framework: it is sustained by *reversible* causes. *Reversible causation* happens when the rise and decline in causes is associated with similar changes in the things they cause.

It may be tempting to presume that causation is either reversible or irreversible, but the research may not actually suffice to show which is the case. This condition is, of course, especially risky if the research is intended to lead to practical recommendations. If researchers mistakenly assume that some important causes of inner-city decline are reversible, then they may be surprised to find that inner cities do not revive as anticipated when city governments start to make sources of capital available, free up planning laws to make changes of land use easier, invest in skills training and so on. This outcome does not necessarily mean that they were wrong to conclude that capital shortages, skill shortages and planning rigidities were important in explaining the decline of the inner cities. But it might be the case that these causes are, in the strict sense, not reversible, and the causes of urban revival might not simply be achieved by the obverse of those forces that are responsible for decline.

The problem of inferring causation from truncated data

A common source of this kind of mistaken inference lies in research design. More specifically, there is a special danger in collecting and analysing *curtailed* or *truncated* data, so that we only see part of the curve that describes the relationship between the causal forces and the outcomes they are considered to explain. Speaking about this issue in terms of 'curves' might suggest that it is only important in quantitative research, but – as the examples relating to memory and spoilt brats show – this issue is just as important in qualitative work. Moreover, thinking about curves will teach us that there are not simply two curves – reversible and irreversible causation – but several possible trajectories. Consider the six graphs in Figure 12.6 that describe possible relationships between a causal variable *C* and an outcome variable *E*.

If we collect and analyse data only on the first third of any of these curves, we might well make the wrong inference. If we projected on in the same way from the observations on the first third of the curve in cases 4 and 5, then we should be broadly right, and we might get our policy prescriptions based on those inferences about right, too. But projecting forward from the first third of case 1 would mislead us into thinking that it was like case 4, when, with more data, we should know that it is

Figure 12.6 Trajectories of reversible and irreversible causation

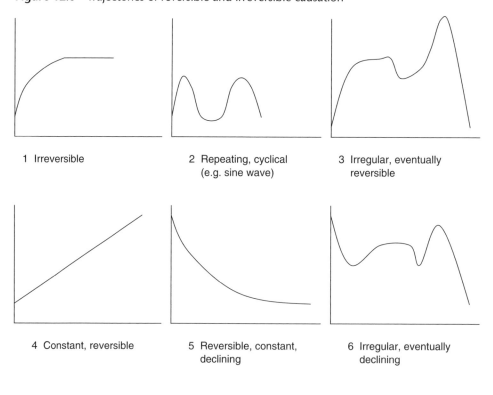

| 1 Irreversible | 2 Repeating, cyclical (e.g. sine wave) | 3 Irregular, eventually reversible |

| 4 Constant, reversible | 5 Reversible, constant, declining | 6 Irregular, eventually declining |

ACHIEVEMENTS

not. Similarly, the first third of the curve in case 2 could mislead us into the mistaken inference that C's causal force was already exhausted.

These examples show why making extrapolations from irregular sections of curves is very risky. To do much with data supporting the curves in cases 3 and 6 would require us to know a great deal more about what is going on, especially with the causal mechanism. Suppose the causal mechanism has to do with the exhaustion of supplies of raw materials that are critical for an industry such as 'rare earth metals'. Data on the position of firms producing goods which rely on rare earth metals might well look like cases 3 or 6 above. But firms can innovate. They might find alternative ways of making these goods so that they do not need these metals. Or they might diversify into other fields. So we might be wrong to project forward the plummeting of the curve on the right hand side in cases 3 and 6. The lesson is that, until we know more about the fuller set of interacting and confounding mechanisms, we ought to be very cautious in projecting trajectory curves like these.

EXERCISE 12.3. REVERSIBLE SUICIDE?

A recent book by authorities in the field (Pape and Feldman, 2010) claims that there were 350 suicide bombing attacks in the world between 1980 and 2003, but that there were 1833 between 2004 and 2009. In the same period since 1980, the volume of other kinds of terrorist attack has substantially declined.

What might be the causes of such changes in the pattern of terrorist attack? Which of them might be reversible or irreversible, constant or repeating, regular or irregular?

Over what period would you collect data, if you wanted to make reliable inferences from research about how these causes work?

Trade-offs in moving from factors to mechanisms and beyond

The last two chapters have examined the main types of crane used for explanatory heavy lifting in social research, especially factors – which may be represented by variables, configurations of factors, mechanisms and contexts, and trajectories. We have argued that each improves the capacity of our research design to capture the nature of causality. As always in the methodology of social sciences, we might, however, have to pay a price for this gain, by foregoing other virtues of good research design.

In particular, there may well be a trade-off between the richness of our understanding of causality and generality. We have seen that Ragin criticises the very process of abstracting from the different ways in which individual factors might be related to each other, because it risks conflating causation. This may not matter if what we want is a reasonable general account of *what* matters, but it would matter greatly if we need to know more precisely *how* it matters. So if our purpose in conducting research is to test a theory of high generalisability about increases in the volume of suicide bombing or rough sleeping or to test the efficacy of a new drug, we would be right to settle for a large-*N*, VOR project with a strongly parsimonious set of variables.

Nevertheless – as we have seen in the examples used in this chapter – policy interventions in complex social problems might be better informed by research that produces a much finer understanding of how, exactly, causation works in specific contexts. Of course, if that choice involves a focus on really fundamental distal causal mechanisms, then our research would inevitably sacrifice some goodness of fit with its underlying theory. In turn, that would limit any claim to have 'tested' that theory and would also inhibit the *direct* transfer of practical findings to a much larger set of apparently similar cases.

Whether we choose to gain or lose virtues such as parsimony, generality, goodness of fit and richness of causal understanding – and what trade-offs we should make between them – are not questions to which there is a universally correct answer. Rather, our design strategy will depend on our research question and particularly on the reasons we have for wanting it to be answered.

Whatever those reasons, we also need to know exactly what warrant we can claim for the explanatory inferences we draw from our research. As we saw in Chapter 10 as we embarked on this discussion about explanation, this is a core issue for methodology in social science, because understanding the warrant for explanatory inference helps us to know to what degree we can mitigate the fundamental problem of causation in claiming to be building knowledge about the social world. So it is to this issue that we now turn in Chapter 13.

Basic reading

Pawson R and Tilley N, 1997, *Realistic evaluation*, London: Sage, provides a clear introduction to variable and mechanism-based explanation, and makes the case for configurations of contexts and mechanisms.

Advanced reading

More advanced discussion of mechanisms is provided by Cherkaoui M, 2005, *Invisible codes: essays on generative mechanisms*, Oxford: Bardwell Press. Also helpful are: Bunge M, 2004, How does it work? The search for explanatory mechanisms, *Philosophy of the Social Sciences*, 34, 2, 182–210; Goldthorpe J, 2000, Causation, statistics and sociology, in J Goldthorpe, *On sociology: numbers, narratives and the integration of research and theory*, Oxford: Oxford University Press, 137–60; Mayntz R, 2004, Mechanisms in the analysis of social macro-phenomena, *Philosophy of the Social Sciences*, 34, 2, 237–59; Steel D, 2004, Social mechanisms and causal inference, *Philosophy of the Social Sciences*, 34, 1, 55–78; Steinberg PF, 2007, Causal assessment in small-N policy studies, *Policy Studies Journal*, 35, 2, 181–204.

Gambetta D, 1998, Concatenations of mechanisms, in P Hedström and R Swedberg (eds), *Social mechanisms: an analytical approach to social theory*, Cambridge: Cambridge University Press, 102–24, discusses how chains of mechanisms can lead to trajectories.

On feedback trajectories, see Jervis R, 1997, *System effects: complexity in political and social life*, Princeton, NJ: Princeton University Press.

On reverse causation, see Lieberson S, 1985, *Making it count: the improvement of social research and theory*, Berkeley, CA: University of California Press.

King G, Keohane RO and Verba S, 1994, *Designing social inquiry: scientific inference in qualitative research*, Princeton, NJ: Princeton University Press, 185–96, discuss strategies for dealing with endogeneity when modelling causation using variables rather than mechanisms.

THIRTEEN
Warranting explanations

This chapter will:

- examine the relationship between necessary and sufficient conditions in ascribing causality;
- discuss issues raised by claims that some cases are unique and require 'narrative' explanations;
- consider whether the differences between probabilistic and deterministic explanations are substantive ones or artefacts of research designs; and
- contrast and discuss the relationships between the principal inference strategies of deduction, induction and abduction.

Warrant

The previous chapter examined how different kinds of explanations used in social sciences are structured. This chapter examines what is required to provide warrant for these types of explanations, and the problems of inferring that they are supported – or not – by the patterns found in data collected in empirical research.

In order to be warranted, an explanation requires:

- evidence that the phenomena pointed to in the *explanans* really can be found in the focal case(s) or population at the right stage or in the right place; and
- evidence that the *explanans* is related *in the right causal way* to the *explanandum*.

These conditions are simply stated, but these simple statements hide important methodological issues which are what this chapter is all about.

Explanations using necessary and/or sufficient conditions

In Chapter 9 we considered conditions that events, states of affairs or trends should meet, before they could be considered *cases of* a concept. In so doing, we distinguished necessary from sufficient conditions. The same logical features are important in distinguishing necessary from sufficient conditions in warranting causal explanations. A necessary condition is one that must be met for the outcome to occur, even if other conditions are also required. Sufficient conditions may not be the only ones that need to be met for the outcome to arise. Perhaps the same result could emerge from other circumstances; but when these conditions are found, the outcome will indeed arise. In rare but tidy cases, a condition may be both necessary and sufficient.

Understanding how these conditions are used in explanations is central to providing warrant for inferences, to show validity. But, in making causal inferences, we have to ask the counterfactual question that we need not ask in concept formation: what would we expect – given our existing knowledge and our understanding of context and mechanisms – in the absence of a necessary condition or of a set of sufficient conditions?

Two criticisms are often levelled at attempts to offer causal explanations for particular outcomes and both use between-case comparison, either implicitly or explicitly. One claims that a proposed explanation is not *sufficient*, because the same outcome did not transpire in other cases where the same conditions were in place. The other claims that the proposed explanation is not *necessary*, because the same outcome transpired in other cases where the same conditions were not in place. If these claims are upheld, then a researcher is faced with only two choices: to abandon the explanation or else show why the case in the study is different from the ones cited by the critic. Example 13.1 shows how this works.

EXAMPLE 13.1. MAY I SEE YOUR CARD, MADAM?

Why did the former Labour government in the UK become committed in 2001 to introducing ID cards, after having previously opposed the idea?

Ministers themselves have claimed that it was a response to growing identity fraud. In short, the measure was a straightforward response to a growing problem.

But there is a problem with this explanation. The problem of identity fraud was just as serious in Canada, for example, and no political party seriously proposed ID cards there. At best, our explanation appears *insufficient*, though only if we accept that Canada was similar to the UK in its vulnerability to identity fraud.

We could also reply to the criticism by trying to show that, even if the explanation is insufficient, it offers a necessary condition. That is, we could claim that no country would adopt an identity card scheme *unless* it had a problem with identity fraud.

The critic of our identity fraud explanation might then reply, 'France is a well-developed modern economy with a democratic government that is also concerned about the risks posed to its citizens by identity fraud risks. And it is true, they have ID cards there. But they adopted them long before identity fraud became a significant problem.'

This time, the criticism is that our explanation is *unnecessary*, but it has force only if France is like the UK case in relevant ways. This time, the argument is that the same outcome is observed, but the supposed causal factor is missing, because the French scheme was adopted for quite other reasons.

(Continued)

So if we are blocked on that count, too, then we can only salvage our identity fraud explanation by denying the critic's claims that the cases are relevantly like ours.

In so doing, we would have to enrich our explanation. We would have to argue that there was something about the UK in relation to ID cards that, at least in this period, makes it a very different case from Canada and France. For this purpose, we might bring in other conditions. For example, we might argue that concern about identity fraud does its explanatory work in relation to the introduction of ID cards only when (1) certain ideological configurations influence governments and (2) institutional blockages preventing adoption of ID cards are removed, and that both these conditions held true in the UK after 2001 but not in Canada.

But this means that 'concern about identity fraud' now shares the explanatory burden with ideology and institutional factors. We are moving to a more complex explanation and refining the *type* of case to which our explanation applies. But using ideological and institutional factors may well face the same kind of criticism as the ones that have just been rehearsed above. If so, we shall be forced to enrich our explanation still further – or else abandon it. And so on, until we find an explanation that fits.

The kind of iterative process – by which candidate explanations are tried out upon data, and then restricted to subsets of cases defined by particular criteria or additional conditions, until the explanations fit the data – at least, as well as can be expected given the nature of those data, is called *analytical induction*.

These two kinds of criticism each rest on the assumption that demonstrating causation depends upon demonstrating relationships of necessity and sufficiency between conditions and the outcomes we are trying to explain. For this purpose, necessary or sufficient 'conditions' for outcomes may be variables, sets of variables or configurations, or contexts and mechanisms.

Limits to the usefulness of demonstrating necessary and/or sufficient conditions

Many methodologists believe, however, that demonstrating necessary and/or sufficient conditions has limited utility in helping us understand causation.

Suppose, for example, that the only way to achieve high social status within a certain branch of medicine is:

a to have at least fifteen years' experience in practice;
b to take the most difficult and complex cases that one can find; and
c to hold the post of professor in a university medical school that was founded before the First World War.

In that case, we can say *each* of (a), (b) and (c) is a *necessary condition* for high social status in that branch of medicine. But suppose that in the profession of architecture, one can achieve high status by:

d   designing major public buildings in at least three medium-sized European or North American cities that are written about in certain trade journals, and also being lionised in the Sunday supplements of the broadsheet press for at least two buildings which are not domestic homes; or

e   designing a major and innovative financial district skyscraper, and being the subject of a profile in *Time* magazine; or

f   having made £1 million from contracts for building offices, public buildings or innovative houses, and also having received contracts from at least one member of a Middle Eastern royal family and being written about in the architecture trade press.

Then, in this case, we can say that any of the sets of conditions (d) or (e) or (f) would be *sufficient conditions* for high social status in architecture.

Note, however, that the conditions listed above are not, *as a simple matter of law, logic or formal association*, necessary and/or sufficient causes of high status in either of these fields. Rather, these lists depend for their utility and accuracy on an underlying theory – one which could be empirically tested – about *how* causation works to ascribe status in such professions.

Consider, by way of contrast, the statement that it is both necessary and sufficient for introducing a government bill for consideration in the British House of Commons that the government's legislation committee finds time for it to be debated and that it goes through the requisite parliamentary procedures to achieving a first reading. This is an example of an explanation that is true because it stipulates conditions that are based in procedure, entitlement or qualification. 'Explaining' that a person receives a free bus pass because they are over sixty years of age is a statement of the same type. Specifying these kinds of conditions does not provide an adequate account of causation in any but a formal sense, because these conditions do not deal with the underlying reasons why the state continues to grant elderly people free bus travel or why the government originally decided to legislate on the issue at all. Rather like the argument we looked at in Chapter 7 about whether bankers caused the economic crisis of 2007–8, the explanation is unsatisfactory at the level of meaning.

It is important to remember, too, that not all social phenomena *must* have necessary causes. Indeed, we have already seen in Chapter 8 that an effect can arise from multiple causes – some acting with or alongside each other (multi-causality), and others forming alternative routes to the same outcome (equifinality) – so that no cause is uniquely and absolutely *necessary*. Unless we believe that some events have no causes (e.g. the Big Bang that many scientists think created the Universe, perhaps?), it is more plausible to claim that all events must be caused by some condition – or, perhaps, a set of conditions – that is *sufficient* to explain them. But this claim, in itself, does not help us much because it leaves us with the problem of limiting the causal forces we should consider in any particular case. If we do not sort out what causal forces are likely to be most important, we may well encounter the problem raised by the old nursery rhyme:

> For want of a nail the shoe was lost.
>
> For want of a shoe the horse was lost.
>
> For want of a horse the rider was lost.
>
> For want of a rider the battle was lost.
>
> For want of a battle the kingdom was lost.
>
> And all for the want of a horseshoe nail.

If so, we would find that some conditions are so trivial, so remote (distal) from the effect we are trying to explain, and so contingently linked to this effect, that trying to track them down would be absurd and the explanations they provide unsatisfying. A chain of distal, but trivial, necessary causes alone provides no very powerful explanation.

Unsurprisingly, then, researchers are divided on whether searching for necessary and sufficient causes is either helpful or possible. Our view is that, in many practical research settings, it can often be helpful to analyse a data set to identify necessary and sufficient conditions for an outcome. But this will not work well, unless we have a theory that tells us what causal forces are likely to matter, how relationships of sufficiency and necessity arise, and why they are likely to be of interest for the purposes of our research. In turn, thinking about such issues may point to the need to refine concepts and revisit the structure of our candidate explanations, as we discussed in Chapters 10 and 11.

Suppose, for example, we find, on examining the data produced by the project described in Example 9.1 and Exercise 12.3, that there are some putative causes of factors found in some cases, but not in others, in explaining changing patterns of 'suicide terrorism' in recent years. Should we conclude that this is because 'suicide terrorism' is not, after all, a well-formed concept? If so, we could try to redefine it, to enable us to look for causes in smaller, more precisely defined, subsets of the phenomenon of interest – thus following the strategy we discussed in Chapter 9 in relation to the use of typologies.

If this procedure fails, should we then give up on the idea of there being any general causal paths which explain its rise? Or – as Ragin recommends (2000: 109ff.) – we could develop an account that talks about conditions being 'usually necessary' or 'almost always necessary'. Or would that process simply obscure what we mean by 'necessary'? And if so, does that matter? We shall explore this important question in the next section.

Stochastic versus deterministic causal explanations

A claim that something is sufficient to explain a result implies that, if that condition is present, the outcome is more or less certain to follow. We can call this relation *deterministic*.

By contrast, a claim that something is a necessary condition at most raises the *probability* of that outcome: whether the outcome transpires usually depends on the presence of other factors or mechanisms, too, although perhaps a few mechanisms may be inherently 'hit and miss' in their causal power, whatever else is going on.

Some factors are neither necessary nor sufficient causes in themselves, and raise the probability of the outcome by quite modest degrees. And sometimes we find sets of conditions which seem to be 'sometimes sufficient', because we cannot identify any further conditions that turn them into deterministic ones. In these cases, the identifiable causes lead to the outcome sufficiently often to be important (or 'statistically significant'), but not always. And in the cases where they do not lead to the outcome, we do not observe any negative conditions that block them: it seems that, on some occasions, the causation just does not 'work'. It is as if chance is playing a part. These causal relations we describe as *stochastic*.

But do differences between deterministic and stochastic causes reflect real differences in the nature of causation in social life? Or do they simply result from the design of our research? Do stochastic causes really measure our failure to identify the features of the condition that would make the causal relation a deterministic one? Could these features be found if only we could design our research better?

Is stochastic causation a result of differences in social life or differences in research design?

Some methodologists would answer that causation does work in different ways in different social settings. Some social institutions seem to depend on relationships between causes and outcomes working rather like the causal effect of a deftly applied cue to a billiard ball. In the army, for example, obedience to orders is so thoroughly instilled that, in most contexts, disobeying a direct order from a superior becomes unthinkable for the ordinary soldier. Indeed, it is argued that instilling this kind of automatic obedience is necessary to ensure that soldiers can be relied on to respond to orders in the confusion of battle. Sustaining this kind of institution is, in fact, a complex and costly business. But it means that for most practical purposes the institutional background can be taken for granted and a *deterministic* relationship established between, say, the order to go out on patrol and the action being done.

In most other social settings, we do not expect causation to be so consistent and reliable. Suppose, when we apply the scheme discussed in Chapter 10 for incentivising cardiac patients to travel to distant hospitals for elective care, we find that 45% of patients take up the offer. We might well decide that this study offers sufficient evidence to justify the provision of this incentive. In a social setting that values patient choice, establishing the probability that the behaviour of nearly half of the patients could be changed in this way would be considered very acceptable.

In other cases, still, as Lieberson (1997) points out, the rules governing social life specifically provide that causation *must be* stochastic. Examples include lotteries or sudden-death play-offs in sports competitions, where brute luck is intended wholly or partially to determine outcomes.

Despite such variations in the ways that social settings generate causation, some social scientists argue that, in practice, *all* causal effects are stochastic, and any determinism perceived in the course of research is a function of the research design. They argue that small-*N* research designs, in particular, are prone to encouraging the mistaken perception that causation is being exhaustively mapped, and that studying more cases would almost certainly uncover more variation in outcomes. Certainly, we should find it unsatisfying for a study of just five or six cases to offer accounts of causation which could not explain all the variation observed, for that would miss the whole point of doing in-depth within-case analysis on so few cases.

Other social scientists argue, conversely, that the causation found in many large-*N* studies – such as the one undertaken to measure the effect of financial incentives on the take-up of out-of-area surgical treatment – appears to be stochastic only because this research design necessarily sacrifices granularity for parsimony. If only we knew more about the patients in the study and about how the offer was communicated to them by their doctors, then we could know which of them would respond to a financial incentive and which of them would not. That is, if we had much more data of a sufficiently fine-grained kind, we could show that causation is really deterministic.

Imagine, for example, that we break down our heart patients by age, sex, educational attainment, disposable income, severity of condition, degree of pain or strength of ties to relatives in the locality of their home. Suppose, further, that we recruit sufficient numbers of patients in each of these categories to draw inferences about how each type of patient might respond to a cash incentive. But suppose we still find within-group variation in the take-up of this offer. If so, should we conclude that the effect is really stochastic, or should we continue to claim that we would find that it is deterministic, if only we had even more finely-grained data about the differences between patients? Only if our research design enables us to *rule out* all other plausibly relevant factors can we conclude, with appropriate qualifications, that the effect could well be stochastic.

It may be that for some *practical* purposes, it does not matter which view on this issue is right. We often do not need to know whether observed causal effects are *really* stochastic or deterministic, because we can estimate conditional probabilities perfectly well, given the information that we happen to have and the question we actually need to answer. For example, we probably do not need to know about the factors that determine individual patients' response to the offer, so long as we have enough information to judge that offering financial incentives for out-of-area treatment is broadly worthwhile.

But for *methodological* purposes, however, this debate does matter. This is because – as this example reveals – scholars who believe that all causation is more or less stochastic and those who cleave to the possibility of deterministic causation would design their research differently. In particular, they would stop analysing their data at different points in the research process. That is, they would strike different trade-offs in dealing with one of the most fundamental dilemmas in social science – one that arises in every research design – between the virtues of parsimony and goodness of fit. Exercise 13.1 explores this point further.

EXERCISE 13.1. WHY ARE YOU SLEEPING ROUGH?

In Exercise 2.2, we asked you to develop several explanations for the association between the economic recession and the rise in rough sleeping in British towns.

In Exercise 11.2 you were asked to develop flow charts to represent causal relationships between variables in these explanations. Did they assume causes that are stochastic or deterministic?

Can you think of a *case-based* research design that would enable us to tell whether causal processes were deterministic or not?

Suppose, further, that, in reading the literature on rough sleeping, you discovered a study that claimed to have found that people with low educational attainment (defined as leaving school without passing the school-leaving examination, i.e. GCSE at least at grade C) make up 75% of rough sleepers. Does this finding satisfactorily 'explain' anything at all important about why people become rough sleepers? If not, why not, and what more do you think we need to know to understand what might really explain this apparent association?

Unique cases? 'Narrative explanation'?

If we keep adding factors in the search for determinism, we shall also distinguish each case more strongly from the others by establishing yet more specific conditions for this determinism to work. The logic of this procedure is that we shall end up arguing that there are, in the event, *no* other relevantly similar cases and that the whole complicated concatenation of evidence and analysis provides a sufficient explanation for the outcome only in that case. Since it is now being treated as a unique case, we could claim that it is a necessary explanation too, so the distinction between necessary and sufficient conditions collapses. Just as in physics, where conventional models fail in the presence of singularities, so in social science: when the case is truly unique, some standard distinctions between types of explanation break down.

Some social scientists would regard searching for determinism in ever-more limited cases as a strategy that undermines the whole point of social science, which is to produce theories of high generality. On the other hand, many historians, and quite a number of ethnographic anthropologists and sociologists, would say that this is precisely the sort of explanation that they are proud to offer. They would argue, furthermore, that, in building up a complicated skein of factors and understanding their complex interrelations in a particular case, they shall produce not only the richest possible explanation, but a different *type* of explanation. This type of explanation is what, in Chapter 7, we called a *narrative explanation*.

Narrative explanations do not necessarily have to be presented in story-like prose: we could, for example, attempt to draw a complicated diagram to summarise the narrative's structure. But, however presented, the aim of a narrative explanation is not to 'model' the case, in the sense of simplifying and reducing data to expose each of the essential causal relationships separately. Its purpose is, instead, to achieve a full and rich account of a case as a whole. Likewise, none of the factors in a narrative explanation is assumed to be working independently of the others, in the way that is assumed in the process of statistical inference. Rather, the whole point of narrative explanation is to trade parsimony for goodness of fit and closeness to the data.

On the other hand, whether narrative explanations are satisfying depends on our view of the extreme trade-off they demand in favour of goodness of fit at the expense of parsimony and generality.

Inference strategies

Many traditional methods textbooks distinguish between 'induction', 'deduction' and 'abduction' as principal strategies for arriving at explanations. We examined the meaning of the first two of these terms in Chapter 5, and showed that each forms the basis of inference. Here, we add another term to this set. *Abduction* is the process of using data to eliminate explanations to leave, in the ideal case, all but one standing as the most plausible explanation.

The distinctions between these three strategies are highly problematic. For example, *every* type of inference relies, to some extent, on deduction, so these strategies are not, in practice, mutually exclusive. For example, inductive inference relies on deductive processes in coding data. Thus, the classification developed in Example 13.2 is developed – in the first instance, at least – bottom up from data collected from unstructured interviews: most people would therefore regard it as 'inductive'. But, to order and make sense of these data, it becomes necessary to attach concepts – for example, the concepts of 'ideology', 'instrumentality' and 'social conformity' – to the five types of motivation thus discovered. In so doing, it is practically impossible to escape from ideas in currency in social science and their theoretical baggage. There is, inevitably, an important element of deduction involved in the inductive process of drawing out and labelling 'themes'.

EXAMPLE 13.2. A CASE OF BAD CONSCIENCE?

In Example 7.2, we considered how we might find out how households make decisions about dealing with their waste, and their motivations for recycling. Let us assume that – among other methods – we decided to conduct loosely structured, in-depth interviews with members of a sample of thirty households that reliably sort their household waste, to discover why they choose to do so and how much effort they put into it.

We analyse the data in the interview transcripts, by drawing out key 'themes'. In so doing, we become aware that 'conscience' is not a single code, but seems instead to reflect five

(Continued)

---

different primary motivations for recycling. We label these motivations: *ideological/environmental* (recycling as a manifestation of strong commitment to saving the planet); *ideological/anti-corporate* (recycling as a stand against excessive packaging, air-miles and other ills associated with contemporary retailing); *tokenistic* (recycling as a convenient, relatively costless way to do 'something for the environment'); *instrumental* (recycling through the local authority's scheme as the most convenient way to store and dispose of household waste); and *social conformity* (recycling because everyone else round here does it).

As we code – and also check and recheck our coding to ensure reliability of coding across the data set – we make increasingly firm and confident rules about what kinds of interview data are coded to which type. In this way, we establish an iterative relationship between data and coding.

Abduction

Abduction is sometimes called 'inference to the best explanation'. Textbooks sometimes define it as reasoning from effects back to causes: 'The next-door lawn is wet, but the street is, too, so it must have rained. So the neighbours probably haven't broken this summer's hosepipe ban again.' Because it is sometimes presented as a rapid, even intuitive, process of identifying the most likely explanation, it can sound suspiciously like 'jumping to conclusions'.

Properly understood and practised, however, abduction can be both rigorous and useful. The task is, first, to identify all the plausible explanations and then – at least in the ideal case – to rule out all but one explanation which can be shown to have face validity, coherence and clarity of causal mechanism. Example 13.3 gives a very simple example.

EXAMPLE 13.3. NINE OUT OF TEN CATS PREFER…

There is a dying fieldmouse on the mat, and we have a cat. The cat is looking rather pleased with itself and there are faint signs of mouse fur about its front claws. What explains the field-mouse on the mat?

Well, someone else's cat could have pushed it through the catflap. And there is another cat in the street. But the one down the street is a feeble and ancient mog, hardly up to catching even the slowest fieldmouse, and it has never shown the slightest tendency to deposit any prey, or indeed anything else, beyond its own litter tray.

Conceivably, one of the neighbours' children might have pushed the fieldmouse through our catflap 'for a laugh' (on the part of the child, not the mouse). But if that were the case, the poor beast would surely be lying more or less in front of the flap, not three feet away on the mat. And in any case, the children were all in school today.

In practice, we are unlikely to go through such careful reasoning. The inference to identifying the culprit would be made rather straightforwardly. And surely in ninety nine cases of dying fieldmice out of a hundred – had there been a data set so large – the self-satisfied puss would have no grounds for appeal.

Moreover, in the case of the cat's smile, the causal hypothesis quite literally has face validity…

Followers of the American pragmatist philosopher Charles Sanders Peirce are enthusiastic about using abduction to explain novel and surprising observations by creating innovative and original hypotheses, for which they claim a specially high probability of being right. But in practice, abduction is not best understood as a better strategy than – or even as an alternative to – the other two listed above.

As we saw in Example 13.1, identifying ways of ruling out rival explanations is a necessary part of warranting *any* kind of explanation, once we seek to enhance its warrant beyond a simple claim that an explanation is plausible or is one that 'the evidence tends to support'. Abduction is the principal strategy by which any kind of explanation is first developed. Furthermore, we shall see below that much empirical research with explanatory ambitions relies upon a process of falsification to rule out successive hypotheses. It follows that abduction is not best regarded as a *distinct* explanatory strategy, but rather as a process that is integral to much explanatory work in social sciences.

Abduction relies upon deduction to eliminate hypotheses: it simply reverses the process used in standard deduction. In the pure case of deduction we derive hypotheses from theories. We could, for example, easily deduce from a relevant theory a hypothesis about what a relatively young, healthy cat will do when the opportunity of a sluggish fieldmouse presents itself, and test it with an appropriate sample of domestic felines. By contrast, abduction does not begin with a set of theories. Instead, we find hypotheses in our empirical data, and then systematically eliminate them in the hope of leaving a single explanation standing, one that will be capable of reverse deductive inference to a larger theory. But the basic structure of the inference is essentially the same, in that warrant is established deductively. Conversely, in using standard deductive explanatory strategies, we have no way of choosing between deductively derived hypotheses without empirical research that necessarily involves a measure of induction.

Conclusion

These, then, are the main strategies that are used to warrant explanatory inferences in social science research. We have seen that they are by no means distinct strategies and, particularly, that deduction, induction and abduction each have essential tasks to perform, often within the same piece of research.

We shall see in the next chapter that, as we already began to see in Chapter 5, a more useful way of distinguishing different approaches to social science research is that between between-case and within-case analysis. The next chapter will therefore look at the ways in which causal explanation is attempted by means of each of these approaches.

Basic reading

For a readable discussion of necessary and sufficient explanations, see Ragin CC, 1987, *The comparative method: moving beyond quantitative and qualitative strategies*, Berkeley, CA: University of California Press.

Advanced reading

Mackie JL 1965, Causes and conditions, *American Philosophical Quarterly*, 2, 4, 245–55, reprinted in E Sosa and M Tooley (eds), 1993, *Causation*, Oxford: Oxford University Press, is a canonical statement on necessary and sufficient conditions; it provides some subtle twists and nuances for which we have no space here.

FOURTEEN

Between-case and within-case strategies

This chapter will:

- examine further the distinction introduced in Chapter 5 between within- and between-case analysis;
- demonstrate the use of causal inference in between-case analysis, using data drawn from a classic study in the sociology of education; and
- discuss causal inference in within-case analysis, and demonstrate the use of causal process tracing.

We saw in Chapter 13 that, in practice, induction, deduction and abduction are not alternative inferential strategies but that elements of each are used in varying degrees and in different combinations, in most explanatory work. It has therefore become more common (e.g. Mahoney, 2003) to distinguish between:

- inferences based on *between-case comparisons*, as is done in variable-oriented research (VOR) and case-oriented research (COR); and
- inferences based on within-case analysis, as is done in case-based research (CBR). It can also be done *within* cases used in COR.

For reasons set out in Chapter 5, it is much more useful, too, to focus discussion about inference on the distinction between between-case and within-case reasoning than on the distinction between qualitative and quantitative data. 'Qualitative' and 'quantitative' are epithets that describe types of data, not types of inference. Quantitative data can be used in both kinds of inference. And, as we also saw in Chapters 10–12, causal forces must, at some stage in the process of making explanatory inferences, be conceived qualitatively, even if the evidence used in the inference is heavily quantitative.

It remains true, nevertheless, that within-case research designs tend to use a lot of qualitative data, because CBR is typically adopted for its capacity to produce richer, less drastically reduced data sets through a more open-ended research process. But it is also true that many between-case inferences are qualitative in nature, especially in COR where the number of cases is limited either by practical considerations – for example, by the simple fact that there are not many cases of, say, global hairdressing businesses – or because of the nature of the sample that happens to be appropriate.

Between-case comparisons: deduction and hypothesis testing

Readers of earlier chapters should now be convinced that the first condition for valid inference – whether to an interpretation or an explanation – is that we have good reasons to believe that our criteria for including cases, or the relevant aspects of cases, are sufficiently robust to ensure that the data set is well formed. With a well-formed data set, we can use comparative techniques to identify patterns and associations between cases, or between aspects of the same case. If the number of cases is sufficiently large – and if we have cardinal numbers – we may be able to use statistical techniques for such purposes. But if it is not sufficiently large – or if we have only ordinal numbers – we must use either qualitative comparisons or simpler quantitative techniques.

In some cases, we can use deduction and hypothesis testing: by this, we mean the successive testing of theory-derived hypotheses about expected associations, with a view to making an inference to an explanation. But, of course, establishing association does not mean we have established causation. At most, associations *tend to confirm* or *tend to disconfirm* a theory about causation, where that theory yields an expected association or correlation that is then observed – or not – in its expected strength and distribution. Indeed, *only when an association is one that would be expected, if a particular causal explanation were true, can an association provide support for an explanation.* Even then, it is necessary to show that the association is not spurious, that it has in all probability been produced in the expected way, and that no other explanation for the association fits better.

In his classic book on methodology, *The logic of social action* (1979), Raymond Boudon offers a much cited example of how the process of deduction and hypothesis testing works. The data are old, but we shall discuss this example in detail because the debate it addresses is still important, and because the example illustrates particularly well the structure of inference and the extent of warrant that can be claimed for candidate explanations on the strength of the data. Note that this discussion employs the concept of 'distance' between variables we explained in Chapter 6: readers may like to refresh their memory before reading further.

The study used straightforward statistical data collected in 1962 (Girard and Clerc, 1964) on a sample of 20,000 pupils in France, to examine the relationship between educational achievement in the early teenage years and socio-economic background. At that time, French schoolchildren could leave full-time education any time after the age of eleven, provided they had successfully completed their primary education. The other option for pupils was to go on to secondary education. What explains whether or not children from different classes proceeded to secondary schooling? Consider Table 14.1 (from Boudon, 1981 [1979]: 138, using Girard and Clerc, 1964).

Table 14.1 Educational achievement and age of leaving primary school by socio-economic background

Educational achievement and age of completing primary school	Weekly paid manual workers (%)	Salaried workers (%)	Middle-rank executives (%)	Senior executives (%)
Pupils judged excellent or good				
Up to 11 years old	2.4	6.1	14.5	20.2
11 years old	16.4	24.2	38.4	32.7
12	13.9	12.7	10.0	7.9
13	2.4	2.1	1.6	1.0
14 and over	0.1	0.1	–	–
Pupils judged average				
Up to 11 years old	0.5	1.6	2.3	5.0
11 years old	11.7	12.5	11.8	13.3
12	16.7	16.3	8.6	8.1
13	5.7	3.3	1.7	1.6
14 and over	0.6	0.5	0.5	0.3
Pupils judged mediocre or poor				
Up to 11 years old	0.1	0.3	0.3	0.7
11 years old	4.6	3.7	3.5	4.1
12	14.7	10.2	4.8	3.4
13	8.5	5.1	1.9	1.3
14 and over	1.7	1.3	0.1	0.4
Total	100	100	100	100

Source: from Boudon (1981 [1979]: 138), using Girard and Clerc (1964); used with permission of Taylor & Francis

As we would expect, Table 14.1 shows that the children of parents from higher socio-economic groups stayed on longer in primary education and tend to have a higher chance of being judged good or excellent. Now compare these data with those in Table 14.2 (from Boudon, 1981 [1979]: 139, using Girard and Clerc, 1964) which use the same measures to show rates of entry into secondary school.

Table 14.2 shows that the probability of entering secondary school fell for the children of manual workers who were judged to be excellent or good, if they did not complete primary school before thirteen years when the percentage dropped to 45%. Children of manual workers who were judged to be mediocre showed a

Table 14.2 Rates of entry into secondary school by age of leaving primary school and educational achievement

Educational achievement and age of completing primary school	Weekly paid manual workers (%)	Salaried workers (%)	Middle-rank executives (%)	Senior executives (%)
Pupils judged excellent or good				
Up to 11 years old	79	95	84	98
11 years old	90	96	99	99
12	79	91	96	98
13	45	63	77	69
14 and over	–	–	–	–
Pupils judged average				
Up to 11 years old	69	90	87	90
11 years old	57	78	81	99
12	45	59	71	90
13	11	33	65	86
14 and over	14	27	–	–
Pupils judged mediocre or poor				
Up to 11 years old	–	–	–	–
11 years old	18	45	73	85
12	9	15	29	52
13	3	10	12	59
14 and over	8	8	–	–

Source: from Boudon (1981 [1979]: 138), using Girard and Clerc (1964); used with permission of Taylor & Francis

steadily falling chance of entering secondary school, the later they completed primary school. By contrast, unless they were judged to be mediocre or poor, children in the highest socio-economic group entered secondary school in high numbers even though they might have completed primary school as late as thirteen.

These data provided early evidence for helping us to understand a problem that continues to occupy sociologists: why do children from lower socio-economic classes have lower chances of accessing secondary – and indeed higher – education than those from higher social classes? Three theories – each specifying a particular causal mechanism – were in currency in 1962, and continue to be important in this field of research. They are set out in Box 14.1.

Rejecting competing hypotheses

The data in the two tables allow us to follow Boudon and Girard in saying something about each of these theories. Consider first the class subculture theory. If it were true, then the causal mechanism at work in a subculture would, presumably, be a *pervasive* one, and we should observe differences across the whole subset of data, irrespective of the age at which children complete primary education. We would also expect the effect to show up only for children in the lowest socio-economic class, or perhaps moderately, at most, in the next lowest class.

Table 14.2 shows, however, that this hypothesis did not hold for this population. Among pupils judged excellent or good, the differences between children from different socio-economic classes are not striking. The exception to this finding is among children who do not complete primary school until age thirteen or later: in this group, the propensity of manual workers' children to stay on in education fell much more sharply than that of the children of the salaried and executive classes. It seems, then, that for a great many children of manual workers, any class subculture that *might* have been at work is being overwhelmed by the effect of completing primary school relatively early.

Let us now consider the nature of the inference we have just made. The theory rests on identifying a particular kind of causal mechanism, from which we derived a hypothesis about the associations that we would expect to observe in the data. These data do not show conclusively that there is no class subculture effect whatsoever. Rather, as we noted above, this effect *might* have been present but has been offset or overwhelmed by other forces. So, if any effect is to be salvaged from the class subculture theory, it would have to be one that works only if other causal forces are neutral. The inference we are drawing, then, is that the class subculture explanation is *not sufficient*. The data do not enable us to draw any inference about whether or not it is a *necessary* condition to explain class inequalities in access to secondary education in 1950s France.

Next, let us look at the cognitive disadvantage theory. Again, we should expect its effect to be pervasive, because of the nature of the causal mechanism on which it rests. That is, we should predict an observable difference for all the children of manual workers. Yet we have already found that manual workers' children who completed primary school before twelve years of age seem to have had almost as high a chance of entering secondary schools as those of higher socio-economic groups with similar patterns of primary school achievement.

The structure of the inference here is the same. We examined the nature of the causal mechanism proposed by our theory, to derive an hypothesis about the expected distribution of distances on key variables. Again, we are warranted in concluding, not that there is *no* such effect, but only that it does not support a *sufficient* explanation.

Finally, let us consider the differential returns putatively expected from investing in education. What theory can we develop to tell us how this mechanism would be expected to work? Well, there is every reason to predict that expected returns from investment in education will be differentiated by the extent of prior educational achievement. For a manual worker's family, the fact that a child had performed well enough to complete primary school young and to be judged excellent or good might well be taken as *prima facie* evidence that further investment in education was worthwhile. Conversely, we should expect that more parents from executive and other better-off backgrounds would be better able to bear the costs of further education – including those whose child has not achieved highly or easily in primary school – but that even parents from these groups will not support every child into secondary school, irrespective of whether or not the child's primary performance was promising.

Can we derive anything more from this theory? It may be worth considering whether families from different socio-economic classes have different capacities to care about the 'sunk costs' of education – that is, the previously incurred costs of education. Better-off families might be less willing to 'treat sunk costs as sunk', which, economics insists, is the most rational basis for decisions in future investments. This is because better-off families might find it easier than manual workers' families to sustain the hope of offsetting sunk costs, because they may have greater overall confidence that both the education system and labour market will work well for their children. Alternatively, it may be that the absolute cost of the investment will matter more for manual workers' families, whereas the ratio of the cost of the investment to expected total future family earnings may matter more to families that are better cushioned financially against risk. If this is the case, then having already supported a child for a longer period in primary school – even for a high or moderate level of achievement – may discourage a higher proportion of manual workers' than better-off families from supporting their child into secondary education. If so, we should expect to find that the distances on the variables of age of completion matter, even within the group of high achievers but especially for less successful children.

Again, we are developing an explanation by theorising about the nature of the causal mechanism that might be at work, to derive a hypothesis about the expected distances we would find on the variables we are measuring. And indeed, this hypothesis seems to be consistent with what we observe in Table 14.2 in the differences between the socio-economic groups for children that are judged to be mediocre or poor. Moreover, fewer manual workers' children who were judged to be mediocre or poor went on to secondary school than did comparably achieving children of the better-off. Indeed, fewer of them went on to secondary school than did better-achieving children from manual workers' families. Again, the top third of the table shows that children from manual workers' families entered secondary school at a comparable rate to that of their better-off peers, provided they both achieved highly and completed primary school at a relatively young age.

The secondary hypothesis that sunk costs might matter more to manual workers' households also seems to be supported. We find in Table 14.2 that achieving high, but completing late, markedly reduced the chances of children from manual workers' families entering secondary school: it fell to just 45% of those from manual backgrounds who were judged to be excellent or good if they delayed completing primary school until thirteen years of age. Likewise, the gradient in the fall of rates of entry into secondary education was steeper for those judged average in their primary school performance, and the bottom rung was lower, too.

Inference to an explanation?

So what can we infer from these findings? Can we infer, for example, that the two limbs of the returns-to-investment theory are sufficient to explain *all* the data in Tables 14.1 and 14.2? This would be too heroic a claim, because we cannot rule out effects from class subculture and class cognitive disadvantage. All that we can say is that they must be amenable to being offset by other effects, including that which is explained by the returns-to-investment hypothesis. So our inference to an explanation based in the expected returns on educational investment is not quite complete. However, the data are *consistent with* the hypothesis, so *tend to support* it much better than any other available explanation.

The procedure we followed in this example is summarised in Box 14.2. The important point is that the qualifications we carefully inserted into our conclusions about what can and cannot be inferred from the data are not simply the product of scholarly caution. Rather, they flow from our central argument about inference to explanation which can be summarised as follows.

- Association does not in itself prove causation. Rather, explanation requires a theory that offers some reason to think that an observed association matters, in the absence of good reasons for believing that the association is not spurious.
- Absence of an observed association of the right strength, scale or direction does not in itself prove the absence of a predicted causal effect. Any effect that is operating might be offset by other effects.

Most analysis undertaken to support between-case comparative inference is much more sophisticated than this example. Today, most studies would use multivariate statistics for large-N data sets, or perhaps Boolean techniques or other structured case-comparative methods for smaller-N sets, as recommended, for example, by Ragin and his followers. Nevertheless, the *principles* of warranting an inference to an explanation are common to between-case research designs, and are neatly illustrated by this example.

BOX 14.2. DEDUCTION AND HYPOTHESIS TESTING

1 From a *theory*, identify a mechanism linking cause and effect.
2 From the *nature of cause and mechanism*, derive a *hypothesis about the expected associations, that is to say, about the expected and associated distances* on sets of key variables that can be observed and measured.
3 Examine the observed differences and determine whether the differences, if any, are of the expected *direction* and *scale*.
4 Infer from the absence of differences, or insufficient scale, that the hypothesised explanation may be *insufficient*.
5 Infer only from differences of the reverse of the expected direction and of very significant scale, and in the absence of other supporting evidence, that the hypothesised explanation may be false.
6 Infer from the presence of observations consistent with a hypothesis that they tend to support it, all other things being equal.

In the terms of our discussion in Chapter 13, the effect of class on access to education as shown by Girard's data, as it operates through the two prongs of the 'return-on-investment' mechanism, appears to be a stochastic rather than a deterministic one. It clearly does not operate in every case. Unless we believe that whether this effect works or not for a *particular* child is simply a matter of chance – because for the *whole data set*, the effect is probabilistic – it must be the case, as we suggest above, that the effect is being reinforced or offset in particular families by other effects or is working through other mechanisms that produce different outcomes. In other words, one explanation of the apparent stochastic effect in this example is that the research design is insufficiently sensitive to different family contexts. Exactly how causes, mechanisms and contexts interact to produce outcomes in particular cases requires, of course, within-case analysis, and this is why explanatory research sometimes needs to use this approach, too, even if the case will also be compared with others in the same or similar projects. This is because – as we saw in Chapter 7 – within-case analysis is distinguished for its capacity to exploit the richness of a data set and for its sensitivity to context.

Within-case investigations: process tracing

In this section, we are concerned with how within-case analysis can enable us to:

- develop explanatory theories; and/or
- reject explanatory theories, by showing that associations identified by between-case comparative analysis are in fact spurious, or that claims about necessary conditions fail because, in at least one case, the relevant mechanism or association is absent.

For reasons that we explored in Chapter 12, these explanatory ambitions place great demands on building schematic representations of causal processes by means of the *qualitative* analysis of contexts, mechanisms and outcomes (Hedström and Swedberg, 1998; Pawson, 1989, 2006, Pawson and Tilley, 1997). This is so, even when the data employed are primarily *quantitative* in nature, because – as we saw above – we need a qualitative specification of how a causal explanation is expected to work before can we derive a hypothesis that shows us what to do with any quantitative data we collect on a case.

Within-case analysis that is intended to support inferences to causal explanation is often done by using *causal process tracing*. This term is mainly used by researchers studying large-scale historical processes, but the inference procedures it describes are essentially the same as those used by researchers undertaking explanatory studies on small-scale causation in contemporary societies. It is therefore worth spending time, here, to discuss how causal process tracing is used in the process of rejecting and warranting explanatory hypotheses.

Examples of causal process tracing

Let us first look at some work by the late, great American historical sociologist Charles Tilly who uses causal process tracing *inductively* to *reject* a hypothesis and to show that the evidence *provides some support* for a better one (Tilly, 1997a). The study cited in Example 14.1 uses data from a single case to:

- make a descriptive inference about that historical case;
- draw an inference to a causal explanation, which Tilly believes to be important but which has been neglected by other historians; and then to
- reject a commonly accepted causal theory.

EXAMPLE 14.1. DOWN WITH THE REVOLUTION!

In his article 'Cities, bourgeois and revolution in France', Tilly (1997a) offers an explanation of certain aspects of the French Revolution, to the significance of which, he argues, other historians have failed to give adequate recognition.

His article concerns the period in France after the revolution of 1789 – the period on which Hollywood films such as stories of the Scarlet Pimpernel have tended to dwell. The conventional story is that, having imprisoned King Louis XVI and his wife Marie Antoinette, the revolutionaries quickly secured control of the rest of France, because – after decades of oppressive taxes and bread shortages – a majority of the population was only too glad to be rid of the monarchy and aristocracy and also the power of the clergy. Tilly casts doubt on this story, by carefully tracing the large-scale resistance to revolutionary rule.

First, then, consider his descriptive inference. Much conventional history has suggested that resistance to the revolution was generally confined to the privileged classes and their direct retainers, that it was geographically confined, and that such counter-revolts as occurred were special cases inspired more by religion than by politics. Wrong, on all counts, says Tilly. Close attention to data relating to the very local level suggests that there was resistance – and sometimes outright rebellion – against the revolution involving all classes, in almost every part of France except Paris. Tilly claims, too, that the counter-revolutionaries resented the exclusion of nobles and priests from the system of governance even though most of them were not from these groups, nor were they their retainers. Why would such people become counter-revolutionaries?

Comparing urban and the rural areas, Tilly (1997a) is able to identify, in particular, two causal context–mechanism–outcome configurations which, he believes, offer an explanation:

a   In some rural areas agrarian capitalism was well advanced prior to the Revolution, and feudalism was, in practice, long gone (context). This meant that, the formal abolition of feudalism in 1789 did not, of itself, have a huge effect. However, the centralisation of power into the hands of the Parisian revolutionaries stripped many agrarian leaseholders, as well as the nobles, of local power and influence. In particular, the lesser leaseholders, the peasantry and other landless groups were disempowered by the growing intrusiveness of the central state, by the loss of paternalistic protection previously offered by the nobility and priesthood, and by the prospect of new taxes and military conscription. Disappointment and frustration (mechanism) induced them to rebel against the new order (outcome).

b   Revolutionary France was re-organised into new *departements*, superseding old local administrative arrangements. Several cities in the north and west lost status by failing to become capitals of their new localities (context). In other areas, too, where the revolutionaries lacked bourgeois allies, they had to impose new systems on smaller cities that had economic activity associated with their former status. So, the revolutionaries faced geographically widespread opposition from displaced leaders who were still able to command loyalty (mechanism) and to mobilise counter-revolutionary resistance (outcome).

Tilly's inferences are suitably qualified. He does not claim that these two context–mechanism–outcome configurations are, even together, *sufficient* to explain the whole of the variation he observes in the social and geographical distribution of different types of resistance or in their intensity. But he makes the explicit claim that, using causal process tracing, he can warrant the claim that important causal processes explain a significant part of this variation.

It is possible, too, to use causal process tracing to warrant stronger claims of the sufficiency of causal explanations. In practice, this can only be done for cases on a much smaller scale than those used by historical sociologists like Tilly. Such cases might consist, for example, in studies of a single organisation over a limited period of time, one where fewer mechanisms are likely to operate, and where there might, in consequence, be fewer offsetting effects.

Consider again, our recycling example. Example 14.2 sets out in some detail how within-case analysis could be used first to reject a hypothesis deduced from an explanatory theory and then to warrant a better one.

EXAMPLE 14.2. A RUBBISH POLICY REVISITED

In Chapter 12 (Example 12.2 and subsequent discussion), we considered a local authority which adopted a policy on recycling which resulted in an increase in the dumping of rubbish in streets, canals, parks and other urban open spaces, and which also increased the number of disputes among neighbours. In assuming that introducing a new rule (only separated waste is collected from the kerbside) would have a particular effect (i.e. increasing the proportion of domestic waste that is recycled), the council assumed a mechanism of 'rule compliance' driven by respect for authority. We hypothesised that a 'rule evasion' mechanism might also be at work, but this hypothesis failed to explain why one mechanism operated in some areas and the other mechanism in other areas. So we needed to develop and warrant an explanation that took more account of context. Here we explain *how* causal process tracing could be used in this case to develop a satisfying explanation:

1 We interview local authority managers to develop a *narrative* based on their understanding of how the policy was supposed to work.
2 From this narrative we deduce the hypothesis underlying their policy: that the new rule is, in practice, both a sufficient and necessary condition of the hoped-for change in recycling behaviour.
3 This hypothesis is then easily rejected deductively by showing (a) that some households engaged in recycling of household waste before the rule was introduced and (b) that its effect was not consistently found throughout the geographical area covered by the rule. Let us imagine, too, that, in the course of demonstrating (b), we also discover that the local authority's data show clearly that illicit dumping of garbage and disputes about uncollected rubbish have increased since the rule was introduced.
4 We then begin to develop an alternative hypothesis, by identifying an appropriate social theory capable of explaining this particular mix of effects. For this purpose, we draw on what institutional theory says about the ways that informal institutions like neighbourhoods lead people who live in them to conform to, or to defy, formal rules, and how non-compliance or workarounds are enforced.
5 We decide to develop this theory, initially by conducting interviews with illicit dumpers. In the course of these interviews we begin to spot a 'fear of reprisal' mechanism which seems to explain the reluctance of illicit dumpers to comply with the local authority's rule. We also spot the significance of the fact that the use of differently coloured bags for kerbside collection of waste makes householders' compliance or non-compliance with the scheme highly visible to their neighbours, thus reinforcing neighbourhoods' behaviour norms in relation to recycling waste.

(Continued)

---

6   This insight suggests why behaviour in relation to recycling varies in different neighbour-hoods. We explore it further in interviews with a sample of households that conform to the rule, and this work suggests the presence of a 'social pressure to conform to formal rules' mechanism in their neighbourhoods.

7   We examine the available quantitative data on the geographical distribution of illicit dumping and the volumes of recycled waste. Together with our interview data, these patterns enable able us to develop a more refined theory about how the same rule triggers different mechanisms in different neighbourhoods.

8   Developing this theory requires us to do some formation work on key concepts. What, for example, is meant for the purposes of this study when we say that a 'neighbourhood' is an informal social institution, and what counts as 'compliance' with a formal rule? We also do some work on how variations in behaviour might be measured or coded, and how cases of 'neighbourhoods' might be selected and bounded.

9   We are then in a position to make a deductive inference about the differences we would expect to find in context–mechanism–outcome configurations if this theory holds,

10 We then seek to test this inference. We consider running a statistical test to determine whether the expected observations are present, but this requires a larger number of discrete neighbourhoods within the local authority's area than the case can provide. So we develop a COR study to compare the interaction of contexts, mechanisms and outcomes in fewer neighbourhoods, to test their congruence with our hypotheses. Because we are interested in explaining differences in outcome, a most different case selection principle is used, as discussed in Chapter 8.

If this study can show support for the hypotheses, then we could have some confidence in claiming to be able to explain why different outcomes are produced in different contexts.

The studies cited in Examples 14.1 and 14.2 – though very different in other ways – were both stimulated by the fact that the empirical evidence failed to support hypotheses derived from existing theory, and both use a mix of deductive, inductive and abductive inference to provide better ones. In principle, it is also possible to use causal process tracing in a strongly deductive piece of research, one designed primarily to test and refine existing theory. It would differ from the study discussed in Example 14.2 in that *case selection* would be theory driven and the hypotheses to be tested would be more exclusively derived from the theory rather than being informed, too, by inductive insights.

Whatever its purpose and ambitions, causal process tracing benefits greatly from the construction of flow diagrams to identify and display causal relations, including the labelling of key causal relationships. It is also helpful to employ *counter-hypothetical reasoning* to test causation. That is, for each causal influence, we would ask, 'what would have happened, if the causal influence were absent?' This process enables us to compare our observations with a counterfactual scenario to see more clearly what contribution to causation is being made by each of our postulated causal influences.

All within-case analysis also has to cope with the fundamental problem of trade-offs between competing virtues in research design. As we have emphasised throughout this book, small-N research trades generality for goodness of fit, and – in the case of process tracing – for richer understanding of causality. So the explanatory inference we can make from such studies is necessarily of qualified generality. This is not an issue for social scientists who are concerned with unique historical cases of high intrinsic interest. What matters for Tilly, for example, is whether the causal processes he traces satisfactorily explain the observed variations in resistance to the French Revolution in different parts of France; he does not aim to show that these processes explain similar variations in resistance to revolutions in other countries or at other times.

It is, nevertheless, sometimes possible to generalise the explanatory inference made in within-case analysis to similar cases. For example, our theory about the context–mechanism–outcome configurations involved in recycling of household waste might work in other local authority areas, but to make this inference, we would first need good data to show that these areas are, in fact, similar in all relevant respects. For the most part, however, the explanatory inferences that can be expected from using causal process tracing are best limited to within-case analysis, including within-case comparison (in this case, between different neighbourhoods covered by the same recycling scheme).

Similarly, within-case analysis regards the relative weighting of explanatory factors as, at most, a secondary matter. The main purpose of causal process tracing is – as it says on the tin – to trace the processes through which explanatory influences work to produce outcomes, including the way they interact.

EXERCISE 14.1. TRACING THE CAUSAL PROCESSES DETERMINING ACCESS TO HIGHER EDUCATION

In the UK, there is currently a major policy debate about why children from poor families – usually defined as children who are eligible for free meals in school – are very under-represented in the student populations of high-ranking universities.

Assume that the three candidate theories for explaining this phenomenon are those we set out in Box 14.1 in relation to differential access to secondary education.

Explain how you would use between-case and within-case analysis to test the application of these theories to the issue of access to higher education, with a view to confirming, refining or replacing them.

Conclusion

The last four chapters have shown that the ways in which we can develop satisfying explanations follow the basic principles of research design laid out in Chapter 5. In so doing, these chapters have considered ways in which we can use the controls available to observational research to mitigate the fundamental problem of causal inference.

Careful concept formation enables us to select cases or samples on the basis of deductive hypotheses about what similarities and dissimilarities in those cases or samples might be causing similar or different outcomes. Because we care about explanatory satisfaction, the causal claims for which warrant is most worth seeking are those which capture carefully specified variables or configurations of variables, or – better still – context–mechanism–outcome configurations. For the same reason, we shall usually be more interested in distal contextual factors and mechanisms than in proximate ones.

From theories about how these causal forces would be expected to work, we can derive testable statements for empirical examination. In CBR and COR, we might use causal process tracing approaches, whilst in VOR, we might use statistical tests for differences in distances. Causal process tracing might be used where we want to explore trajectories of the kind we examined at the end of Chapter 12. Doing that with VOR designs requires a great many points of quantitative data on the causal timeline. But the underlying logical structure of inference remains essentially the same, whether we use causal process tracing or certain kinds of statistical tests. The differences between these procedures have to do more with the trade-offs each procedure makes between causality and other design virtues such as parsimony and goodness of fit, and with the extent to which each procedure tends to leave us with causality which appears to be deterministic or stochastic.

The next few chapters will examine interpretation. As we shall see in Chapter 15, interpretation can sometimes provide richer accounts of the *explananda* than we might otherwise possess in *explanatory* research. Sometimes, however, interpretation is undertaken for its own purposes, rather than in support of better explanation. So we need to examine how far interpretation can actually be conducted without implying some causal claims, how far the trade-offs involved in interpretation differ from those in explanation, and how far the inferences from data to interpretation represent quite distinct strategies of argument from those used in explanation.

Basic reading

For a discussion of within-case analytic methods and causal process tracing, see Mahoney J, 2003, Strategies of causal assessment in comparative historical analysis, in J Mahoney and D Rueschemeyer (eds), 2003, *Comparative historical analysis in the social sciences*, Cambridge: Cambridge University Press, 337–72.

Good introductions to causal process tracing are also offered by George AL and Bennett A, 2004, *Case studies and theory development in the social sciences*, Cambridge, MA: Massachusetts Institute of Technology Press, and in the chapter by A Bennett in D Collier and HE Brady 2010 [2004], *Rethinking social inquiry*, Lanham, MD: Rowman & Littlefield, 207–220. This chapter is published only in the second edition.

An excellent example of deductively-driven causal process tracing is to be found in Richards P, 2011, A systematic approach to cultural explanations of war: tracing causal processes in two West African insurgencies, *World development*, 39, 2, 212–20.

Advanced reading

Valuable advanced texts on causal process tracing are the following: Gerring J, 2007, *Case study research: principles and practices*, Cambridge: Cambridge University Press, Chapter Seven; Bennett A and Elman C, 2006a, Complex causal relations and case study methods: the example of path dependence, *Political Analysis*, 14, 3, 250–67; Bennett A and Elman C, 2006b, Qualitative research: recent developments in case study methods, *Annual Review of Political Science*, 9, 455–76; Blatter J and Blume T, 2008, In search of co-variance, causal mechanisms or congruence? Towards a plural understanding of case studies, *Swiss Political Science Review*, 14, 2, 315–56; Steinberg PF, 2007, Causal assessment in small-N policy studies, *Policy Studies Journal*, 35, 2, 181–204.

FIFTEEN

Interpretation

This chapter will:

- examine the use of interpretation in social science, both as part of the research process and as a distinctive product of research;
- identify the types of, and contexts for, interpretation in social sciences;
- examine the structure of interpretations;
- show how interpretations differ from, and relate to, explanations as products of social research; and
- argue that all forms of 'interpretivism' provide poor ways to understand what is valuable about interpretation.

Introduction

In the next two chapters we turn to the issue of interpretation in social science. As in our examination of explanation, the focus will be on interpretation as a *product* or *achievement* of research.

The structure of these two chapters mirrors our discussion in the last four chapters on explanation. We shall first examine what is meant by interpretation and how interpretations are used and structured, before going on in Chapter 16 to focus on the core methodological question: how are inferences to interpretations warranted?

Interpretation: product and process

In common parlance, an interpretation provides an account of what something means or signifies, by showing why it is intelligible. This is also how many social scientists use the term. 'Interpretation', in this sense, describes one product or outcome of research. An *explanation* tells us *why and how* events take place, conditions exist or trends develop. An *interpretation* tells us about their *significance or meaning*, either to the people involved, or to those who observe or study them, or both. This simple definition serves to start our discussion of its place in social science research, although, by the end of the next chapter, we shall have arrived at a more exact characterisation.

But as well as being a particular kind of research *product*, interpretation is, of course, also an integral *process* in *all* social research, in that coding, analysis, synthesis and, indeed, all kinds of reasoning about our findings depend upon 'interpreting' data. Indeed, we shall see that even explanatory research involves a lot of interpretation.

Interpretation as a process

As a *process*, interpretation is conducted for fundamentally the same purposes, whether we are using variables or cases, within- or between-case analysis, or qualitative or quantitative data.

Consider first its use in VOR and, in particular, in what is commonly called 'statistical interpretation'. Four basic tasks must be carried out in designing, and then in drawing inferences from, statistical analysis (Moser and Kalton, 1971: 447–67). Together they constitute the process of interpretation in VOR: each captures a distinct element of the significance or meaning of the research. They are:

Categorical significance. As we said in Chapter 1, the first task is to determine whether the things we examine really do fall within the concepts in which we are interested. Using our prior understanding of the topic, we carefully *select* the relationships between variables which are worth exploring; which findings are most relevant to answering a research question; and which results to report as the headline ones.

This activity depends on sound work, both in forming concepts and in specifying the theory to be tested, because the things interpreted at this stage are concepts and theories. For example, the exercises and examples on recycling household waste we examined in Chapters 6 and 7 depended on interpreting difficult concepts such as 'conscience' and 'trust'. Their selection as variables follows from preliminary theorising about why these variables might be important in explaining the behaviour of households. Operationalising them to select all and only relevant cases to form our population is part of the statistical interpretation of categorical significance.

Instrument significance. In designing and adjusting instruments to ensure their construct validity, we must determine – perhaps on the basis of supplementary research – what research participants might have *understood*, say, by questions administered in questionnaires, or by games or roles played in experiments. This judgement involves attributing aspects of mental life to the people being studied, and interpretation, in this sense, involves making judgements about risks to *validity* and *reliability* from the design and use of research instruments.

Error significance. Next we must *weigh* the confidence that can be placed in the findings of the research, and indicate how much certainty the data provide in their support. This judgement might rest upon the result of an appropriate statistical test, but, when using qualitative data, it might equally rest on a broader judgement about the nature of the sample and the instruments used to collect and analyse the data. In other words – as we have discussed several times before – it will be informed deductively by the theories we hold about the nature and appropriateness of our research design.

Inferential significance. Finally, we must draw *inferences* from statistically significant relationships between variables. This task involves explanatory inference, as discussed in the last four chapters. Interpretation here consists in our judgement about the *degree of support* lent by our empirical findings to the larger claims we might venture to make in answering the research question. Whereas the first three tasks in statistical interpretation are conducted upon discrete statistics or discrete relations between statistics, the fourth depends upon the whole body of the analysis.

Much the same process is used in CBR and COR, or when qualitative data are used. Here too, interpretation consists in working out what analysis to carry out; how to operationalise key concepts; and what significance to attach to the resulting analyses, both for interpreting facts about the particular cases and for answering the overall research question.

Silverman's (1993) text on interpreting qualitative data in CBR and COR, for example, treats interpretation as a process involving the same four features we identified above. In the first instance, interpretation is done piecemeal by interpreting a strip from a written text, from a transcript of an interview, or from the record of an observation of some behaviour. It involves allocating a category or code stipulated in an analytic frame. Only secondarily, for Silverman, does interpretation provide an overall *synthesis* – the interpretation – as the product of the study. As with statistical interpretation, the selection of relationships to be studied rests on sound concept formation. But COR or CBR undertaken for the purpose of developing theory does not rest on deductive specification of the theory to be tested so heavily as does interpretation in VOR.

It can be seen, then, that the four tasks of interpretation are an essential part of the *process* involved in conducting *any* research. Although they are rather different from the activities commonly discussed by those who call themselves 'interpretivists' – about whose methodological arguments we shall say more below – they are, nevertheless, the fundamental activities by which *significance* is captured in the processes of designing, carrying out and reporting the findings of social science research.

Subjective and objective interpretation

In Chapter 1, we distinguished between subjective and objective interpretations as products of research. Some historians claim to provide objective interpretations that tell us what patterns of historical events signify for our own age, or what they signify for the general direction of historical change.

An example might be Colley (1992) who explores the development of a particular idea of nationhood, defined as a twentieth-century destination with which at least some readers will identify. Like much of this kind of work, it is teleological: it builds upon causal explanations to suggest that their meaning lies in their culmination; history is shown to lead to outcomes, the significance of which readers will recognise and can appreciate more fully from the interpretive argument. Teleological interpretations take trajectories: they work backwards from a point taken to be a destination, and proceed to argue that the significance of the whole trajectory stems from that destination point.

Elements in recent history that are widely thought to be causally significant for contemporary events often attract objective interpretations, too. For example, historians of the Cold War have often argued the case for or against adopting particular strategies for managing international relations subsequently (cf. Gaddis, 1997) on the basis of the normative meanings bestowed by the 'lessons of history'.

In this chapter, however, we shall not be concerned with objective interpretation, because most methodological discussion of interpretation in the social sciences – especially in sociology, criminology, business studies, anthropology and, more recently, in political science – has been about 'subjective interpretation'. By this term we mean the researcher's account of how the people being studied think and feel about a condition, an event, a problem or whatever.

The scope of subjective interpretation

'Subjective interpretation' is usually described as the study of 'meanings', in the sense of that word which we set out in Chapter 2. Researchers interested in subjective interpretation are interested in three kinds of meanings. First, they are interested in people's mental lives, including their:

- ways of classifying things;
- thought patterns, ways of arguing, ways of moving between topics;
- biases;
- attitudes;
- beliefs;
- desires, including both general aspirations and specific goals;
- motives, or reasons for action;
- intentions, acts of will and commitment;
- anticipations of the future;
- narratives about the past; and
- emotions, including hope, fear or anxiety.

Some meanings are shared by *people in the actors' context*, and so interpretive research is, second, also interested in a social group's:

- ways of categorising and classifying things;
- symbols;
- myths;
- narratives and histories (both overtly fictional and non-fiction), collective memories, historical analogies, points of reference;
- ideologies or world views;
- values;
- moral standards;
- legitimate and accepted reasons for action;
- etiquette;
- standards for work done, or normative expectations, and so on.

Third, social scientists are interested in 'thought styles', by which we mean not *what* people think but the *way* in which they think. For example, for some research purposes it may be important to interpret how rigidly people mark their categories; how dogmatically they insist on their beliefs or world views; or, conversely, how easily they accommodate negotiation and compromise (Fleck, 1979 [1935]; Douglas, 1986).

In attempting to order such long lists of things that are of interest in interpretive research, Kincaid (1996: 192–3) offers a helpful summary of the principal kinds of *meaning* which subjective interpretation seeks to capture. They are:

- *Perceptual meaning* – how an actor perceives the world, including the actions of others and the actor.
- *Doxastic meaning* – what an actor believes.
- *Intentional meaning* – what an actor intends or desires to bring about.
- *Linguistic meaning* – how an actor's verbal behaviour is to be understood.
- *Symbolic meaning* – what an actor's actions or creations, or what the phenomena in which the actor participates, represent.
- *Normative meaning* – what behavioural expectations, rules and norms an actor's actions reflect or embody.

In practice, it is very demanding for a single study to capture all of these things. In the mid-twentieth century, anthropologists sometimes had the luxury of being able to spend several years – or perhaps parts of each year for up to a decade – living with the people they studied, and were able to develop very full interpretations. Resources today rarely permit such extensive data collection. Contemporary social scientists therefore tend to concentrate their modestly sized projects on a few aspects of actors' mental and emotional lives.

Interpretive and explanatory inference

Interpretive inference is the making of arguments from evidence about what people say and do in the context in which they operate. The purpose is to draw conclusions about what they think or mean, and what significance they and other people attribute to it. Interpretation can therefore be regarded as a *special case of descriptive inference*, because its purpose is to describe a state of affairs that cannot be directly observed. Indeed, a famous advocate of interpretation in anthropology, Clifford Geertz, describes his particular method for generating interpretations as 'thick description' (Geertz, 1973b).

Questions about what people 'mean' are perfectly respectable research questions in their own right, and interpretive researchers may legitimately restrict their research to answering them. Going on to ask *why* people have come to think the way they do, or what the consequences are of their ways of thinking, involves a different type of question because answering it requires an *explanatory* inference.

Interpretations and types of research design

It is common for researchers to develop and test interpretations using case study approaches. Especially in CBR, interpretations are usually developed and tested using qualitative data.

But this need not be the case. Many attitudinal surveys – including the kinds regularly reported in the press – are used to support inferences about people's beliefs and values, and most of them use VOR designs and quantitative data. Although most attitudinal surveys are not generally regarded as interpretive work, this is nevertheless what they are, as the types of 'meanings' listed above make clear. And in Chapter 17, we shall examine a study that uses quantitative data not only to test an interpretation by using predefined codes – as do most attitudinal studies – but also to develop one of considerable richness.

Conversely, the previous chapters on explanation made clear that much CBR is conducted for explanatory purposes. So it is a mistake to suppose that CBR, qualitative research and interpretation coincide exactly, excluding other research design principles.

Researchers' and actors' interpretations

We need next to understand the distinction between *primary* and *secondary* interpretations:

- *Primary* interpretations are the claims made by *actors themselves*, expressed in speech or text or implicit in other behaviour, about how they understand their world, their problems, their relations with others and so on.

- *Secondary* interpretations are *researchers'* accounts or reconstruction of actors' primary interpretations, and are inferred from speech, writing and other behaviour. The more accurately a secondary interpretation captures the essential structure and detail of actors' primary interpretations, the greater its validity.

A closely related distinction to the one between primary and secondary interpretations is that between *emic* and *etic* interpretations. The terms were introduced by the linguistic anthropologist Kenneth Pike (1967). They are taken from the suffixes to the terms 'phonemic' and 'phonetic' which refer respectively to the *meanings* and the *sounds* of linguistic expressions; that is, what people mean to say and what other people hear:

- *Emic* perspectives on cultural life use categories which make sense to the actors being studied. Pike's – controversial – view was that emic perspectives can be validated only by the people being studied.
- *Etic* perspectives use categories that make sense independently to scientific observers, but which may not necessarily make sense to the actors themselves. They are validated by scientific procedures intended to capture their correspondence with facts. Rarely, for example, do ordinary people talk about themselves, family, friends and colleagues as being in 'cognitive dissonance', or having 'bridging social capital', although these terms may well be used by social scientists who write about them. These, then, are etic rather than emic terms.

Clearly, emic and etic styles of research can apply as much to explanation as to interpretation, but these terms are used mainly by interpretive researchers. For example, the anthropological theorist Marvin Harris developed an account of methodology (Harris, 1976) which argued that etic perspective is the goal of social research, whilst emic perspectives – or primary interpretations – are the raw material, the things to be interpreted. Pike argued, to the contrary, that capturing and documenting emic or primary interpretation is – or should be – the central goal in its own right, not least because he was sceptical about claims for the objectivity of independently generated scientific perspectives (Headland *et al.*, 1990).

For many, but not all, contemporary interpretive social researchers, the distinction between emic and etic interpretation is not the same as the one between primary and secondary interpretation. This is because they believe that secondary interpretation can and should faithfully capture and recapitulate the categories used in primary interpretation, so it should not rely on etic categories. There are few, if any, secondary interpretations written by social researchers which have succeeded in entirely eliminating etic categories, although there are plenty of examples of bad interpretive work where etic categories are smuggled in without being acknowledged as such.

In practice, emic and etic *interpretation* should probably be understood as constituting a spectrum, not a dichotomy, even though any individual *term* might be unambiguously emic or etic. We might aim to rely on emic categories, and to move our interpretation as far as we can to the emic end of the spectrum. But it is very difficult – and may, strictly, be impossible – to make any kind of permanent record that simply replicates – without *any* selection or translation – the ways in which a group of people think about their social life. This is because in the very act of recording raw data – let alone analysing them – we cannot avoid imposing our own concepts and types. This fact need not be catastrophic for secondary interpretation. But it is important for researchers to be explicit about the limits of their ability to capture all and only emic categories, and about the ways in which they have translated, selected and related concepts they take to be emic.

Two classic interpretive studies

To illustrate this point, we examine two examples of research which interpreted how groups of people understood their own practices. Example 15.1 cites research by a famous cultural anthropologist, the late Roy Rappaport.

EXAMPLE 15.1. WHAT DO YOU MEAN BY UPROOTING THAT BUSH AT ME?

Rappaport studied the Maring people in highland New Guinea (1984 [1968], 1999). He developed a rich account of the way in which conflict and war, religion, commercial exchange and kinship relations were closely related, rather than being relatively separated activities as they are in some societies. He found that they were connected by a ritual order that was closely tied to the planting of gardens, and that this was significant, because horticulture was the economic foundation of New Guinea agrarian social organisation.

He traced the important symbolic role of the *rumbim* bush, which was uprooted in declarations of war, planted in peacemaking, clasped by men, avoided by women and so on. So Rappaport's work showed how *rumbim* is to be understood not merely as a shrub, but also as a central emic concept in Maring life. In making such a large claim about the centrality of the concept, '*rumbim*', Rappaport is offering an interpretive theory of the organisation of Maring thought.

Rappaport's secondary interpretation uses concepts such as 'ritual order' – and indeed the notion of the 'centrality of a concept' – that would never appear in Maring accounts of the way their lives are organised, even if their own accounts were translated literally into English. Indeed, Rappaport's work was not intended to fall at the extreme 'etic' end of the emic–etic spectrum, but mixed emic and etic categories. Rappaport would, nevertheless, claim that his secondary interpretation has captured something of real importance about the primary interpretations of Maring life.

EXAMPLE 15.2. WHY LADS HATE EAR'OLES

Our second study is a sociological classic which interpreted the social life of a Midlands school in the 1960s and 1970s, as it was experienced by the 'lads', a group of twelve disenchanted schoolboys. Unlike Rappaport's interpretation of Maring social life, Willis's account in *Learning to labour* (1977) revealed very different understandings of authority and adolescence among groups of people in the school, including 'the lads' and a group of more conformist schoolboys known to the 'lads' as the 'ear'oles'. He explored how their different primary interpretations were involved in the conflicts between 'the lads' and 'the ear'oles'. Willis's study demonstrates the difficulty of reporting primary interpretations entirely in emic concepts. The interpretations offered by 'the lads' – and particularly the categories they used to frame their experiences, such as their references to the despised 'ear'oles' and their framing of their resistance to authority as 'avin' a laff' – occupied a central place in Willis's account of their thought style. That centrality was chosen in relation to etic concepts such as 'authority', institutions such as 'education', structural divisions between social and ethnic groups, and the labour market. This marking off of Willis's sociological interests would almost certainly not be recognised by the lads themselves. The very structure of his account of their primary interpretations makes an implicit – and, by the end of the book, an explicit – appeal to causal processes that are unambiguously theoretical and etic. Willis offers a Marxist analysis of how emic categories – particularly being a 'lad' and the disdain for education and learning that went with it – selected certain boys for, and encouraged them willingly to accept, manual jobs at the bottom of the labour market.

Why primary interpretation cannot use only emic categories

This example shows that it may sometimes be methodologically desirable to rely, at least in part, on etic categories, so long as we use them explicitly. Indeed, many researchers in sociology, business studies and political science harbour a suspicion that 'insiders' tend to provide self-serving accounts that gloss over aspects of their lives that may be unpalatable to those who read the research or to their bosses, political masters or funders. If we rely exclusively on emic interpretations we risk having our research captured by their interests or world views. Researchers who lack the resources to live and work for long periods with those they study – and who consequently rely heavily on such methods as interviews and focus groups – are especially vulnerable to this risk. Using etic categories to guide the research will not solve problems of missing or skewed data, but may help to direct questioning in ways that alert us to anomalies that should qualify our inferences.

EXERCISE 15.1. BUS CULTURE

You are conducting a study to find out how bus drivers think about their passengers, supervisors and managers, and the purposes, risks and rewards of their jobs.

You conduct interviews. You go out with for a shift with each of a sample of the drivers to watch and listen. What would you have to do to transform your field notes on what they say and do into a secondary interpretation of your own?

Now suppose that you find some drivers who feel very positive about their passengers and value providing a service for them, but are very cynical about their supervisors and the company managers. You find others to be cynical about passengers, suspecting many of being fare-dodgers or unreasonable in their demands for punctuality or cleanliness when the drivers feel they have little control over these things. These latter drivers feel they have more in common with their supervisors, although perhaps not with the managers, than they have with passengers.

Would you expect each of the drivers' emic accounts to be internally consistent? Why, or why not?

Now suppose that none of the bus drivers uses the term 'cynical'. It is therefore an etic term. However, you decide that it is entirely apposite. Do you now think you could frame the etic significance of the contrast between their two views of passengers and supervisors in a way that also makes or implies no explanatory claims?

A short definition of a secondary interpretation

We can now enrich the simple definition of interpretation with which this chapter began, by saying that a secondary interpretation provides:

- rich, patterned, structured, context-heavy categorisation and description of a set of human phenomena; either
- by reference to the ways in which actors themselves understand or feel about the phenomena of which they are part, and/or by reference to the wider trends, contexts or situations carefully selected as most relevant by the researcher; or
- by drawing upon actors' own accounts – preferably their private ones, if we can access or infer them, not just their public ones – about how they understand these phenomena, set forth in their own speech and text (i.e. the *primary interpretation*).

The structure of a secondary interpretation

Methodologists have not settled upon agreed standards for the structure and content of secondary interpretations. Standard textbooks are rather coy even about the conventional elements of a secondary interpretation, yet they are quite clear about what constitutes a decent explanation.

Many writers list elements of primary interpretations, as we have done above. They typically tell us in some detail what methods are used to create a secondary interpretation or to provide an account of a primary one: for example, open coding of data; the identification of themes; identifying relationships between categories; classifying categories; and so on. They also tell us to how check our interpretation, once we have developed it. And they provide advice about how to write up our interpretation. But they offer no more than hints about what the secondary interpretation should consist in, if it is to do its job.

The following set of elements provides our own reconstruction – based on interpretive studies we admire – of what a secondary interpretation needs, assuming a 'best practice' study in which all our assumptions and claims are explicit and clear:

1 *Unit*: the definition of the unit of analysis. In the case of Willis's *Learning to labour*, the unit for studying the schoolboys' relationships with authority is 'a Midlands school in the 1960s', whilst in Rappaport's work, the unit is '1960s' Maring social organisation'. Even if it is not always made explicit, the choice of unit reflects some background theory. If spelled out, that theory would, first, account for the unit's *relevance* for the research question. Secondly, it would give us some reason to believe that it has the *coherence* required to be treated as a unit of analysis. Ideally, third, the theory might tell us something about the *relationships* we should expect between the unit and the *context*. It should also show, fourth, how the beliefs, categories and so on, which will be reconstructed in interpretation, can be seen to be *intelligible* ones. Chapter 16 below provides a full discussion of various ways to judge the intelligibility of beliefs ascribed in interpretations.

2 *Contextual factors*: the specification of the scope of the factors that would be recognised by the people being studied as being significant for the study. In Willis's study, two key contextual factors were the limited authority of the teachers and the bleak prospects offered by the labour market. In Rappaport's study, they were the nature of military, commercial and kinship relationships among peoples in the New Guinea highlands.

3 *Context boundaries*: the specification of criteria of relevance of contextual factors for answering the research question. This raises the question of how far from the phenomena observed it is necessary to go before something is too indirectly or distally linked to the focal interest of the study. For example, Willis clearly believes that the family background of the twelve lads is beyond the scope of his interpretation of their experiences of school life.

4 *Measures*: the specification of indicators and, ideally, thresholds, to determine 'what counts' for actors as cases of things of focal interest for the study. Willis does not tell us, for example, exactly *how* conformist a boy had to be before the 'lads' would classify him as an 'ear'ole', but he does provide some indicators. In his study of how coroners form the judgement – often on the basis of limited and ambiguous information – that a death is a suicide, Taylor (1982) is careful to explore in detail the thresholds that deaths have to pass before different subgroups of coroners would classify them as suicide.

5 *Attribution* of mental life: an account of the *content* of those parts of the actors' primary interpretation of their world that are relevant for the research question; their classifications and categories, beliefs, desires, emotions, memories and so on. In Willis's study, they are the desire to 'ave a laff' and their norms of competitiveness and fair play. This element constitutes the central claim in a conventional secondary interpretation about people's primary interpretations. But without the other elements, it is hard to make sense of what is being attributed or why the particular attributions are *important*.

6 *Thematics*: the specification of particular themes and tropes – that is, the turns of speech or metaphors that frame primary interpretations – to be analysed in the study, on which the 'interpretation as synthesis' will rest. These themes and tropes are selected as being particularly central to the primary interpretations, in that they account for aspects of mental life that relate most closely to the research question. In Rappaport's work, the meaning of the *rumbim* bush is a key element in his thematics. In Willis's case, a key emic trope is the 'ear'ole', whilst a central etic one is 'manual labour'.

7 *Thematic relations*: an account of the relations between tropes and themes; for example, their mutual reinforcement, tension and fragmentation. Clearly, an interpretation must show how each is related to the others, and how strongly a claim for coherence and integration is being made. For example, a study should clearly show if it is being claimed, as Willis does, that the people being studied – in his case, the teachers and the different groups of boys in the school – operate with fragmented cognitive frames, and whether these frames are firmly structured or change with the flow of conflict.

8 *Actor–context relations*: the specification of ways in which sense-making links context and mental life either (a) for the actors themselves – for example, the lads' identification with each other in the context of the school – or (b) for other observers – for example, the meaning of Maring dances signifying peace, war, welcome, suspicion, openness to trade, and so on, to visitors from neighbouring peoples.

A secondary interpretation that sets out explicitly each of these things can be regarded as well structured. It can also be regarded as accountable, in the sense that it would be much easier for another researcher to go back to the raw data – fieldwork notes, perhaps – to check the procedures by which the interpretation was derived.

EXERCISE 15.2. MIND YOUR LANGUAGE

Consider again your interpretation for Exercise 15.1, and think, this time, about the social environments that buses constitute at different times in the day, such as the morning rush hour; late afternoon when children are going home from school; late shopping evenings; and night time after the bars have closed.

Suppose you suspect that some emic terms used by bus drivers to describe important elements in the context in which they work have different meanings at different times in the day. How would you tell? And if that were the case, what would you have learned?

Suppose, too, that bus drivers speak of passengers who cause difficulties, for example over fares, as 'irates' (the term that Hochschild's (1983) air stewards used to describe their difficult passengers). How would you work out the thresholds that the drivers use for applying this label?

Interpretation and explanation

Are secondary interpretations, of the kind we set out above, a kind of explanation? Or are they quite different from explanation, and if so, are they to be preferred to causal explanations? Some methodologists think they are both different and preferable. To see why, we first need to revisit what is meant by 'explanation'.

There is a loose, everyday sense of this word, to mean a general account of something. Perhaps that account tells us something about its nature. It might show us how it fits among other related events, states of affairs and so on. Or perhaps it tells us what notions people associate with this phenomenon; what stories are told about it; what it has come to symbolise; how people appeal to ideas of it when justifying their behaviour; and so on. If we were to allow the word 'explanation' to cover these kinds of things, then all secondary interpretations would be 'explanatory'. But this is not the meaning we have given in the previous four chapters to explanation in social sciences. Rather, we have concentrated on causal explanations which answer questions about *how* and *why* events happen, states of affairs arise and conditions occur, by tracing the influence of factors, configurations or mechanisms, or combinations of these things.

The *central* work of interpreting is not causal explanation. Rather, it is the descriptive attribution to people of any of the things we listed above, encompassed by the capacious term 'meanings'. But we need next to discuss whether, in carrying out that central task, we nonetheless have to make, or at least imply, some causal assumptions or claims.

In practice, most interpretive work in social science is undertaken as part of research which examines the causes and consequences of people's mental lives, as well as describing those lives. Most classical anthropology provided detailed examinations of people's beliefs and emotions about such things as kinship, trade or religion to provide material for building causal explanations, and this is still true of most interpretive work across the social sciences.

If we say that a householder was willing each week to separate eight kinds of household waste into different boxes and bins, and even willing regularly to drive her collections of garbage to the local recycling centre, *because* she had come to believe that this was the duty of a good citizen to the environment, then we have gone beyond interpretation. Interpretation might discover that belief, and describe how important it is to her. It might even document how the householder came to form it. But it requires an explanatory inference to argue that her newfound commitment was *caused* by her acquiring that belief, rather than, for example, the belief being a rationalisation adopted after beginning the practice. In particular, it is an *ideational* explanation because it appeals to a factor rooted in her ideas.

Many methodologists and philosophers of social science have argued that interpretation should and can be done in ways that neither make assumptions about causation nor imply causal statements of this kind. The view that interpretation *should* be done without carrying any explanatory baggage – and indeed that it should be done *instead* of explanation – is called 'interpretivism'.

Three types of 'interpretivism'

'Interpretivism' is used to describe those views about the status of social science knowledge which consider causal explanation to be epistemologically suspect. Interpretivism holds that knowledge achieved in secondary interpretation is valuable but that it is fundamentally different from that claimed for explanation. It follows from this view that interpretivists must believe that interpretation can be done without carrying any explanatory freight.

To complicate matters, there are several interpretivist positions. Each uses slightly different arguments.

Type I interpretivism: reasons not causes

If ideas motivate, inspire or lead people to act or refrain from acting in particular ways, then it might be supposed that there is a causal relation between ideas and action. But some interpretivists deny that *reasons* for actions *cause* them. Those who take this view can be called Type I 'interpretivists'. The best-known advocates of this view are Wittgenstein (in his later work in 1953) and Winch (1958). Winch presents several arguments for rejecting the claim that reasons have causal force on actions. He argues, first, that reasons are used in primary interpretations in *justification* (not, Winch emphasises, necessarily wrongly so): they appeal to the standards prevailing in the actor's situation to make actions acceptable. The relationship between reason and action then is one of story-telling and making action intelligible, not one – in his view – of causal explanation.

Second, he argues that if something is amenable to causal explanation, then it must be capable, at least in principle, of being predicted, just as a law in physics predicts the consequences of applying a force. He insists that human life in general is not like this, and that, however regular and patterned they might be, reasons or motives for an action are not like physical laws. Indeed, he claims that, as an empirical generalisation, human actions are unpredictable.

Third, Winch doubts the value of regarding reasons, as realistic accounts would do, as objective and independent mental states which are caused by, and in turn cause, actions. Instead he insists that they are better conceived as moves in games in which actors engage in challenging each others' primary interpretations.

His fourth argument is that the relationship between the content of a reason and the action is 'internal' to an institution. Winch uses the example of a sergeant calling 'eyes right!' and the troops obeying. For Winch, obedience is intrinsic to the institutions of military life, so invoking the reason and acting in the way that it suggests are connected by the logic of the institution rather than causally. Contemporary interpretivists call this connection a 'constitutive' one (Wendt, 1999).

These arguments have several weaknesses. The first is that they tend to imply that we should not look behind the primary interpretation but they do not explain why, other than by appealing to scepticism about the independent existence of abstract states of mind. Second, whilst it is not obvious that human affairs are as unpredictable as Winch assumes, this argument is not relevant to this debate. Not all causal explanations do imply *point* predictions. They may imply only general trends, and may involve stochastic rather than deterministic causation. Third, the general scepticism about invoking states-of-mind is unwarranted, as we showed in Chapter 4 when we offered criticisms of the general positivistic argument against realism about things that cannot be observed directly, but about which we must make inferences. Fourth, the fact that people often violate institutions – whether by outright rebellion, quiet subversion, ridicule or by circumventing or even just ignoring them – makes it difficult to sustain the idea that our reasons typically have only, or even mainly, constitutive relations with our actions. Institutions often have a more fragile hold over us than Winch's argument suggests; moreover, the people studied by social researchers invariably recognise the fact. In fact, many reasons have no constituent relations with an institution. For example, there is no institution of 'everyday environmentalism' to which the householder's sense of duty to recycle is intrinsic.

Many contemporary social scientists who follow Winch's position regard interpretation as superior to causal explanation, because they believe that it allows for: (1) richer, subtler accounts of thought than the crude, mechanical relations which, they believe, is all causal explanations permit; (2) richer roles for contextual factors than causal explanation allows; or (3) more contingent relations between thought and action than the law-like generalisations which, they believe, are insisted upon by causal explanation.

Yet, as the previous four chapters have shown, if causal explanation is done well, then it can capture subtlety, richness, context, particularity and contingency. Indeed, the point of careful causal process tracing is precisely to produce fine-grained, within-case analysis. Indeed, we would argue that causal process tracing aspires to greater satisfaction than can be offered by interpretation, which is restricted to actors' thought worlds.

Type II interpretivism: no determinate facts about reasons

This position claims that there is no way of determining which of a variety of plausible secondary interpretations is true. Readers of Chapter 4 will already be familiar with this view under the title of relativism. Relativism may be compatible with denying that reasons are causes, but the non-causal view of reasons does not deny that there are determinate facts about people's reasons. It is logically possible to hold, as Type I interpretivism does, that there may be determinate facts which help us decide something is, or is not, a reason for the actions of a given person or a group, but at the same time to deny that its relation to action is causal. We gave some reasons in Chapters 3 and 4 for finding this view unconvincing.

Type III interpretivism: indefinite variety in primary interpretations

Finally, there is an influential type of interpretivism which is usually associated with 'postmodernism' or some kinds of 'poststructuralism' (e.g. Rorty, 1979). Some scholars argue that there is, in principle, an indefinite variety of *primary* interpretations. People are so various in their ways of thinking that it is possible for them to believe, feel, classify and so on in almost any way at all. This is of course a highly controversial *empirical* claim. For the record – although we have no space to argue this in detail here – we think it implausible, on the evidence that empirical social science offers about the patterns of diversity in human culture. And surely, thought could only float so freely from its subject if there were *no* systematic causal connections between experience and belief – which amounts to Type I interpretivism – or if there are no determinate facts for which experience stands proxy – which amounts to Type II interpretivism or relativism. That is, it is not obvious that Type III interpretivism is a distinctive position from the other two types.

Weber and 'understanding'

Max Weber, one of the founding figures in social science, adopted a weaker position which is close to, but not the same as, interpretivism as we have defined it. He argued that explanation and 'understanding' are fundamentally different strategies for generating knowledge, even if, in practice, interpretation provides materials used in larger explanations. Weber appeared to suggest that 'understanding' – which captures the way that people think and value – is achieved by 'empathy' which, in turn, is not a form of inference but a direct insight.

Few commentators on Weber's work are convinced that he clearly elucidated what non-inferential empathy would be, and how it would deliver reliable and valid knowledge sufficiently robustly to count as social science (Hollis, 2002 [1994]). In his empirical work, Weber proceeded by conventional inference, using historical and contextual evidence, weighing it carefully and qualifying his claims. Indeed, Kincaid (1996: 191–221) argues that no one has been able to show that there is a non-inferential strategy of empathetic reconstruction which meets standards of validity and reliability, let alone the other standards discussed in this book.

Second, however, Weber argued that even secondary interpretations must be '*adequate* at the level of cause'. He recognised that interpretations cannot avoid being judged by standards appropriate to explanation, even if demonstrating the structure of a causal relation is not their principal purpose. But does this mean that interpretation can never be done without bringing in the explanatory assumptions or implications which the strict interpretivist seeks to exclude?

Does interpretation necessarily involve explanation?

Can interpretation – *in practice* – remain silent about explanation and causation? Can we perform secondary interpretations coherently and satisfyingly without implying any explanatory claims about how people came to acquire their beliefs, emotions and categories, or about the consequences of their mental lives for their actions or for their ways of organising?

These questions matter not only for philosophical debates about the status of interpretations, but also for the practical task of designing research and qualifying inferences. If we cannot exclude all explanatory claims from our interpretations, then we had better be explicit about them. In particular, we should be clear which claims are untested or unfounded assumptions; which rest on well-researched evidence; which are deduced from other theories; and which are empirically tested in the study which developed the interpretation.

There are three good reasons why we should expect that interpretation will rest upon, and in turn imply, causal claims. The first has to do with how we select certain categories, beliefs, emotions and so on as being *important*. Why is the *rumbim* so important for Rappaport's account of Maring thought? Why is the distinction between the 'lads' and 'ear'oles' so important in Willis's work on Midlands schoolboys? A simple answer could be that the Maring thought *rumbim* to be important and told Rappaport so, and the schoolboys likewise insisted to Willis that these categories mattered to them. But that answer would not have satisfied those researchers, nor should it satisfy us. If – having looked at actions as well as claims, and at context as well as individuals – we decide to accept people's claims about the importance of certain categories in their thought, we shall start to think about the work those categories do for these people and why they matter so much. We could refer to the ways in which these categories inspire people to act or refrain from acting. We might point to the role they play in shaping relations with each other and outsiders. But these would be causal claims. 'Inspiring action' and 'shaping relations' are placeholders for causal relations between ideas and behaviour: otherwise, they have little meaning.

The second reason has to do with the inferences that people – not only social scientists – make from what actors say and do to what they think. Human beings readily rely on abductive inferences that 'only someone who thought in this way would produce the sort of speech and behaviour we are observing' or 'we can only understand what these people are doing, if we understand this behaviour to mean a particular thing'. For example, we can only understand what we observe people doing in church if we have some understanding of worship and its purposes. But these are causal inferences, because they are schematic arguments about *what must have brought* about the patterns of speech and/or behaviour we have observed.

The third reason is that to design research capable of developing an interpretation, we select methods of data collection, analysis and even data interpretation, using the four processes identified at the beginning of this chapter. Those methods rest on a theory. The theory postulates that, if we collect only these data in only these ways, and then record and analyse them using only our selected procedures, then we shall capture valid and reliable information from which we can draw sound inferences about how actors think. If that theory is true, then it must involve some causal mechanism by which carrying out particular activities of data collection – say, observing or interviewing – will induce actors, knowingly or unknowingly, to reveal evidence about their mental lives. So the very act of doing interpretive research rests on a causal claim about how primary interpretations reveal themselves in ways that can be satisfactorily captured in secondary ones.

For these three reasons, most interpretive researchers cannot, in practice, achieve interpretations that are free from explanatory claims. In Example 15.3 we illustrate the first reason, by demonstrating that even an interpretive researcher who claims to develop interpretations that carry no explanatory freight cannot do so. This is because, without implying explanatory claims, the researcher cannot show us what is important about actors' mental lives.

EXAMPLE 15.3. COCKFIGHTING MEN

In a famous interpretive study, the anthropologist Clifford Geertz identifies the explicit and implicit rules that governed behaviour within the institution of the cockfight which held a central place in the life of Balinese males in the 1950s and 1960s. Here is a selection from Geertz' own list of the informal, unspoken rules (1973a: 437–41):

- A man should almost never bet against a cock owned by a member of his own kin group.
- If your own kin group is not involved, you should bet on the cock of your nearest allied kin group.
- Cocks from villages some distance away from the location of the fight are almost always the favourites, because only a man confident of his cock's fighting prowess would dare to travel any distance for it to fight.
- Seldom will two cocks fight, in neither of which any local group has both a social reason and a financial stake.
- People involved in the *puik* relationship of hostility will and are expected to bet very heavily, even maniacally, against each other to attack the other's masculinity and defend their own.
- The centre bet is made up of bets from allies who are locally central to the social order, not outsiders' money.
- You may borrow for a bet but not in one.
- It is a bad thing to bet against the centre bet, unless it is small and you do not do it too often.

From informal rules and norms like this, Geertz detects institutional constraints and imperatives that clearly had causal force in shaping the behaviour of Balinese men. Second, he explains in terms of status-seeking why men enter their prize cocks for tournaments which commonly led to the death of the cocks. Finally, he explains the persistence of cockfighting, by referring to its role in providing Balinese men with a means of acting out and 'commenting upon' their social organisation.

Geertz goes on to show how the function of display fits alongside other episodes of ritualised social display in the Balinese social order of the period, and enriches the claim that it is functional in managing passion and providing a conduit for status conflict and competition with a distinctive and much quoted twist:

> What sets the cockfight apart from the ordinary course of life, lifts it from the realm of everyday practical affairs, and surrounds it with an aura of enlarged importance is not, as functionalist sociology would have it, that it reinforces status discriminations (such reinforcement is hardly necessary in a society where every act proclaims them) but that it provides a metasocial commentary upon the whole matter of assorting human beings

(Continued)

> into fixed hierarchical ranks and then organising the major part of collective existence around that assortment. Its function, if you want to call it that, is interpretive: it is a Balinese reading of Balinese experience, a story they tell about themselves. (1973a: 448)
>
> The tenor of this passage makes it clear that Geertz wants to explain the institution of cock-fighting by reference to the imperative to provide such commentaries. In short, *primary interpretation* carried out by means of a cockfight is something that can be explained by reference to the social imperatives that create a demand for such lay interpretations:
>
>> Attending cockfights and participating in them is, for the Balinese, a kind of sentimental education. What he learns there is what his culture's ethos and his private sensibility ... look like when spelled out in a collective text. (1973a: 449)
>>
>> [I]t brings together themes – animal savagery, male narcissism, opponent gambling, status rivalry, mass excitement, blood sacrifice – whose main connection is their involvement with rage and the fear of rage, and binding them into a set of rules which at once contains them and allows them play, builds a symbolic structure in which, over and over again, the reality of their inner affiliation can be visibly felt. (1973a: 449–50)
>
> This sentence is nothing other than a functional explanation of an institution by reference to its causal role. Geertz would loathe this description of his work, but it seems hard to deny the tissue of explanations running throughout his interpretation. Nor could it be otherwise: for without them, we should not understand why the ideas he attributes to Balinese men are ones that are intelligibly related to what Geertz observed them doing.
>
> His defenders might argue that his purpose is to use the case study to develop rather than to test his theory, but even this process requires careful warrant.

This example suggests that, instead of trying to peel interpretation away from explanation, we should do two things. First, we should make the explanatory claims in our interpretations more explicit, and, second, offer evidence for them. In short, we should regard the causal implications of these claims not as untested – or untestable – *interpretive insights*, but rather as *hypotheses* for further explanatory research. The explanatory stage of the research may, of course, be postponed for practical reasons, if, for example, PhD students and other new researchers lack resources for large-*N* explanatory work. But, nevertheless, the significant contribution to knowledge made by the explanatory claims on which interpretations rest should be recognised as such.

Conclusion

Interpretation is an important strand of social science in its own right. It has, for example, been the core business of much anthropology for over a century. Increasingly in recent decades, and especially since the abandonment of aspirations – never realised – for behavioural approaches, other disciplines, too, have committed more resources to interpretive studies. Understanding how people think is central to a great deal of social science.

We have shown that there are important tensions in deciding just how far we can hope to rely on primary interpretations in constructing secondary interpretations. Interpretation is much more systematic and analytic than simply recapitulating what we hear. It must follow a structure. It must emphasise what is important in the primary interpretation and show why it is important. This depends on theory.

The best interpretive research has often been done in conjunction with explanatory work. Researchers want to know *why* people think the way they do, and what the *consequences* are of their climates of ideas. We have argued that it is very difficult to construct secondary interpretations which convince readers that they are interesting and important, without making at least some causal claims. Often, it is useful to test at least some of these claims in the same study. Even if that is impossible – for reasons of time, funding or limitations in the data – it is important to declare the explanatory cargo in your research report.

For such reasons, the various positions which attract the label 'interpretivism' provide misleading accounts of what in interpretation is valuable to social science.

The next chapter will examine in more detail what has to be done, to test, evidence and provide warrant for interpretations.

Basic reading

Hollis M, 2002 [1994], *The philosophy of social science*, rev. edn, Cambridge: Cambridge University Press, is useful on the status of subjective interpretation.

Geertz C, 1973, Deep play: notes on the Balinese cockfight, in C Geertz, *The interpretation of cultures*, London: HarperCollins, 412–53, is an accessible classic study using interpretive inference.

An early, influential, short and readable statement of a philosophical argument for interpretation and against explanation is to be found in Winch P, 1958, *The idea of a social science and its relation to philosophy*, London: Routledge & Kegan Paul.

One of the best-known contemporary advocates of interpretation is Norman Denzin; see Denzin N, [1989] 2001, *Interpretive interactionism*, London: Sage.

Advanced reading

For a critique of risks in statistic interpretation, see King G, Tomz M and Wittenberg J, 2000, Making the most of statistical analyses: improving interpretation and presentation, *American Journal of Political Science*, 44, 2, 341–55.

For a philosophical critique of interpretivism, see Kincaid H, 1996, *Philosophical foundations of the social sciences: analysing controversies in social research*, Cambridge: Cambridge University Press.

For a defence of interpretation by an historian of political thought, see Bevir M, 2004, Interpretation as method, explanation and critique, a reply, *British Journal of Politics and International Relations*, 6, 156–61.

SIXTEEN

Warranting interpretations

This chapter will:

- consider various standards for assessing whether an interpretation is sound or otherwise, or better or worse than another;
- discuss how to make more, rather than less, intelligent trade-offs between different virtues in interpretive research design; and
- examine standards and procedures for demonstrating that an interpretation is warranted.

In Chapters 13 and 14 we discussed standards used to warrant inferences from empirical research to explanations of states of affairs in social life. One important conclusion was that there are better or worse explanations, and so an important issue in designing good research is to understand what makes them so. In this chapter, we examine whether there are also standards to tell us which are better or worse *interpretations*, by discussing how we can make warranted inferences from data to interpretations. In so doing, we shall underline, yet again, an important theme that has run throughout the book – that is, all research designs must trade off important virtues, such as goodness of fit, parsimony, causality and generality. So we must also consider how we can make more, rather than less, intelligent trade-offs between such virtues in making interpretations, particularly secondary ones.

Warranting secondary interpretations

You will recall that in Chapter 15, we defined a secondary interpretation as a special kind of descriptive inference about actors' thought worlds, as they relate to phenomena of significance for our research. At the end of that chapter, we concluded that this inference comprises, in effect, descriptive *hypotheses* about:

- what kind of *mental life* people have in relation to these phenomena, including what they believe, feel, hope and fear about them; how they classify and categorise them; and how they understand the past and anticipate the future;
- how those mental phenomena are *anchored* in their situation and context.

We further concluded that, in so far as secondary interpretations involve some causal claims, hypotheses offered by interpretations may be explanatory ones and, if so, should be capable of being stipulated and tested as such.

In this chapter, we shall build on these arguments by considering what makes a *good* secondary interpretation. We shall assume that readers accept our previous arguments (Chapters 3 and 4) for a realist epistemology, our critique of relativist epistemological claims both generally (Chapter 4) and in respect of interpretation (Chapter 15), and our arguments for the potential for validity in explanatory inference (Chapters 10–13). It follows from these arguments that we reject the claim that there is no independent basis for judging one interpretation to be better warranted than another. This chapter therefore examines how we can make this judgement.

In discussing what makes a better or worse interpretation, we shall focus on methodological issues. By contrast, much of the literature on interpretive research deals either with method – by describing procedures for checking interpretations, especially with the people being studied – or with the kinds of epistemological issues we discussed briefly in Chapter 15. In particular, few previous discussions of interpretive research deal with trade-offs between competing virtues in research design.

The first problem we need to address has to do with our responsibilities, respectively, to the people we study and to the people who read and use our research. This problem is usually captured in the claim that interpretations should, above all, be 'intelligible'.

Intelligibility of interpretation

It is often claimed that the purpose of an interpretation – as opposed to that of an explanation – is to render intelligible to the reader the phenomenon being interpreted. It follows that a better interpretation is one that renders it more intelligible, whilst a worse one renders it less intelligible. This statement seems indisputable and clear, but, in practice, intelligibility is not a straightforward notion, and it does not offer an unambiguous standard for good interpretation.

Consider the problem of interpreting the thought worlds of peoples whose beliefs and practices are very different from our own, and indeed from those of most readers of social science research. For example, some important aspects of the thought world of the highland New Guinea people we looked at in Chapter 15 are quite different from that of most Western Europeans. Similarly, as we shall see below, urban street criminals operating in downtown St Louis use *argot* which reveals a thought style and a view of the world that are in important respects very different from those of upright citizens living in the same city.

So the problem is this. On the one hand, the criterion of *goodness of fit* requires that we describe the mental lives of such people as faithfully and fully as possible. In so doing, we must set out beliefs, categories and emotions that are not held, used or felt by most readers. But, on the other hand, the aim of making their lives intelligible to readers requires us to presume that, in many relevant respects, the people being studied are, at least in some respects, *similar to* them.

All human beings have to eat, drink, find shelter, reproduce, bring up children and deal with illness and death. They also have to co-operate on projects that no human being or nuclear family alone can manage; sustain an appropriate standard of living; find some institutionally stable way of distributing any surplus they produce; develop systems of social cohesion to contain risks of schism or violence; and hold individuals to account for the performance of whatever functions they are allotted. The constraints of a recognisably human existence cut in at an early stage in human history, at fairly low levels of technological development and at relatively small scales of social organisation. So if we cannot recognise that aspects of the thought worlds of the people we study relate to these common activities, then we are, in effect, taking our study outside the social sciences.

To render the lives of those we study intelligible, social science therefore extends to them some rather elementary principles, variously labelled *rationality*, *charity* and *felicity*. All three principles teach us to assume that the activities and beliefs of people we study make sense in relation to activities that any human beings will have to undertake, and that at least some of their categories and beliefs will be of a mundane and straightforward kind. This is usually considered to be a helpful way to proceed, even if we go on later to identify and interpret categories, beliefs and emotions that are less familiar to us, and to explore their relationships to these more fundamental ones.

Rationality

But these three principles are also, in practice, rivals, for they offer prescriptions that are not altogether compatible with each other. Consider first the philosopher Karl Popper's principle of *rationality* (Popper, 1983 [1967]: 359). Popper recognises that – as an empirical claim – the proposition that people generally behave in ways that are 'appropriate' to their situations and their purposes is false. But he nonetheless believes that – as a maxim of good methodology – we should always be willing to jettison other parts of our theories before we are prepared to jettison the principle that people are fundamentally rational in this respect.

Founding a methodological maxim on a false generalisation is, of course, highly problematic. And it is not clear what would count as 'appropriate' (Popper's word) behaviour. If we assume that any behaviour is 'rational', then the concept of rationality loses any independent content and meaning. But, if we assume that 'rationality' implies some standards that are independent of a particular context, then we would need to work out where exactly the line is to be drawn between rational and irrational behaviour. And if, in the process, we come to believe that the actions or beliefs of the people we study are 'irrational', does that necessarily make them uninteresting, or less worthy of being interpreted in ways that are faithful to their own perceptions of their experiences? Or does it just mean that we have drawn the standard of rationality too narrowly, and failed to make our interpretation meet the standard of making the people we study intelligible? For people's thought worlds can be intelligible, even when they do not follow an economist's standard of rationality. Consider Example 16.1.

EXAMPLE 16.1. HE'S A SNITCHER, BUT I SNITCH ONLY WHEN I MUST

In their much cited criminological study of street criminals in St Louis, Missouri, Rosenfeld *et al.* (2003) discuss the apparent irrationality involved in 'snitching' – the practice of criminals informing on other criminals to the police in return for material rewards or reduced punishments. Data collection for this study consisted in interviews with twenty street offenders, who are actively involved in such activities as shoplifting, illegal drug use and dealing, assault and armed robbery. Interviewees were recruited through the agency of an active member of this underworld, but the study demonstrates that it is not necessary for researchers to live for a long time among the people to do good interpretive research.

Snitching offends against the strong code of behaviour – what the authors call the 'code of the street' – that governs behaviour and relationships between street criminals in St Louis. It can attract terrible retaliation and long-term stigma, if discovered. It might, therefore, be considered irrational for street criminals to snitch, and none of those interviewed considered themselves to be 'snitchers'. Yet the interviews suggested that snitching is widespread and that most street criminals sometimes snitch.

The authors reconcile these apparent contradictions by making an important statement about how street criminals classify 'snitching': criminals distinguish between *playing* the snitch and *being* a snitch. In a social context in which their everyday lives are not generally protected by law-enforcement agencies, street criminals are often forced to *play* the role, to access police protection, or to escape police harassment, or perhaps to get a reduced sentence once caught. But this does not count as *being* a snitcher, as long as (a) they do not offer information *voluntarily* to the police in the hope of gain, (b) they inform only in self-defence and (c) their snitching is victimless, in that it is not intended to result in harm to a fellow criminal – except, perhaps, in retaliation for a wrong or to 'take down' someone who has become over-mighty.

The authors show, then, that the decision to inform is a complex and constrained one, and can be understood only in the particular context of life on the street. They argue, too, that while the code of the street is a powerful constraint on behaviour, it is not followed unthinkingly. Rather, street criminals are constantly involved in making careful and rational calculations about the anticipated costs and risks involved in following or departing from it, within the system of categories of 'being' and 'playing'. Classification forms part of the constraint, as well as a resource for self-justification.

(Continued)

But they show, too, that snitchers make such judgements in an unstable world where risks and costs are unpredictable. As a result, snitching is an important source of violence on the streets, because it gives rise to huge tensions among street criminals, ones that the 'code of the street' can only partly control. Furthermore, the authors argue, life on the street has become less predictable as a result of the recent shift toward harsher penalties and lower tolerance even of minor crime, because this shift has ratcheted up the pressures on street criminals to snitch and also the violence of the retribution for snitching.

Rosenfeld *et al.* do not refrain from offering an independent commentary on their respondents' accounts of their snitching behaviour. They acknowledge, for example, that the practice is dysfunctional for the street-crime community and point to the self-delusion involved in the claim that snitching can be victimless. In such ways, they demonstrate the 'irrationality' in the snitches' accounts of their behaviour, at least when judged in narrow terms.

Yet, the authors also claim that their interpretation of the 'meaning' of snitching to those involved in street crime is a useful one, not least in understanding the interrelationships between criminal justice policy, policing strategies and increasing levels of street violence. They show, moreover, that presenting an intelligible interpretation of snitching involves understanding not only the complex and competing pressures on criminals that result from the life they lead on the streets, but also the ways in which even their deluded and self-serving accounts of snitching help to frame the ways that they perceive, manage and choose between different risks. Thus, the authors' secondary interpretation reveals that both the behaviour of snitches and their accounts of their behaviour are – in emic terms, and in the specific context in which the snitchers find themselves – consistent and rational.

Charity

Because of the difficulties in determining how far we can extend the standard of rationality from that used in economics, some researchers might prefer Davidson's principle of *charity* or 'rational accommodation' (2001 [1984, 1977]) to Popper's rationality principle. Translated into a methodology for interpretive research, Davidson's principle implies that secondary interpretations should always seek to interpret the categories and beliefs of the people being studied in ways which make as many as possible of them true and which also make them as consistent as possible with each other, in so far as this aim is also consistent with what we, as researchers, think we know – from independent evidence – about their environment, situation, relationships and so on. Davidson subsequently (2001) qualified – and in the process weakened – his principle, by insisting that what matters more than the congruity of primary with secondary interpretations is ensuring that actors' claims – and, presumably, their actions and behaviour – are intelligible in the light of our theories about their context and condition.

But as McGinn (1977) pointed out, we can often render people's mental lives *intelligible* using etic concepts: it is not necessary to rely exclusively on their emic concepts to comply with this maxim. For example, Example 16.1 contextualises changes in life on the street in wider changes in criminal justice policy and policing practices which, the authors show, are not fully intelligible to the snitchers, except in terms that Rosenfeld *et al.* understand but do not endorse. The snitchers perceive the increasing involvement of the police in the everyday life of the street – even at moments when no crime is being committed – as oppressive and unfair, whereas the readers are invited to understand it as a response to political pressures to bear down on crime by more strongly regulating and inhibiting the activities of street criminals.

If we accept the interpretive strategy of Rosenfeld *et al.*, it would be difficult also to accept Grandy's (1973) reformulation of the charity maxim as a principle of *humanity*. Grandy's principle asks us to interpret actor's beliefs, desires and behaviour – and the relations between them – in ways that make them as similar as possible to our own. This formulation has been widely criticised (e.g. Lukes, 2007) for being even more chauvinistic than Davidson's, because it would make us reluctant to grant that other people think in ways that are different from our own.

Felicity

Whereas Popper offered a maxim for explaining actions, and Davidson and Grandy one for interpreting people's beliefs, the sociologist Erving Goffman offered one for understanding what people mean in the flows of their conversation. Goffman (1983) argues for a methodological principle of interpretation which he calls 'Felicity's Condition' (with capital letters). He claims that it should underpin all good interpretations of talk and text, and that it should 'lead us to judge an individual's verbal acts not to be a manifestation of strangeness' (Goffman, 1983: 27).

Goffman's argument places great emphasis upon 'felicity conditions' for different kinds of utterances. This concept was taken from work in the philosophy of language by JL Austin and John Searle which postulates that it is possible to specify general conditions in which a particular utterance can be interpreted as being sincere, and in which, therefore, its 'real' meaning is the same as its face meaning.

Goffman distinguishes truth from felicity conditions. Consider the following exchange:

A: There's a good film on tonight.

B: Don't think you can get around me like that.

On the face of these utterances, a factual claim combined with an evaluation is offered, but answered with a brusque imperative. Literally, the exchange is a *non sequitur*. B refuses to answer A on the matter of A's sentence. What do A and B *mean*? The conditions under which we can say whether it is true that there is a good film on tonight are largely irrelevant to answering that question. And there are no truth conditions for a command like B's. Instead, Goffman's argument would be that we need to attend to the circumstances presupposed by A and B, within which their intentions can be made intelligible. More precisely, to interpret what they mean we need to identify the situations they each want their utterances to bring about.

Suppose A and B are sexual partners who have had a serious argument, B has not forgiven A, but A wants to make peace, but without offering an apology. If we can show evidence for these conditions, then we can venture the hypothesis that A's sentence is an invitation, and that it is intended to create a situation in which A and B make up, while B's reply is intended to reject that invitation and to signal a continued feeling of grievance. Then the exchange makes sense, and B's reply follows from A's utterance. The interpretation process then has the following structure. A set of contextual conditions is supplied. These constitute the felicity conditions for the attribution of intentions for the effect speakers want their utterances to have (what the speakers *mean*). That effect is called the illocutionary force (Austin, 1962; Searle, 1969). When we have identified and evidenced felicity conditions and illocutionary force, we have shown that the utterances are sincere, sane and appropriate responses to the speakers' circumstances. That, in Goffman's view, is the essence of interpreting what people mean.

Goffman also points out that on the face of utterances, we constantly breach the formal conditions for sincerity, yet do so in ways that can be shown to be felicitous. For example, we can use the same sentence with quite different meanings when we utter it straightforwardly and when we use it as a joke, a rhetorical question, a deliberate exaggeration or with an intention to deceive. Goffman (1974) calls the use of the same word or phrase with different meanings 'keyings'.

Thus, in his own work on the behaviour of patients in psychiatric hospitals, Goffman took a particularly humane and broad view of sanity. Indeed, he argues that, if we can find a way of understanding and specifying the premises on which a paranoid person acts, then we should be able to interpret their behaviour in ways that will make sense under the conditions in which they find themselves. And it should usually be possible – on this principle – to make sense of the cognitive processes, emotions and behaviour of most people, even those who experience ways of thinking and ways of speaking far from our own.

So, as a rule of thumb, the intelligibility principle seems sensible, but is not altogether satisfactory, because it has no single, uncontested meaning. We have argued against narrow rules such as rationality as economists would understand it, or a presumption of rule-following as constituting 'appropriate' behaviour. Likewise, we have suggested that the principle of charity too may be too rigid if it insists on interpretations that make people's beliefs more accurate or more consistent than they actually are – ones that, in other words, trade too much goodness of fit for too much parsimony.

Felicity's Condition was formulated for speech rather than action. But in many ways its injunction to specify circumstances is a better guide, although it remains insufficiently precise. Understanding the circumstances in which ideas and behaviour are formed usually involves making some explanatory claims which rule out 'strangeness' by rendering behaviour an explicable response to context. Moreover, it represents a better trade-off specifically for interpretation – given the variety of primary interpretations and their scope for people to hold erroneous beliefs – because it privileges causality and goodness of fit more than parsimony.

EXERCISE 16.1. FELICITY AND TENSIONS WITHIN INTERVIEWEES' ACCOUNTS

In previous chapters, we have asked you to think about the possible causes of a recent increase in rough sleeping in British towns.

Let us suppose that you decide to enrich your work on this problem by researching how young homeless people think about their situation, their own and other people's responsibility for it, and what counts as 'rough sleeping' So you interview a twenty-year-old man who alternates living on the streets with short periods in hostels. You capture a number of statements from him, including those below.

You treat the following statements as being about responsibility. The first set appears to attribute some responsibility to his parents, but not consistently:

I got kicked out ... I took a lot of bashing because my mother split from my father, yeah and I stuck with my father. He used to do what he did to my mother to me ... I thought 'I don't want to go through what she's been through. I'm off!'

But the following statement appears to suggest that the main responsibility is his own:

I'm a fool to myself as well like. I've got to admit that. I've had some problems and some I've brought on myself because I'm stupid.

You treat the following statements as being about his framing of his relationship with his accommodation:

I mean look at this [car and tarpaulin sheet] – it's not much, is it? But it's my home. It's the home that I've chosen. I've chosen to live like this. That's why I'm not homeless.

But when asked directly whether he thinks he is homeless, he thinks of the home of the parent who 'kicked [him] out', and replies:

Well, no, because I've got a home to go to, and, yes, because I can't go there.

Try to develop two alternative hypotheses that would supply felicity conditions which would make all these statements intelligible and make the young man's relationship to those statements intelligible, too. How would you design research to test whether either is correct?

[These are all quotations reported in Hutson and Liddiard (1994: 123–42), but were taken from interviews with *different* young homeless people. However, one of us worked with homeless people in the early 1980s and can remember many young people describing their situation in ways that exhibited complicated internal tensions between different parts of their account in the manner this exercise suggests.]

Relevance

A central challenge, which arises from the imperative to pursue intelligibility in secondary interpretations, is that of *relevance*. Which of an actor's beliefs, desires, emotions and so on are relevant to the secondary interpretations in question?

This might be a problem, for example, in developing interpretations of how people think about past events. For example, how far back would we want to go in reconstructing collective memories of previous business recessions in interpreting how they shape current beliefs and attitudes in a particular firm? Similarly, how far forward should we go in interpreting attitudes to future events, especially when we move from specific anticipation to vague aspiration or fear? To revert once again to our recycling example – and particularly to Example 12.2 – how firm a conception or expectation of future environmental disaster does a household member have to possess for his or her motivation for recycling household waste to count as an 'ideological/environmental' one? And again, how prominent in the householder's consciousness does this expectation have to be, to be relevant to the study?

Such problems in doing interpretation are analogous to problems encountered in explanation-building in deciding how far to go in tracing distal causes. Both problems are special cases of the general one of setting bounds to cases. In interpretive research, this means bounding the range of ideas, beliefs and other aspects of actors' mental lives that are relevant to a study. And as with explanation, developing a specific strategy for addressing this problem must depend on the research question, and particularly on the purpose for which the interpretation is required. The precision in determining whether a person is an 'ideological environmentalist' might, for example, matter a great deal less in a study of the local implementation of a recycling scheme than in a study of the changing character of green politics. And above all – as we saw in the previous chapter – there is no way to determine what counts as important or relevant in developing an interpretation, without relying, at least in part, on specific explanatory theories about the actors we study, and their situations and conditions. These points are all illustrated further in Example 16.2.

EXAMPLE 16.2. DE-TRACKING EDUCATIONAL REFORM

Wells *et al.* (1995) undertook an interpretive study of reforms designed to eliminate what in the USA is called 'tracking' and what, in English schools, is called 'streaming by ability'.

In line with previous research on implementing change in schools, they began by defining the 'unit of analysis' as the process of reform within each of the ten schools in the study, but quickly found that perceptions of the change process in schools needed to be contextualised in the wider politics of the communities served by the schools. So the boundaries of the cases were extended, for example by interviewing parents and school board members. In extending the scope of the study in this way, they also drew on theory originally developed for the study

(Continued)

---

of community power. This theory was influential in political science in the 1960s and 1970s but had never been applied to institutional change in schools.

An iterative process was thus established between theory-building and data collection – and between induction and deduction – which, they claim, led to theoretical insights that would never have been developed if they had worked rigidly with pre-set boundaries of cases. For example, extending the scope of the cases led the researchers to recognise both the commitment to educational reform of parents from minority groups and their belief that their views were marginalised by the politics of school reform. In consequence, as Wells *et al.*'s research proceeded, it became increasingly focused upon developing new theory about the political context of school reforms, rather than to exploring theory about institutional reforms within schools.

The three dimensions of good interpretation

But what does this discussion mean for good methodological practice, especially when we are interpreting the mental lives of people whose experiences are relatively foreign to the researchers and the anticipated readers? Our view is that sooner or later we shall need to invoke rather fundamental, general concepts to label, order and make sense of the content of interpretations. That is, to be both intelligible and relevant, it is necessary to show that people's beliefs, systems of ideas, emotions and ways of categorising and classifying their world are, in the context in which they live:

- *Either more or less integrated with each other.* For example, if Geertz (1980) is to be believed, nineteenth-century Balinese thought was highly integrated, consistent, coherent and unified. By contrast, Feldman's (1989) study on the US Department of Energy found its thought world to be rather 'loosely coupled', and the diaries of the 1960s British cabinet minister Richard Crossman (1975) displayed the conflict and instability in the thought worlds of the Labour administration in which he served.
- *Either instrumental* or *non-instrumental* in character. For example, in the examples used in Chapter 15, Rappaport shows that 'clasping the *rumbim*' makes instrumental sense in communicating states of war and peace among the Maring people. Similarly, in the work cited in Example 16.1, Rosenfeld and his colleagues demonstrate that the snitchers' way of classifying different kinds of informing is highly instrumental, because it allows them both to co-exist with law-enforcement agencies and, at the same time, to believe that they live in conformity with the norms of the 'code of the street'. But, as we can see, references to instrumentality require explanatory factors to enter into interpretation, because both these interpretations explain *why* these people behave and account for themselves, as they do. Conversely, of course, interpretations may also deal in aspects of people's mental lives for which no instrumentality is claimed. Some things that feature in our interpretations of their lives may have, for example, purely religious or aesthetic meanings.
- *Either broad or narrow* in contextual frame. Suppose we develop an interpretation of the way that a cluster of people think about their household waste which shows that the

way they think about rubbish is based on categories generated in and describing their home, their family life, or their domestic practices. That would be a narrow view of their thought world about waste, because it would mean that their primary interpretation was mainly local to the activity of handling waste. By contrast, suppose we developed a secondary interpretation which showed the impact of categories from their working lives, from the environmental movement, or from their economic relationships with retail businesses which supply goods in extravagant packaging. That interpretation would be broader. It would use ideas about things that are relatively distal from the immediate business of separating types of waste into bags and putting them by the kerb or driving them to the recycling centre.

The more clearly a researcher can show where on these three dimensions the subject matter of interpretations – beliefs, ideas, emotions and ways of classifying and so on – falls, the more successfully his or her interpretation can be said to have met the conditions of intelligibility and relevance.

EXERCISE 16.2. INTELLIGIBLE ROUGH SLEEPING?

Think again about the work you did for Exercise 16.1.

Let us suppose that you have a set of transcripts and field notes from interviewing and observing a sample of twelve rough sleepers. Most show a similar range of attitudes to, and beliefs about, their situations to the quotations from the young man in Exercise 16.1. That is, they show that sometimes the rough sleepers wish to deny that they find their situation a problem, and that at others they blame themselves or other people for it. Only three rough sleepers explicitly link their plight to wider economic factors, such as high levels of youth unemployment, or social factors such as inadequate mental health care or the withdrawal of local authority outreach work with the homeless.

Think about whether, in forming a secondary interpretation of the mental worlds of these twelve rough sleepers, you can make judgements about the extent to which they are more or less integrated with each other; instrumental or non-instrumental; and narrow or broad. If not, think about the additional evidence you would need to make such judgements. And consider how such judgements could make your secondary interpretation a better one.

Virtues of good interpretation

Even if 'intelligibility' and 'relevance' offered more precise guidance to the art of interpretation than they do, they would still not, in themselves, be sufficient to determine what counts as good interpretation. Both explanatory and interpretive research must strike trade-offs between different virtues in research design, especially parsimony, goodness of fit and generality. So the question is what virtues are particularly relevant to interpretive research: are they the same as for explanatory research, and what trade-offs between them might be required?

We have already argued, in discussing rationality, charity and felicity, that goodness of fit may be more important than parsimony. By goodness of fit, we mean giving adequate coverage to the significance for the study of as much detail in the data set as possible, both within and between cases. Indeed, the claims of interpretive researchers to capture more richness and nuance than is usual in explanatory research – at least, in explanatory designs that rely heavily on data reduction techniques – suggest that we should value this virtue above others for interpretive research, and be prepared to trade some parsimony for goodness of fit.

This is not to say that interpretation should discount *parsimony* altogether. It is a reasonable principle of research design that if two interpretations of the same phenomena are available, then – other things being equal – we should prefer the one that invokes fewer ideas, beliefs, emotions and categories to make sense of the data. Rappaport's interpretation of Maring life offers considerable parsimony, because he is able to show that a relatively modest number of concepts – such as that of the *rumbim* – play central roles in the thought worlds of his subjects, across a variety of settings.

A virtue that was originally proposed for explanation by Kitcher (1989) but which is often held to be especially important in interpretation – and which is related to parsimony – is *unification*. An interpretation exhibits unification to the extent that it uses a single argument to provide a systematic reconciliation of beliefs, emotions, ideas and so on in a given social domain. However, there are several risks in giving unification heavy emphasis. We must make sure that the people we study do, indeed, have a unified, coherent, integrated primary interpretation of their situation, by testing this hypothesis empirically: that is, we need first to be sure of its goodness of fit. Otherwise, we run the danger of imposing a unity on the phenomena being interpreted that derives, in practice, only from our secondary interpretation.

To state the obvious, strong unification is most – or indeed only – of value when the phenomena being studied are unified. In interpreting the thought world of a strongly integrated and cohesive community – one with limited conflict and limited internal diversity in thought styles – unification may well be much more appropriate than in interpreting the mental life and practices of communities that are fractured, fragmented and conflict ridden. Thus, we might surmise that the interpretation eventually developed by Wells *et al.* was not particularly unified, because the research design was extended specifically to take account of multiple, competing perceptions of the states of affairs in the ten focal schools.

Other design virtues have less relevance to interpretation. We saw in the previous chapter that – strictly speaking – interpretation is a special kind of *descriptive* inference. But does that render interpretation exempt from demonstrating causality? We have seen already that the process by which some elements of an interpretation are assembled rests upon explanatory hypotheses, not least because it is very difficult indeed to describe the mental lives of a cluster of people without making some explanatory claims about the causal relationship with their actions. Indeed, we saw that felicity conditions are often causal explanations. For this reason, we must ensure that any explanatory claims which underpin our secondary interpretation are transparent and explicit; that they represent a reasonable trade-off between the various virtues of explanations; and that the available data are used rigorously to provide warrant for them, in the same ways as we discussed earlier in this book in the chapters on explanation.

Generalisation need not be a central virtue of secondary interpretations. A central purpose of accurate, detailed interpretations of actors' mental lives is to account for their distinctive, rather than their general, features. Generalisation should be only as broad or narrow as the contextual frame argued to be the relevant one.

Validity and reliability in interpretation

Even if researchers do not use their interpretive resources to explain the actions of the people they are studying, it seems reasonable to expect that standards of validity and warranted inference should apply to interpretations, just as they do to explanatory hypotheses (Hammersley, 1992).

At this point in this chapter, we should remind ourselves of what we mean by validity and reliability in the context of explanatory research – and to invite any readers who have not yet read the discussion in Chapter 1 to do so. In Chapter 1, we said that:

- External validity is a standard of correspondence with facts.
- Internal validity measures the extent to which the inference supported by the research is well designed to eliminate bias, and free from the effects detected from those of confounding variables.
- Reliability is a measure of the extent to which our measures return consistent results.

So what equivalent standards are there in interpretive research?

Validation strategies

The following are offered by leading writers as sub-concepts of 'validity' that are especially relevant to interpretive research (Kvale, 1995; Sandberg, 2005; Lincoln and Guba, 1985; Sandelowski, 1986):

Construct validity: This term refers to the question of whether the concepts used to capture the beliefs, ideas, categories and other aspects of people's mental lives are accurate representations of them, or whether they systematically distort them in some way, thus rendering the interpretation invalid.

The education researcher Joseph Maxwell uses 'interpretive validity' to refer to the external validity of constructs – and to relations between constructs – used in interpretations, and argues (Maxwell, 1992) that these standards apply in the same way as they would to explanatory research. In much of the literature, achieving construct validity seems to rely heavily on the skills of the researchers; the depth and thoroughness of their engagement with their cases; and their willingness to engage in open-minded and explicit discussion of concepts with others in the relevant research community, including research participants. Some of the literature speaks, for example, of the 'craft' of interpretation and the need for engaging in 'deep enquiry', for 'triangulation' and for securing 'consensus' about concepts (e.g. Lincoln and Guba, 1990).

Construct validity is clearly important in any research. However, it is not clear that such comments offer a good route to achieving construct validity; for what matters more for an interpretation is that the inference from the data is clear, accountable and warranted and that the etic concepts used have clear empirical and theoretical justifications.

Communicative validity: The problem of construct validity in interpretive research leads some interpretive researchers to argue that a stronger claim to validity can be made by achieving consensual confirmation of our constructs through dialogue with the community of participants. Denzin, for example, asserts baldly that 'the interpretations that researchers develop about a subjects' life must be understandable to the subject. If they are not, they are unacceptable' (2001 [1989]: 65). We have already argued that, if this means that even primary interpretations must be restricted to the use of emic categories, it is clearly impossible to meet this standard. But in any case, it is not clear why this criterion is important, since Denzin himself acknowledges in the same paragraph that researchers may be able to identify things that subjects cannot see, and may even hope to know the subjects better than they know themselves.

Nevertheless, as a checking procedure, the activity of running interpretations past participants to see how they react is often a valuable part of the research process. For example, it is doubtful that, if they had been asked, the Balinese men of the 1950s would have recognised the etic categories (e.g. 'sentimental education') used by Geertz in his account of their cockfights (Example 15.3). Yet, whatever the limitations of his interpretation – and it has been much contested over the decades on both empirical and methodological grounds – on its own, this seems not to be a compelling criticism of it. Even the manner in which people might reject etic categories might be informative or even – in some circumstances – positively confirm the candidate interpretation. Let us suppose, for example, that we conduct an interpretive study in a secondary school, similar to the one by Willis that we looked at in Chapter 15. If a head teacher vigorously contested our interpretive claim that talent in sport is less highly valued than academic prowess, we might ask ourselves why this interpretive claim hit a particular nerve. As a result, the head teacher's challenge might lead us to open up a new line of fruitful enquiry.

Pragmatic validity: This is achieved if participants – or indeed other people with an interest in our research, such as the funders of a piece of evaluation research – are able successfully to rely on our constructs in making decisions and taking actions on the basis of our interpretation. Again, this is thought to be important by leading methodologists of interpretive research, for example Lincoln and Guba (1985, 1990). Yet Giddens (1987) argued that etic categories used in social science are often adopted by the people we study, especially if the study changes their behaviour and leads them to adopt new practices. This suggests the ease with which they pick up our *argot* might not indicate its goodness of fit with their previous practices and thought styles, so much as its flexibility in informing their accounts of their new styles, or its power to influence and change their thought rather than to capture it unchanged.

Transgressive validity: This is achieved if our constructs are found to be robust against alternative ones, of if they can be synthesised from constructs developed by means of rival approaches. In principle, this standard is sensible and obvious. But, in practice, there is a paucity of interpretive studies that report comparisons between alternative interpretations, and this suggests that this standard is honoured more in the breach than in the observance.

Reliability in interpretive research

The following sub-concepts of 'reliability' are often claimed to be used in interpretive research, usually by the same authors whose work we cited on validity above:

- *Applicability*: The fit of the method and the resulting interpretation to the data, and its transferability to other domains that are similar in relevant respects.
- *Consistency*: The ability of other researchers to follow the methods used to build the interpretation; and the dependability of the ways they are applied.
- *Reliability as interpretive awareness*: The extent to which the researchers demonstrate that they have identified, and taken account of, any tendencies in their practice for inconsistency of, or bias in, interpretation.

Again, the standards offered by these sub-concepts are unexceptionable, but they apply, too, to explanatory work and are not distinctive to interpretive research.

It can be seen that, in practice, much of the discussion of validity and reliability noted above has to do with *procedures* or *heuristics*. It reminds us of the importance of checking our preliminary or provisional findings, and may suggest *methods* for doing so. But it does not deal with the *methodology* of interpretation. That is, it does not define the general relationships that should be in place between our secondary interpretation and the mental worlds being studied, for acceptable standards of validity or reliability to be met, irrespective of the particular heuristic procedures we use. Second, they do not tell us why we should be interested in whether our interpretation meets those standards.

In these respects, the textbook categories of validity and reliability for interpretive research are less informative than – and therefore not clearly equivalent to – those for explanatory research.

Warranting good interpretations

So can we say anything that is specific to *interpretive* research about the relations we might want to find between our data and our secondary interpretations? Or must we agree with relativists who claim that any or no relationship will serve equally well?

It should be clear from the discussion in this chapter and the previous one that, in our view, interpretation has an important part to play in social research, first in providing a particular kind of descriptive inference and, second, in developing explanatory hypotheses. We suggest that, for these purposes, a *good* interpretation should meet the following standards:

- *A descriptive relationship with reality*: It should provide accurate descriptions of actors' beliefs, ideas, emotions about the phenomena in question, use well-formed concepts for describing, cohering and ordering them, and apply clear and defensible thresholds for deciding what empirical phenomena count as examples of which concepts.
- *An appropriately selective relationship with reality*: It should clearly identify the phenomena being interpreted as being relevant for the research, and demonstrate why the concepts and typologies applied to the phenomena are not only relevant but also justified by good theory or by empirical propositions already accepted on independent grounds. It should specify how the phenomena being interpreted are associated with the relevant population or cases, and how the cases or population are related to others to which the interpretation might appropriately be extended or generalised.
- *A pre-explanatory relationship with reality*: It should make transparent any implicit causal claims contained within the interpretation. It must then clearly identify and distinguish the elements that are expected to be used as important variables, configurations, mechanisms or contexts in further research to test these claims and offer confidence that they could be effectively operationalised for the purpose.

To illustrate how these standards might be applied, let us return to our study of the recycling of household waste. In Examples 7.2 and 13.2 we discussed the need for, and a process for achieving, an understanding of the motives of people who are prepared to make the effort to recycle their household waste. The explanation clearly rests upon an interpretation of their ideas, beliefs, values, norms and claims about behaviour in respect of the management of garbage, and the ways in which these aspects of mental life are linked through the concept of 'motive'. As described in those examples, it offers a descriptive inference, which makes sense by claiming that 'motives' fall into five distinct bundles which we labelled, respectively: *ideological/environmental*; *ideological/anti-corporate*; *tokenistic*; *instrumental*; and *social conformist*. Example 16.3 discusses what would make this a good interpretation.

EXAMPLE 16.3. PUTTING OUT THE GARBAGE: INTERPRETING RELATIONSHIPS BETWEEN IDEAS, BELIEFS AND BEHAVIOURAL NORMS

In the first place, we need to be confident about the *descriptive relationship* of our interpretation with the 'reality' of our respondents' mental lives, so far as they think about rubbish disposal. To do this we would need to be confident that – despite being etic rather than emic ones – each of the five bundles or 'types' of motives we ascribe to recyclers is, within the limits of the data, an accurate, full, distinctive and coherent description of their ideas, beliefs and values about waste and how these things are linked to claims about how householders ought to behave.

This confidence could be achieved by exploring how householders understand waste disposal problems that recycling is supposed to solve; how much they care about this problem and why; what they think are the root causes of the problem; how confidently they regard recycling as a solution; what normative claims they make about how householders should manage their rubbish; and whether they claim that their beliefs affect their own behaviour. In so doing, we need especially to understand how the relevant aspects of beliefs, ideas, norms and claims about behaviour are linked.

We need, too, to be sure that each of the concepts used for labelling the five types has both internal and external validity and captures intension appropriately. For example, 'ideological environmentalism' is potentially a tricky type, because both 'ideology' and 'environment' are capacious and slippery concepts. And how, exactly, would we distinguish casual lip-service to saving the planet from strong commitment to specific environmental values?

We would clearly need to stipulate and bound these concepts carefully, by deciding what kinds of statements would be taken as indicating an 'ideological' stance on waste, and how positive, precise and well informed these statements need to be to count as indicating a firm and fixed commitment. We would need to be sure, for example, that the 'environmental' ideology type is being consistently distinguished from the 'anti-corporate ideology' type.

Second, we need to be confident about the *selective relationship* of our interpretation to reality. To do this, we would need to make sure that, between them, the five types cover the full range of ideas, beliefs and reported behavioural norms suggested by the empirical data. Furthermore, if we believe that our sample of householders is reasonably typical of people who live in areas with recycling schemes, we should ensure, too, that the way we conceptualise different types of motivation is not so idiosyncratic as to prevent their extension to similar populations of householders in other areas. We might decide, too, that the interpretive power of our types would be weakened if they are insufficiently distinguished from each other. So – to use the account of typologies we built in Chapter 9 – we would probably try to build a *classical* typology consisting in exhaustive, mutually exclusive types.

Third, we need to recognise explicitly that we are interested in motives for recycling because we assume that 'motives' explain why some people bother to recycle their household waste. In other words, the exercise has been done because we have a theory about the *causal* relationship between ideas, beliefs, behavioural norms and actions. We might further hypothesise that the *different* types of motives developed in our interpretation might be associated with *different* patterns of recycling behaviours in that, for example, being motivated by ideology of some kind leads to more consistent recycling of a wider variety of rubbish than do

(Continued)

other types of motivation. If so, we could plausibly claim to have developed an interpretation that has a positive *pre-explanatory relationship* with reality.

Developing this hypothesis more fully, and then testing it by means of explanatory research, depends, of course, on finding ways of operationalising the independent variable (ideological motivation) and dependent variables (more consistent recycling; recycling of more rubbish; recycling of a greater variety of rubbish). The relationships between them could perhaps be tested in a VOR study, but it is more likely that we could trace the causal processes linking ideas, beliefs, norms and action in a COR study.

Induction and pluralism in interpretive research

Much interpretive research is primarily inductive. Whereas in explanatory research, researchers commonly present theories *deductively* first and then present the empirical data, in interpretive work it is very common to begin with the empirical material and then to show *inductively* how the inference builds up to the interpretation. Indeed, some relativist scholars insist on this approach, on the epistemological ground that all interpretations are subjective. So none can be more valid or virtuous than any other, and therefore the whole idea of testing competing deductive hypotheses is misguided.

A realist perspective regards an interpretation as a hypothesis about how people think and what things mean to them, and holds that such things are matters of fact that ought, in principle, to be amenable to inference from empirical research. So there can be no principled objection to using deductive designs for comparing the performance of interpretations in making sense of people's primary interpretations to see which might be superior in goodness of fit, parsimony, accuracy or other virtues. Approaching interpretive research in this way would start with *explanatory* theory. For example, researchers working in the sociology of knowledge might, on the basis of institutional theory, develop various hypotheses about the specific patterns of thought that would be adopted by people in consequence of living or working together in a particular kind of social institution and of relating to their family, friends and colleagues in particular ways. In Chapter 17, we shall examine in more detail a research project of this type.

Although most interpretive studies develop a single secondary interpretation, without attempting to compare rival ones, some studies contrast rival *primary* interpretations of different people involved in the same events. For example, in her monumental work, *The Challenger launch decision*, Diane Vaughan offers careful interpretive work on NASA and its contractor companies in the years immediately before the fateful day in 1986 when the Space Shuttle exploded (Vaughan, 1996). She contrasts the primary interpretations of different companies and professionals of the evidence from previous launches about damage to the 'O' rings. Vaughan grounds her comparative analysis of primary interpretations in detailed explanatory work, showing how the relations between people with contrasting primary interpretations led them to take decisions which, in their circumstances, appeared sensible to them, but led directly to the disaster.

Comparison is sometimes done on *objective* interpretations. For example, one interpretation of the emergence of, say, punk rock in the 1970s might emphasise the continuities between the punks and the wider arts and fashion scenes of the 1970s. Another interpretation that focused on the different kinds of people who became punks might emphasise the discontinuities, as did Hebdige's (1979) work in cultural studies which viewed punk as a distinct 'subculture' within the wider scene. By picking out different lineages, aspects or perspectives on the same cultural or social phenomena, each interpretation can supplement the other, rather than being rivals. The point is that objective interpretations of the same phenomena need not be incompatible or mutually contradictory, so long as each illuminates *different aspects* of a complex phenomenon and none claims to be complete.

But suppose, though, that someone were to argue that Rappaport was wrong in claiming that the *rumbim* was central to the thought world of the Maring, or that Willis misunderstood the roles played by the categories of 'avin' a laff' or the 'ear'ole' in the way that the 'lads' understood their relations with their peers. In such cases, we should have genuinely rival secondary interpretations between which we should want to try to judge, if the requisite data could be obtained. To claim that both views might simultaneously be correct is to allow contradictions in *social science accounts* of people's thought worlds. This, we have argued, is an unsatisfactory claim, both in principle (Chapter 4) and in practice. Whilst it is an empirical fact that some actors' primary interpretations may contain contradictions, researchers' accounts ought to aim for consistency.

Conclusion

Good interpretive research is both valuable and very hard to do.

Contrary to what purist explanatory researchers sometimes claim, careful work to build descriptive inferences about people's thought worlds in their particular social and institutional context is important in explanatory research, for two reasons. It may provide a clear account of what is to be explained and it can identify the explanatory factors, contexts or mechanisms. Interpretive research always rests on a structure of explanations – whether they are implicit or, as they should be, explicit – which define what counts as the relevant context and as the focal interest of the case or population of cases that is being interpreted. Whether or not the researcher goes on to use the findings of an interpretive study for explanatory research, real contributions to knowledge can be obtained by careful and rigorous interpretive work. The interpretive studies in the developed world of the great mid-twentieth-century researchers such as Goffman or Whyte (1993 [1943]), or social anthropologists such as Rappaport in New Guinea, are major contributions to social science, independently of their *explanations* of the phenomena they interpreted.

But we have argued too that using interpretation as the starting point of explanation adds much value to social science research. This chapter has made clear that there are distinctive trade-offs among virtues of good secondary interpretation, and dovetailing them with the trade-offs required to support the explanatory inferences involved in meeting the standard of felicity requires very careful work to bound cases and integrate the two kinds of inferences.

It is therefore misleading and dangerous to believe, as many people seem to do, that good interpretive work is easier to do within the confines of a small project than explanatory work, or that interpretive work is easier to bound and manage because it involves fewer inferential stages. On the contrary, the richness and depth of the empirical data needed for convincing interpretive research means that they are often *more* demanding to collect and especially to analyse than the kind of reduced data required for some kinds of explanatory research, especially VOR. For this reason, it is often easier for people with limited resources to achieve a contribution to knowledge by means of a small-scale explanatory design that uses secondary or archival data – by means, for example, of a study in qualitative historical social science – than it is to develop and bound a well-designed piece of interpretive research and to convincingly warrant the interpretation. Indeed, it is no coincidence that much of the very best interpretive work – including some of that cited in this chapter and in Chapter 15 – is produced only after decades of intensive fieldwork.

Basic reading

For arguments about what counts as validity in interpretation, see Altheide DL and Johnson JM, 1998, Criteria for assessing interpretive validity in qualitative research, in NK Denzin and YS Lincoln (eds), *Collecting and interpreting qualitative materials*, London: Sage, 283–312; Kvale S, 1995, The social construction of validity, *Qualitative Inquiry*, 1, 1, 19–40; Lincoln YS and Guba EG, 1990, Judging the quality of case study reports, *Qualitative Studies in Education*, 3, 1, 53-59, reprinted in AM Huberman and MB Miles (eds), 2002, *The qualitative researcher's companion*, London: Sage, 205–15; Maxwell J, 1992, Understanding and validity in qualitative research, *Harvard Educational Review*, 62, 3, 279–300, reprinted in AM Huberman and MB Miles (eds), 2002, *The qualitative researcher's companion*, London: Sage, 37–64; Sandberg J, 2005, How do we justify knowledge produced within interpretive approaches? *Organisational Research Methods*, 8, 1, 41–68; Sandelowski M, 1986, The problem of rigour in qualitative research, *Advances in Nursing Science*, 8, 3, 27–37.

Advanced reading

Goffman E, 1983, Felicity's condition, *American Journal of Sociology*, 89, 1, 25–51, sets out his proposed standard.

For his account of principle of charity, see Davidson D, 2001 [1984, 1977], *Inquiries into truth and interpretation*, Oxford: Oxford University Press.

For Popper's rationality principle, see Popper K, 1983 [1967], The rationality principle, from D Miller (ed.), *The pocket Popper*, Oxford: Fontana, 357–65.

PART IV

Synthesis

Combinations and trade-offs

SEVENTEEN
Combining research designs

This chapter will:

- examine the range of logically possible ways in which the design principles associated with explanatory and interpretive research can be combined in a single study;
- identify some important challenges and benefits in so doing; and
- examine the services that explanation and interpretation can provide for each other in a combined study.

Readers of standard texts on explanatory and on interpretive methodologies could be forgiven for believing that we have to make a once-and-for-all choice between explanatory and interpretive research, because the epistemological gulf between them is unbridgeable. In practice, however, many researchers find ways to combine elements from these different kinds of research design, and there are good reasons for so doing.

In previous examples and exercises on recycling household waste and the rise in rough sleeping, we have suggested that the findings of explanatory, VOR-type explanatory research might be enriched by conducting interpretive research, or that interpretive research might supply hypotheses for testing in explanatory research. Readers may, for example, like to remind themselves of how different styles of research were used to illuminate different aspects of the same problem in Examples 6.1, 7.2 and 12.2. Potentially, of course, these different styles of research could be combined in the same project. A similar point is made in Example 17.1.

EXAMPLE 17.1. MAKING RISKY INFERENCES ABOUT CHANGING RISKY BEHAVIOUR

If, for example, we want to understand how different groups of people respond to an advertising campaign about the dangers of sexually transmitted infections, it seems risky to make inferences only from data about, say, changes in the rates of infections reported to hospital

(Continued)

clinics or the sales of condoms. This is because we cannot be sure that changes observed in such data can really be attributed in large part to the advertisements. Likewise, if the data do not change, it does not necessarily follow that the information campaign has had absolutely no effect. Some effects may take a while to show up, or they may have an effect only when something else intervenes, for example the death of a celebrity from AIDS. So as well as examining the data, we might also want to know how the target groups react to the advertisements, and what they remember, thought and felt about them. But conversely, it would be risky to draw inferences about how their behaviour might change only from an interpretation of their reactions to the campaign. To achieve a full understanding, we probably need to combine explanatory and interpretive research.

Why combine design principles?

Researchers sometimes work with elements from both types of research designs for some combination of the following six reasons:

1   to identify trends for richer description;
2   to identify possible hypotheses, especially about *how* a causal process might run through thought, feelings or classification;
3   to make an inference to the best explanation, or an abduction;
4   to map discrepancies between actors' understandings and researchers' independently observed conditions;
5   to explain actors' understandings by reference to researchers' independently observed conditions; or
6   to test hypotheses against patterns.

But combining styles of research in such ways often turns out to be a more complex issue than might first appear. This chapter explains why, and discusses why we might nevertheless attempt to combine elements from different styles in our own research.

Triangulation's too good for 'em, I say

Many textbooks urge us to start by 'triangulating' data. 'Triangulation' is what land surveyors or ships' navigators do to fix an exact position in a landscape or a sea, by plotting it on lines to two or more other points whose positions are already known. In social science, 'triangulation' is used as a metaphor. It usually involves combining quantitative and qualitative data, or data from different sources, or data derived from different methods, or data collected by different researchers, or perhaps interpretations based on different theories (Miles and Huberman, 1994; Henn *et al.*, 2009

[2006]). Its primary purpose is to provide a check on external validity (see, for example, the review by Shih, 1998, of classical sources such as Garner *et al.*, 1956, and Campbell, 1956). If we can achieve the same substantive result by using more than one method or data set, then we can have greater confidence in it.

Clearly, triangulation only works if we have some procedure by which we can map what we learn from using one method or type of data onto what we learn from the other. Some scholars talk about the analysis they carry out to do this as a 'meta-matrix': this is, in essence, a table showing, on the same rows, findings about what the researcher believes to be the same thing, on the basis of some criteria of linkage (Wendler, 2002). This process, in turn, relies on having a good theory that demonstrates how the instruments used for each part of the project tap into the same underlying phenomena. In short, we need a theory that enables us to match categories and classifications used in data derived from different methods or sources (Kopinak, 1999; Erzberger and Prein, 1997; Meijer *et al.*, 2002).

If, however, these methods use very similar categories, it may be more honest to say – as Meijer *et al.* (2002) do – that triangulation is really a way of enhancing our confidence in internal validity. Or we could simply say – as yet other writers do – that it offers us a richer picture (see Shih's, 1998, review).

'Triangulation' is not, however, a helpful metaphor when we want to combine, in the same research project, elements from different kinds of research design that address, not the same or similar questions, but different ones. (cf. Tarrow, 2004: 178–9). We may need to do this when the theories that inform our research design suggest that we have two or more research questions that are related in some critical way, especially when one question calls for an explanation and another for an interpretation. It is this problem that we discuss in this chapter, and we consider it to be an important one. Whereas triangulation, correctly understood, is concerned with combining data types to answer the same question, the really interesting challenges are presented by combining explanatory and interpretive research to answer related but distinct questions.

Consider, for example, a famous study by Weick and Roberts (1993) on sense-making among naval and fleet air arm personnel on US aircraft carriers. They start with an interesting puzzle: why are more people not killed in risky operations? That question clearly calls for a causal explanation. But Weick and Roberts do not begin by taking a sample of aircraft carrier operations and collecting data on independent and dependent variables. Instead they ask: how do various types of naval and air force personnel make sense of what they do together? They look, for example, at the vocabulary these personnel use to describe what they do; they examine the narratives they tell about situations in which they are obliged to trust one another; and they ask what they believe to be the worst that could happen to them. Out of these apparently unpromising materials, Weick and Roberts build up an interpretation of the thought styles of the teams. Next, they argue, in explanatory vein, about the commitment to the collective endeavour that enables a safe, high-quality team performance. Good risk management, they argue, is less the consequence of following good safety management procedures than of being able to sustain a certain collective style of thought.

If Weick and Roberts had started with VOR, it is far from obvious that they would have been able to develop such a rich account. This, then, is a good example of a research question that requires a combination of *interpretation* – in this case, of the thought world of the carrier personnel – and an *explanation* of the causal consequences of their thought worlds. Moreover, their project proceeds in two distinct stages, so they could not have 'triangulated' different kinds of data to answer their research question.

We need, then, to move beyond the confined issue of triangulation and consider more ambitious combinations of research designs.

A typology of social research and its combinations

In Chapter 5 we distinguished social science research according, first, to the two types of product it offers – explanation or interpretation – and, second, to the two types of data it uses – qualitative or quantitative data. If we cross-tabulate these four types of research we get four spaces into which we can then place most social science research (Figure 17.1):

- In the qualitative/explanatory quadrant, we have *type A*. This is work that chases causal factors, configurations and mechanisms. Examples include the explanatory studies by Heather and Tilly we cited in Chapters 11 and 14.
- In the qualitative/interpretive quadrant, we find *type B*. The studies we used as examples in Chapters 15 and 16 exemplify this type of research.
- In the quantitative/explanatory quadrant is *type C*. This quadrant is where we would put, for example, statistical analysis of associations such as the association we discussed in Chapter 10 between the use of prison and the fall in crime rates.
- In the quantitative/interpretive quadrant is *type D*. We have cited few studies of this type in this book, but it includes descriptive statistical work. So a lot of research commissioned by business and government bodies for the purpose of identifying risks and opportunities and building future strategies would fit here. The Wanless (2002) Report on the future funding of the UK's National Health Service is a case in point. Researchers in this tradition tend to offer multiple projections from past trends into future possibilities, and then work out what would need to be the case for each scenario to be sustained or undermined.

Getting from four to twelve combinations

We have already seen that none of these four styles of research is, typically, adequate on its own to answer many questions about which we care most in social science. So perforce we must sometimes combine the types of research.

Figure 17.1 Four basic styles of research

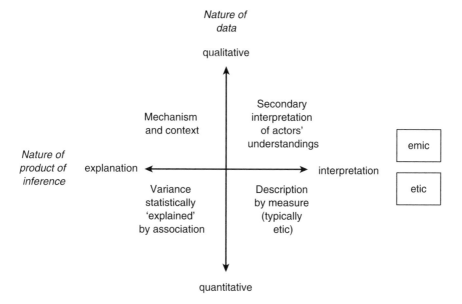

Let us think first about the combinations that are possible in bilateral relations between these four basic styles of social research. Given that each bilateral combination can run in either direction – and the styles can be combined horizontally, vertically and diagonally – twelve combinations are logically possible. It may be possible that there is more than one type of combination running in the same direction between any two styles of research, but we discount that possibility here, leaving twelve possibilities, as follows:

1 a causal mechanism helps us to develop or test a secondary interpretation of actors' understandings;
2 a secondary interpretation of actors' understandings helps us to understand a causal mechanism;
3 a causal mechanism helps us to understand a statistical association;
4 a statistical association helps us to understand a causal mechanism;
5 a secondary interpretation of actors' understandings helps us to understand a statistical description;
6 a statistical description helps us to understand a secondary interpretation of actors' understandings;
7 a statistical association helps us to understand a statistical description;
8 a statistical description helps us to understand a statistical association;
9 a causal mechanism helps us to understand a statistical description;
10 a statistical description helps us to understand a causal mechanism;

11 a secondary interpretation of actors' understandings helps to us understand a statistical association; and

12 a statistical association helps us to develop or test a secondary interpretation of actors' understandings.

In saying that one thing (A) – say, a causal mechanism – 'helps' us to understand or to develop something else (B) could, of course, mean many different things. But in practice, we mean that A might provide:

a ideas, questions, hypotheses, frameworks, concepts for further exploration in B;
b material that supports an account of what is found by B; or
c a contrast with what is found by B, so that discrepancies between them can be examined.

Of course, these services might conversely be provided by B for A. Figures 17.2 and 17.3 show the range of twelve possible combinations and give some examples in each case.

Figure 17.2 Combinations of styles of research – horizontal and vertical

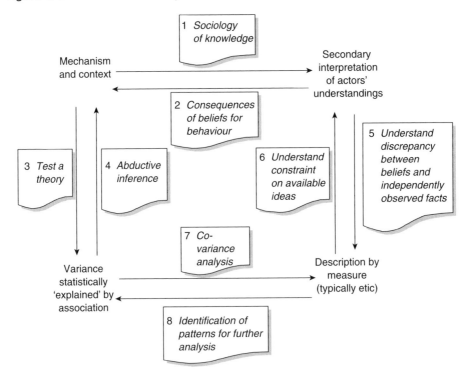

Figure 17.3 Combinations of research styles – diagonals

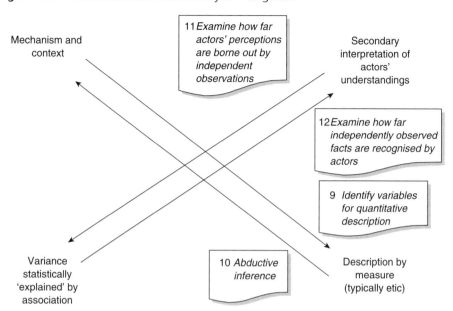

For example, abduction is found in cases 4 and 10, whilst analysis of discrepancies occurs in 11, 12, 8 and 9 and involves taking ideas yielded by one type of research for further examination in another.

Combining research types: an appropriate strategy for modest projects

It is worth looking at some examples where researchers have combined research styles, to see more clearly what can be achieved by combining styles of research. In so doing, we shall assume that you are already persuaded of the merits of the vertical combinations: that is, of the usefulness of combining quantitative and qualitative research. Because there are often supposed to be much higher barriers to combining interpretive and explanatory research, we shall concentrate in the next part of this chapter on the horizontal – and on a few of the diagonal – combinations in the above figures.

We have deliberately picked examples of research undertaken in modestly scaled projects. We have done this, partly because we assume that most readers of this book do not have easy access to large research grants. But, even more important, we want to challenge the idea that combining research styles can be successfully undertaken only in large, lavishly funded projects that employ big research teams and involve two or more distinct phases of work. Instead, we hope to show that any trained researcher can do it. Indeed, we venture to suggest that combining styles of research is a particularly appropriate strategy for doctoral students, not least because it is rather rare for a researcher subsequently to have three years to devote to a single piece of research. Moreover, if one purpose of doctoral research is to provide an apprenticeship in both the core and advanced craft skills of the trade, then experience in using and combining different research styles might be useful.

We first discuss two exemplary studies combining interpretation and explanation, albeit in very different ways.

A causal mechanism enriches a secondary interpretation

In an exemplary piece of doctoral research conducted some thirty years ago in the sociology of knowledge, the anthropologist Steve Rayner studied a variety of Trotskyist, Luxemburgist and Maoist revolutionary sects in London (Rayner, 1982, 1988). In the proper anthropological manner, he undertook participant observation. He posed as a true believer in their various faiths, and managed to be admitted to meetings of revolutionary cells, central praesidiums, study groups, worker–intellectual fraternity courses and so on. The picture he paints of their world views is remarkable. One challenge he faced in writing about these people is the one we discussed at length in Chapter 16: how to represent the groups' thought styles to a readership that might conclude that the people in them are so different from themselves as to be completely incomprehensible or, even, irrational. He found that all these groups were entirely committed to the belief that the socialist revolution was imminent; that capitalism was about to collapse; and that its collapse would be followed inevitably by their own triumph as leaders of a dictatorship that would represent the interests of the working class and institute distributive justice under a system of collective ownership. Clearly, they did not spot the imminent coming of Thatcher, Reagan and Mulroney.

On the dependent variables, Rayner (1982) undertook extensive studies of the ways in which the actors understood their world. In particular, he decided to focus on the conceptions of time in the world views of his subjects. He found that they all had long historical memories for defeats and betrayals, and for the achievements of great but deceased leaders. But their long memories of the past contrasted with their very short time horizons in thinking about the future. Because the revolution was supposed to be at hand, and because speculation about the details of post-revolutionary life was severely frowned upon as being, at best, a distraction – and, at worst, as demonstrating a lack of commitment to the contemporary struggle – the future was effectively foreshortened.

One part of Rayner's research consisted in classical ethnographic interpretive work to develop a secondary interpretation of the actors' understandings. His writing about these groups pursued the goal of emic interpretation. But like every ethnographer, he wrote for a readership of social scientists, and this meant that he could not entirely avoid the imperative to develop interpretations that are etic, at least to some degree. While his subjects probably recognised much of themselves in his writing, they would probably have found many questions that were asked about them, and the dimensions on which he interpreted their thought styles, to be ones that they would find irrelevant, if not downright repellent.

Rayner was not content, however, simply to provide an interpretation of the way in which these sectarians thought. Indeed, in his subsequent writings on theory, he has made clear his distance from the postmodernist view that nothing more than interpretation is possible. Rayner wanted an explanation. He was persuaded that the way in which the Marxist sectarians thought had consequences for the ways in which they behaved and lived, and for how they conducted their politics and their organising. He certainly did not want an explanation that explained *away* their thought style, by redirecting attention to other factors with causal effects on behaviour.

So Rayner turned to the work of his supervisor, the great anthropology theorist, Mary Douglas, to help him formulate an explanation. Although she was personally somewhat repelled by the world of sectarians, Douglas was always intellectually fascinated by it, and much of her work was devoted to puzzling out why sects emerge, why they go through the trajectories they do, and why their thought styles develop as they do. As an institutionalist theorist in the Durkheimian tradition, Douglas argued that sectarians are not subject to intrinsically different causal processes from anyone else: to suppose otherwise is akin to invoking the lazy charge of 'irrationality' that used to dominate debates in anthropology about African religious beliefs or to adopting the equally unhelpful postmodern notion of incommensurability. Douglas held, rather, that people in all social settings think in much the same way, but – Douglas learned from Durkheim and from her own teacher, Edward Evans-Pritchard – they do so under different institutions (Douglas, 1986). In turn, Douglas's work reminded Rayner that Marxists buy the weekly shopping, do the washing up, pay rent or do not, and make friends and fall out with them, in much the same way as everyone else. What mattered for his study was how they operated in the institutional context of their political life and how their politics spilled over into the rest of their lives which were lived under quite different institutions.

An institutionalist explanation of the thought styles of leftist sects

So Rayner developed an institutionalist explanation for the way in which his sectarians thought about time. He argues that the institutions of the sects reinforced strong social bonds within the groups and therefore emphasises internal equality among the groups' members: they also heavily underscored the boundaries between the groups and everyone else. These boundaries are defined strongly around the rejection of accountability to 'mainstream' institutions of London social, political, economic and cultural life in the 1970s. A large part of their point is to weaken the degree of social regulation by wider institutions in order to strengthen members' accountability to the sects.

This dynamic creates a problem for sectarians. In this institutional situation, maintaining cohesion is quite difficult. The demands the group made on its members' time and emotional energy are very great. Members often 'burn out'. Sects are unable to use formal authority to hold the group together, because that would violate the commitment to internal equality. They are equally unable to rely on entrepreneurial energy or on philanthropic patronage because those institutions would corrupt the principles of the sects. So sects are thrown back on shared principles as the only available basis for cohesion. And this leaves them open to the danger that members can differentiate themselves from other members only by being more committed to their shared principles than are other members. This process reinforces the institution of the group, but it demands ever more energy and commitment from members, and therefore increases the risk of burnout. It also risks schism as members compete for the fragile leadership roles which are all that the institutional context affords by way of reward.

Because principles alone cannot solve the cohesion problem, it makes sense to try to maintain levels of energy and commitment by stressing the urgency of the sects' tasks. That is best done by foreshortening the future: if we know that an urgent crisis is about to reward the faithful with power or salvation, then we have an incentive to work harder for the cause. But this strategy alone does not solve the problem. For if the rejection of mainstream institutions is to be maintained, and the purity of the sect's ideas and practices to be protected, then members need to be reminded constantly of their duties to maintain the boundaries between their sect and the rest of the world. Moreover, the danger of schism is so great that memories of past betrayals and their catastrophic consequences for the cause are a good way to keep the true faith before members. Similarly, constant reminders of the founders' sacrifices reinforce commitment to the duties of membership. Finally, nothing keeps the flame of passion for justice burning so bright as memories of past injustice. So long historical memory makes every kind of sense.

In short, Rayner uses Douglas's theory to offer a parsimonious, functional explanation of the sects' world views by pointing to two institutional factors: the degree of social regulation and the degree of social integration of the sects. But nothing in Rayner's argument implies that the mechanisms he describes will always work. On the contrary, many sects fell apart from schism, burnout and failure to evade the long arm of regulation by governments, long before the positive feedback mechanism of the institutions produced the perceptions of time that characterised the extreme Marxist left in the 1970s. Moreover, Rayner's is a theory of conflict, not of harmony: it explains how internal conflict can be overcome only with difficulty and at the expense of a process that can in the longer term exhaust sects and involve them in external conflict with other institutions in the wider city or polity.

Rayner evidenced his causal theory with two kinds of data. He used archival and documentary material made available by his subjects and their enemies – often other Marxist sects seeking to accuse them of betrayal – to describe and explain the long-term dynamics of the sects. And he observed the ways in which members used meetings of various kinds to hold each other to account. In so doing, he coded the institutions to which they appealed as consistently as he could. Finally, he considered and criticised as inadequate a range of other explanations of what he observed.

Rayner's work elegantly combines an interpretive study of actors' understandings and mental life with a causal account of the processes by which the sects' biases in thought style are systematically produced. The relationship between explanation and interpretation is that of type 1, because he explains the actors' understandings of time by reference to institutional conditions independently observed by the researcher.

A secondary interpretation helps to account for a causal mechanism

Our second example is Charles Tilly's work on the 'parliamentarisation' of 'popular contention' in Great Britain in the last half of the eighteenth century and first three decades of the nineteenth century (Tilly, 1993, 1997b). This celebrated study shows how interpretive research can be used to support explanatory research.

In practice, as we have said more than once in this book, all explanations of actions or social organisation involving attitudes, ideas or motives depend on interpreting them. But, just as the explanatory claims embedded in interpretations are not always acknowledged as such, so the same goes for interpretations developed in the course of explanatory research. This example is a particularly interesting and valuable one, because it develops a formal, explicit secondary interpretation to enrich an explanation. This interpretation uses mainly etic categories but – unusually for this type of research – depends on systematic, rigorous analysis of emic categories using techniques more commonly used in explanatory social research.

The interpretive work in this example may, in consequence, be different from that which you may previously have come across. First, it does not involve observation of people, groups or organisations. Nor does it involve doing qualitative interviews. Instead, it draws its data from historical documents. Second, it uses quantitative as well as qualitative analysis, and does so, moreover, in highly structured ways that involve significant data reduction and parsimony. So, third, the trade-off in design values is very different from that involved in most interpretive research, which tends more strongly to emphasise goodness of fit.

The approach used in this study is also a long way from Rayner's, in that it is historical rather than ethnographic; and there is not a whiff of Durkheimian theory in Tilly's articles. But there is an illuminating relationship between the two pieces of work, because Tilly's argument proceeds by reversing the methodological direction of Rayner's. That is, interpretation is done to support and enrich explanation, not the other way around.

Explaining the significance of changes in collective political action

This work links Tilly's macro-level interests in the changing nature of the state with his micro-level interests in social ties. It starts from the widely accepted thesis that, in this period, the nature of government and politics in Great Britain changed in ways that were hugely important in laying the foundations for parliamentary democracy. In this period, politics and government became much more centralised and focused on Parliament, replacing a system in which governmental authority was exercised in large part through local elites based largely in the landed aristocracy and gentry, and in which popular demands or resistance often found expression in riots and other unplanned and often violent modes of political contention.

Tilly goes along with standard explanations of this change, by citing three closely linked causal mechanisms which, he shows, are mutually reinforcing in bringing change about.

First, the ruinously expensive wars of the eighteenth century required new sources of finance that ultimately redounded to taxation. This process strengthened the power of Parliament (which had won the right to approve taxation in the constitutional settlement of 1688). Furthermore, Parliament used its growing authority to engage in regulatory action that, in turn, triggered the making of political claims by new social and economic groups and led to demands for more efficacious ways of making them. Second, growing capitalisation of both agriculture and industry gave birth to new forms of economic organisation among landowners, capitalists and workers. These, in turn, created new reasons and capabilities for making claims against the state, not least in relation to the governance of their mutual relations. Finally, there were changes in the processes by which people – particularly those who were largely excluded from pre-parliamentary politics centred on the monarchy and local elites – engaged in collective action and made political claims. Tilly refers to such processes as ones of 'political contention'.

Tilly's special contribution to our understanding of this change is to underscore the significance of this third mechanism, which he regards as setting Great Britain on the path to a democracy based in the equal political rights of all citizens. For this purpose, he investigated exactly what 'parliamentarisation' of claims-making and collective action meant; how it worked; and what stock tropes of speech – what Tilly calls 'repertoires of political contention' – were drawn upon in recording and learning about it.

To do this, Tilly turned from explanatory to historical–interpretive research. His methodology was informed by his claim that:

> Popular contention is deeply cultural, in the sense that it relies on and transforms shared understanding concerning what forms and ends of action are desirable, feasible, and efficacious; collective learning and memory strongly limit the claims that people make and how they make them. (1997a: 248)

To trace changes in this 'shared understanding', Tilly's small research team developed, as its major analytic resource, a machine-readable catalogue of over 8000 'contentious events' that occurred in the south-east of England between 1758 and 1820, and in Great Britain as a whole between 1828 and 1834. The data in this catalogue were taken from qualitative historical documents – especially the official Hansard record of parliamentary debates, newspapers and widely circulating periodicals. They were coded under ten headings, including: the type of event; where it took place; who took part; and how it was described by contemporaries. The process of coding respected the broad parameters of emic interpretation, by recording how contemporaries perceived and labelled these events, but etic categories were also superimposed through the coding system which forms the basis for Tilly's etic interpretations of changes in understanding political contention in this period.

Tilly uses the data in his catalogue for two main analytic purposes. First, he uses the ways in which contemporaries referred to political movements, groups, events and actions to produce statistical descriptions – simple frequencies, for example – to show trends in the occurrence of different types of events and in the behaviour associated with them. He also traces patterns in the use of different verbs of contention – such as 'claim', 'demand', 'attack', 'control' and 'cheer' – to track changes in the nature of claims about modes of political claims-making.

Second, Tilly uses sociometric block-modelling techniques – which are more often used in social sciences to identify and map social network structures – to analyse contemporary descriptions of types of political actors and the changing relations between them in particular sub-periods. This analysis enabled him to achieve a more finely grained analysis of who typically opposed, or allied with, whom, and thus of the detailed dynamic of the 'parliamentarisation' of British politics in times of particularly rapid or significant change.

The process of building interpretations of change is theory driven, in that Tilly makes his selections of periods and data on the basis of his prior knowledge of his case. He is able to make descriptive inferences from his extensive data set, because his wider historical knowledge enables him to relate the trends he discovers to other processes in British history in the relevant period. In turn, he relates his inferences back to his three causal mechanisms and demonstrates their significance. He thus enriches the explanation of the broad set of changes in this important period in British history, in three main ways.

First, he infers from his close empirical analysis that, by 1834, popular contention was much less frequently recorded as being expressed by means of unplanned – and sometimes violent – demonstrations, riots and strikes. Instead, making claims was increasingly recognised as an activity that was most frequently and most efficaciously channelled through assemblies, campaigns and events designed to develop and declare collective opinions on public issues in the context of a system of representation focused on Parliament.

Second, Tilly's interpretation provides much greater specificity and detail than would be provided by a general account of the causal mechanisms of change. Third, Tilly's analysis enriches our understanding of why the 1830s are both a high point in levels of contention and a defining moment in a process in which Parliament became a much more powerful locus within the newly configured central state. The growing involvement of Parliament in the 1830s in what would, in earlier decades and centuries, have been purely local agrarian conflicts, is a fitting symbol of a ratchet effect created by the interplay of the three causal mechanisms.

To sum up, Tilly's articles offer us an elegant example of combining at least two styles of research – case 2 where a secondary interpretation of actors' understandings helps us to understand a causal mechanism, and case 10 where a statistical description helps to understand a causal mechanism. Whereas Rayner shows us the consequences of institutional accountabilities in producing pressures for certain aspects of mental life to become entrenched, Tilly shows us how the mental life captured in emic categories can help illuminate the significance of underlying causal processes.

Other combinations of research designs

Some of the other combinations of explanation and interpretation that run between left and right of Figure 17.2 can be disposed of quickly, because they are less interesting or because they raise few interesting epistemological or methodological challenges. For example, the two horizontal combinations along the bottom of the diagram – between quantitative description and statistical explanation of variance – are ones that are extremely common but they raise no special problems, other than the usual ones about the status of an inference from an association to causation. That inference is made through the presence of other, reasonably robust, theories – probably of a qualitative character – about the underlying causal mechanisms (see Chapter 12).

Similarly, the diagonal combinations running from left to right in Figure 17.3 are not especially challenging. Consider the two combinations on the positive diagonal. They differ only in the direction of priority for comparison between the subjective perceptions and framings of the people being studied and observations made independently by the researcher (which can stand for the purpose of analysis as objective 'facts'). For many years, for example, this kind of research was used to map the nature, extent and direction of deviation of actors' subjective biased perceptions from scientifically measured facts and dominated the study of risk perception (Example 17.2).

EXAMPLE 17.2. MEASURING SUBJECT PERCEPTIONS OF RISK

Many psychometric studies were conducted to show just how erroneous different groups of people were in their assessment of probabilities of death or serious injury from a variety of causes – including road accidents and flying – by comparison with the rates identified by risk analysts using quantitative data sets (see for example some of the earlier papers collected in Slovic, 2000).

(Continued)

In recent years, this approach has been criticised on a number of grounds. Adams (1995), for example, questioned the averaging used in compiling the data sets. What, he asks, is our risk of being run down when we cross the road? But which sort of road are we crossing? An 'A' road in the centre of a city, perhaps? But is the city typical? Is this road typical? Typical of what exactly? And what about the time of day? Surely it matters whether we cross at rush hour or in the middle of the night? Again, our age and fitness might matter: how quickly can we run; are we disabled in any way?

The problem is that we would have too few observations to provide reliable inferences if the available data were disaggregated to meet such cases. But without such analysis, can we be sure that we are being as irrational as some of the older studies would have insisted, if we rate our estimates of injury particularly high or low? Perhaps we have some informal and tacit knowledge that reflects a more finely grained judgement of the probabilities in the light of our age; fitness; time of day; the nature of the road; traffic conditions; and the phasing of the local traffic lights. Perhaps it is the experts, not us, who are relying on too thin a data set, albeit a quantitative one.

Consider, finally, case 10 in which a statistical description helps us to understand a causal mechanism. In the hands of a skilled practitioner like Charles Tilly, this combination can be undertaken in ways that can support intelligent inference, albeit one that requires careful qualification based on detailed knowledge of the particular case or cases. But in less skilled hands, it may be risky. Certainly, it is not a combination that will bear the weight of a claim to 'help us to understand' in every case.

To make inferences from a description – even a very rich and multi-dimensional statistical description – to support for a particular causal mechanism is a form of abduction or inference to the best explanation, as we discussed in Chapter 11. We saw in that discussion that to validate an abduction, it is necessary to show that the evidence available is not plausibly compatible with any other explanation, leaving only one explanation for which there is a causal mechanism that is well founded in an existing theory. This is a tall order. In everyday contexts of very simple problems, we are able to perform abduction with some degree of reliability, as we discussed in Chapter 11. But in more complex social science contexts, it may be much more difficult. It is worth noting that, in the example we used above, Tilly does not attempt anything so strong as a crucial test to support an abduction from his interpretation to his explanation. On the contrary, he offers an explanation based on independent sources in the historical literature, and uses the interpretation to enrich it.

This reinforces the general point that there are risks in making very strong inferences from findings in one style of research to conclusions in another style of research, in each of the twelve possible combinations. But the risks are especially great in making strong inferences that run from right (interpretation) to left (explanation). One can make errors in drawing inferences for interpretation from explanation. But they are likely, in general, to be less serious than the converse errors from interpretation to explanation, because we mostly look to explanations to provide interpretations with sets of anchors, categories, variables, definitions of cases and hypotheses.

Conclusion

We have attempted in this chapter to persuade you that many of the really interesting questions in social science – whether they are very small or very large in scale – call for combinations of explanatory and interpretive research styles and of qualitative and quantitative data. This is not surprising, because the six types of task that we identified at the beginning of this chapter, and for which we might want to combine explanatory and interpretive styles, are the core tasks of social research.

We have shown, too, that combining styles is not without risks and challenges. Trading off the risks of combining styles against the potential gain in the richness of our explanations and the solidity of our interpretations involves a judgement that ambitious researchers may have to make if they are to grapple with more, rather than less, interesting research questions.

Advanced reading

For an approach to combining interpretive and explanatory designs in the study of political identities, see Smith RM, 2004, The politics of identities and the tasks of political science, in I Shapiro *et al.* (eds), *Problems and methods in the study of politics*, Cambridge: Cambridge University Press, 42–66.

For philosophical rather than methodological reflections on relationships between, and on possibilities of, combining explanation and interpretation, see Hollis M, 2002 [1994], *The philosophy of social science: an introduction*, Cambridge: Cambridge University Press.

EIGHTEEN

Trade-offs in research design

This chapter will:

- show how the central arguments of the book about inference and warrant work together to explain the status of methodology in social sciences;
- review the qualifications that have to be made upon warrant and inference;
- explore in particular the qualifications that arise from the trade-offs we make in research design; and
- conclude briefly by considering how far methodological debate has come in recent decades and where it now appears to be moving.

Inference and warrant revisited

This book has presented a series of closely linked arguments for designing social research in particular ways.

Our central argument has been that there is a limited number of primary routes through which we can make inferences from data relevant to a research question, to the conclusions we draw to provide a good answer to that question. Understanding these primary inferential routes, and being able to judge which one to use in any part of our research, is what we learn from methodology.

Methodology is, we have tried to show, not the same thing as method. It follows that the choice of a particular method or technique depends on methodological arguments which justify, for example, the choice of a deductive, explanatory, comparative-case-oriented design to answer the research question, rather than, say, an inductive, interpretive, case-based one. That is why there is no such thing as 'quantitative' or 'qualitative' methodology. In Chapter 14 we showed that explanatory inference proceeds by the same basic argument, whichever types of data are used. Chapter 17 used an example from Tilly's work which shows that the same thing is true in interpretive inference. Drawing the inference that a certain explanation for, or description or interpretation of, a phenomenon is better warranted than another rests on methodological arguments.

We have argued, too, that methodology is also not the same thing as the philosophy of social science. There is no 'realist methodology', nor is there a 'positivist methodology' nor yet a 'constructionist methodology'. These epistemological positions do not mandate the choice between variable-oriented, case-based or case-comparative designs, nor between deductive and inductive designs, nor do they demand or rule out designs for descriptive, explanatory or interpretive inference. Methodology's relationship with philosophical argument is – like its relationship with method – an intimate one. But an argument in philosophy does not mechanically determine a particular methodological approach.

Philosophy is, nevertheless, important for methodology in two ways. First, as we saw in Chapters 2–4, philosophical arguments help us to understand the status of the claims to knowledge made by descriptions, explanations and interpretations. Second, philosophical arguments help us to understand the standards to which our inferences aspire: for example, those associated with virtues in explanation, such as causality, parsimony, generality and goodness of fit, or those with virtues in interpretation, such as those we discussed in Chapter 16 as the principles of rationality, charity or felicity.

The unity of social science

A large and important conclusion follows from the arguments in this book. It is that social science is essentially a single enterprise. It is not bifurcated according to the type of data we use, for the same logics of argument underpin inferences from both counting and describing. Nor is social science rent by irreconcilable approaches associated with different philosophical positions: people who hold different philosophical positions simply take different views about the status of the claims to knowledge yielded by well-designed research.

Nor, again, is social science divided by principles of research design such as deduction and induction, or description, explanation and interpretation, because, in practice, the best research often combines these principles in ways that demonstrate their fundamental compatibility, Finally, we have used examples throughout this book from disciplines as diverse as political science, criminology, anthropology, sociology, organisation and business studies, education research and public administration to show that the same methodological considerations apply across these artificial divisions of social science, which have, in any case, been separated only recently and for reasons of intellectual convenience.

Just as in the natural sciences, inference in social research proceeds from the analysis of well-selected and well-structured observations to arguments about things that cannot be directly observed. The point about methodology is that it allows us to argue that our research design gives us warrant for believing that our analysis constitutes good evidence for claims about these unobservable things. Even in descriptive research, we must often make inferences from observation to claims about things that we cannot directly observe. If we want to know – as descriptive researchers interested in 'social capital' do – whether citizens in selected twenty-first-century countries have fewer or more friends than did their parents and grand-parents, or whether they rely more or less upon those they count as friends, then we have to make inferences from people's answers to, say, survey questions or in-depth interviews to claims that their relationships really are ones of friendship. This process requires concept formation work on 'friendship', and inferences to be drawn from reported claims about how it currently works in these countries.

In interpretive research, the unobservable things in which we are most interested are mental states: people's beliefs, desires, intentions, emotions, or their shared background resources for mental states such as ways of classifying issues and problems, or their narratives about the past. Explanatory research calls, perhaps, for inferences to the widest variety of things that cannot be directly observed, including interests, pay-offs, constraints, institutions, conventions, organisations, social relations and networks, practices, skills and capabilities, as well as mental states such as ideas, intentions and motives.

We saw in Chapter 4, however, that people holding different philosophical positions about social science disagree about the status of knowledge claims about things which cannot be observed directly. Positivists and relativists are very cautious here, for strikingly similar reasons. By contrast, realists consider that there are good reasons for treating these claims as being true or false on the basis of determinate facts, even if we are forced to make inferences to those facts. On this question, we have nailed our own colours firmly to the realists' mast.

What matters in making inferences from facts that can be directly observed to things that are not observable is that our choice of research design enables us to be precise about the qualifications that we must make to our confidence in the claims of warrant we can make for these inferences.

This fact is, in itself, not especially interesting for methodology, although its correct interpretation matters greatly for philosophy. What *is* methodologically interesting is, for example, whether we can design a crucial test, such that we can rule out all other explanations than the one which remains standing, so that we need make fewer qualifications than otherwise. Even then, we would need to acknowledge any risks we may have taken in concept formation. There will also be matters of method – such as risks of measurement error – that should also be declared as qualifications of our inferences.

Nevertheless, using a crucial test in this way would enable us to be more confident about inferences than, for example, if they were drawn from a piece of research that was designed to develop a new hypothesis. Of course, a study to develop a hypothesis or to refine a difficult but critical concept *could* represent scientific progress of a more significant kind than a routine test of a hypothesis that has already been well examined and from which we can learn rather little more than we previously knew. So another lesson we hope you will take from this book is that confidence in our inferences and the scientific value of these inferences are very different things.

Qualification and trade-offs

Throughout this book, we have also argued that an important reason for requiring careful qualifications of our inferences is that every descriptive, interpretive or explanatory inference we make must strike some trade-off between the competing virtues, respectively of good descriptions, interpretations and explanations. It is impossible in any single study to maximise all of these virtues at once.

If a body of research in a particular field develops and, with luck, begins to converge in its findings – that is, it begins to accumulate knowledge – the particular trade-offs made in each of the studies that form that body of work may come to matter less. But in each study, a critical part of the way we qualify our inference is to be explicit about the particular trade-offs we have made. Indeed, only when a review of a body of developing knowledge can identify findings that are common to studies which have clearly made different and, even, contrasting trade-offs can that review be justifiably confident of the robustness of the findings around which the field appears to be converging.

We have argued that the same basic virtues apply to explanatory and to interpretive inference, even though different trade-offs between them may be required for a study – or for a part of a study – that is principally interpretive from those made in an explanatory one. The four virtues which are conventionally listed (Przeworski and Teune, 1970) – and on which we have focused most heavily in this book – are the following:

- *Parsimony*: the virtue of economically using a limited number of important factors to explain or, perhaps, interpret a wide range of events or conditions or social phenomena.
- *Goodness of fit with the data*: the virtue of capturing as much of the available empirical information as possible and its significance, in order to explain or interpret as many *aspects* of the cases studied as fully and comprehensibly as possible.
- *Generality*: the virtue of supporting inferences from the data on one or few cases in an empirical study, to a wide range of other possible cases which are similar in relevant ways; this virtue allows us to explain as many *cases* as possible within the category from which the study takes its sample.
- *Causality*: the virtue of supporting inferences that clearly show the structure of variables, causal mechanisms, contexts and outcomes.

This list is, however, not exhaustive. We have already glimpsed other important virtues that also have to be traded off. They include the following:

- *Precision*: the virtue of enabling a precise and exact statement of the structure of the explanation or interpretation offered by the study.

In Chapter 9, we saw the importance of being precise in defining and operationalising concepts. But we also noted, there, that in some kinds of interpretive research, we

---

have to work with 'family resemblance' concepts and that, even in some explanatory research designs, we must use radial concepts. In so doing, we accept less precision in exchange for some other virtue. In interpretive research, for example, we might accept reduced precision in a concept, such as that of a 'game', that we attribute to the people we study, in exchange for greater goodness of fit.

- *Fundamentality*: the virtue of emphasising the most basic factors that are used in explaining conditions, events or other phenomena.

In Chapter 10, we discussed what is at stake in designs which privilege more distal or more proximate factors in explanation. All other things being equal, and depending on the research question, we showed that distal explanations can be more satisfying. On the other hand, proximate ones may allow greater goodness of fit or greater generality.

- *Interactivity*: the virtue of securing an understanding of the complex interactions between different factors that may be part of the explanation, rather than simply identifying and listing them.

In Chapter 6, we examined both the power and also the limitations of conventional statistical analysis which gives to each explanatory factor a coefficient showing the proportion of the variance on the dependent variable. As Ragin has emphasised, one limitation of such studies is that – at least on their own – they tell us little about just *how* factors work together.

Mechanism-chasing studies may be more informative on this point. As social science becomes increasingly interested in the 'complexity' of interactions between factors, this virtue is coming to be increasingly prized. On the other hand, it is difficult to achieve it without sacrificing some parsimony, and sometimes even some generality, because the same factors may interact differently in different subsets of a population, as we saw in Chapter 11 in our discussion of the causation of revolutions.

- *Contribution to scientific progress*: the virtue of advancing either empirical knowledge or theoretical capability or the richness of our conceptual apparatus.

A study may, for example, provide only empirical information of an unsurprising kind in a well-worked field. Being able to place strong confidence in inferences from it may, undoubtedly, be valuable if, say, the point is to use descriptive inference to identify small changes in trends – for example, in retail crime – about which policymakers and businesses may care very deeply.

The scientific value of such a study is, however, rather different from a study which opens up a previously unexplored question, develops a fresh hypothesis, redefines a central concept, identifies a major anomaly in a body of well-regarded theory, or produces a surprising or counter-intuitive empirical finding which calls for fresh theoretical work to explain or interpret it. On the other hand, such studies may well be ones which require us to place greater qualifications upon their inferences, precisely because of the risks they have taken.

This discussion shows that it is difficult, in the same study, to maximise its contribution to scientific progress and also its generality. Similarly – unless the innovation is one of method – it is hard to maximise both a study's contribution to scientific progress and its goodness of fit. This is because most innovative developments tend to be in concept formation or in theoretical development which prizes causality and fundamentality.

Trade-offs in research design

This discussion underlines the argument made at several points in the book – that it is always necessary in conducting any research to choose some virtues as being more important than others and to design the project accordingly. How this choice is made depends on the nature of our research question and our reasons for wanting to answer it.

There are, unfortunately, no hard, fast and universal rules to help us make the judgements involved in this choice. Judgements about trade-offs are, therefore, always open to challenge: some will necessarily be better than others, and, indeed, some may, in the view of critics or referees, be downright misguided. Making design choices that are capable of being rigorously and convincingly defended is the best to which we can aspire: none can be put entirely beyond challenge.

There are, however, some rules of thumb. By a rule of thumb, we mean a maxim that often or usually produces valuable results, but does not do so automatically or invariably. There is always scope for designers of research to argue that, for their purposes, a rule of thumb should be set aside, that it is inapplicable or inappropriate for their project, or that some other trade-off would be more valuable for the particular research question. So all rules of thumb are rebuttable. But, nevertheless, we venture to offer three of the most important ones for making trade-offs in research design:

1 *Causality in explanatory research*. This rule of thumb is that explanatory research should, if possible, optimise the capture of causality, even at the expense of generality and some loss of goodness of fit. As we said in Chapter 6 and many times subsequently, VOR can identify causal factors. But it may need to be supplemented with CBR and COR studies if we want to capture more information about just how, or by what mechanism, those factors work, both severally and together. If so, the supplementary studies may reasonably sacrifice some generality for that gain in precision and interactivity.
2 *Goodness of fit in interpretive research*: Interpretive research often, quite properly, prizes goodness of fit above other virtues. Many of the great classic anthropological studies, as we discussed in Chapters 15 and 16, for example, captured the significance of data both widely and deeply. To sustain these achievements, it may well be reasonable to sacrifice some parsimony and generality.

3 *Goodness of fit on* explananda *in CBR and COR.* Because much of the point of case-based and small-*N* comparative research is to identify differences in causation or actors' mental lives within or between a small number of cases, we expect it to prize that particular element of goodness of fit which consists in providing a full and exhaustive account of the significant differences on these cases.

In case-based and comparative research, therefore, we might reasonably be prepared to sacrifice generality for this particular aspect of goodness of fit. By contrast, statistically unexplained variance in VOR work is perfectly normal: indeed, we are usually suspicious of a large-*N* VOR study which claims to have provided a statistical explanation for one hundred per cent of the variance or an absolutely perfect correlation. Ineliminable measurement error alone ought to make that unlikely. In other words, large-*N* VOR studies routinely sacrifice goodness of fit for generality.

Defending trade-offs in design

These three rules of thumb cannot provide complete guidance, because, as we said above, everything in the end depends on the research question. In Example 18.1, we use a recently published major study on change in the organisation and management of public services in Europe to show, first, how the trade-offs were informed by the purposes of the research and, second, the grounds on which they could be criticised and defended.

EXAMPLE 18.1. CHANGE AND DECAY IN ALL I SEE

Two internationally renowned scholars of public management, Christopher Pollitt and Geert Bouckaert, of the University of Leuven, recently published a book (Pollitt and Bouckaert, 2009) reporting how public services change over time. This study used a case-comparative design of the kind we described in Chapter 8, with a complicated selection of cases and complex levels of analysis.

 Their initial hunch was that change follows different dynamics in different countries. The hypothesis was that public services (1) in countries with first-past-the-post electoral systems, which tend to produce highly adversarial politics and big pendulum swings, and (2) with highly centralised political systems, where localities have less scope to decide for themselves how far to follow or resist national policies, (3) will differ from those in countries with (4) proportional representation, which tends to lead to coalition governments and mutual accommodation, and with (5) decentralised political systems, where localities can choose, if they wish, to insulate themselves from national pressures to some degree.

 This hypothesis led them to compare the nations of the UK and Belgium, and the localities of Brighton and Leuven.

(Continued)

They also hypothesised that patterns of change will be different among services run by many different professions from those where the service is staffed largely by a single profession. This hypothesis led them to compare health care – particularly secondary care in hospitals – with policing.

So far, so deductive. However, they did not start with a hypothesis derived from a causal theory about what would drive change. Instead, they decided to specify, in advance of conducting the research, a typology, not of causal mechanisms, but of *trajectories* of change. They suggest that change might be either abrupt or incremental, and might either occur within a path, or occur between paths.

Cross-tabulating these two dimensions gave them four types of change. Change might show the form of a *tortoise* (incremental, within a path), a *stalactite* (incremental, but between paths, to produce something quite new), a *boomerang* (abrupt, but returning to its original path) or an *earthquake* (abrupt, between paths once and for all).

Pollitt and Bouckaert sought to apply their typology by examining which of the four types best fits each service in each period of the thirty-five years or so of their study. There is a very close analogue for this procedure in certain kinds of non-parametric statistical research. In approaches of this kind – such as 'joinpoint' analysis – the researcher works with a predefined set of previously specified patterns for curves, and examines the distributions observed for goodness of fit of these 'splines', as they are called. These splines – like any curves – smooth out some movements in the data, and interpolate to some degree where data are missing. Although Pollitt and Bouckaert used qualitative data, they provide an illustrative diagram – which they compare with a medical cardiogram – of how their four types might be sequenced over time.

Having analysed their data about change, coded for these four types and found the best fit they could, they proceeded to identify quite a long list of factors – they call them 'mechanisms', but, in the terms we have used in this book, they are perhaps better thought of as factors – that appear to have been causally responsible for these patterns of change.

Now consider the trade-offs they have struck in this design. Their priority was *goodness of fit*. In using only four types, they have also preserved a degree of *parsimony*. *Generality* was not a major goal, if by that we mean direct generalisation to other countries or to other cities. Rather, they wanted to develop an account – as opposed to testing it – that might suggest what has gone on elsewhere.

But, arguably, they have sacrificed the capture of *causality*. The four types of trajectory are not themselves causes or mechanisms – as we have understood them in this book – and the list of factors they identify toward the end of their empirical analysis is developed inductively rather than tested directly.

This sort of trade-off is in fact not uncommon in the study of change. Indeed, some of the most influential and respected scholars make a very similar trade-off (Streeck and Thelen, 2005; Mahoney and Thelen, 2010). Pollitt and Bouckaert – and for that matter, these other authors – would be able to defend their chosen trade-off on the following grounds.

First, they could say that the field is too underdeveloped in its understanding of causation to enable them to have pre-specified a hypothesis about causal relations that would be more than a menu of candidate factors. Second, they could say that, for the understanding of trajectories – as opposed to causation – of change (which is after all their principal question), a focus upon splines rather than mechanisms is a reasonable one. Third, they could say that the trade-off they have achieved is a consequence of their choice of research question and analytic framework. So – for all these reasons – it was appropriate to trade-in *causality* and *generality* for *goodness of fit* and *parsimony*.

(Continued)

A critic of the trade-offs in their research design might worry about two things. First, one of the risks of non-parametric statistical designs is that of curve-fitting. Maybe the procedure works almost too well: if one selects from the available data in ways that make that possible, it is always possible to find that one of the available curves shows goodness of fit. Pollitt and Bouckaert's work may display the equivalent risk in qualitative work. Although they tried to control for this risk by fixing their periods as far as possible by major political changes, we might wonder whether the bounding of those changes actually helps to avoid the problem or is actually the means by which they fall into this hazard.

Second, we might wonder if anything that occurred only at local level could ever meet the standards for being an earthquake, in the way that an event at national level – such as, say, the need for a country's public finances to be bailed out by the EU or the International Monetary Fund – might be. In other words, one risk that flows from their case selection procedure is that coding becomes an artefact of research design, rather than a consequence of evidence. A critic might worry that their typology of change patterns biases the findings at local level toward tortoises and stalactites. The point to notice for this chapter, however, is that it follows directly from the trade-offs involved in making goodness of fit the key virtue, and, consequently, in settling for a two-level case selection principle involving this set of splines.

In fact, Pollitt and Bouckaert do have a case of a local earthquake: the traumatic splitting of the University of Leuven in 1968, when the Flemish authorities took over the university and the Walloons set up a new university a few miles away. But of course this event may be better understood as a local sub-case or local implementation of a much greater, and rather unusual, national earthquake.

The point of Example 18.1 is neither to praise nor to criticise Pollitt and Bouckaert. For the record, we think they have produced a genuinely valuable and interesting study about change which leads us to think about trajectories in ways that are rather different from those put forward by previous research in this field. Their study therefore merits a respected place in the literature on institutional change. We use it here only to illustrate how the trade-offs made in this study relate to its purposes. Our discussion identifies the ways in which their study is deductive or inductive, its case selection principles and the reliance it places, respectively, upon between-case and within-case analysis. As a result, we have, first, been able to identify the virtues that have been least prized and most prized, and, second, to consider whether the risks taken with the virtues that are least prized were worth taking to secure the gains achieved in knowledge.

Methodological gambles in research design

In this example we have considered these trade-offs and their outcomes retrospectively. But in designing any piece of research we must, of course, consider them prospectively. Essentially the same process of reasoning must be gone through in advance, but with one critical – and obvious – difference: we are, in effect, taking out a bet on the gain in understanding and knowledge that our research will afford.

Planning a piece of research is always a methodological gamble on trade-offs. But the gamble can be a more or less defensible one.

In placing the bet, it is rarely worth privileging one virtue above all others. As in other walks of life, 'moderation in pursuing virtue' is a good maxim. A study that sacrificed everything for goodness of fit would be hard to justify. Without some effort to pursue at least two or three of the other virtues, it would collapse either into description or else into forced curve-fitting. You might think that Pollitt and Bouckaert ran that same risk, but they did preserve some degree of parsimony and disciplined their case selection by an interest in developing – although not testing – theory with aspirations for future generality.

Similarly, a study that pursued causality at the expense of all parsimony would be so specific to its case that it would, in effect, lose all potential for aspiring to develop theory of more general application. And it would certainly become less interesting, as a result. So in planning a new piece of research, it is wise to consider whether we are taking too great a gamble by focusing too much on one – or a very few – virtues.

Trade-offs are contingent

It is also worth bearing in mind that we shall probably not find ourselves making the same trade-offs for different pieces of research, even within the same project. Some trade-offs may be justified in the early stages of the development of a body of research but become less appropriate as the field matures. For example, in the early stage of the development of a field of literature, we might be prepared to sacrifice parsimony and causality for a design that told us something fairly coarse about the range of factors at work in a wide, general population. As the field develops and the literature matures, we should want the reverse trade-off. Likewise, one set of trade-offs may be the right one to make at one stage in a multi-stage project, and another in a later stage. Consider Example 18.2 which looks at the way in which the maturity of the body of existing literature might influence the choice of trade-off.

EXAMPLE 18.2. MY PATIENT LIST IS BIGGER THAN YOURS

There is a large body of work – mainly done through large-*N* VOR studies – that tells us that there is a strong relationship between the size of the hospital units that carry out a range of surgical activities and the outcomes for the patients in terms of risks of death on the operating table, five-year survival chances, readmission to hospital and so on. That is, there is a great deal of work that claims to identify the key variables with a high degree of generality and a high level of parsimony.

This is useful in identifying the exact nature of the condition we need to explain, but, of course, it leaves us knowing far too little about causes and mechanisms that produce it. There is a range of candidate explanations:

(Continued)

- Do larger teams exercise greater internal discipline over the quality of their work, because size makes for better supervision and training (this would be a causal effect directly associated with size)?
- Do older, more established teams do better because they have built up their systems and they just happen to be larger (if so, size is not a cause, and to imply that it is, would be misleading)?
- Do bigger units attract people who are better surgeons (if so, the main cause is a staff selection effect)?
- Do larger centres process patients with better prognoses (a patient selection effect)?
- Or is some other cause working in the cases?

It is possible, too, that the relative weight of these factors differs significantly among specialties, so the generality claimed for this body of research may be masking important differences among types of cases.

What this body of research now needs is some studies that prize *causality* and *precision* so that they can determine which of these facts produces the effect and how, even if in so doing they sacrifice some *generality*. In seeking precision, they will probably prize *goodness of fit* and also lose some *parsimony*. If multiple causes seem to be at work, then we may also need further research that values *interactivity*.

Trade-offs and realism

In Chapter 4, we argued that there are good reasons to accept that there are determinate facts about abstract unobservable things such as institutions, constraints, social ties and practices on the basis of which the claims, to which we make inferences, are true or false. Making inferences about them, we argued in Chapter 1, is the whole point of social research.

We have also argued that different studies on the same research question might legitimately use different trade-offs in their design. Some readers might think there is a tension here. You might wonder why we could regard it as defensible that different research projects could draw different trade-offs in their research designs for studying the same determinate facts.

In fact, realism is quite consistent with recognising that there might be quite a range of defensible trade-offs. First, we have shown clearly that we should not try to defend just any trade-offs between design virtues in research. Some are, in general, poor trade-offs, and would fall foul of the rules of thumb proposed above. Some will produce poor results in particular studies for more contingent reasons. So the range of defensible variety is limited.

Second, realism is a claim about underlying facts. It is not a claim that any of the research design principles we identified in Chapter 5, still less about the findings of any particular study, should be accepted as unimpeachable. Indeed, we have shown that each of those design principles – deductive and inductive studies, descriptive, explanatory and interpretive ones and so on – quite reasonably call for slightly different trade-offs between virtues such as parsimony, generality, causality and goodness of fit.

Third and most fundamentally, there may be cases where bodies of literature consisting in studies on the same or closely related research questions, which have used different but defensible trade-offs, converge in their findings. This cumulation provides evidence – gathered, perhaps in systematic (Petticrew and Roberts, 2006) or realistic (Pawson, 2006) research reviews – that social science as a whole is beginning to capture some of the underlying facts about a problem or question. The best explanation for being able to make such a cumulation is that there are indeed determinate facts which are being glimpsed by studies, irrespective of the choice the researchers make among the available defensible trade-offs. Conversely, if the literature shows no such convergence, it does not follow that there are no determinate facts about their questions. It may simply be that the questions or the hypotheses have been too poorly formulated to capture those underlying realities.

Variety in trade-offs among differently designed studies on the same question therefore provides a validity check on the inferences we make – one that is conducted over time, or perhaps in a research review, rather than in any one empirical study. Therefore, recognising a bounded diversity in defensible trade-offs positively assists the realist argument about explaining convergence in findings as the cumulation and confirmation of knowledge.

Methodology in the twenty-first century

This book has been written from the conviction that many of the methodological disputes which dominated much of twentieth-century social science are exhausted, and that we can now discern the shape of future methodological debates.

From the 1960s until the 1980s and even into the early 1990s, the focus of disagreement was about whether quantitative and qualitative data should in general be preferred. It was commonly supposed that the differences in the nature of the data – as between things that are counted and things that are described – made a huge difference to every one of the methodological issues discussed in this book. At every stage in this book, we have shown that this supposition is simply not true. Issues of validity and reliability, problems of concept formation, questions about the kinds of explanation or interpretation that can be warranted on the basis of data, all call for much the same types of inference, whether the data used consist in numbers or in words.

In those same decades, much attention was concentrated on the question of sample size. Advocates of case studies argued that small-N studies could yield valuable information, while the champions of large-scale studies insisted that, in the absence of great numbers of cases, valid inferences could not be achieved. More recently, although peace has not yet been established, at least an armed truce has broken out between these warring parties. In this book, we have argued that – provided we understand the different tasks for which different kinds of studies are conducted, and provided we put appropriate qualifications on what we can conclude from either kind of research – there is ample space in the broad plains of social science for both kinds of work to be pursued. Moreover, there are many methodological issues that both types of research design must address, such as problems of concept formation and the structuring of explanations. And, increasingly, research must find ways of combining within-case and between-case analysis, or adroitly linking explanatory and interpretive strategies.

In the 1970s and 1980s, a growing interest in interpretation combined with a surge of interest in epistemological outlooks that were unsympathetic to realism. The result was a burgeoning methodological literature in an 'interpretivist' register. We have argued in Chapters 15 and 16 that this literature often provides a poor account of what is valuable in interpretation. By the 1990s, the high tide of that movement had probably passed, and across the social sciences interest is returning to causal explanation. In particular, there is growing interest in the methodological case for techniques such as causal process tracing.

Other methodological debates, too, now seem exhausted. Arguments about whether the social sciences were fundamentally different from natural sciences have given way to much more nuanced comparisons between particular social and particular natural sciences, in which there is less room for such coarse duality. The idea no longer seems so convincing that the most important practical choice for a researcher in designing a study is to do with his or her philosophical position on the status of unobservable entities. The relationship between philosophy and principles of design is now widely recognised to be less mechanical than this old formula suggests.

We suspect that, in consequence, methodological debates in social science in the twenty-first century will increasingly look very different from twentieth-century ones. We hope and believe that methodology is being recognised more clearly as presenting questions which are distinct both from those of method and from those of philosophy. Instead of set-piece confrontations around grand dichotomies, we expect attention to shift to more fluid debates about:

- the relationship between deductive and inductive designs, the scope for combination, and the risks involved in writing up research in a deductive logic of justification if the logic of discovery, in practice, combined strong elements of induction (or *vice versa*);
- designs for different ways of combining within- and between-case analysis, including both explanation and interpretation;
- the nature of causal mechanisms and their relationship with causal trajectories, not just as an empirical question but as a problem for research design;
- the integration of developing and testing causal theory with specifying felicity conditions in interpretive work; and
- developing a richer set of more conditional rules of thumb about trade-offs between the partially rival virtues in research design.

There are also some signs, as we noted in Chapter 9, of a revival of interest in older debates, such as those about the status and importance of different kinds of typology in social science.

At the centre of methodological debate, though, will remain the challenge of designing research which provides defensible warrant for the inferences we seek to make from the observations we select to claims about things that we cannot directly observe. Every chapter in this book has been directed to an aspect of that challenge. Social science communities have long been peculiarly self-conscious – even, sometimes, anxious or defensive – about this central challenge, in a way that does not hold so consistently for every research community in the natural and technological sciences.

Even if this self-consciousness may seem oddly precious to outsiders, it has the merit of encouraging social scientists to pay close attention to just what they can infer from their research and how they defend their inferences. We hope that the arguments, examples and exercises in this book will help you to design research which – in encouraging you to strike appropriate trade-offs and to declare suitable qualifications – will enable you to draw confident inferences which will make important and robust contributions to progress in social science.

Glossary

Abduction: use of data to eliminate explanations by falsification to leave, in the ideal case, all but one explanation as the most plausible.

Ad hoc *adjustment*: a change made to the explanatory propositions offered by a theory, where the change is not driven by its main concepts; it adds no new empirical content (i.e. makes no predictions of new observations) but is done to make the theory consistent with anomalous data.

Additive: a conception of causation in which each independent variable is understood to be analytically distinct and to produce an effect without interaction with other variables. Each independent variable that is found to be significant is assumed to make its own independent contribution to producing the outcome described by the dependent variable. The contributions made by these independent variables are added together to provide the causal explanation. 'Additive' causation is contrasted with configurational, conjunctural, mechanism and emergent causation.

Anomaly/anomalous data: data which are inconsistent with the predictions derived from a theory.

'As if' explanation: an explanation which predicts the available data well (i.e. exhibits strong goodness of fit) but in which the assumptions do not necessarily have to be plausible.

Association: a relationship between two variables X and Y, such that when X is observed, with an acceptability level of probability, Y will also be observed.

Auxiliary hypothesis: a hypothesis which is provided in addition to the principal hypothesis or hypotheses; in the presence of anomalous data, an auxiliary hypothesis is changed or even abandoned, in preference to changing or abandoning the principal one(s).

Behaviouralism: the thesis that, *in principle*, theories could be stated without the use of terms describing mental life, but that in practice this is too difficult and/or too cumbersome.

Behaviourism: the programme of trying *in practice* to eliminate terms describing mental life from substantive theories in use.

Between-case analysis: developing an explanation by comparing variables, configurations and so on between cases, to identify potentially causal factors or trends that appear to be common or different.

Causal explanations: explanations that answer the questions 'why?' and 'brought about by what?' They rely on factors, or configurations of factors or contexts and mechanisms.

Causality: a specific virtue in research design: that of supporting warranted inference by demonstrating clearly the formal structure of the causal relationships postulated in a causal explanation, to show the nature of the causation.

Causation: the process by which one phenomenon – or set of phenomena – brings about another.

Coherence theory of truth: a philosophical theory of the meaning of 'truth'. It states that a statement (e.g. in a model or a theory) is true if, and only if, the statement is either consistent with or entailed by other statements that are scientifically accepted as providing the best available description and/or explanation of the data.

Commensurability: a term in one theory is commensurable with those in another theory if the term in the first theory can be translated without loss of meaning into a set of expressions that have meaning in the second theory.

Conceptual framework: a taxonomy and interlocking set of definitions of key elements used in an explanation, or in a hermeneutic reconstruction, to provide understanding.

Condition: a state of being, a state of affairs.

Configuration: combinations of characteristics, aspects of cases, or variables and their interrelations that, when taken together, provide an explanation of a phenomenon.

Confirm: support provided by observations or data for a theory, by virtue of being consistent with a prediction derived from the theory.

Construct validity: the degree to which the measures used to operationalise a concept really capture it.

Construction (of data): see 'data construction'.

Constructionism: (1) the thesis that people understand the issues they face in ways that are influenced by their mental lives, and that their construals of their situations have major consequences for their actions and social organisation; (2) the thesis that institutions are sustained only by the social acceptance of them; (3) *ideational* constructionism: that institutions come into being as a causal consequence of prior sets of ideas and beliefs.

Constructivism: (1) a psychological theory about how individuals learn the meanings of concepts and so on; (2) in the study of international relations, a position equivalent to ideational constructionism (see constructionism (3)).

Context: (1) the set of variables, or their configuration, which remains constant during the period in which a mechanism is operating to bring about an effect, but which has a critical influence upon which effect the mechanism brings about; (2) as above, but where the set of variables, or their configuration, exhibits systematic relations and connections among its elements.

Contextual factor: an empirical phenomenon that affects the causal operation of a mechanism.

Correspondence theory of truth: a philosophical theory of the meaning of 'truth' that holds that a statement (e.g. in a model or a theory) is true if, and only if, the empirical content of the statement corresponds to the facts that actually obtain.

Counterfactual: a claim that 'If C had not happened, then E would not have occurred, where, in fact, both C and E have occurred.'

Crucial confirmation test: a test that allows for no plausible explanation to be developed that would make the theory *inconsistent* with the data.

Crucial disconfirmation test: a test that allows for no plausible explanation that would make the theory consistent with the data.

Data: information gathered in the course of research, which is believed, on the basis of a theory of the research design and of what the instruments used actually do, to relate in some clear way to a population or set of cases.

Data analysis: methods for manipulating the data to enable the research question to be answered, usually by identifying important and relevant patterns. These methods include statistical procedures, and also qualitative analysis techniques, such as open-ended content analysis, Boolean analysis and a variety of theory-based comparative techniques for handling historical qualitative data.

Data collection: procedures for capturing what is important for the research question from the data that have been created, including the use of codes to classify important aspects of the things examined, counting and more advanced quantitative procedures.

Data construction: methods for laying out sets or series of data that have been created and collected on a suitably common basis, so that they can be compared, analysed and otherwise manipulated in order that patterns can be detected.

Data creation: methods for producing the raw material of research, namely well-structured sets of items of information that can be used for analysis. They include participative and non-participative observation, focus groups, interviews, questionnaire surveys and so on.

Deduction: the process of deriving hypotheses about expected associations by logical entailment from theories.

Deductive research design: a research design that begins with the process of deducing a hypothesis from a theory; the purpose is to determine logically what would have to be found to be the case if the hypothesis were true and what would not be observed to be the case if it were false; a procedure is established to collect the necessary data which are analysed to determine whether the findings warrant an inference capable of confirming or disconfirming the hypothesis.

Degenerating (of a research programme): no longer capable of producing theories that furnish explanations from which we can derive novel predictions of facts that we should expect to find or, better still, not find, if the theories were true.

Description: a statement of what is believed, on the basis of evidence, to be the case. It provides answers to questions such as 'What kinds of things are the Xs?' and 'How can we characterise them?'

Descriptive inference: (1) the process of drawing inferences from data to a description, or (2) the process of drawing inferences from a description of a particular sample to a population or from a set of cases to a larger set which cannot itself be observed.

Deterministic: a conception of causation in which a cause C (which can be a variable or a configuration) raises the probability of an effect E to near or absolute certainty.

Disconfirm: undermining of a theory by an instance, case or observation that is inconsistent with a prediction derived from the theory.

Distal variable: an explanatory variable, the content or meaning of which is a long way from the phenomenon it explains.

Emic: the use of categories that are meaningful to the actors being studied, and that are supposed to be validated only by a consensus among them.

Empiricism: the philosophical position that holds that all knowledge comes from experience, or from what we can observe, not just in visual observations but by using our senses or the instruments we possess to extend and enhance them. Empiricists argue, second, that when we develop abstract concepts and theories, we are identifying patterns that recur in the data, and that those recurrent patterns are the real content of explanations.

Endogeneity: a causal path, in which an outcome that has been effected by a causal factor or variable that has, in turn, an effect on the causal factor; endogeneity thus works through a causal feedback loop.

Epistemology: the sub-discipline within philosophy that considers the merits of theories about the status of knowledge, whether that knowledge is drawn from science, from everyday observation or from other practices.

Etic: the use of categories that make sense to scientific observers, and which are validated by scientific procedures intended to capture correspondence with facts.

Explanandum (pl. *explananda*): the phenomena that are being explained.

Explanans (pl. *explanantes*): the things that explain a phenomenon.

Explanations: answers to such questions as 'Why have the Xs done Z or become Y?', 'What brought this about?' and 'What *caused* the Xs to become Y or do Z?'

Explanatory framework: an overarching account of which factors should be examined, to explain a type of phenomenon; examples include rational choice, Marxism, behaviourism, structural functionalism and institutionalism.

Explanatory inference: the process of drawing inferences (q.v.) from data to an explanation.

Explanatory power: the proportion of variance in a phenomenon explained by an explanation.

Explanatory satisfaction: the degree to which an explanation is informative and not banal; typically, satisfaction is enhanced by the use of variables or configurations that are contingent, critical, and distal or fundamental.

Factor: an empirical feature or phenomenon that may exert some causal influence upon an outcome.

Falsify: the use of systematically collected observations which are inconsistent with predictions derived from the theory (i.e. which are anomalous), to argue convincingly that the best scientific judgement would reject the theory rather than amend or reject it, or to save it by amending auxiliary hypotheses.

Framework: see 'paradigm'.

Fundamental problem of causal inference: the problem that, except in strictly controlled experiments, it is impossible empirically to warrant the claim that 'if X had not been present, Y would not have happened, so X must have caused Y'. This is because we cannot observe a situation without X, in which everything else is the same.

Generality: a specific virtue in research design: that it supports warranted inference to an explanation or interpretation that holds for the widest plausible set of unobserved cases that are relevantly similar to those which have been observed.

Generative: a conception of mechanisms which uses a realist (q.v.) understanding of mechanisms, and which stresses the transformative character of the causal process.

Goodness of fit: (1) the measure of how well – how exactly or how closely – a set of data fits the distribution predicted by a theory; (2) a truthful, detailed and close description of phenomena, or analysis of qualitative data, that provides a sufficiently full set of the relevant facts to answer the research question, and that ignores no relevant facts; (3) a specific virtue in research design: that it allows warrant for an explanation or an interpretation because it meets one of the above conditions.

Hard core: explanatory propositions that are central to a research programme (q.v.), and which will be retained, in the face of anomalous data, even if this requires changes to, or even abandonment of, propositions in the 'protective belt'.

Holism: the thesis that a theory cannot be tested by comparing its specific predictions with a discrete set of data, in isolation from all other theories and empirical knowledge. Holism is the proposition that we can always save the theory under test from anomalous data by rejecting or amending some other theories (perhaps theories of the technology used in the research design). Therefore a scientific judgement must be made about which, of all the many theories which could be at risk, it is most reasonable to amend or reject. While relativists claim that such judgements are conventional, realists argue that good reasons are available for following some rules of thumb to guide our decisions about when to save and when to reject theories.

Hypothesis: a precise statement of the observations expected to be found in data which are collected and analysed to establish patterns of association or causal process.

Incommensurability: one scientific theory is incommensurable with another theory if its concepts or terms cannot be translated without loss of meaning into a set of expressions that have meaning in the second theory.

Induction: the activity of observing phenomena empirically, to look cumulatively for patterns of associations, in order to develop a hypothesis or candidate generalisation.

Inductive research design: a research designs that starts with the creation and/or collection of data, not by deriving and testing a prior hypothesis as is required by deductive research. The purpose is to formulate a hypothesis or candidate generalisation, by identifying patterns in the data.

Inference: a claim about a thing or things that cannot be directly observed, on the basis of observations of a thing or things we can observe and a theory about how the unobservable and observable things are connected.

Inferential leverage: the capacity of a research design to support warranted inferences to explanations or interpretations on the basis of a given set of data. It depends on achieving an appropriate, reasonable and defensible trade-off between the key virtues of research design for the purposes of the particular project.

Interpretation: the process of determining the significance or meaning of a phenomenon or a set of phenomena, or making sense of them; normally, this is undertaken in one or more of three ways:

1 determining whether a phenomenon counts for a given research purpose as falling within some category (*categorical* significance, e.g. data coding, statistical interpretation);
2 attributing beliefs, feelings, interests and other aspects of their mental lives to people being researched, and drawing out their significance for them (*subjective* significance, e.g. anthropological or sociological interpretation); and/or
3 developing an integrated account of a phenomenon (i.e. an interpretation – noun) that makes sense of evidence, showing its meaning, significance or importance for readers of the research, either for the sake of understanding the phenomenon or for their practical purposes (*objective* significance, e.g. historical interpretation).

Interpretive inference: the process of making an inference (q.v.) from data to an interpretation.

Logical explanations: explications derived logically that are, in consequence, necessary truths or mathematical facts; or explanations that are true by definition.

Meaning: the significance attached – normally but not exclusively by actors themselves – to events, states of affairs or processes in their beliefs, desires, intentions, emotions and other elements in their mental lives.

Meanings: understandings expressed in mental life through ideas, categories, forms of classification, beliefs, hopes, desires and so on.

Mechanism: an underlying causal process – not directly observable – that may operate upon events, states of affairs or other processes, to bring about transforming effects in the presence of various contextual factors. Mechanisms may be individual (e.g. cognitive dissonance reduction) or social (e.g. 'the invisible hand' of a pure market).

Mental life: people's beliefs, desires, emotions, concerns, categories, classifications and ways of conceiving their relations, themselves and their world.

Method: the set of techniques recognised by most or many social scientists as being appropriately used for the creation, collection, coding, construction and analysis of data.

Methodological soundness: the general or overarching virtue of a research design. A sound design exhibits the capacity for warranted inference from the data to a description, explanation or interpretation which provides a satisfying answer to the research question. In particular, in a sound design, an explanation or interpretation will represent a reasonable and defensible trade-off between the virtues of goodness of fit, parsimony, generality and causality and so on.

Methodology: theories of how, and how far, a research design enables researchers to draw sound inferences to conclusions that offer answers to the research questions, and to determine how far hypotheses are supported or undermined.

Model: a detailed measurable statement, which is capable of being represented formally – or the formal representation itself – describing the realisation of a theory. A model shows how factors are linked, displaying the predicted or retrodicted influence of each element upon each other, and, ideally, the size or relative scale of that influence. In constructing a model, parsimony is usually weighted more heavily in the explanatory trade-off than detailed goodness of fit or wide generalisability.

Narrative explanation: an explanation that uses a rich and complex set of contextual factors and configurations. No factors or configurations are privileged as the primary explanation while the others act as background or moderating factors. Rather, the explanation is seen to lie in the way that all the factors or configurations interact.

Necessary condition: a necessary condition is one that must be met for an outcome to occur. So C is a necessary condition of E if, and only if, in each and every case where E occurs, it could only have occurred because C was present.

Negative feedback: a case of endogenous causation in which the causal force *undermines* the focal process. Thus, where C causes E which then undermines C, there is a feedback loop to C of a negative character.

Observation: (1) value taken by a unit of data collected and defined by a scheme of measurement; (2) any unit of data (e.g. case in a sample or data set); (3) systematic collection of data, where the researcher cannot exercise experimental control values of units; (4) audio/visual inspection of behaviour.

Ontology: the sub-discipline within philosophy that considers the merits of theories about the categories of things that are or exist.

Outcome: an effect of a cause; the consequence of a causal relation; an event, state of affairs or process that is treated for explanatory purposes as the destination or final boundary of the case.

Paradigm: a shared commitment by an identifiable group of scientists about what should be observed or examined; what therefore counts as data; what questions are important; how data should be interpreted; and about what counts as a satisfying answer to a research question.

Parsimony: a specific virtue of a research design: that an explanation accounts for, or an interpretation makes sense of, the set of phenomena being explained or interpreted, using the fewest necessary variables or configurations (in explanations) or concepts or themes (in interpretations).

Positive feedback: a case of endogenous causation in which the causal force *reinforces* the focal process. Thus, where C causes E which then reinforces C, there is a feedback loop to C of a positive character.

Positivism: the philosophical position which holds (1) that science can only defensibly make inferences from what we can actually observe; (2) that we can observe correlation or association, but not causation; (3) that we should measure the power of an explanation by the goodness of fit of correlations and associations between factors; (4) that abstract, unobservable processes and entities posited in theoretical statements should be treated as convenient shorthand for structured patterns of relationships between observational measures which should predict future observations; (5) that in principle a theory could be reduced to a set of empirically testable general statements about expected patterns between things we can observe, so long as we design the right kind of research instruments.

Pragmatism: the philosophical position which holds that (1) science is a problem-solving activity, where success is judged by its capacity to eliminate the puzzles that scientists happen to have; and that (2) we cannot at any point be wholly confident that successful science is true science or describes underlying realities, only that we are successfully solving more problems, or more important or more interesting problems. Some scholars who accept pragmatism also accept relativism, although pragmatism, understood in this way does not logically entail relativism.

Prediction: statements derived logically from theories that set out the observations and data that are expected to be found by empirical research.

Primary interpretation: claims made by actors themselves in speech or text about their own understandings of their situation, beliefs, desires, experiences, relations with others and so on.

Process tracing: the procedure of analysing, within a case, data on candidate causal relations to identify the factors that influence other factors, and to trace the causal paths by which this happens.

Progressive (of a research programme): the capability of producing theories that furnish explanations from which we can derive novel predictions of facts that we should expect to find or, better still, not find, if the theories were true.

Proposal: a detailed statement of a research project. It sets out the research question to be answered, the aims and objectives in answering the question, and the methods to be used, together with a brief statement of the nature of the inference to be drawn from the data to answer the question.

Protocol: a detailed methodological defence of a research proposal, setting out the steps through which the inference will proceed and the degree to which the conclusion is likely to be supported, given the nature of the data and the nature of the methods used to create, collect, construct and analyse them.

Proximate variable: an explanatory variable, the content or meaning of which is near to the outcome to be explained.

Rational choice: a conception of causation in which (1) people pursue preferences under constraints in the light of their beliefs and their information about their situation and the feasibility of their goals; (2) outcomes are explained by actors' pursuit of their preferences and by the interaction of their goal-seeking behaviour with that of others; and (3) in preference schedules, goals and sub-goals that are arranged in rank order of preference and are selected by reference to incentives (which are taken to be exogenous).

Realism: philosophical doctrine that there are determinate facts about unobservable processes, on the basis of which well-specified social science models and/or theories are either true or false, and that scientific judgement can provide good reasons for provisionally accepting models and theories as true or false.

Reduction (by a theory of data): the process of focusing the analysis of data under a small number of codes or variables, so that an explanation can be limited to a small number of factors that are expected to have high explanatory power.

Reduction (one theory to another): elimination of terms from one theory without loss of meaning, to leave statements of a more fundamental character that are derived from a second theory.

Regularity: a generalisation that rests on a very large number of observations, each of which shows the same consistent behaviour or characteristics in the instances or cases observed.

Relativism: the philosophical doctrine that holds that (1) there is no compelling reason to accept that the processes which appear to be posited by scientific explanations correspond to determinate facts on the basis of which those explanations are either true or false; and that (2) scientific methods of research and inference do not alone supply such compelling reasons.

Research design: the specification of the way in which data will be created, collected, constructed, analysed and interpreted to enable the researcher to draw warranted descriptive, explanatory or interpretive inference; standards of warrant are expected to vary slightly – around a core set of virtues – for each type of inference, so a design should also specify why the warrant is calculated to strike a reasonable trade-off between competing virtues.

Research programme: those propositions in a paradigm (the 'hard core') that are retained in the face of apparently troubling evidence because they are central to it, together with a set of propositions that are not so critical to its meaning, which advocates of the programme are sometimes willing to revise (the 'protective belt'), when anomalous data must be accommodated.

Retrodiction: prediction of expected observations for data about cases in the past, or for data that have already been collected.

Scientific judgement: the determination of which theories to accept, amend and/or reject, in the light of anomalous data, based on reasons not limited to goodness of fit, but also taking into account trade-offs between parsimony, generality, causality, conceptual development, elegance, risk of measurement error and so on.

Secondary interpretation: researchers' interpretations of actors' primary interpretations.

Sense-making explanation: explanation of actors' behaviour or its consequences by reference to their open-ended explorations of their environment and the meanings and significance these explorations have to them, both at the time and in retrospect.

Significance: the meaning or importance of a set of phenomena for (1) a group of people being studied or for (2) readers of the research.

Sociology of knowledge: the study of the effect of institutions, interests and capabilities upon the ideas that come to be accepted by groups.

State of affairs: circumstance enduring for a period of time which affects one or more units of observation.

Statistical 'explanations': accounts that show correlations, regularities in association between factors, usually operationalised as variables.

Stochastic: a conception of causation in which a cause C (which can stand either for a variable or for a configuration) raises the probability of an effect E, but typically to a level less than near or absolute certainty.

Sufficient condition: the effect of a sufficient condition is one that is, by itself, enough for a condition to occur. So C is a sufficient condition of E if and only if C occurred, produced E and any other conditions can be disregarded.

Test (of a theory): the process of systematically collecting observations in order to identify potentially disconfirming cases of the theory, in order to inform a scientific judgement about whether the theory should be accepted or rejected.

Theory: an integrated set of statements – ideally, derived from a general framework or paradigm – from which hypotheses can be deduced to explain particular outcomes. A theory may include reference to unobservable entities or processes, from which predictions can be derived of expected observations, including future ones.

Theory-laden (of data, or observations): cannot be described, presented or coded without the use of terms derived from or given meaning by theories (not necessarily those theories which are to be tested by using the data or observations).

Trade-off (in explanation, or more generally in a research design): a settlement about which virtues are more and which are less important in a situation where some virtues can only be achieved or increased at the expense of others.

Trajectory: a sequence of mechanisms, leading to a clear direction of change in outcomes over a period of time.

Trend: a statement of the trajectory or direction exhibited by a data set over a distribution (especially, a trajectory in a data set plotted against time).

Typology: statement of relations among logically possible categories in an ordered scheme of classification.

Under-determination (of theory by data): the fact that no set of statements describing a set of data can ever logically entail only one true explanatory theory capable of accounting for those observations.

Verification: the use of systematically collected observations which turn out to be consistent with predictions derived from the theory (not anomalous), to argue convincingly that the best scientific judgement is to accept the theory that the observations were designed to test.

Warrant: the measure of the confidence that we have in an inference's capability to deliver truths about things we cannot observe.

Within-case analysis: procedures for developing explanations by analysing data on each case separately to identify causal relations.

References

Adams J, 1995, *Risk*, London: UCL Press.

Adcock R and Collier D, 2001, Measurement validity, *American Political Science Review*, 95, 3, 529–46.

Allison G with Zelikow P, 1999 [Allison, 1971], *Essence of decision: explaining the Cuban missile crisis*, New York: Addison Wesley Longman.

Almond GA and Verba A, 1967, *The civic culture*, Boston, MA: Little Brown.

Altheide DL and Johnson JM, 1998, Criteria for assessing interpretive validity in qualitative research, in NK Denzin and YS Lincoln (eds), *Collecting and interpreting qualitative materials*, London: Sage, 283–312.

Austin JL, 1962, *How to do things with words*, Oxford: Oxford University Press.

Bailey KD, 1994, *Typologies and taxonomies: an introduction to classification techniques*, London: Sage.

Barr S, Ford NJ and Gilg AW, 2003, Attitudes towards recycling household waste in Exeter, Devon: quantitative and qualitative approaches, *Local Environment*, 8, 4, 407–21.

Bennett A, 2010 [2004], Process tracing and causal inference, in D Collier and HE Brady, *Rethinking social inquiry*, Lanham, MD: Rowman & Littlefield, 207–220.

Bennett A and Elman C, 2006a, Complex causal relations and case study methods: the example of path dependence, *Political Analysis*, 14, 3, 250–67.

Bennett A and Elman C, 2006b, Qualitative research: recent developments in case study methods, *Annual Review of Political Science*, 9, 455–76.

Berger T and Luckmann P, 1991 [1966], *The social construction of knowledge: a treatise in the sociology of knowledge*, Harmondsworth: Penguin.

Bevir M, 2004, Interpretation as method, explanation and critique, a reply, *British Journal of Politics and International Relations*, 6, 151–61.

Blaikie N, 2007 [1993], *Approaches to social inquiry*, Cambridge: Polity Press.

Blatter J and Blume T, 2008, In search of co-variance, causal mechanisms or congruence? Towards a plural understanding of case studies, *Swiss Political Science Review*, 14, 2, 315–56.

Boudon R, 1979, From description to explanation, in R Boudon, *The logic of social action: an introduction to sociological analysis*, London: Routledge & Kegan Paul, 134–47.

Brady HE and Collier D (eds), 2010 [2004], *Rethinking social inquiry: diverse tools, shared standards*, Lanham, MD: Rowman & Littlefield.

Brewer M, Browne J, Joyce R and Sibieta L, 2001, *Child poverty in the UK since 1998–99: lessons from the past decade*, IFS Working Paper 10/23, London: Institute of Fiscal Studies and ESRC.

Bunge M, 2004, How does it work? The search for explanatory mechanisms, *Philosophy of the Social Sciences*, 34, 2, 182–210.

Byrne D and Ragin CC (eds), 2009, *The Sage handbook of case-based methods*, London: Sage.

Campbell DT, 1956, *Leadership and its effects upon the group*, Columbus, OH: Ohio State University Press.

Cartwright N, 2004, Causation: one word, many things, *Philosophy of Science*, 71, 805–19.

Chan K, 1998, Mass communication and proenvironmental behaviour: waste recycling in Hong Kong, *Journal of Environmental Management*, 52, 317–25.

Cherkaoui M, 2005, *Invisible codes: essays on generative mechanisms*, Oxford: Bardwell Press.

Clarke RV, 1980, Situational crime prevention: theory and practice, *British Journal of Criminology*, 4, 136–47.

Cochrane A, Clarke J and Gewirtz S, 2001 [1991], *Comparing welfare states*, London: Sage and Buckingham: Open University Press.

Colley L, 1992, *Britons: forging the nation, 1707–1937*, New Haven, CT: Yale University Press.

Collier D and Gerring J, 2008, *Concepts and method in social science: Giovanni Sartori and his legacy*, London: Routledge.

Collier D, Laporte and Seawright K, 2008, Typologies: forming concepts and creating categorical variables, in J Box-Steffensmeier, H Brady and D Collier (eds), *Oxford handbook of political methodology*, Oxford: Oxford University Press, 152–73.

Collier D and Mahoney J, 1993, Conceptual 'stretching' revisited, *American Political Science Review*, 87, 4, 845–55.

Collier D, Mahoney J and Seawright J, 2004, Claiming too much: warnings about selection bias, in HE Brady and D Collier, *Rethinking social inquiry: diverse tools, shared standards*, Lanham, MD: Rowman and Littlefield, 123–38.

Collins A, O'Docherty R and Snell MC, 2006, Household participation in waste recycling: some national survey evidence from Scotland, *Journal of Environmental Planning and Management*, 49, 1, 121–40.

Collins R, 1999, *Macrohistory: essays in sociology of the long run*, Stanford, CA: Stanford University Press.

Coser L (ed.), 1992, *Maurice Halbwachs on collective memory*, Chicago: University of Chicago Press.

Crossman RHS, 1975, *The diaries of a cabinet minister*, 3 vols, London: Hamish Hamilton and Jonathan Cape.

Davidson D, 2001 [1984, 1977], *Inquiries into truth and interpretation*, Oxford: Oxford University Press.

Denzin N, 2001 [1989], *Interpretive interactionism*, London: Sage.

Denzin N and Lincoln YS, 1998, *Strategies of qualitative enquiry*, Thousand Oaks, CA: Sage.

Department of Communities and Local Government, 2010, *Consultation on proposed changes to guidance on evaluating the extent of rough sleeping: summary of responses*, London: Department of Communities and Local Government, available at www.communities.gov.uk/publications/housing/evaluatingroughsleepingresponse (accessed 20 May 2011).

Dion D, 1998, Evidence and inference in the comparative case study, *Comparative Politics*, 30, 2, 127–45.

Dogan M and Pelassy D, 1990 [1984], *How to compare nations: strategies in comparative politics*, Chatham, NJ: Chatham House.

Douglas M, 1986, *How institutions think*, London: Routledge & Kegan Paul.

Dunleavy P, 1991, *Democracy, bureaucracy and public choice*, Hemel Hempstead: Harvester Wheatsheaf.

Eisenhardt K, 1989, Building theories from case study research, *Academy of Management Review*, 14, 4, 532–50.

Erzberger C and Prein G, 1997, Triangulation: validity and empirically based hypothesis construction, *Quality and Quantity*, 31, 141–54.

Esping-Andersen G, 1990, *The three worlds of welfare capitalism*, Cambridge: Polity Press.

Evans-Pritchard EE, 1976 [1937], *Witchcraft, oracles and magic among the Azande*, abr. E Gillies, Oxford: Clarendon Press.

Feldman MS, 1989, *Order without design: information processing and policy making*, Palo Alto, CA: Stanford University Press.

Feyerabend P, 1993 [1975], *Against method*, London: Verso.

Fleck L, 1979 [1935], *Genesis and development of a scientific fact*, trans. F Badley and TJ Trenn, Chicago: University of Chicago Press.

Ford J, 1975, I beg your pardon, in J Ford, *Paradigms and fairy tales*, London: Routledge, 1–16.

Friedman M, 1979 [1953], The methodology of positive economics, in M Friedman, 1953, *Essays in positive economics*, Chicago: University of Chicago Press, reprinted in Hahn F and Hollis M (eds) 1979, *Philosophy and economic theory*, Oxford: Oxford University Press, 18–35.

Gaddis JL, 1997, *We now know: rethinking cold war history*, New York: Oxford University Press.

Gambetta D, 1998, Concatenations of mechanisms, in P Hedström and R Swedberg (eds), *Social mechanisms: an analytical approach to social theory*, Cambridge: Cambridge University Press, 102–24.

Garner WR, Hake HW and Eriksen CW, 1956, Operationism and the concept of perception, *Psychological Review*, 63, 149–59.

Geddes B, 2003, *Paradigms and sand castles: theory building and research design in comparative politics*, Ann Arbor, MI: University of Michigan Press.

Geertz C, 1973a, Deep play: notes on the Balinese cockfight, in C Geertz, *The interpretation of cultures*, London: HarperCollins, 412–53.

Geertz C, 1973b, Thick description: toward an interpretive theory of culture, in C Geertz, *The interpretation of cultures: selected essays*, London: HarperCollins.

Geertz C, 1980, *Negara: the theatre state in nineteenth-century Bali*, Princeton, NJ: Princeton University Press.

George AL and Bennett A, 2004, *Case studies and theory development in the social sciences*, Cambridge, MA: Massachusetts Institute of Technology Press.

Gerber A, Green DP and Kaplan EH, 2004, The illusion of learning from observational research, in I Shapiro *et al.*,(eds), *Problems and methods in the study of politics*, Cambridge: Cambridge University Press, 251–73.

Gerring J, 1999, What makes a concept good? A criteria framework for understanding concept formation in the social sciences, *Polity*, 31, 3, 357–93.

Gerring J, 2001, *Social science methodology: a criterial approach*, Cambridge: Cambridge University Press.

Gerring J, 2005, Causation: a unified framework for the social sciences, *Journal of Theoretical Politics*, 17, 2, 163–98.

Gerring J, 2007, *Case study research: principles and practices*, Cambridge: Cambridge University Press.

Glaser B and Strauss A, 1967, *The discovery of grounded theory*, Chicago: Aldine.

Giddens A, 1987, *Social theory and modern sociology*, Cambridge: Polity Press.

Girard A and Clerc P, 1964, Nouvelles données sure l'orientation scolaire au moment de l'entrée en sixième, *Population*, 19, 5, 829–72.

Goertz G, 2006, *Social science concepts: a user's guide*, Princeton, NJ: Princeton University Press.

Goffman E, 1974, *Frame analysis: an essay on the organisation of experience*, Boston, MA: Northeastern University Press.

Goffman E, 1983, Felicity's condition, *American Journal of Sociology*, 89, 1, 25–51.

Goldstone JA, 1991, *Revolution and rebellion in the early modern world*, Berkeley, CA: University of California Press.

Goldthorpe J, 2000, Causation, statistics and sociology, in J Goldthorpe, *On sociology: numbers, narratives and the integration of research and theory*, Oxford: Oxford University Press, 137–60.

Gomm R, Hammersley M and Foster P, 2000, Case study and generalisation, in R Gomm, M Hammersley and P Foster (eds), *Case study method: key issues, key texts*, London: Sage, 98–116.

Grandy R, 1973, Reference, meaning and belief, *Journal of Philosophy*, 70, 14, 439–52.

Green, DP, 2004, Mobilizing African-American voters using direct mail and commercial phone banks: a field experiment, *Political Research Quarterly*, 57, 2, 245–55.

Halpern D, 2005, *Social capital*, Cambridge: Polity Press.

Hammersley M, 1992, *What's wrong with ethnography?*, London: Routledge.

Harris M, 1976, History and significance of the emic/etic distinction, *Annual Review of Anthropology*, 5, 329–50.

Headland T, Pike KL and Harris M, 1990, *Emics and etics: the insider/outsider debate*, Thousand Oaks, CA: Sage.

Heather P, 2009, *Empires and barbarians: migration, development and the birth of Europe*, Basingstoke: Macmillan.

Hebdige D, 1979, *Subculture: the meaning of style*, London: Routledge.

Hedström P and Swedberg R (eds), 1998, *Social mechanisms: an analytical approach to social theory*, Cambridge: Cambridge University Press.

Henn M, Weinstein M and Foard N, 2009 [2006], *A short introduction to social research*, London: Sage.

Hochschild AR, 1983, *The managed heart: commercialisation of human feeling*, Berkeley, CA: University of California Press.

Hollis M, 2002 [1994], *The philosophy of social science: an introduction*, Cambridge: Cambridge University Press.

Humphreys M and Weinstein J, 2009, Field experiments and the political economy of development, *Annual Review of Political Science*, 12, 367–78.

Hunter LM, Hatch A and Johnson A, 2004, Cross-national gender variation in environmental behaviours, *Social Science Quarterly*, 85, 3, 677–94.

Hutson S and Liddiard M, 1994, *Youth homelessness: the construction of a social issue*, Basingstoke: Macmillan.

Janoski, T and Hicks, AM, 1994, *The comparative political economy of the welfare state*. Cambridge: Cambridge University Press.

Jervis R, 1997, *System effects: complexity in political and social life*, Princeton, NJ: Princeton University Press.

John P and Brannan T, 2008, How different are telephoning and canvassing? Results from a 'get out the vote' field experiment in the British 2005 General Election, *British Journal of Political Science*, 38, 3, 565–74.

Kahneman D, Slovic P and Tversky A (eds), 1982, *Judgment under uncertainty: heuristics and biases*, Cambridge: Cambridge University Press.

Kahneman D and Tversky A, 2000, Choices, values and frames, in D Kahneman and A Tversky (eds), *Choices, values and frames*, Cambridge: Cambridge University Press, 1–16.

Kincaid H, 1996, *Philosophical foundations of the social sciences: analysing controversies in social research*, Cambridge: Cambridge University Press.

King G, Keohane R and Verba S, 1994, *Designing social inquiry: scientific inference in qualitative research*, Princeton, NJ: Princeton University Press.

King G, Tomz M and Wittenberg J, 2000, Making the most of statistical analyses: improving interpretation and presentation, *American Journal of Political Science*, 44, 2, 341–55.

Kitcher P, 1989, Explanatory unification and the causal structure of the world, in P Kitcher and W Salmon (eds), *Scientific explanation*, Minneapolis: University of Minnesota Press, 410–507.

Kopinak JC, 1999, The use of triangulation in a study of refugee well-being, *Quality and Quantity*, 33, 169–83.

Kuhn TS, 1970 [1962], *The structure of scientific revolutions*, Chicago: University of Chicago Press.

Kurki M, 2008, *Causation in international relations: reclaiming causal analysis*, Cambridge: Cambridge University Press.

Kvale S, 1995, The social construction of validity, *Qualitative Inquiry*, 1, 1, 19–40.

Ladyman J, 2002, *Understanding philosophy of science*, London: Routledge.

Lakatos I, 1970, Falsification and the methodology of scientific research programmes, in I Lakatos and A Musgrave (eds), *Criticism and the growth of knowledge*, Cambridge: Cambridge University Press, 91–196.

Laudan L, 1977, *Progress and its problems: towards a theory of scientific growth*, Berkeley, CA: University of California Press.

Laudan L, 1990, *Science and relativism: some key controversies in the philosophy of social science*, Chicago: University of Chicago Press.

Levy JS, 1997, Prospect theory, rational choice, and international relations, *International Studies Quarterly*, 41, 1, 87–112.

Lieberson S, 1985, *Making it count: the improvement of social research and theory*, Berkeley, CA: University of California Press.

Lieberson S, 1992, Small *N*'s and big conclusions: an examination of the reasoning in comparative studies based on a small number of cases, in CC Ragin and HS Becker (eds), *What is a case? Exploring the foundations of social inquiry*, Cambridge: Cambridge University Press, 105–18.

Lieberson S, 1997, Modelling social processes: some lessons from sports, *Sociological Forum*, 12, 1, 11–35.

Lincoln YS and Guba EG, 1985, *Naturalistic inquiry*, Beverly Hills, CA: Sage.

Lincoln YS and Guba EG, 1990, Judging the quality of case study reports, *Qualitative Studies in Education*, 3, 1, 53–9, reprinted in AM Huberman and MB Miles (eds), 2002, *The qualitative researcher's companion*, London: Sage, 205–15.

Lipton P, 2004 [1991], *Inference to the best explanation*, London: Routledge.

Lober D, 1996, Municipal solid waste policy and public participation in household source reduction, *Waste Management and Research*, 14, 125–43.

Lukes S, 2007, The problem of apparently irrational beliefs, in SP Turner and MW Risjord (eds), *Philosophy of anthropology and sociology*, Amsterdam: North-Holland, 591–606.

Mackie JL 1965, Causes and conditions, *American Philosophical Quarterly*, 2, 4, 245–55, reprinted in E Sosa and M Tooley (eds), 1993, *Causation*, Oxford: Oxford University Press.

Mahoney J, 2003, Strategies of causal assessment in comparative historical analysis, in J Mahoney and D Rueschemeyer (eds), *Comparative historical analysis in the social sciences*, Cambridge: Cambridge University Press, 337–72.

Mahoney J and Thelen M (eds), 2010, *Explaining institutional change: ambiguity, agency and power*, Cambridge: Cambridge University Press.

Manicas PT, 2006, *A realist philosophy of social science*, Cambridge: Cambridge University Press.

Maxwell J, 1992, Understanding and validity in qualitative research, *Harvard Educational Review*, 62, 3, 279–300, reprinted in AM Huberman and MB Miles (eds), 2002, *The qualitative researcher's companion*, London: Sage, 37–64.

Mayntz R, 2004, Mechanisms in the analysis of social macro-phenomena, *Philosophy of the Social Sciences*, 34, 2, 237–59.

McGinn C, 1977, Charity, interpretation and belief, *Journal of Philosophy*, 74, 521–35.

Meijer PC, Verloop N and Beijaard D, 2002, Multi-method triangulation in a qualitative study on teachers' practical knowledge: an attempt to increase internal validity, *Quality and Quantity*, 36, 145–67.

Miles MB and Huberman AM, 1994, *Qualitative data analysis*, Thousand Oaks, CA: Sage.

Mill JS, 1967 [1843], *A system of logic: ratiocinative and inductive*, Toronto: University of Toronto Press.

Ministry of Justice, 2010, *Breaking the cycle: effective punishment, rehabilitation and sentencing of offenders*, Cm 7972, London: The Stationery Office.

Moore B, Jr, 1966, *Social origins of dictatorship and democracy: lord and peasant in the making of the modern world*, Boston, MA: Beacon Press.

Morse JM, Barrett M, Mayan M, Olson K and Spiers J, 2002, Verification strategies for establishing validity and reliability in qualitative research, *International Journal of Qualitative Methods*, 1, 2, 1–19.

Moser CA and Kalton G, 1971, *Survey methods in social investigation*, London: Heinemann.

Niskanen WA, 1971, *Bureaucracy and representative government*, Chicago: Aldine-Atherton.

Northcott R, 2008, Weighted explanations in history, *Philosophy of the Social Sciences*, 38, 1, 76–96.

Okasha S, 2002, *Philosophy of science: a very short introduction*, Oxford: Oxford University Press.

O'Toole BJ, 2006, *The ideal of public service*, London: Routledge.

Pape RA and Feldman JK, 2010, *Cutting the fuse: the explosion of global suicide terrorism and how to stop it*, Chicago, University of Chicago Press.

Pawson R, 1989, *A measure for measures: a manifesto for empirical sociology*, London: Routledge.

Pawson R, 2006, *Evidence-based policy*, London: Sage.

Pawson R and Tilley N, 1997, *Realistic evaluation*, London: Sage.

Peretz JH, Tonn BE and Folz DH, 2005, Explaining the performance of mature municipal solid waste recycling programs, *Journal of Environmental Planning and Management*, 48, 5, 627–50.

Peters BG, 1998, *Comparative politics: theory and methods*. Basingstoke: Palgrave Macmillan.

Petticrew M and Roberts H, 2006, *Systematic reviews in the social sciences: a practical guide*, Oxford: Blackwell.

Pike KL (ed.), 1967, *Language in relation to a unified theory of structure of human behaviour*, rev. edn, The Hague: Mouton.

Pollitt C and Bouckaert G, 2009, *Change and continuity in public policy and management*, Cheltenham: Edward Elgar.

Popper K, 1959, *The logic of scientific discovery*, London: Routledge.

Popper K, 1983 [1967], The rationality principle, from D Miller (ed.), *The pocket Popper*, Oxford: Fontana, 357–65.

Przeworski A and Teune H, 1970, *The logic of comparative social inquiry*, New York: Wiley.

Putnam RD, 2000, *Bowling alone: the collapse and revival of American community*, New York: Simon and Schuster.

Ragin CC, 1987, *The comparative method: moving beyond quantitative and qualitative strategies*, Berkeley, CA: University of California Press.

Ragin CC, 1994, *Constructing social research*, Thousand Oaks, CA: Pine Forge Press, Sage.

Ragin CC, 2000, *Fuzzy-set social science*, Chicago, University of Chicago Press.

Ragin CC, 2004, Turning the tables: how case-oriented research challenges variable oriented research', in HE Brady and D Collier, *Rethinking social inquiry: diverse tools, shared standards*, Lanham, MD: Rowman and Littlefield, 123–38.

Ragin CC and Becker HS, (eds), 1992, *What is a case? Exploring the foundations of social inquiry*, Cambridge: Cambridge University Press.

Rappaport RA, 1984 [1968], *Pigs for the ancestors: ritual in the ecology of a New Guinea people*, New Haven, Connecticut: Yale University Press.

Rappaport RA, 1999, *Ritual and religion in the making of humanity*, Cambridge: Cambridge University Press.

Rayner S, 1982, The perceptions of time and space in egalitarian sects: a millenarian cosmology, in M Douglas (ed.), *Essays in the sociology of perception*, London: Routledge & Kegan Paul, 247–74.

Rayner S, 1988, The rules that keep us equal: complexity and costs of egalitarian organisation, in JG Flanagan and S Rayner (eds), *Rules, decisions and inequality in egalitarian societies*, Aldershot: Avebury, 20–42.

Richards P, 2011, A systematic approach to cultural explanations of war: tracing causal processes in two West African insurgencies, *World development*, 39, 2, 212–20.

Rihoux B and Ragin C (eds), 2008, *Configurational comparative methods*: *qualitative comparative analysis (QCA) and related techniques*, Los Angeles: Sage.

Rogowski R, 2010 [2004], How inference in the social (but not the physical) sciences neglects theoretical anomaly, in HE Brady and D Collier, *Rethinking social inquiry: diverse tools, shared standards*, Lanham, MD: Rowman & Littlefield, 89–98.

Rorty R, 1979, *Philosophy and the mirror of nature*, Princeton, NJ: Princeton University Press.

Rorty R, 1990, *Objectivity, relativism and truth: philosophical papers, volume 1*, Cambridge: Cambridge University Press.

Rosenfeld R, Jacobs BA and Wright R, 2003, Snitching and the code of the street, *British Journal of Criminology*, 43, 2, 291–309.

Sampson RJ, Raudenbusch SW and Earls F, 1997, Neighbourhoods and violent crime: a multi-level study of collective efficacy, *Science*, 277, 918–24.

Sandberg J, 2005, How do we justify knowledge produced within interpretive approaches? *Organisational Research Methods*, 8, 1, 41–68.

Sandelowski M, 1986, The problem of rigour in qualitative research, *Advances in Nursing Science*, 8, 3, 27–37.

Sartori G, 1970, Concept misformation in comparative politics, *American Political Science Review*, 64, 4, 1033–53.

Sayer A, 1999, *Realism in social science*, London: Sage.

Scott JC, 1998, *Seeing like a state: how certain schemes to improve the human condition have failed*, New Haven, CT: Yale University Press.

Searle JR, 1969, *Speech acts: an essay in the philosophy of language*, Cambridge: Cambridge University Press.

Searle JR, 1995, *The construction of social reality*, Harmondsworth: Penguin.

Searle JR, 2009, Language and social ontology, in C Mantzavinos (ed.), *Philosophy of the social sciences: philosophical theory and scientific practice*, Cambridge: Cambridge University Press, 9–27.

Shapiro I, Smith RM and Masoud TE (eds), 2004, *Problems and methods in the study of politics*, Cambridge: Cambridge University Press.

Shih F-J, 1998, Triangulation in nursing research: issues of conceptual clarity and purpose, *Journal of Advanced Nursing*, 28, 3, 631–41.

Sieber SD, 1981, *Fatal remedies: the ironies of social intervention*, New York: Plenum Press.

Silverman D, 1993, *Interpreting qualitative data: methods for analysing talk text and interaction*, London: Sage.

Sjöberg L, 2003, Distal factors in risk perception, *Journal of Risk Research*, 6, 3, 187–211.

Skocpol T, 1979, *States and social revolutions: a comparative analysis of France, Russia and China*, Cambridge: Cambridge University Press.

Slovic P, 2000, *The perception of risk*, London: Earthscan.

Smith RM, 2004, The politics of identities and the tasks of political science, in I Shapiro, RM Smith and TE Masoud (eds), *Problems and methods in the study of politics*, Cambridge: Cambridge University Press, 42–66.

Stake R, 1978, The case study method in social inquiry, *Educational Researcher*, 7, 5–8, reprinted in Gomm R, Hammersley M and Foster P (eds), 2000, *Case study method: key issues, key texts*, London: Sage.

Stake R, 2005, *Multiple case study analysis*, New York: Guilford Press.

Steel D, 2004, Social mechanisms and causal inference, *Philosophy of the Social Sciences*, 34, 1, 55–78.

Steinberg PF, 2007, Causal assessment in small-N policy studies, *Policy Studies Journal*, 35, 2, 181–204.

Stinchcombe AL, 2005, *The logic of social research*, Chicago: University of Chicago Press.

Strauss A and Corbin J, 1997, *Grounded theory in practice*, London: Sage.

Streeck W and Thelen M (eds), 2005, *Beyond continuity: institutional change in advanced political economies*, Oxford: Oxford University Press.

Sutton M, Schneider J and Hetherington S, 2001, *Tackling theft with the market reduction approach*, Crime Reduction Research Series Paper 8, London: Home Office.

Taagepera R, 2007, Predictive versus postdictive models, *European political science*, 6, 2, 114–23.

Taagepera R, 2008, *Making social science more scientific: the need for predictive models*, Oxford: Oxford University Press.

Tarrow S, 2004, Bridging the qualitative-quantitative divide, in HE Brady and D Collier (eds), *Rethinking social inquiry: diverse tools, shared standards*, Lanham, MD: Rowman & Littlefield, 171–80.

Taylor S, 1982, *Durkheim and the study of suicide*, London: Macmillan.

Tilley N and Laycock G, 2001, *Working out what to do*, Crime Reduction Research Series Paper 11, London: Home Office.

Tilly C, 1993, Contentious repertoires in Great Britain, 1758–1834, *Social Science History*, 17, 2, 253–80.

Tilly C, 1997a, Cities, bourgeois and revolution in France, in C Tilly, *Roads from past to future*, Lanham, MD: Rowman & Littlefield, 133–63.

Tilly C, 1997b, Parliamentarisation of popular contention in Great Britain, 1758–1834, *Theory and Society*, 26, 2/3, 245–73.

Tilly C, 2008, *Explaining social processes*, Boulder, CO: Paradigm.

Vaughan D, 1996, *The Challenger launch decision: risky technology, culture, and deviance at NASA*, Chicago: University of Chicago Press.

Wanless D, 2002, *Securing our future health: taking a long term view – final report*, London: HM Treasury.

Weber M, 1946, Bureaucracy, in HH Gerth and CW Mills (eds), *From Max Weber: essays in sociology*, Oxford: Oxford University Press, 196–244.

Weber M, 1947, *The theory of social and economic organisation*, trans. AM Henderson and T Parsons, New York: Free Press.

Weick KE and Roberts KH, 1993, Collective mind in organisations: heedful interrelating on flight decks, *Administrative Science Quarterly*, 38, 8, 357–81, reprinted in KE Weick, 2001, *Making sense of the organisation*, Oxford: Blackwell, 259–83.

Wells AS, Hirschberg D, Lipton M and Oakes J, 1995, Bounding the case within its context: a constructivist approach to studying detracking reform, *Educational Researcher*, 24, 5, 18–24, reprinted in AM Huberman and MB Miles (eds), 2002, *The qualitative researcher's companion*, London: Sage, 331–48.

Wendler MC, 2002, Triangulation using a meta-matrix, *Journal of Advanced Nursing*, 35, 4, 521–5.

Wendt A, 1999, *Social theory of international politics*, Cambridge: Cambridge University Press.

Whyte WF, 1993 [1943], *Street corner society: the social structure of an Italian slum*, Chicago: University of Chicago Press.

Willis P, 1977, *Learning to labour: how working class kids get working class jobs*, Farnborough: Saxon House.

Winch P, 1958, *The idea of a social science and its relation to philosophy*, London: Routledge & Kegan Paul.

Wittgenstein L, 1976 [1953], *Philosophical investigations*, trans. GEM Anscombe, Oxford: Blackwell.

Index

concepts *cont.*
  use in social science 129–134, 150
  see also conjunctive and disjunctive,
    family resemblance, radial, scalar,
    typological concepts
conceptual framework 173, **300**
conclusion validity 22
conditions (distinguished from causes)
  99 107, **300**
  necessary 97–100, 103, 107, 125, 200–4,
    216–8, **306**
  sufficient 97, 100, 200–5, 221, **309**
configurations (of variables) 175–9, 180–1
conjunctive and disjunctive
  concepts 138–9
construct validity 21–22, 259–60
  see also concepts
constructivism 57–58, **300**
constructionism 57, **300**
content validity 92–3, 95, 228
context/contextual factors 105, 135,
  187–189, 220–5 *passim*, 237, **301**
control (in observational research) 74–5, 78,
  86, 118–20, 157–8
correspondence theory of truth 61, **301**
counterfactual inference 17, 157–158, 201,
  223, **301**
crime reduction 28, 34, 45, 52, 55, 60,
  63, 180–3
  see also market reduction, 'prison works'
criterion validity 92–3
crucial test (of a theory) 40, 95, 287, **301**
Cuban missile crisis 26–7, 31, 34–5, 63
curve fitting 41

data
  achieving richness in 104–5, 114, 266
  anomalous 40–44 *passim*, 51,
    56, **299**
  interpretation of 11, 42–4 naturalistic 74
  reduction of 28, 54, 86, 103, 279, **307**
  stages of working with 9–11
  truncated, problems of 196–7
  use always dependent on theory 42–4,
    52–3, 56, 208, 270–1
  see also historical data, quantitative vs
    qualitative data
data analysis 10, 43, **301**
data coding 10, 21–3 *passim*, 55, 85, 94,
  114, 118–9
data collection 10, 42
data creation 9, 94, **301**
data organisation 10, 90–92, 94, 114,
  177–9, 220
data sharing 43–4, 150

deduction 33, 76–78, 95, 113, 208–211,
  213–218, 220–5 *passim*, 264, **301**
  use in theory-building 110–111
democracy, concept of 130–141 *passim*
description 16, 26–8, **302**
  relationship with explanation and
    interpretation 18–19, 272–275, 282–3
descriptive inference 12, 16, 18–19, 27–8, 36,
  38, 262, **302**
design *see* research design
determinacy 95, 108, 207
deterministic causation 97, 204–207, **302**
displaying (data) *see* data organisation
disciplines in social sciences, their common
  history 3
distality *vs* proximity (in explanation) 88,
  159–163, 185–187, 198, 204, 225, 237,
  255, 257, 289, **301**, **307**

education and social mobility 213–220, 224
emic and etic categories (in interpretation)
  233–4, 235–238 *passim*, 279, **302**
empiricism 50, **301**
endogenous causation 189–190, **302**
epistemology, realist 61–62
equifinality 126, 176, 178
experimental research 29, 69–74
explanation
  combined with interpretation 246, 272–5,
    275–83
  forms of 165–172, 172–5
  positivist understanding of 50–5
  relationship with interpretation
    17–20, 31, 59, 232, 239, 241–6,
    254–5, 264–6
  satisfaction in 54, 63, 99, 110, 159–162,
    172, 185–88, 189, 224–5, **303**
  structure of 180–199 *passim*, 218–20
  trade-offs in 163–165, 197–8, 290
  see also historical explanation, narrative
    explanation, variable-oriented
    research
explanatory inference 12, 17, 36, 198,
  218–20, 223–4, **303**
  distance in, 159–60
  warrant for 200–211 *passim*

factors 35, 93, 159, 174–6, 197, **301**
  variables as proxies for 85, 103, 107–8,
    174–5, 180–81
  see also configurations, mechanisms
falsification (of a theory or hypothesis) 34,
  39, 48, 52, 97, 103, 107, 125, **301**
family resemblance concepts 139–140, 289
feedback, in causation 30, 191–194

virtues in research design 19–20, 286, 288–90, **309**
  trade-offs between 4, 36, 41, 51, 54–5, 95–96, 178, 197–8, 205–208, 223–225, 247–9, 254, 258–9, 265–6, 288–296

warrant 11–13, 19–20, 49–51, 163, 200–211 *passim,* 220–5 *passim,* 248–266 *passim,* 286–7, 298, **309**
  demonstrating 15–16, 36–7, 82, 95, 158, 198, 238
  see also inference

Weber, M.
  on ideal type of bureaucracy 170–1
  on interpretation 242
  on *verstehen* 110
  see also ideal type
Willis, P. (*Learning to Labour*) 235–328, 243
Winch, P. on interpretation 240–241
within-case analysis 78–79, 220–224, **309**